THE CONTINUITY OF CHANGE

THE
CONTINUITY
OF
CHANGE

THE SUPREME COURT AND INDIVIDUAL LIBERTIES
1953–1986

Melvin I. Urofsky

Virginia Commonwealth University

WADSWORTH PUBLISHING COMPANY
BELMONT, CALIFORNIA
A DIVISION OF WADSWORTH, INC.

History Editor: Peggy Adams
Editorial Assistant: Cathie Fields
Production Editor: Donna Linden
Designer: James Chadwick
Print Buyer: Barbara Britton
Permissions Editor: Jeanne Bosschart
Copy Editor: Margaret Moore
Compositor: Omegatype Typography, Inc., Champaign, Illinois
Cover Illustration: Rebecca Archey

Printed in the United States of America   49

1 2 3 4 5 6 7 8 9 10 — 95 94 93 92 91

Library of Congress Cataloging-in-Publication Data

Urofsky, Melvin I.
    The continuity of change: the Supreme Court and individual liberties,
1953–1986 / Melvin I. Urofsky.
        p.   cm.
    ISBN 0-534-12960-9
    1. Civil rights—United States—History.   2. United States. Supreme Court—History.
I. Title.
KF4749.U76   1991
342.73'085'09—dc20   90-36833
[347.3028509]   CIP

For Jonathan and Lindsay Meyers
Lisa and Mark Miller
and their parents

Contents

PART IV   EQUAL PROTECTION OF THE LAWS

Preface

Felix Frankfurter once commented that when he had been a law professor, he watched and studied the Supreme Court intensely, indeed obsessively, "as closely as a mother watches a sick child."[1] I cannot make that same claim, but I, too, have been a long-time court watcher, first as an amateur, and in the past few years on a more professional basis. In teaching constitutional history and in running a variety of teacher institutes on the Court and the Constitution, I have come to appreciate the cliché that the Supreme Court is the least understood branch of our federal government. People who talk knowledgeably about Congress, the President, and even the administrative agencies appear to know little about the Court other than a rather simplistic understanding of some major decisions. The legislative and executive branches are *political*, but the judiciary is *legal* and therefore comprehensible only to lawyers and the like.

This is both a false and lamentable situation. Anyone who has ever tried to read an act of Congress, with multiple titles and innumerable sections written in a language that bears only the slightest resemblance to English can turn with relief to the elegance and simplicity of Earl Warren's decision in the segregation cases or William O. Douglas's exposition of why we enjoy a right to privacy. Moreover, while there is no question that what Congress does affects all of us, so too do the decisions of the Supreme Court. A black child's right to attend public school without being segregated by race, a woman's right to have an abortion, an accused person's access to an attorney, a political activist's right to voice unpopular views—all of these derive from how the Supreme Court interprets the Constitution.

Because its decisions are so important, the Court often becomes a participant in the political process, and the justices are well aware of this fact of life. While they do not have to run for office, they know that their decisions, especially unpopular ones, can often trigger a firestorm of political protest. One does not have to go very far back in history to find evidence of this; both President Bush and the Congress rushed to make political capital following the Court's decision that burning an American flag constituted symbolic speech and therefore came under the protection of the First Amendment.[2]

Although the justices are protected from political retaliation by the life tenure they enjoy under the Constitution, they understand that the prestige and institutional integrity of the Supreme Court can be damaged by ill-conceived decisions or the failure to provide for proper implementation. They also understand that major changes in doctrine should be avoided, because the country relies on the Court for constitutional stability. We expect that when we elect a president or congressional representative, changes will be made; the candidates often run on a platform that calls for significant alterations in governmental policy. The nation would be appalled, however, at the prospect of a Supreme Court justice who openly avowed the idea of reversing established judicial doctrine. The defeat of the nomination of Robert Bork to the high court in 1987 can be attributed in part to the widespread perception that he opposed much of what the Court had decided in the previous three decades and would consciously work to repeal those decisions.

In 1968 Richard Nixon also declared that he believed the Warren Court was wrong on a number of issues, especially those cases involving the rights of accused persons, and that if elected president, he would nominate people to the courts who would have a different view of what the law should be. Probably in no campaign since 1860[3] had the Court been so central a theme in a presidential election. When in early 1969 Nixon named Warren Burger as Chief Justice, the President implied that the nation could look forward to a significant conservative shift in the Court's doctrinal decisions.

This book is a study of just how much of a shift took place. Was the Court headed by Earl Warren as radical as its critics claimed? Was the Burger Court as reactionary as its opponents charged? The answer I have reached is that in the area of individual liberties, while the Warren Court certainly moved the nation into a greater sensitivity to civil rights and liberties, its decisions for the most part devolved out of earlier doctrinal developments. The Burger Court, on the other hand, while more conservative in some areas, essentially continued and consolidated the major Warren Court doctrines, and in some areas, such as equal rights for women, pushed far ahead of its predecessor. In terms of judicial activism, that is, the willingness of the Court to establish policy through constitutional interpretation, the Court from 1953 (when Earl Warren became Chief Justice) to 1986 (when Warren Burger retired) has been the most activist of any Court in the nation's history. In the pages that follow, I hope to convince the reader of this thesis.

*   *   *   *   *

While writing a book is an individual (although not always a lonely) process, getting that book published is a group enterprise, and one of the pleasures of authorship is thanking the talented men and women who transformed what I tapped out on my word processor into the book the reader now holds in his or her hands. David Follmer found the thesis of continuity and change interesting enough to sign a contract for this book when he headed the Dorsey Press. About a year later, Wadsworth bought Dorsey, and Peggy Adams inherited both author and eventually manuscript, and as the history editor she has done a fine job of nurturing both. Donna Linden and Cathie Fields oversaw production, and they did so in a friendly and painless manner for which I am most grateful. James Chadwick designed the final product. Margaret Moore is an author's dream of a copy editor, and her sharp eye saved me the embarrassment of many an error. My agent Audrey Adler Wolf does all the things that agents are supposed to do, including keeping her authors more or less on schedule, but she does it as a friend and not as a taskmaster. I would also like to thank the reviewers of the manuscript: Kermit Hall, University of Florida; Paul Murphy, University of Minnesota; and Rebecca S. Shoemaker, Indiana State University.

My son Philip, now associated with Shearman & Sterling in New York, helped out as a research assistant in the early stages, and my wife Susan continues to show her love by ignoring my less than charming behavior during the writing process. The book is dedicated to my nephews and nieces, and their parents, as a token of happy family gatherings.

MELVIN UROFSKY
Richmond, Virginia

THE CONTINUITY OF CHANGE

I

INTRODUCTION

The honorable, the Chief Justice and the Associate Justices of the Supreme Court of the United States. Oyez, oyez, oyez, all persons having business before the honorable, the Supreme Court of the United States, are admonished to draw near and give their attention, for the Court is now sitting. God save the United States and this honorable court.

1

"God Save This Honorable Court"

Continuity and Change on the Supreme Court

The quaint, simple formula that opens each session of the Supreme Court of the United States is as old as the Republic, and its message as enduring. In the most powerful nation on earth, the rights of every citizen are protected by the Constitution, and the meaning of those rights ultimately rests in one court. Yet unlike the presidency and Congress, a majority of Americans know relatively little about the Supreme Court, its members, or how it goes about its business.[1] When great cases are decided, headlines and television stories carry the news to nearly everyone who can see and hear, but there are only a few cases each term that command such attention. Analysis of the Court's work, trends and changes in doctrinal development, and criticism of particular decisions are usually limited to scholarly law journals.

This is unfortunate, for the work of the Court, the cases it decides as well as which ones it chooses not to hear, affect American life in ways as profound as any congressional statute or presidential policy. Moreover, despite Alexander Hamilton's assurances that the judiciary would be "the least dangerous branch" of the government,[2] in modern times the Court has proven itself a powerful coequal partner to the executive and legislative branches. Certainly the revolution in civil rights does not bespeak an ineffective judiciary, nor does the Court's standing up to the president and/or Congress indicate a sense of powerlessness. The decisions of the Court can and do affect many aspects of our society, and it is important that an enlightened citizenry at the least understand the rationales behind those decisions and the importance of the Court as chief arbiter of the meaning of the Constitution.

This book examines an important aspect of that judicial impact: the way the Court interpreted the meaning of certain basic rights between 1953, the year Earl Warren became Chief Justice of the United States, and 1986, when his successor, Warren E. Burger, stepped down from the center chair. I have chosen this period for a number of reasons, most importantly because this third of a century marked one of the greatest expansions in the meaning of American liberties in our history, and that expansion resulted directly from doctrinal changes announced by the Court. Critics and admirers alike often used the term *judicial revolution* to mark the Warren years (1953–1969), and in the 1968 presidential election, Richard Nixon promised that, if elected, he would nominate justices who would turn back that revolution. Nixon had the opportunity to place four men on the Court, and his successor, Gerald Ford, who as a member of Congress had also been a bitter critic of the judiciary, named a fifth. Yet an examination of the Burger Court, published in 1983, carried the subtitle "The Counter-Revolution That Wasn't."[3]

In fact, the Warren Court was never as radical as its critics charged, nor did the Burger Court prove as conservative as its detractors claimed. That is the central theme of this book, and an elaboration of that statement constitutes the majority of subsequent chapters. By this I do not mean that the Warren Court did not hand down decisions that significantly affected constitutional doctrine in a "liberal" manner, which placed a higher value on individual liberty and autonomy as against the authority of the state. Nor do I mean that the Burger Court did not hand down its share of "conservative" decisions, favoring the state as against the individual. If we take a look at these decisions in the larger sweep of constitutional history, however, we will find far more doctrinal continuity than change.

INSTITUTIONAL CONSTRAINTS

The Court itself, as nearly all legal institutions are, is basically conservative in a Burkean manner, meaning that it is reluctant to give up that part of the past it deems good. Common law courts have for centuries relied on past precedents to guide their decisions in current cases, and unless a very good reason can be presented, courts will follow the rule of *stare decisis*—let the prior decision stand. The Court will, of course, ignore precedent when it is inapplicable, but the rule encourages uniformity and stability, two characteristics greatly valued in law. So unless a strong argument can be made for change, the justices as a matter of judicial policy will tend to follow precedent.

Another institutional constraint is the fact that a majority of the Court must agree not only that a particular result is right; it must also agree on the reasons for that result. This tends to keep doctrinal holdings fairly narrow and centrist. A majority may be willing to make a minor adjustment in a rule but not willing to go along with an opinion incorporating more radical changes. Thus the ideological purist on the Court, a Hugo L. Black on the left or a William H. Rehnquist on the right, may often write an opinion that is intellectually and doctrinally far clearer than the majority opinion. But if their colleagues are unwilling to travel that far in altering the doctrine, it comes down as a lone dissent or concurrence. The effective justice is the one who can define a consensus position and build a majority coalition for that holding. The opinion may be a little fuzzy, and it may not change the previous doctrine in any radical manner, but it is still good law and will be difficult to dislodge. In such a setting, doctrinal change is most often slow and incremental in nature.

Perhaps the greatest restraint against sudden change is the fact that men and women, once appointed to the bench, enjoy life tenure. The average term of a chief justice is a little over thirteen years, whereas associate justices serve an average of fifteen years and three months. George Washington named ten people to the Court and Franklin Roosevelt nine, but most presidents do not have the opportunity to name a majority; some, including Jimmy Carter, never got to name any. Normally, one appointment, by itself, can rarely alter a Court's doctrinal path, but when the Court is closely divided, one or two appointments can shift the balance, as when Earl Warren and William Brennan took the Court on a distinctly liberal path in the 1950s. Moreover, presidents have no assurances that the man or woman they name will continue to support any particular doctrinal line. Eisenhower regretted putting Warren and Brennan on the bench, and Byron White proved far more conservative than Kennedy had anticipated.

People are, at bottom, the key element in judicial decision making, and it is not easy to identify the factors that make some justices effective, perhaps even great. Longevity on the Court is by itself not critical; Gabriel Duvall served twenty-four years, Bushrod Washington thirty, and John McLean thirty-one, yet their names are practically forgotten today. On the other hand, their longevity certainly magnified the influence of John Marshall (thirty-four years), Joseph Story (thirty-three), Stephen Field (thirty-four), Hugo L. Black (thirty-four), and William Brennan, who has sat for thirty-four years as of this writing.

This longevity is also a reason why historians are leery of naming Courts after chief justices, even though we use this shorthand device as much as anyone else. It is true that certain chiefs—John Marshall is the outstanding example— so dominated their colleagues that one can speak of the "Marshall Court." The conservative William Howard Taft also exercised effective leadership over his conservative brethren in the 1920s. Most often, however, we find associate justices who preceded the Chief and remained to greet his successor. Hugo L. Black and William O. Douglas served under five chief justices—Hughes, Stone, Vinson, Warren, and Burger. If one asks who has been the effective "leader" of the Court since the 1950s, many court watchers will name William J. Brennan, and one scholar has suggested that rather than talk about a "Warren Court" or a "Burger Court," we should in fact discuss the "Brennan Court."[4]

Another problem in using terms such as "Warren Court" is the question "*Which* Warren Court?" The nine men who joined in the first desegregation case in 1954 are not the same men who handed down the reapportionment decisions a decade later; both the inner dynamics of the Court and its doctrinal tinge changed as some men left and others took their place. The continuity and the change in Court personnel can easily be seen in Figure 1.

Figure 1

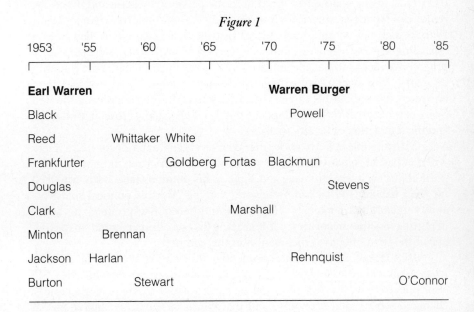

With these caveats in mind, let us take a brief look at the twenty-two men and one woman who, collectively, made up the Warren and Burger Courts.

THE WARREN COURT

When Earl Warren (1891–1974) arrived in Washington in the fall of 1953, few people expected great things of him. As part of a political deal for the Republican presidential nomination the year before, Dwight Eisenhower had promised Warren, the popular three-term governor of California, a seat on the high court if Warren would endorse the Eisenhower candidacy.[5] Eisenhower no doubt thought of Warren as a side judge, an associate justice, rather than as the nation's highest judicial officer, and he, like many others, probably subscribed to journalist John Gunther's description of Warren as a genial second-rater, "honest, likeable, and clean . . . with little intellectual background, little genuine depth or coherent philosophy." He will, Gunther concluded, "never set the world on fire or even make it smoke."[6] Fred Vinson's unexpected death, however, left the center chair open, and Eisenhower somewhat reluctantly named Warren.

The man who would one day be called "Super Chief" had risen slowly but steadily in California politics. His record, generally good, had one major flaw: During the war he had given in to the patriotic hysteria and urged the removal of Japanese-Americans from the West Coast. Aside from that incident, Warren had run an enlightened local district attorney's office, had been a crusading attorney general, and as governor of California had compiled a progressive record that made him attractive to the liberal wing of the Republican party. Moreover, despite the Japanese-American stain, Warren had demonstrated throughout his career a sensitivity to civil liberties; during the Red Scare of the early fifties he had spoken out forcefully against Joseph McCarthy and the imposition of loyalty oaths.

Many people failed to notice that Warren's genial exterior covered a steely will that had been hardened in the political furnace. Warren did not have any great ability as a legal thinker, and some of his opinions have been criticized for their naiveté and lack of systematic analysis. But his political skills, his ability to work harmoniously with people of different backgrounds, his talent in putting together majorities, while keeping his own vision in mind, made him one of the most effective chief justices of this century.

If he lacked a coherent jurisprudential philosophy, Warren had definite ideas about what the Constitution meant in protecting individual liberties. He also believed that government in general had a positive role to play in a rapidly changing society and economy, and that courts in particular had a special obligation to articulate civil rights and liberties and to protect them from intrusion by the state. As his biographer and former law clerk G. Edward White described it, Warren came to the Court with "a penchant for activism" and a strong "moral passion."[7]

Traditionally the chief justice sits in the center chair, with the senior associate justice on his right and the next senior associate on his left; the alternation continues down to the most junior associate justice, who sits at the end on the chief's left. During the entire time Earl Warren presided over the Court, Hugo LaFayette Black (1886–1971) sat at his right hand. Black had been a populist senator from Alabama and a firm supporter of Franklin Roosevelt's New Deal. He had also been suspicious of courts interposing their will against that of the elected representatives of the people, and thus had enthusiastically backed Roosevelt's attack on the Supreme Court in 1937. As a reward, Black received Roosevelt's first appointment to the Court, and he served there from 1938 until his death in 1971.[8]

Black's deficiencies in legal knowledge embarrassed his brethren during his first few terms on the bench. Justice Stone took the unusual step of appealing to Professor Felix Frankfurter of Harvard to advise Black: "You might be able to render him great assistance. He needs guidance from someone who is more familiar with the workings of the judicial process than he is."[9] Frankfurter gladly took up the task, and soon reported to his mentor, Louis Brandeis, that while Black was not "technically equipped," he had a "good head" and was "capable of learning."[10]

Black indeed did learn, and sometime in the early 1940s a clear constitutional vision emerged in his opinions, one that he would advocate consistently for his more than three decades on the bench. While courts should defer to legislative policy decisions, he believed they had a clear obligation to play an activist role in the defense of civil rights and individual liberties. Black read the constitutional mandate literally and absolutely. Where the First Amendment said that Congress shall make no law abridging freedom of speech, it meant just that—Congress shall make *no* law limiting speech. Moreover, Black believed that the Fourteenth Amendment "incorporated" the protections of the Bill of Rights and applied them to the states as well. On the other hand, Black did not believe in so-called natural rights, which could be grafted on to the Constitution by judges, and dissented from the Court's ruling that a right to privacy existed; he could find no mention of privacy in the Constitution.[11]

His close friend William O. Douglas recalled Black as one of the two great proselyters on the Court.[12] A skilled political infighter as well as one who knew how to charm, Black believed in his causes, and, just as he had worked the floor of the Senate, he worked the chambers of his colleagues trying to round up votes for his position. What made Black one of the great forces on the bench in this century is that although it took him some time to reach his ideological lodestar, once there he preached a clear vision that could be understood by the academies, lower courts, and the general public. By 1953 Black stood as the acknowledged leader of the activist, liberal segment of the Court.

During Warren's first four terms, Stanley Forman Reed (1884–1980) sat on his immediate left, although ideologically, Reed tried to crowd the center on most issues. Educated at Yale and Columbia Law School, he had enjoyed a successful practice in his native Kentucky before coming to Washington, where he served as counsel for the Federal Farm Board and general counsel for the Reconstruction Finance Corporation in the Hoover administration. A moderate Democrat, he stayed on under Roosevelt and became solicitor general in 1935, carrying the heavy burden of defending New Deal measures against a hostile Court. He had been competent rather than brilliant, but he had shown enough promise that upon his appointment, Brandeis had passed the word to the Roosevelt administration that Reed would be welcome on the bench. Once on the bench, Reed tended to be a follower rather than a leader and could usually be counted on to vote along with Frankfurter. He supported government power, and seemingly had little sympathy for either civil rights or civil liberties, which led Justice Douglas, who personally liked the gentle, courtly Reed, to term him "one of the most reactionary judges to occupy the Bench in my time."[13]

To the right of Black sat the intellectual leader of the conservative wing of the Court, former Harvard law professor Felix Frankfurter (1882–1965).[14] A protégé of Oliver Wendell Holmes and Louis Brandeis, Frankfurter had been the outstanding academic commentator on the Supreme Court and its business for the two decades prior to his appointment to the bench in late 1938. Like the other Roosevelt nominees, Frankfurter still carried the scars of the battle between the Court and the New Deal, and held the firm belief that courts should in nearly all instances show deference to the policy-making prerogatives of the elected political branches. Far too bright not to recognize that judges did indeed make law, he believed in a very circumscribed area for that role.

Frankfurter, as well as his many admirers, had believed that once on the Court he would as a matter of course assume the intellectual leadership of the bench. During his first few terms he had, in fact, been acknowledged by the other Roosevelt appointees as a sort of "first among equals," and he had taken the lead in several opinions supporting New Deal legislation and down-playing judicial prerogatives. Frankfurter related well to his superiors, to a Holmes or Brandeis or Franklin Roosevelt, and to his students, for whom he could act as mentor, but he had poor skills in relating to his equals; he kept trying to treat them as students, and they would have none of it.[15] For all his study of the Court and the interaction of its members, he could never fathom why his colleagues resented his trying to teach them the law. He could never understand why they fidgeted as he lectured to them in conference nor why they seemed insulted when he told them they did not understand the law.[16]

Every time a new member came on the Court, Frankfurter would attempt to take him under his wing. At first, the new justice would be grateful for the advice of someone who knew the Court and its work so well, but within a short time the newcomer would learn his way, and Frankfurter would still be treating him as if he had just showed up and wanted to know where the library was. Frankfurter tried this on Warren, with predictable results. Warren had not gotten where he was by having someone else tell him how to think; before long, relations between the Chief and Frankfurter had become strained, especially as Frankfurter realized that Warren seemed headed toward an alliance with the liberal forces led by Hugo Black.[17]

Personal relations between Frankfurter and Black always remained relatively pleasant, at times even cordial, despite the fact that ideologically they stood poles apart.[18] "Open warfare" is as good a description as any of Frankfurter's attitude toward Black's friend and ally William Orville Douglas (1898–1980).[19] Douglas had been Sterling Professor of Law at Yale and one of the leading lights of the Realist movement, which, among other things, acknowledged that judicial prejudices played a major role in decision making. He had gone to Washington to join the Securities and Exchange Commission, and in the late thirties, as its chairman, had led the SEC fight to force Wall Street to accept reform and regulation.[20] Douglas had appeared willing to follow Frankfurter's lead when they first went on the Court (Douglas took his seat two months after Frankfurter), but before long he found himself drawn to the judicial activism and concern for individual liberties advocated by Hugo Black.

Douglas may have been the smartest man on the Court at the time, but he never seemed to have been totally submerged in the business of being a judge. In his first years he wrote some very well-reasoned opinions,[21] but as time went on his opinions grew shorter and deliberately avoided the type of analysis (law review opinions, as he called them) that could influence lower court judges and help refine doctrine. Probably more than any other member of the Warren and Burger era, Douglas can be characterized as a results-oriented justice, interested only in the right result and not too concerned with explaining the jurisprudential steps one took to get there.[22] As the years went on, he moved ever closer to Black's absolutist view of constitutionally protected rights, but it would be a mistake to see him as merely Black's shadow. Douglas, more than any other member of the Court, was willing to constitutionalize rights not found there, so long as he considered them basic to individual liberty. In the best common law tradition, Douglas ignored contemporary reliance on either precedent or textual analysis to discover a right to procreation[23] as well as to privacy.[24]

Douglas also proved the Court's most visible extrajudicial presence. His enormous energy barely tapped by demands of the Court (he worked hard, but claimed it never took more than four days a week to do his Court assignments), he became an avid world traveler and lecturer, and with the exception of topics he thought might come before the Court for adjudication, believed he had as much right as anyone to speak out on the issues of the day. Both Roosevelt and Truman considered him as a likely running mate, and throughout the forties rumors abounded that Douglas had political ambitions. But he stayed on the Court, traveled, engaged in causes, divorced and remarried, and lived his individualistic creed to the end.

Next in seniority came Robert Houghwout Jackson (1892–1954), whose last years on the Court were embittered by unfulfilled promise, both those made to him as well as of his own talent. Jackson had overcome family poverty and a mediocre legal education to become a successful attorney and then a highly regarded solicitor general and attorney general in the Roosevelt administration; Brandeis so admired Jackson's performance at oral arguments that he reputedly said Jackson should be made solicitor general for life. Probably more than any other man on the Court in the forties, he had the gift for the well-turned phrase that could capture a broad idea in a few words.[25] It was Jackson who once summed up the reality of the Court's power when he declared that "we are not final because we are infallible, but we are infallible only because we are final."[26] According to Paul Freund, Jackson had one of the most inquisitive and open minds on the bench; "fresh and unconventional ideas were welcome to him as they can only be to a lover of irony and paradox. . . . [H]e never ceased to rethink and redefine his premises."[27]

Roosevelt had once promised Jackson that he would make him Chief Justice, but by the time Charles Evans Hughes retired in 1941, the president had already made seven appointments, all from Democratic ranks. With the war on in Europe and a good chance that the United States would soon be involved, Roosevelt believed he should appoint a Republican as a gesture of national unity, so he elevated the highly respected Harlan Fiske Stone to the center chair. He then told Jackson that he would get it next time, and in the meantime nominated him to take Stone's place as associate justice. After the war, Jackson agreed to serve as the American prosecutor at the Nuremberg war crimes trials, and while there Stone died; Truman, either unaware of Roosevelt's promise or considering it no longer binding, named his good friend Fred Vinson. A bitter Jackson believed that Hugo Black had somehow contrived to block his appointment as Chief, and in a moment of anger and frustration let fly a public letter accusing Black of conflict of interest and mentioning "feuds" on the Court.[28]

Jackson's closest friend on the bench, and his ideological ally, was Frankfurter, who for reasons of his own nurtured Jackson's resentment of Black and Douglas. Jackson rarely voted against the government, and thus one is surprised at his opinion for the Court in the second flag salute case, in which he wrote a ringing defense of freedom of conscience, while his usual ally, Felix Frankfurter, penned an angry dissent.[29] By the time Warren came to the Court, Jackson was an ill man; he had a heart attack over the summer of 1953 and died a few months after the Court handed down its decision in *Brown* v. *Board of Education*.[30]

The three most junior members of the Court had all been appointed by Harry Truman, and none of them could be considered "distinguished" jurists. When a vacancy occurred shortly after Truman entered the White House, political prudence dictated that he extend an olive branch to the Republicans by naming one of their own to the Court. Harold Hitz Burton (1888–1964), a moderate Republican senator from Ohio, fit the bill perfectly. He had impeccable party credentials but did not belong to the GOP's right wing; he had been progressive on economic and social issues and an internationalist; above all, he had hit if off well with Harry Truman when the two served together on the special committee to investigate defense contracts. Once on the bench, Burton quietly fell in with the conservative wing, as he had been expected to do, although he had, as Justice Douglas recalled, "a strong humanitarian impulse that shone through at odd times."[31] Through most of his tenure on the bench, he tended to support the government, especially in national security cases. His biographer described Burton as "an average justice . . . not a bright, witty intellectual like a Frankfurter or a Black."[32]

Tom Campbell Clark (1899–1977) provided further evidence of Truman's tendency to appoint political cronies to the bench. A protégé of Sam Rayburn, the Texas-raised Clark had come to the Justice Department in 1937 and had uncomplainingly helped direct the relocation of Japanese-Americans during the war. He had also prosecuted war contract frauds uncovered by the Truman Committee, and he and Truman soon became friends. When Truman became president, he wanted some people he knew and trusted in his cabinet and named Clark attorney general.

Described by one writer as "an able administration hatchet man,"[33] Clark became the Truman administration's chief "cold warrior" and enforcer of the loyalty programs, and he later brought these attitudes with him to the Court, especially as they related to security cases. But to his credit, Clark realized that the prosecution of Communists in the name of democracy also required him to protect civil rights for the same reason. He entered the government on the side of the Negro for the first time in the restricted covenant case,[34] and despite his southern origins, backed Truman in his civil rights program.

Truman later called Clark "my biggest mistake. . . . He's about the dumbest man I think I've ever run across."[35] The acerbic Fred Rodell concurred in this view of a man so incompetent that he relied totally on his clerks.[36] Court historian Bernard Schwartz disputes this judgment and suggests that Clark may be the "most underrated Justice in recent Supreme Court history." His files show that he did, in fact, write his own opinions and that he was easily the most competent of the four Truman appointees. Although basically conservative, Clark remained open-minded and, according to Schwartz, under Warren's tutelage grew receptive to viewpoints he would have earlier dismissed.[37] Clark, for example, delivered the Court's opinion in the landmark case of *Mapp* v. *Ohio* (1961), which applied the Fourth Amendment warrant requirements to the states.[38]

Sherman Minton (1890–1965), another of Truman's pals, had been a one-term senator from Indiana and a strong New Deal supporter. After his defeat for reelection, Roosevelt named him to the Seventh Circuit Court of Appeals, and he supposedly lobbied his friendship with Truman into a seat on the high court.[39] As Felix Frankfurter noted, "Shay" Minton "will not go down in history as a great jurist, but he was a delightful colleague."[40] His pleasant personality may be the only positive thing people could say about him, because in his case conservatism (except in regard to civil rights) was compounded by incompetence.[41]

The Court that Warren took over in the fall of 1953 gave little promise of becoming either liberal or activist. Black and Douglas had staked out their position on the left and believed—correctly, as it turned out—that Warren would join them. Shortly after the nomination, Douglas described Warren as "a fine and a good man [who] is going to make an excellent Chief Justice."[42] Frankfurter, despite his poor personal relations with some of the brethren, remained the ideological leader of the conservative wing, which included Reed, Jackson, and the three Truman appointees. It would be a mistake, however, to assume a unity on the right akin to the jurisprudential agreement between Black and Douglas. The "Frankfurter" wing agreed in principle on judicial restraint but differed on particulars. Frankfurter, for example, had a purist view of the Fourth Amendment, which led him to scrutinize search-and-seizure cases, whereas Burton and Minton, despite economic conservatism, stood strongly for civil rights, as did Clark.

This lineup began to change fairly quickly. Robert Jackson died in 1954, Minton retired in 1956, Reed in 1957, and Burton the following year. To replace Jackson, Eisenhower named the highly respected Wall Street lawyer John Marshall Harlan (1899–1971), whose grandfather had been the sole dissenter in *Plessy* v. *Ferguson*, the case that established the "separate but equal" doctrine.[43] Although Harlan would first join Frankfurter and then take his place as leader of the conservative wing of the Court, he was anything but a stodgy reactionary and had none of the acerbity that had so poisoned Frankfurter's relations with the brethren.

The patrician Harlan brought great learning and high legal skills to the Court and quickly earned a reputation as a "lawyer's judge," one whose opinions spoke not only to the theoretical concerns of academics but also to the practical issues that lawyers, prosecutors, and others needed to know and understand. Numerous clerks reported that a Harlan opinion always received great respect and a careful reading in the other eight chambers, even if one stood on the opposite side of the argument. One scholar declared that Harlan's opinions "have not been exceeded in professional competence by any Supreme Court Justice since Brandeis."[44]

After Frankfurter's retirement in 1962, Harlan "came to be looked on as the conservative conscience of an ever more activist Court."[45] His conservatism, however, was a far cry from that of the Truman appointees and certainly from that of the New Deal opponents of the 1930s, such as James McReynolds or George Sutherland. A respecter of precedent, Harlan did not make it an icon but demanded an extremely strong case before he would vote to overturn a prior ruling. Like Brandeis, he did not believe that every wrong could be righted by the Court and that under a federal system there had to be great flexibility and diversity accorded to the states. He could not accept Black's blanket application of the Bill of Rights to the states, and like Frankfurter, would sustain a state criminal procedure if it passed a "fundamental fairness" standard. Harlan's conservatism had a Burkean flavor to it, as well as a sensitivity to individual rights, particularly those protected under the First Amendment.

Harlan had grown increasingly unhappy with the Warren Court's activism in the 1960s and felt more at home with the arrival of Warren Burger. There is little doubt that he would have been an intellectual leader of the Burger

Court, but he fell ill and had to resign in the fall of 1971; a few weeks later he died.

Harlan's appointment replaced one conservative with another, but the nomination of William Joseph Brennan, Jr. (b. 1906) to take Minton's place dramatically shifted the balance of the Court toward liberal activism. Supposedly Eisenhower wanted to name a Catholic and a Democrat just prior to the 1956 election, and his attorney general, Herbert Brownell, had recently met and been impressed with Brennan, then a member of the New Jersey Supreme Court. Right after Eisenhower sent Brennan's name to the Senate, Justice Douglas put his law clerk to work reading Brennan's state court opinions to see if they could get a measure of how the new man would vote. The clerk concluded that one could not predict Brennan's future behavior on the basis of his writings.[46] It took little time, however, for Brennan—a former Frankfurter student—to align himself with Black and Douglas, and the latter wrote enthusiastically that the new justice

> is a wonderful person and a grand human being. He has courage and independence. He is imbued with the libertarian philosophy and I would be willing to give odds that he will leave as fine a record on this Court as Holmes, Hughes, Murphy or any of the great.[47]

Brennan eventually emerged as a dominant member of the Warren Court and as one of the great consensus builders in the Court's history.[48] He developed a special relationship with Earl Warren, which gave him added leverage in determining the direction of the Court. In the 1960s the regular conference would inevitably be preceded by a private meeting between the two to plan strategy. As one of Warren's biographers and former law clerks termed it, Brennan served as the Chief's "judicial technician."[49]

Brennan's influence, however, derived not from his judicial skills which, while impressive, were not overwhelming. Instead, much of it derived from his personality, his friendliness, his political instincts, and above all, from his uncanny ability to define a liberal consensus that could bring in centrists and even some conservatives. Brennan could massage an opinion to cut away the sharp jurisprudential edges and thus make it palatable to those who would never have accepted the results if stated as a Black or a Douglas or a Frankfurter would have done. Brennan could get on well with his colleagues and understood that a vote against him on one case never precluded a future vote for his position in another. During the Warren years Brennan's influence on the Court was often underestimated, because the liberal activists seemed so dominant. In the Burger years, however, and even into the Rehnquist era, Bill Brennan kept building consensus and winning over majorities.[50] If he did not win as many as he had in the Warren era, and if he found himself dissenting more often,[51] he still managed to pull out some astounding victories. Moreover, Brennan's suggestion that state courts might go further in establishing state-based protections for civil liberties led many state judges to do just that, at a time when the Supreme Court seemed to be setting limits to the reach of constitutional protections.[52]

Brennan's priorities in terms of individual rights emerged fairly clearly. The Bill of Rights gives to every person enormous protection against the state. We cannot be stopped from expressing our views, from petitioning the government, from exercising the full range of those liberties we hold dear. The government, on the other hand, must always be held in check, and the judiciary must assure that there is no established church, no infringement on the rights of persons accused of crimes, and above all, no interference with individual privacy and personal autonomy. Brennan is probably the judicial activist *par excellence*, and he has been the leading advocate of the Court reinterpreting constitutional provisions to make them applicable to modern society.[53]

The year Brennan joined the Court also marked the term Warren broke away from Frankfurter's efforts to corral him in the conservative camp.[54] As a result the liberal wing now had four firm votes—the Chief, Black, Douglas, and Brennan—and depending on the issue, could often pick up the fifth vote necessary for a majority. One could not say that the balance had swung over from conservatism to liberalism, from judicial restraint to judicial activism, as Frankfurter and Harlan still exerted considerable influence. But one could say that the pendulum had started to swing and had reached a middle position that swung one way and then the other depending on the issue.

Of the five appointments Dwight Eisenhower made, Charles Evans Whittaker (1901–1973) is the least distinguished; Bernard Schwartz suggests that "he may have been the worst Justice of this century."[55] A farm boy who had quit high school at sixteen, Whittaker had never gone to college and had attended an unaccredited law school at night. He worked hard, however, and became a fairly prosperous lawyer and an active Republican in Missouri. Eisenhower named him to the federal district court in 1954, elevated him to the Eighth Circuit two years later, and then appointed him to the Supreme Court the following year when Stanley Reed retired.

Whittaker tried hard, but he was in over his head. He lacked intellectual capacity and could not make up his mind. In a Fourth Amendment case, Douglas had circulated a draft dissent that drew three votes away from what had been an 8-1 decision assigned to Frankfurter. Whittaker was reportedly wavering, and Frankfurter, furious at the possibility of losing his majority, hounded him mercilessly. Finally Whittaker fled from Washington to the country for the weekend, taking his clerk with him, and declared he would announce his decision when he returned on Monday. After three days of agonizing, he stayed with Frankfurter, but entered a one-paragraph concurrence that made no sense.[56]

Douglas described Whittaker as "an affable companion" with extremely reactionary ideas who had trouble making up his mind and writing an opinion.[57] Ultimately the pressure of the Court's work proved too much for him to handle, and he resigned. As one scholar aptly noted, "[T]here is little that Whittaker has done which shows he had the talents, skill, or temperament that a Justice on our highest Court requires."[58]

Eisenhower's last appointment, Potter Stewart (1915–1985) to replace Burton, proved one of the most able and interesting men on the bench. At age forty-four he was the youngest person to be appointed in a century, with the exception of Douglas, and gave off an air of vigor and youth that at times seemed almost out of place on the bench. Stewart, however, loved being a judge and once remarked that it involved "all the fun of practicing law without the bother of clients."[59]

Although Douglas offhandedly characterized Stewart as a conservative, labels such as liberal, conservative, or activist are nearly meaningless when applied to this man. Stewart himself said that he had enough trouble trying to figure out what these terms meant in the political world and that they had no meaning on the Court. Asked to describe himself, he declared simply: "I am a lawyer."[60] Although he dissented from many of the Warren Court's more activist decisions in the 1960s, Stewart had little in common with Frankfurter or even Harlan. One of his law clerks once described him as the quintessential common law judge, and that may be the best clue to understanding his jurisprudence.[61]

Although common law judges are nominally bound by *stare decisis*, they also have the obligation of squaring the legal rules of the past with current needs and conditions, fulfilling Holmes's famous aphorism that "the life of the law has not been logic; it has been experience. The felt necessities of the time . . . have had a good deal more to do than the syllogism in determining the rules by which men should be governed."[62] Stewart could parse past cases with the best of his colleagues, but he had a keen sensitivity to how law would actually work in the real world and of the danger of erecting inflexible and irrelevant rules. He felt bad that many people would only remember him for his comment in a 1964 case when he declared he would not attempt to define pornography, "But I know it when I see it."[63]

This common-sensical approach reflected Stewart's pragmatic view of life, and it led him to examine each case not only on its own legal merits but also in terms of how the rule would work in the real world. He was never as results-oriented a judge as Douglas, but in his own way Stewart sought the right solution, the workable solution, and then could weave the legal ropes to support it. If one tries to analyze his opinions over twenty-three terms from a strictly jurisprudential context, one might conclude that Stewart lacked any doctrinal consistency at all. His decisions make far more sense if we view them in terms of a somewhat conservative, but certainly not hidebound, common law judge trying to figure out what rules will do the least harm to past decisions and still keep the law flexible and in tune with modern needs.

With the accession of John Kennedy to the White House, one might have expected that his appointments would give the four activists a consistent fifth vote. That is, in fact, what happened, but not with Kennedy's first appointment, Byron R. White (b. 1917), who brought an impressive list of firsts with him to the Court—first former All-American back, first former pro football player, and first former Supreme Court clerk to become a member of the Court. White had impressed Kennedy with his personal courage in handling the Freedom Riders' protest in Alabama in the spring of 1961. Aside from civil rights, however, White tended to be pragmatic and conservative, somewhat like Stewart, but more dispassionate and reserved, and during the Warren years could not be counted as firmly anchored in any particular doctrinal grouping. He seemed to grow more conservative with the years, however, and after the Nixon appointees joined the bench in the early seventies, White appeared to have found his jurisprudential home with Burger and Rehnquist. Like Stewart, though, he retained an independence that occasionally surprised those who took his conservative vote for granted. There has been practically nothing written about his jurisprudence, because, as one scholar noted, "[H]is basic judicial philosophy has never been clearly defined."[64]

Kennedy's second appointment, Arthur Joseph Goldberg (1908–1990), finally gave the liberals a solid fifth vote, and there is a certain irony that the activist Goldberg replaced this century's chief exponent of judicial restraint, Felix Frankfurter. The youngest of eleven children of an immigrant fruit peddler, Goldberg had worked his way through Northwestern Law School, graduating first in his class. He then developed a highly successful labor law practice, became counsel to the AFL-CIO and then Kennedy's secretary of labor. The politically sensitive president knew that Jewish groups would want one of their own to replace Frankfurter, and he was not about to disappoint them.

Goldberg differed from Frankfurter in almost every way. He got along well with the brethren, championed an activist role for the Court, and was not afraid to take on new issues. The new justice easily articulated the differences between himself and his predecessor. Frankfurter, he said, "always was fearful that the Court would injure itself [by taking controversial issues]. . . . Well, it's not the function of a Supreme Court Justice to worry about the Court injuring itself. It's the sworn duty of a Supreme Court Justice to do justice under law and apply the Constitution."[65] His good friend Bill Douglas could not have said it better.

The years 1962 to 1969 are the heyday of Warren activism. The liberal bloc not only had five sure votes on most issues but also could often count on one or more of the moderate/conservative group to join them. Tom Clark seemed to grow more susceptible to Warren's influence as the years went by. Harlan remained closest to the Frankfurter view of judicial restraint, but without the inflexibility that had isolated Frankfurter in his last years on the

Court. Stewart and White, while they frequently disagreed with the liberals, found many occasions when they could vote with the majority. The only problem, from the liberal point of view, seemed to be Black's growing conservatism after 1964, but even that did not diminish the liberal strength significantly.

Goldberg, the last to join the Court, was the first to leave; after the rough and tumble of labor law and Democratic politics, he found the marble temple somewhat quiet.[66] There is a difference of opinion whether Goldberg wanted to leave the Court or whether he just could not resist Lyndon Johnson's arm-twisting, but in 1965 he agreed to take over the thankless job of American ambassador to the United Nations.

To replace him, Lyndon Johnson named his good friend Abe Fortas (1910–1982) and thus began one of the more tragic stories involving the Court in this century. Johnson practically had to beat Fortas over the head to go onto the Court. An "insider among insiders" in Washington, he was a close personal friend of the president and had direct access to the Oval Office. He had a lucrative law practice, enjoyed an opulent life style, and his wife opposed the appointment because of the enormous salary reduction involved. Yet Fortas had found time to do public interest work as well and had been the counsel for Clarence Earl Gideon in that landmark case.[67] It might have been better for all concerned if the president had just left Goldberg on the bench and Fortas at his side.

Yet there is no doubt that Fortas had one of the best legal minds of any member of the Court this century, and many compared him to the greatest legal craftsman ever to sit on the high court, Louis Brandeis, in terms of legal skill. John Harlan, the "lawyer's judge" on the bench, admired the quality of Fortas's work. Like his former teacher and close friend Bill Douglas, Fortas was an activist, and he had all of Goldberg's proclivities but far more skill as a judge. He might have made a great justice, perhaps even a great chief justice, but his inability to remove himself as an advisor to Johnson ultimately led to his downfall.[68]

Johnson made his second appointment in 1967—Thurgood Marshall (b. 1908), who became the last member of the Warren Court and the first black appointed to the nation's highest bench. Douglas, in his memoirs, stated baldly that Johnson named Marshall "simply because he was black, and in the 1960s that was enough."[69] No one, certainly, represented the black legal struggle for equal rights as did Marshall. The grandson of a slave and the son of a railroad steward, he had been the chief strategist for the NAACP in its long campaign to *Brown* and one of the most successful attorneys ever to appear before the Court.[70]

The successful litigator, however, turned into a mediocre judge. John Kennedy had named Marshall in 1961 to the Court of Appeals for the Second Circuit (perhaps the nation's most important circuit), and at least some of

Marshall's colleagues there questioned his judgment and judicial ability. He left the bench in 1965 to become solicitor general, a job where he could fully exercise the skills he had honed over many years. Then Johnson named him to the high court, where he quickly became a vote without an identifiable voice. He supported the activists down the line but never developed any identifiable jurisprudential philosophy he could call his own.[71] A decade later, when only he and Brennan remained from the liberal bloc, the joke among law clerks was that Burger might have the center chair, but Brennan had two seats.

On June 13, 1968, Earl Warren went to the White House to inform the president that he intended to retire, "effective at your pleasure." Johnson's acceptance letter indicated he would accept Warren's decision "at such time as a successor is qualified."[72] For once Warren's famed political skills had failed him. He had hoped that by resigning before the election, he would give Lyndon Johnson the opportunity to name a new chief sympathetic to Warren's philosophy. Johnson's nomination of Abe Fortas certainly pleased Warren but ran into a firestorm of criticism in the Senate. Aside from the fact that he had continued to advise Johnson while on the bench, the critics had nothing substantive to deny confirmation. But members angry and frustrated at the Warren Court's liberalism on any number of issues joined with partisan Republicans and antiwar Democrats to block the nomination. Finally Johnson withdrew the nomination, and Earl Warren agreed to stay on as Chief Justice until a successor had been named and confirmed by the Senate. The nomination now fell into the hands of the new president.

THE BURGER COURT

In the 1968 presidential election, Richard Nixon had run against the Supreme Court as much as he had run against the Democratic nominee, Hubert Humphrey. "Some of our judges have gone too far," he charged, "in assuming unto themselves a mandate which is not there, and that is, to put their social and economic ideas into their decisions." If elected, Nixon promised, he would put strict constructionists, law-and-order advocates, onto the bench.[73] Soon after his inauguration, Nixon called Warren Earl Burger (b. 1907), then a member of the Court of Appeals for the District of Columbia Circuit, to the White House to swear in some minor officials and invited him back to the Oval Office for a chat afterwards. Nixon had been impressed with an article Burger had written critical of recent Supreme Court decisions in criminal procedure.[74] He also knew that as a member of an American Bar Association committee, Burger had traveled around the country and knew many people. Nixon wanted his advice on conservatives he could appoint to the federal judiciary, and over the next several weeks Burger would be consulted by Attorney General John

Mitchell and offer his own advice on appointments. Nearly everyone in the inner circle of the White House recognized Burger as the front-runner to succeed Earl Warren, and on May 21, 1969, the president made the appointment on national television.

Warren Burger's career had been solid and stolid. He helped secure the Minnesota delegation for Dwight Eisenhower at the 1952 Republican presidential convention and was rewarded with an appointment as assistant attorney general in charge of the Claims Division. In 1956 the president named him to the D.C. Court of Appeals, where he quickly became the lone and outspoken conservative on a bench renowned for its liberalism. Burger's opinions did not espouse a reactionary ideology, but instead argued that judges ought to exercise restraint and leave policy making to the elected branches of government. In criminal procedure cases, however, he did tend to take a tougher stand, favoring the prosecution rather than the defendant. *New York Times* columnist James Reston described Burger as "experienced, industrious, middle-class, middle-aged, middle-of-the-road, Middle-Western, Presbyterian, orderly and handsome"—just the type of "Middle American" that Nixon saw as the backbone of his political support.[75]

In his seventeen years in the center chair, Burger never did succeed in bringing the Court around to the strict constructionist posture that Nixon had envisaged. In fact, it is questionable if Burger led the Court—as Taft, Hughes, and Warren had done—in any direction. Appraisals of the Court talk about two or even three periods in which the majority swung from conservative to moderate and back again,[76] and as the following chapters demonstrate, one can find far more continuity than change between the Warren and Burger Courts.

The failure of leadership may be ascribed to several causes, not the least of which is the high intellectual caliber and equally great individualism of the men and woman appointed to the Court. The comment made about one of the justices—"no one leads Douglas"—could apply to nearly all of them. The Chief Justice does not enjoy any inherent powers greater than that of his colleagues, and like them, has only one vote. Technically "first among equals," he can only lead if he demonstrates superior intellectual, legal, or political skills, none of which Burger had. Individualists such as Douglas and Brennan respected Warren and would often—but not always—follow his lead; they had no similar respect for Burger.[77] The intellectual power on the conservative side of the Court belonged not to the Chief but to William Rehnquist.

Burger also chose to emphasize his role as Chief Justice of the United States over that of Chief Justice of the Supreme Court. The Chief Justice is charged by statute to oversee the judicial branch of the government, make sure it operates efficiently, and recommend to Congress any changes needed to make the system work more smoothly. Earl Warren had practically neglected this aspect of his job, and as a result Congress, whose conservative members bitterly opposed many of the Warren Court's decisions, did not prove receptive to his requests for more court personnel or greater funding for administration. Nonetheless, as William Brennan noted, "To those who served with him, Earl Warren will always be the Super Chief."[78]

Burger worked very hard at the job of Chief Justice of the United States, and by all accounts did an excellent job as judicial administrator.[79] He repaired relations with Congress, secured additional funds and personnel for the judicial system, and streamlined many administrative procedures. This, however, took an enormous amount of his time, so that he often came to conference ill-prepared; he usually read summaries of the cases prepared by his clerks rather than the briefs prepared by the lawyers, and thus he often knew less about the facts and legal issues surrounding a case than did his colleagues.[80] All of this made it unlikely that he could lead the Court, a situation that an unnamed colleague on the Court of Appeals had forecast at the time of Burger's nomination: "To suggest that he can bring the Court together—as hopefully a Chief Justice should—is simply a dream."[81]

The same year that Burger took over the center chair, Abe Fortas resigned from the Court, and Nixon had his second appointment to make in order to swing the Court over to the "peace forces." He had implicitly promised to name a southerner to the Court as part of his 1968 campaign strategy, and he now moved to make good on that promise. He sent in the nomination of the highly respected Clement F. Haynsworth, Jr., of South Carolina, chief judge of the Court of Appeals for the Fourth Circuit. Liberals, however, uncovered a relatively minor conflict of interests which, by itself, should not have doomed the nomination. But one year after Nixon's election, political opposition had built to the point where the Senate rejected Haynsworth, 45-55.

Nixon then sent in the name of G. Harrold Carswell of the Fifth Circuit, a man whose legal credentials did not measure up to those of Haynsworth. The description of him as a mediocre judge elicited a defense from Senator Roman Hruska of Nebraska, who said that there were a lot of mediocre people in the world and "they are entitled to a little representation, aren't they?" When investigators uncovered racist speeches supporting segregation as well as his involvement in a scheme to use federal funds to build a segregated golf club, the Senate voted Carswell down as well.

An infuriated Nixon declared that "I will not nominate another Southerner and let him be subjected to [such] malicious character assassination." Shortly afterward he named an old friend of Burger's, Harry Andrew Blackmun (b. 1908), a member of the Court of Appeals for the Eighth Circuit. Blackmun had been Phi Beta Kappa at Harvard and, after graduating from Harvard Law School, had been in private practice for sixteen years, including a stint as counsel to the Mayo Clinic. One commentator described Blackmun's roots as those of a "White Anglo-Saxon Protestant Republican Rotarian Harvard Man from the Suburbs."[82] Both as an attorney and as an appellate court judge, Blackmun had been quiet, hard-working, and generally considered capable. His opinions on the circuit court had been moderately conservative and had tended toward a strict constructionist view of the Constitution.

Once on the Court, newspaper reporters started calling Burger and Blackmun the "Minnesota Twins," a tag that annoyed Blackmun a great deal. While it is true that in the early years the two men tended to vote alike, by the mid-seventies Blackmun had moved away from Burger and had become one of the two key swingmen in the middle, along with Lewis Powell. The middle actually seemed a good place for Blackmun, as he had always emphasized pragmatism above ideology. Like Potter Stewart, he did not support change for its own sake, nor did he seek to read new rights into the law as did Douglas; neither would he take a rigid view that did not allow adjustment to changing conditions. By the early eighties, however, Blackmun's voting pattern moved even further to the left, and as often as not he wound up voting with the liberals, Brennan and Marshall. He enjoyed the fact that the press had long since stopped referring to him and Burger as the "Minnesota Twins."[83] Reporters might well have recalled his answer to a question at the time of his appointment: "I've been called a liberal and a conservative. Labels are deceiving."[84]

Just before the Court opened its October 1971 Term, it lost two of its most illustrious members, Hugo Black and John Harlan. They had both checked into Bethesda Naval Hospital in August, and both submitted their letters of resignation in September. Black died on September 25, and Harlan not long after. To replace Black, Nixon named Lewis Franklin Powell, Jr. (b. 1907) of Virginia, a senior partner in an influential Richmond firm and former president of the American Bar Association.

At age sixty-four, Powell had no desire to go on the Court and turned down the seat when Attorney General Mitchell made the offer. Then the president called and said that Powell had a duty to accept, and as Powell recalled, one can hardly say no to the president. Once again, Nixon had found a political moderate with strong ties in the corporate and legal communities. Moreover, Powell's support of legal services for the poor, his opposition to Virginia's massive resistance against school desegregation in the 1950s, and his efforts to secure peaceful integration of Richmond schools won him the endorsement of many liberals as well. At the same time, more militant blacks considered him a supporter of the status quo, charges that did him no harm with conservatives.[85]

Those who sought to label Powell might well have taken heed of his statement to a reporter, a statement similar to that made by Blackmun: "I don't categorize myself. My views may be liberal on one issue and conservative on another."[86] Although a statistical analysis found Powell voting mostly with the conservatives during the seventies,[87] the author failed to take into account that often Powell agreed with the result but would enter a concurrence stating a more moderate rationale to justify the holding. He favored individual rights but insisted on placing them in the context of communal values; conversely, he believed in majoritarian rule, but not at the expense of individual or minority rights.[88] For Powell, moderation and balance appeared to have been the uppermost virtues during his fifteen years on the bench.[89]

This eventually led Powell to be the proverbial "man in the middle" on any number of 5-4 votes, and perhaps this role is best exemplified in his 4-1-4 opinion for the Court in *Regents of the University of California* v. *Bakke*.[90] Powell's influence tended to moderate the Court's extremes, because neither liberals nor conservatives could hope for a majority without his vote. In the latter years of the Burger Court, Powell can be seen as the leader of the center, usually joined by Blackmun, Stevens, and occasionally White. To their left stood Brennan and Marshall, to their right Rehnquist, O'Connor, Burger, and occasionally White. Powell's innate conservatism led him to oppose extremism from any quarter; change had to take place, but it had to come in its own pace. "It is well to remember," he remarked, "that the course we are running is a long one."[91]

At the same time Nixon sent in Powell's name, he nominated William Hubbs Rehnquist (b. 1924) to take Harlan's seat. Rehnquist also had good credentials, including an undergraduate degree from Stanford, a master's in history from Harvard, and a law degree from Stanford where he edited the law review. After that he served as a clerk to Justice Jackson before entering private practice in Phoenix, where he also was active in the Goldwater wing of the Republican party. Following Nixon's election, he had joined the Justice Department as head of the Office of Legal Counsel, which serves as the attorney general's lawyer. During his stint, Rehnquist took on several special assignments for the president, including memoranda justifying the administration's views on wiretapping, executive privilege, and the war powers.

Of all Nixon's appointments to the Court, Rehnquist proved by far the most ideologically conservative. To forestall Senate rejection, Nixon sent up both the Powell and Rehnquist nominations at the same time, and Senator James Eastland, the powerful head of the Judiciary Committee, made sure that Powell's supporters understood it was a package deal. Once on the Court, Rehnquist quickly became the intellectual leader of the conservatives, arguing steadfastly over the years for strict construction, adherence to original intent, and judicial deference to the legislature. He has been a "law-and-order" man on criminal procedure issues and has refused to recognize the creation of new rights such as abortion or privacy.[92] Had Nixon named others like him, as Reagan tried to do in the 1980s, he might well have turned the Court 180 degrees from Warren activism.

In 1975 a stroke forced William O. Douglas, the last of the Roosevelt appointees, to retire after a record tenure of thirty-six years. Ironically, Gerald Ford, who had tried to impeach Douglas in 1970, named his successor, John Paul Stevens (b. 1920) of Illinois and a member of the Court of Appeals for the Seventh Circuit. After graduating first in his class from Northeastern Law

School, Stevens had clerked for Wiley Rutledge in the 1947 Term and had met and admired Douglas, so he was particularly pleased to be taking his seat. Quiet and self-effacing, Stevens had a reputation while in private practice as a "lawyer's lawyer" and on the appeals court as a "judge's judge." Both scholars and lawyers considered his opinions thorough and sophisticated; at the same time, he had eschewed partisan politics and easily won unanimous Senate confirmation.

While in private practice Stevens had become an expert on antitrust law and probably had a better understanding of economic issues than did any other member of the Burger Court. Some observers expected him to become the intellectual leader of the Court, because his views could command wider support than could the extreme conservatism of Rehnquist. But although Stevens developed some highly original and idiosyncratic theories, they failed to win the support of his colleagues. A centrist on most issues, he alone of the post-Johnson appointees favored the liberal view on rights of the accused.

Ronald Reagan appointed the last member to join the Burger Court, and the first woman in the Court's history, Sandra Day O'Connor (b. 1930). A classmate of Rehnquist at Stanford Law School, she entered private practice in Arizona and in 1969 was appointed to fill a vacant seat in the state senate; her constituents elected her to two subsequent terms. In 1975 she won election to state court, and in 1979 became the first woman appointed to the Arizona Court of Appeals. Despite O'Connor's solid political and conservative credentials, some members of the political right opposed her appointment because she had supported liberalized abortion laws while in the Arizona Senate; she later became one of the most persistent critics of *Roe* v. *Wade* on the Court.[93]

In her first few terms on the Court, O'Connor kept a low profile but tended to vote consistently with Rehnquist and Burger. She then began to establish her own position which, while still conservative, differed significantly from that of her former classmate. She still took a narrow view of civil liberties but found room to allow for judicial review of gender discrimination. She also tended to pay more deference to precedent and valued continuity of doctrine, while allowing for modest changes to accommodate changing conditions. O'Connor's willingness to take an expansive view of the Equal Protection Clause in gender discrimination cases made it possible for the Burger Court to go further in this direction than some of its more conservative members believed prudent or permissible.

These twenty-two men and one woman constituted the membership of the nation's highest court for a third of a century. Widely different in background and philosophy, their differences on key issues accurately reflected the various views held among the general population. They served as the final arbiters of what the Constitution meant in one of the most turbulent periods of American constitutional history.

SOCIAL CHANGE AND THE LIBERAL LEGAL CULTURE

Between the 1880s and 1937, property issues dominated the docket of the Supreme Court. Most of the major cases involved the justices attempting to mediate between the police powers of the state to regulate economic and labor affairs for the public welfare and the right of private property owners to use their property as they saw fit. Conservative judges erected the doctrines of substantive due process and freedom of contract to thwart reform, and the unyielding opposition of the conservative majority on the Supreme Court led to the constitutional crisis of 1937.[94]

However, even while conservatives dominated state and federal courts, legal thinkers in the academies had begun to reformulate legal philosophy. By World War II the basic outlines of the modern liberal legal culture had emerged. Kermit Hall has summarized the basic points of that culture as follows:

> The concept of distributive justice . . . took on a new meaning, one in which government under law was supposed to diminish economic risk taking and heighten individual economic opportunity. Lawmakers had an affirmative duty to provide for rights and liberties, not just to refrain from interfering with their enjoyment. If the courts were to restrain themselves in considering economic regulatory measures, the new configuration of rights consciousness encouraged them to act assertively to promote individual rights and liberties. This new approach raised powerful expectations among groups long disadvantaged, such as blacks, ethnics, native Americans, and women, that judicial institutions were on their side and that through them old wrongs could be legally righted.[95]

As a result, the courts' agendas changed significantly. The old questions of property rights practically disappeared, to be replaced by questions of criminal procedure, access to the ballot, free speech, privacy, and equal protection of the laws—issues which courts had rarely dealt with in the past.

The Court's agenda accurately reflected the growing social turmoil in the country that followed World War II. The Depression years had led many Americans to question not only the economic wisdom of the old order but its social and moral priorities as well, a questioning that had been temporarily stilled during the war. The New Deal, both in peace and war, had shown that the government need not stand by in the face of suffering, that it could respond to the plight of its citizens, and that its solutions could work. Moreover, if the nation could expend its blood and treasure to fight tyranny abroad, then certainly it could no longer tolerate injustice at home.

The example of the NAACP in its quest to overturn legally sanctioned segregation set the model for other groups to follow. The acknowledgment by the Court of one right often led other litigants to put forward their claim to new and different rights. In some ways we became a litigious society,[96] but in other ways this was nothing more than a new version of an old song. Long ago that most perceptive of foreign observers, Alexis de Tocqueville, noted in the 1830s that "scarcely any political question arises in the United States that is not resolved, sooner or later, into a judicial question."[97] If we are to remain a nation of laws rather than of men, then any other recourse is unthinkable; courts must resolve disputes, not only between people but also between the citizenry and their governments. The rule of law and respect for that rule have made it possible for this nation to survive.

So instead of taking to the streets to demand an end to segregation or greater protection of the rights of the accused or the reform of malapportioned legislatures, people went to court and asked for either a broader application of a specific constitutional guarantee, such as the right to an attorney, or a wholly new interpretation of vaguer sections, such as the Equal Protection Clause. The important change is not to be found solely in the number of cases initiated but also in the subject matter of those cases. It is hardly imaginable that a judge sitting on a federal bench in the early thirties would recognize the Bill of Rights as expounded even by conservative jurists a half-century later.[98]

This placed an explicit burden on modern justices that remained somewhat hidden in the past. Common law courts have always had to accommodate law to social change, but normally this rate of change has been slow and incremental, so that minor adjustments to precedent have sufficed. Judges could pretend that all they did was discover already existing law and at most clarified a minor point. In this century, however, the rate of social and economic change has accelerated, and courts have been under constant pressure to keep the law abreast of this change.[99] Incremental change may not be enough, especially when basic rights are concerned; the Supreme Court kept trying to refine the *Plessy* doctrine of "separate but equal" until it had to face the issue head on. *Brown* is certainly a "right" decision from nearly any angle one wishes to view it, but there is no doubt that it is judicial policy making in response to changing social conditions. Not just in race relations but in many other areas as well, a variety of groups in American society looked to the courts to use judicial review as a tool of social change. "The power of judicial review," wrote Eugene Rostow at the beginning of the Warren Court, stands "as an integral feature of the living constitution, long since established as a working part of the democratic political life of the nation."[100]

Given these conditions, the "liberal" majority of the Warren Court had less trouble defining and expanding rights than did the "conservative" majority of the Burger Court, but one question that the following chapters explore is whether any other configuration of justices attuned to modern legal culture as well as the great changes taking place in society could have charted a course significantly different than that followed from 1953 to 1986. What if the Court had ignored the rising tide of black frustration and refused to overrule *Plessy?* We might now have a country torn by violent racial strife, as is South Africa. Did *Brown*, therefore, represent a "radical" or a "conservative" response to an imminent crisis? Similar questions can be asked in regard to gender discrimination, privacy issues, criminal procedure, and freedom of expression. While it is unlikely that civil war would have erupted had the Court decided some Establishment Clause cases differently, civil strife need not always take a violent form.

In the following chapters we look at certain major areas. Part II deals with the various guarantees of freedom of expression contained in the First Amendment; Part III looks at the most criticized and least understood area of the Constitution, the rights of accused persons; Part IV examines the new meaning of equal protection of the laws, especially regarding racial equality but in some other forms as well. In all areas, the inherent institutional constraints, the personalities of the justices, and the changes taking place in society made for constitutional interpretations that, despite some significant departures, have emphasized continuity in our law.

II

THE FIRST AMENDMENT

Congress shall make no law respecting an establishment of religion, or prohibiting the free exercise thereof; or abridging the freedom of speech, or of the press; or the right of the people peaceably to assemble, and to petition the Government for redress of grievances.

2

"No Part of the Business of Government"

The Warren Court and the Religion Clauses

F ew decisions of the Warren Court engendered as much continuing controversy as did its rulings on religious matters. The
segregation cases in the early 1950s caused a major social upheaval in the
country, but within a relatively short period a majority of Americans acknowledged legally sanctioned racial discrimination as constitutionally and morally
wrong. The average person heard charges that the Court had been "soft on
criminals" in cases affecting the rights of accused persons, but aside from
the Miranda warnings seen on television police shows, few people understood
what the Court had done in expanding Fourth, Fifth, and Sixth Amendment
rights.

The religion decisions, however, affected millions of Americans personally—and in ways many did not like.[1] They believed that because of the Court's
decisions, their children could no longer pray in school or read the Bible or
receive religious training on school property. The fact that critics of the Court
distorted the actual rulings certainly exacerbated the situation, but many
people just could not agree that the Framers of the Constitution had intended
to excise religion from the public arena.[2] Long after the furor had died down
over *Brown* and *Miranda*, agitation—and misunderstanding—continued over
the religion rulings. Conservatives demanded a constitutional amendment to
allow prayer in schools, and in 1985, in one of his weekly radio addresses to
the nation, Ronald Reagan declared that "the good Lord who has given our
country so much should never have been expelled from our nation's classrooms."[3] The fact that the president of the United States, more than two
decades after the original school-prayer decisions, publicly misinterpreted
what the Court had said is but one sign of the continuing confusion on this
issue.

THE ESTABLISHMENT CLAUSE PRIOR TO *ENGEL*

The First Amendment to the Constitution contains two clauses concerning religion: "Congress shall make no law respecting an establishment of religion, or prohibiting the free exercise thereof." For most of the first 150 years following the adoption of the Bill of Rights Congress obeyed this injunction,[4] and not until 1947 did the Court rule that the religion clauses applied to the states. Justice Black, in his majority ruling in *Everson* v. *Board of Education*, expounded at length on the historical development of religious freedom in the United States and concluded:

> The "establishment of religion" clause of the First Amendment means at least this: Neither a state nor the Federal Government can set up a church. Neither can pass laws which aid one religion, aid all religions, or prefer one religion over another. Neither can force nor influence a person to go to or remain away from church against his will or force him to profess a belief or disbelief in any religion. No person can be punished for entertaining or professing religious beliefs or disbeliefs, for church attendance or non-attendance. No tax in any amount, large or small, can be levied to support any religious activities or institutions, whatever they may be called, or whatever form they may adopt to teach or practice religion. Neither a state nor the Federal Government can, openly or secretly, participate in the affairs of any religious organization or groups and vice versa. In the words of [Thomas] Jefferson, the clause against establishment of religion by law was intended to erect "a wall of separation between church and State."[5]

In this paragraph we find the fundamental rationale for nearly every religion case decided by the Court in the last forty years, whether it involves the Establishment Clause (in which the government allegedly promotes a religious function) or the Free Exercise Clause (in which the government supposedly restricts an individual from adhering to some practice).

Yet the *Everson* decision provided an interesting twist. A New Jersey statute authorized school districts to make rules providing transportation for students, "including the transportation of schoolchildren to and from school other than a public school, except such school as is operated for profit." One local board allowed reimbursement to parents of parochial school students for fares paid by their children on public buses when going to and from school, and a taxpayer in the district challenged the payments as a form of establishment.

After his lengthy review of the history of the clauses, and language which implied that no form of aid—direct or indirect—could be tolerated under the

Establishment Clause, Justice Black concluded that the reimbursement plan did not violate the First Amendment, which only requires that

> the state be a neutral in its relations with groups of religious believers and non-believers; it does not require the state to be their adversary. . . . [The] legislation, as applied, does no more than provide a general program to help parents get their children, regardless of their religion, safely and expeditiously to and from accredited schools.
>
> The First Amendment has erected a wall between church and state. That wall must be kept high and impregnable. We could not approve the slightest breach. New Jersey has not breached it here.[6]

The opinion evoked dissents from four members of the Court, and Justice Jackson noted that Black, after marshaling every argument in favor of a total separation of church from state, weakly allowed that no breach of the wall had occurred. "The case which irresistibly comes to mind as the most fitting precedent is that of Julia who, according to Byron's reports, 'whispering "I will ne'er consent,"—consented.' "[7] Justice Rutledge took the logic of Black's historical argument and reached the inevitable conclusion that if "the test remains undiluted as Jefferson and Madison made it, [then] money taken by taxation from one is not to be used or given to support another's religious training or belief, or indeed one's own. [T]he prohibition is absolute."[8]

In fact, by the time the Court heard its next religion cases, Justice Black had moved to the position Rutledge had suggested—that the prohibition had to be absolute. In a 1948 decision, *McCollum* v. *Board of Education*, the Court struck down a so-called released-time program in Illinois, in which classrooms in the public schools were turned over for one hour each week for religious instruction.[9] Local churches and synagogues could send in instructors to teach the tenets of their religion to students whose families approved. To Justice Black, writing for the 8-1 majority, the issue could not have been clearer: "Not only are the state's tax-supported public school buildings used for the dissemination of religious doctrines, the State also affords sectarian groups an invaluable aid in that it helps to provide pupils . . . through use of the state's compulsory public school machinery."

Response to the decision varied. The attorney general of Virginia, Lindsay Almond, declared that programs, even those with shared public classrooms, might continue, a ruling applauded by both school officials and church leaders.[10] In northern states where the released-time program followed the Illinois model, with religious instruction taking place in school classrooms, there appears to have been general compliance with the Court's decision. But where local officials could differentiate between the Illinois model and their own, no matter how fine the distinction, the programs remained in operation.

Four years after *McCollum*, the Court issued what might be called its first "accommodationist" ruling on the Establishment Clause. To continue the released-time program, a number of states had moved religious instruction off school property; New York officials, for example, established times in which students left the school grounds and went to religious facilities for instruction. Taxpayers challenged the program on grounds that it still involved the state in promoting religion. The authority of the school supported participation in the program; public school teachers policed attendance; and normal classroom activities came to a halt so students in the program would not miss their secular instruction.

Justice Douglas's opinion for the six-member majority indicated that the Court had heard the public outcry over the *McCollum* decision, and he went out of his way to assert that the Court was not antagonistic to religion. "We are," he intoned, "a religious people whose institutions presuppose a Supreme Being."[11] Although the First Amendment prohibition against an establishment of religion was "absolute," this did not mean that "in every and all respects there shall be a separation of Church and State." Douglas went on to argue that historically the amendment had been interpreted in a "common-sense" manner, because a strict and literal view would lead to unacceptable conclusions: "[M]unicipalities would not be permitted to render police or fire protection to religious groups. Policemen who helped parishioners into their places of worship would violate the Constitution." Such a view would make the state hostile to religion, a condition also forbidden by the First Amendment.

Douglas distinguished between the Illinois and the New York programs primarily on the basis that the former had taken place on school property (a direct aid forbidden by the Constitution) and the latter off the school grounds (indirect assistance not forbidden). Justices Black, Jackson, and Frankfurter dissented. Black put the issue in its bluntest form: New York "is manipulating its compulsory education laws to help religious sects get pupils. This is not separation but combination of Church and State."[12] Justice Jackson, who sent his own children to private church schools, objected as strenuously. The schools did not close down during the released-time period; instead, they suspended teaching so that students who did not choose to attend religious instruction would not get ahead of the "churchgoing absentees." The school, with all the power of the state behind it, thus "serves as a temporary jail for a pupil who will not go to Church."

The three opinions, *Everson*, *McCollum*, and *Zorach*, provided the context in which the Warren Court would hear its religion cases, and the conflicting opinions left very little clear, other than that the religion clauses now applied to the states as well as to the federal government. In all three cases the majority as well as the dissenters had seemingly subscribed to the "wall of separation" metaphor and to the absolute nature of the First Amendment prohibitions, but they disagreed on how "absolute" the separation had to be. Justice Black, after fudging in *Everson*, moved to the absolutist view that characterized his interpretation of the First Amendment for the remaining two decades he sat on the high court. Justice Douglas, who joined Black in that view, also abandoned the temporizing stance he uncharacteristically took in *Zorach*.[13] Although the Warren Court heard no major Establishment Clause cases in its first terms, it appeared likely that a majority of the members would take a strict stand when the issue did arise.

THE REGENTS PRAYER

For many years, ritual marked the beginning of each school day all across America. Teachers led their charges through the Pledge of Allegiance, a short prayer, the singing of "America" or "The Star-Spangled Banner," and possibly some readings from the Bible. The choice of ritual varied according to state law, local custom, and the preferences of individual teachers or principals. In New York, the statewide Board of Regents had prepared a "non-denominational" prayer for use in the public schools. The brief invocation read: "Almighty God, we acknowledge our dependence upon Thee, and we beg Thy blessings upon us, our parents, our teachers and our Country." After one district had directed that the prayer be recited each day, a group of parents challenged the edict as "contrary to the beliefs, religions, or religious practices of both themselves and their children." The New York Court of Appeals, the state's highest tribunal, upheld the school board, providing that it did not force any student to join in the prayer over a parent's objection. The Supreme Court reversed in *Engel* v. *Vitale*.[14]

In his opinion for the 6-1 majority,[15] Justice Black (who had taught Sunday school for more than twenty years) held the entire idea of a state-mandated prayer, no matter how religiously neutral, as "wholly inconsistent with the Establishment Clause." A prayer, by any definition, constituted a religious activity, and the First Amendment "must at least mean that [it] is no part of the business of government to compose official prayers for any group of the American people to recite as part of a religious program carried on by government." Black went on to explain what he saw as the philosophy behind the Establishment Clause:

> [Although] these two clauses may in certain instances overlap, they forbid two quite different kinds of governmental encroachment upon religious freedom. The Establishment Clause, unlike the Free Exercise Clause, does not depend upon any showing of direct governmental compulsion and is violated by the enactment of laws which establish an official religion whether those laws operate directly to coerce nonobserving individuals or not. . . . When the power, prestige and financial support of government is placed behind a particular religious belief, the indirect coercive pressure

upon religious minorities to conform to the prevailing officially approved religion is plain. But the purposes underlying the Establishment Clause go much further than that. [Its] most immediate purpose rested on the belief that a union of government and religion tends to destroy government and degrade religion. [Another] purpose [rested upon] an awareness of the historical fact that governmentally established religions and religious persecutions go hand in hand.[16]

For Black the content of the prayer, its actual words, or the fact that its nondenominational nature allegedly made it religiously neutral, had no relevance to the case. The nature of prayer itself is religious, and by promoting prayer, the state violated the Establishment Clause by fostering a religious activity that it determined and sponsored.

Justice Douglas concurred with the decision, but his opinion shows how far he had traveled both from *Everson* and from *Zorach*. He acknowledged that the former case seemed "in retrospect to be out of line with the First Amendment. Mr. Justice Rutledge stated in dissent what I think is desirable First Amendment philosophy." The man who had approvingly noted the practice of starting sessions of the Court or of legislative bodies with prayers now argued that even those prayers ought to be ruled unconstitutional. Only Justice Stewart dissented, and he quoted Douglas's *Zorach* opinion that "we are a religious people whose institutions presuppose a Supreme Being." The practice in New York and elsewhere did no more than recognize "the deeply entrenched and highly cherished spiritual traditions of our Nation," as did the opening of Court and Congress with prayer.

The *Engel* decision unleashed a firestorm of conservative criticism against the Court which, while it abated from time to time, never died out. In the eyes of many, the Court had struck at a traditional practice that served important social purposes, even if it occasionally penalized a few nonconformists or eccentrics. Taken in concert with the Court's other decisions, it appeared as if Earl Warren and his colleagues were hell-bent on overturning decades, even centuries, of cherished American values. One newspaper headline screamed "COURT OUTLAWS GOD." An outraged Billy Graham thundered "God pity our country when we can no longer appeal to God for help," while Francis Cardinal Spellman of New York denounced *Engel* as striking "at the very heart of the Godly tradition in which America's children have for so long been raised."[17]

The level of abuse heaped upon the Warren Court for the prayer decision reached its peak in Congress. "They put the Negroes in the schools," Representative George W. Andrews of Alabama complained, and "they have driven God out."[18] Senator Sam Ervin of North Carolina charged that the Supreme Court "has made God unconstitutional,"[19] while Congressman John Bell

Williams of Mississippi condemned the decision as "a deliberately and carefully planned conspiracy to substitute materialism for spiritual values and thus to communize America."[20] In an obvious swipe at the Court, the House of Representatives voted the following September to place the motto "In God We Trust" behind the Speaker's chair, and a number of congressmen and senators introduced constitutional amendments to reverse the ruling.[21]

The Court had its champions as well. Liberal Protestant and Jewish agencies saw the decision as a significant move to divorce religion from meaningless public ritual and to protect its sincere practice.[22] The National Council of Churches, a coalition of liberal and orthodox denominations, praised the *Engel* decision for protecting minority rights, while the Anti-Defamation League applauded the "splendid reaffirmation of a basic American principle." President John F. Kennedy, who had been the target of vicious religious bigotry in the 1960 campaign (from many of the groups now attacking the Court), urged support of the decision, and told a news conference:

> We have, in this case, a very easy remedy. And that is, to pray ourselves. And I would think that it would be a welcome reminder to every American family that we can pray a good deal more at home, we can attend our churches with a good deal more fidelity, and we can make the true meaning of prayer much more important in the lives of all of our children.[23]

Kennedy's common-sense approach captured the Court's intent in *Engel*. The majority did not oppose either prayer or religion, but did believe that the Framers of the Constitution had gone to great lengths to protect individual freedoms in the Bill of Rights. To protect the *individual's* freedom of religion, the state could not impose any sort of religious requirement, even in an allegedly "neutral" prayer. As soon as the power and prestige of the government is placed behind any religious belief or practice, according to Justice Black, "[T]he inherently coercive pressure upon religious minorities to conform to the prevailing officially approved religion is plain."

BIBLE READING IN THE SCHOOLS

One year after the school prayer decision, the Court extended this reasoning in *Abington School District* v. *Schempp*.[24] A Pennsylvania law required that

> [a]t least ten verses from the Holy Bible shall be read, without comment, at the opening of each public school on each school day. Any child shall be excused from such Bible reading, or attending such Bible reading, upon the written request of his parent or guardian.

In addition, the students were to recite the Lord's Prayer in unison. This time Justice Tom Clark, normally considered a conservative, spoke for the 8-1 majority in striking down the required Bible reading. He built upon Black's comments in *Engel* that the neutrality commanded by the Constitution stemmed from the bitter lessons of history, which recognized that a fusion of church and state inevitably led to persecution of all but those who adhered to the official orthodoxy.

Recognizing that the Court would be confronted with additional Establishment Clause cases in the future, Clark attempted to set out rules by which lower courts could determine when the constitutional barrier had been breached. The test, he said, may be stated as follows:

> What are the purpose and the primary effect of the enactment? If either is the advancement or inhibition of religion then the enactment exceeds the scope of legislative power as circumscribed by the Constitution. That is to say that to withstand the strictures of the Establishment Clause there must be a secular legislative purpose and a primary effect that neither advances nor inhibits religion.[25]

In this last sentence, Clark set out the first two prongs of what would later be known as the *Lemon* tripartite test, which the Court has used to evaluate all Establishment Clause challenges. The legislation (1) had to have a secular purpose and (2) could neither advance nor inhibit religion. Clark also sought some criteria for distinguishing between the two religion clauses. The Establishment Clause prohibited state sponsorship of religious activities, while the Free Exercise Clause prohibited state compulsion. "The distinction between the two clauses is apparent—a violation of the Free Exercise Clause is predicated on coercion while the Establishment Clause violation need not be so attended."

In this case there had been no formal coercion, because students could be excused from the exercises, but Clark correctly noted that nonparticipating students inevitably called attention to themselves by their absence and thus invited retribution in the form of peer ostracism. Justice William J. Brennan in his concurrence quoted from his teacher, Felix Frankfurter, that "non-conformity is not an outstanding characteristic of children. The result is an obvious pressure upon children to attend."[26] The Court thus apparently held that the coercion needed to trigger a free exercise claim might be indirect, one resulting from the situation created by the government's actions.

In response to Justice Stewart's criticism that in protecting the religious freedom of a few dissenters the Court violated the free exercise rights of the majority who wanted to read the Bible, Clark declared that the Court

> cannot accept that the concept of neutrality, which does not permit a State to require a religious exercise even with the consent of the majority of those

affected, collides with the majority's right to free exercise of religion. While the Free Exercise Clause clearly prohibits the use of state action to deny the rights of free exercise to *anyone*, it has never meant that the majority could use the machinery of the State to practice its beliefs.[27]

Only Justice Stewart dissented,[28] and he argued against either the necessity or the desirability of having a single constitutional standard. "Religion and government must interact in countless ways," most of which were harmless and should not be subject to a "doctrinaire reading of the Establishment Clause." He chastised the majority for violating the free exercise claims of those who wish their children to start the school day with exposure to the Bible. He also objected to the majority's assumption that every involvement by the state necessarily led to coercion; such an assumption would cast suspicion on every type of activity in which one might find some religious component, and he wanted to shift the burden of proof from a presumption of coercion to an actual showing that it had occurred.

Although the *Schempp* case did not trigger quite the uproar that had followed *Engel*,[29] Justice Stewart's dissent did reflect the feeling of many people that *their* rights had been restricted for the sake of a few kooks.[30] Moreover, the Court seemed to say (despite Clark's specific assurances to the contrary)[31] that the Bible could no longer be read in the schools. Americans had been reading the Bible ever since the Puritans had established schools in Massachusetts in the 1630s; generations of settlers had taught their children to read poring over the Bible by the light of oil lamps. Public officials from the president down often took the oath of office with one hand on the Bible. How could it be religious coercion to require schoolchildren to hear a few verses from the Good Book each day? One still finds many people who cannot understand why the Court should find the Bible so threatening.

The discussion might begin with the question "Which Bible?" Most of the statutes or regulations called for the King James version of the Bible, which, without anything else, is anathema to Catholics. The King James also includes both the Old and New Testaments, and Jews object not only to the New Testament but also to the phrasing of certain passages in the Old Testament. Whatever the literary qualities of this seventeenth-century masterpiece, it is riddled with errors in its translations from the ancient Hebrew and Greek, and many of the resulting passages are unacceptable to current dogma in several Protestant sects. And given the patterns of recent immigration, one might well ask whether the Koran or any one of several Far Eastern texts might also be demanded in some schools.

Another consideration is that whether one uses the King James or the Revised Standard or the Douay or the Jewish Publication Society or the Good News version, one is dealing with a book that is essentially a religious appliance. It is designed to promote belief and faith, and that is what every Jewish and Christian sect uses it for. It is the Good Book, the Holy Scriptures, and its official reading over the school public-address system cannot fail but to remind of its reading from the pulpit as part of a religious service.

The fact that a majority of people—even a large majority—are not affronted by prayer in the school or Bible reading is, to a large extent, irrelevant in constitutional adjudication. The purpose of the Bill of Rights is not to protect the majority but rather the minority. As Justice Oliver Wendell Holmes once said of freedom of speech, it is not for the speech we agree with, but for the speech we detest. Freedom of religion, like freedom of speech, does of course protect the majority, but we need not invoke it when nearly everyone is Protestant and subscribes to middle-class values. The protection of the First Amendment is invoked when the majority, attempting to use the power of the state, tries to enforce conformity in speech or religious practice. Very often, to protect that one dissident, that one disbeliever, the majority may be discomfited; it is the price the Founding Fathers declared themselves willing to pay for religious freedom.

Civil libertarians also express concern about state agencies, especially schools, advocating particular religious doctrines or practices as society grows ever more heterogeneous. Those who do not accept the norms of the majority, as Justice O'Connor wrote in a later case, "are outsiders, not full members of the political community."[32] The dissenters are merely tolerated, because of their religion or lack of it, and they are made to feel as inferior members of the society, a situation the Framers of the Constitution wanted to avoid.

Finally, while fundamentalist religious groups attacked the Court's decision in *Engel* and *Schempp*, many of the mainstream religious bodies soon came to see that the Court had actually promoted religion rather than subverted it.[33] The Framers of the famed "Memorial and Remonstrance,"[34] which Virginia Baptists addressed to the General Assembly in 1785, believed that not only the state's antagonism, but also its efforts at assistance, could damage religion and religious liberty. Their intellectual descendants have argued along similar lines and believe that the state can never help religion, but only hinder it. To establish any form of state-sanctioned religious activity in the schools threatens to introduce denominational hostility. Moreover, sincere believers do not need the state to do anything for them except leave them alone; those with confidence in their faith do not need Caesar's assistance to render what is due to God.[35]

EVOLUTION AND CREATION

One can describe the school prayer and Bible cases as instances in which a benign majority unthinkingly imposed its views, unaware that the results restricted the religious freedom of a minority. In the third major Establishment

Clause case of the Warren Court, however, a local majority deliberately attempted to establish its views as official dogma in defiance of what the rest of the country believed.

One of the most famous battlegrounds of the 1920s between the forces of tradition and modernism was the Scopes "Monkey Trial" in Dayton, Tennessee.[36] The legislature had passed a bill outlawing the teaching of evolution in the state's schools. Civic boosters in Dayton had gotten a young teacher named John Scopes to test the law, and the American Civil Liberties Union then provided a lawyer for Scopes. To sleepy Dayton came William Jennings Bryan to thunder against science and uphold the literal interpretation of the Bible, and Clarence Darrow, the greatest trial lawyer of his time, who spoke for science, reason, and intellectual toleration. Darrow exposed Bryan as a narrow-minded bigot, but the local jury still convicted Scopes. The Tennessee Supreme Court reversed the conviction on a technicality, which forestalled Darrow's plan to appeal to the Supreme Court. The law remained on the Tennessee statute books, and similar laws could be found in other "Bible belt" states, but following Dayton they remained essentially dead letters, unenforced and in many cases nearly forgotten.

In Arkansas, the statute prohibited teachers in state schools from teaching the "theory or doctrine that mankind ascended or descended from a lower order of animals." An Arkansas biology teacher, Susan Epperson,[37] sought a declaratory judgment on the constitutionality of the statute. The Arkansas Supreme Court, aware of antievolution sentiment within the state, had evaded the constitutional issue entirely, by expressing "no opinion" on "whether the Act prohibits any explanation of the theory of evolution or merely prohibits teaching that the theory is true."[38]

On either ground the law ran afoul of the Constitution. Without a dissenting vote the Court struck down the Arkansas statute as a violation of the Establishment Clause.[39] Justice Fortas concluded that the Arkansas law "selects from the body of knowledge a particular segment which it proscribes for the sole reason that it is deemed to conflict with a particular religious doctrine, that is, with a particular interpretation of the Book of Genesis by a particular religious group." The Court, having found what it considered a sufficiently narrow ground on which to rule, ignored the larger issues of academic freedom.[40]

Justices Black and Stewart concurred in the result, though they considered the statute void for vagueness. But Black raised some troubling questions in his opinion that foreshadowed some of the issues which would come back before the Court in the Burger years.[41] The majority, in his view, had raised several "troublesome" First Amendment questions. A state law, for example, which prohibited any teaching of biology would be constitutionally different from one that compelled a teacher to teach that only a particular theory is true. Black also was not prepared to hold that a teacher had constitutional rights to teach theories—be they economic, political, sociological, or religious—that the school's elected and appointed managers did not want discussed.

Black's most interesting point, however, involved the question of whether the majority opinion actually achieved the constitutional desideratum of "religious neutrality." If the people of Arkansas considered evolutionary theory antireligious, did the Constitution nonetheless require the state to permit the teaching of such doctrine? Had the Court infringed "the religious freedom of those who consider evolution antireligious doctrine"? Because the record did not indicate whether Arkansas schools taught a literal reading of the Genesis creation story, could a state law prohibiting the teaching of evolution be considered a neutral statute, if it removed a contentious issue from the classroom? Black saw no reason "why a State is without power to withdraw from its curriculum any subject deemed too emotional and controversial for its public schools."

Black's reasoning, or rather its obverse, proved the vehicle by which antievolutionists in Arkansas and elsewhere sought to bypass the *Epperson* ruling a generation later. Instead of removing biology and the evolutionary theory from the schools, they added so-called creation science, which advocated the biblical narrative as supported by allegedly scientific evidence and required that any school teaching evolution had to give "equal time" in the classroom to creation science.

A federal district court found the Arkansas equal-time statute defective,[42] but the Louisiana Balanced Treatment Act of 1982 reached the Supreme Court the year after Warren Burger retired. Justice Brennan spoke for a 7-2 majority in striking down the statute as a violation of the Establishment Clause.[43] The Court denounced the stated purpose of the law, to advance academic freedom, as a sham, because the sponsors of the bill had made it clear during the legislative debate that they wanted to inject religious teachings into the public schools. It is unlikely that the issue will go away; as with the issues of prayer and Bible reading, the true believers will keep seeking some way to get their views grafted onto the school curriculum.

THE FREE EXERCISE CLAUSE

In some ways, but only some, free exercise cases are easier than establishment problems, because they involve the state restricting an individual's religious practices. There is, of course, much overlap between the two clauses, and often a governmental program that tries to help religion in general may in fact restrict the freedoms of individuals. The school prayer and Bible readings offended the Court not just on establishment grounds, but also because they limited the free exercise of those who disagreed with the prayer or worshipped from another Bible.

Free exercise claims also overlap with claims to freedom of expression; several important cases prior to 1953 involved Jehovah's Witnesses, who claimed a right to proselytize, without state regulation, as essential to the free exercise of their beliefs. In these cases, the Court's analysis concentrated almost solely on the criteria used to safeguard speech.[44] In addition, there are some issues unique to free exercise claims.

First is the belief/action dichotomy originally enunciated by Chief Justice Morrison Waite in the Mormon bigamy case in 1879.[45] While the First Amendment absolutely prohibits government efforts to restrict beliefs, it does not prevent the state from forbidding practices that threaten public order or safety. In the example Waite used, if a sect believed in human sacrifice, the government could do nothing to restrict that belief;[46] but it could, without violating the Free Expression Clause, bar the actual sacrifice. The Court soon recognized, however, that one could not divide belief and action so easily, and in 1940 it modified Waite's rule; while action remained subject to regulation, it deserved some protection under free exercise claims.[47]

A second problem involves limits placed by the Establishment Clause on the Free Exercise Clause. The two clauses overlap in their protection, but there are also instances where they conflict. A state's efforts to accommodate certain groups by exempting or immunizing them from general laws may also be seen as providing a preference to one sect.

Undoubtedly the most famous of the early free exercise cases involved the Jehovah's Witnesses and their refusal to salute the American flag. The Witnesses took literally the biblical command not to "bow down to graven images" and considered the flag as an icon. In the first case, *Minersville School District* v. *Gobitis*,[48] Justice Frankfurter sustained the school board requirement that all students participate in the morning ritual. He rejected the free exercise claim almost summarily: "The mere possession of religious convictions which contradict the relevant concerns of political society does not relieve the citizen from the discharge of political responsibilities." Only Justice Stone dissented in that case, arguing that freedom of expression as well as religion had been violated.

One has to recall that the *Gobitis* decision came down with Europe already at war and the United States rearming. But the Witnesses refused to compromise their principles, and the Court soon realized that its decision had been interpreted as a green light to harass those who refused to conform. Moreover, as stories of Nazi atrocities seeped out of Europe, many Americans questioned the right of the state to impose its will on minorities in the name of patriotism.

In 1943 the Court reversed itself in *West Virginia State Board of Education* v. *Barnette*.[49] Justice Jackson, writing for the majority, found the central issue to be less one of religious liberty than freedom of expression. In a passage often quoted in subsequent free exercise cases, he declared:

The very purpose of the Bill of Rights was to withdraw certain subjects from the vicissitudes of political controversy, to place them beyond the reach of majorities and officials and to establish them as legal principles to be applied by the courts. . . . [If] there is any fixed star in our constitutional constellation, it is that no official, high or petty, can prescribe what shall be orthodox in politics, nationalism, religion or other matters of opinion or force citizens to confess by word or act their faith therein.

Probably no other passage so captures the modern meaning of religious freedom.

SUNDAY CLOSING LAWS

The flag salute cases indicated how closely free exercise and freedom of expression are intertwined; the Sunday closing laws show the interconnectedness of the two religion clauses. A number of states had, and many still do have, laws requiring the majority of businesses to close on Sunday. In 1961 the Court heard four cases challenging these laws as violations of the First Amendment, and in three of them the Court refused to consider free exercise claims. In *McGowan* v. *Maryland*,[50] Chief Justice Warren conceded that "the original laws which dealt with Sunday labor were motivated by religious forces." He rejected, however, the argument that this constituted an establishment of religion, because in modern times the laws represented an effort by the state to enforce one day's rest in seven. "The fact that this day is Sunday, a day of particular significance for the dominant Christian sects, does not bar the State from achieving its secular [goals]. Sunday is a day apart from all others. The cause is irrelevant; the fact exists."[51]

In the companion case of *Braunfeld* v. *Brown*,[52] orthodox Jewish merchants attacked the Sunday laws on free exercise grounds. Their religious beliefs required them to close on Saturdays, and having their shops closed two days a week would seriously undermine their ability to earn a livelihood. Chief Justice Warren recited the accepted distinction between belief and action and noted that nothing in the law forced the appellants to modify or deny their beliefs; at worst, they might have to change occupations or incur some economic disadvantages.

There is a striking insensitivity, almost callousness, in Warren's opinion to the problem raised by the Jewish merchants, especially when one considers the great sensitivity he showed to the plights of other minority groups. The opinion is mechanical in its recitation of previous cases setting forth the belief/action dichotomy, and then apparent relief in finding that the law affected only action and was therefore valid.[53] While it is true that nearly all laws have adverse affects on some groups, the Court had imposed a closer scrutiny on laws affecting First Amendment rights. To say that the law did not affect beliefs, but only made it economically difficult for adherents of Judaism to practice those beliefs, showed a complete misunderstanding of the spirit of the Free Exercise Clause.

Justices Stewart and Douglas[54] dissented, but Justice Brennan in his objections pointed the way toward future First Amendment jurisprudence. He had no doubt but that the Sunday closing law imposed a great burden on the Jewish merchants, forcing them to choose between their business and their religion, and this, he believed, violated the Free Exercise Clause. To impose such a burden, the state had to prove some compelling state interest to justify this restriction on freedom of religion, and the "mere convenience" of having everybody rest on the same day did not, in his eyes, constitute a compelling state interest.

Did Pennsylvania have any options, by which the state's interest in fostering one day's rest in seven would not conflict with the appellants' religious freedom? Of course it did. Of the thirty-four states with Sunday closing laws, twenty-one granted exemptions to those who in good faith observed another day of rest. The Court, he charged, had "exalted administrative convenience to a constitutional level high enough to justify making one religion economically disadvantageous."

SATURDAY WORK

Justice Brennan not only pointed out that a common-sense solution existed; his opinion also showed greater sensitivity to the problems economic hardship would cause religious freedom, and the Brennan view triumphed fairly quickly. Two years after the Sunday closing-law cases, the Court heard a case in which a Seventh-Day Adventist in South Carolina had been discharged from her job because she would not work on Saturday. Her refusal to work on her Sabbath prevented her from finding other employment, and then the state denied her unemployment compensation payments. South Carolina law barred benefits to workers who refused, without "good cause," to accept suitable work when offered.[55]

In what we would now term the "modern" approach to First Amendment issues, Justice Brennan posed the same question he had in *Braunfeld:* Did the state have a compelling interest sufficient to warrant an abridgment of a constitutionally protected right? This is, of course, the same question the Court asks in regard to speech restrictions, because the analytical processes in speech and free exercise claims are similar. Free expression of ideas is involved in religion just as in speech, press, assembly, or petition, namely, the right to say what one believes, whether it involves political, economic, social, or religious ideas. Justices Black and Douglas over the years argued for what they termed a "preferred position" for First Amendment rights, because the two men believed these rights to be at the core of a democratic society. Only the most compelling societal need can warrant any restrictions on these rights.[56]

Justice Brennan found no compelling interest presented by the state, and in fact the state could do little more than suggest that some applicants might file fraudulent claims alleging that they could not find work for religious reasons. Brennan did recognize, however, the difficulties Justice Potter Stewart raised in his concurrence, that in ruling that the state had to pay unemployment compensation benefits to Ms. Sherbert, South Carolina was favoring the adherents of one particular sect.[57] He went out of his way to indicate the very limited nature of the decision:

> In holding as we do [Brennan wrote], plainly we are not fostering the "establishment" of the Seventh-day Adventist religion in South Carolina. . . . [Nor] do we . . . declare the existence of a constitutional right to unemployment benefits on the part of all persons whose religious convictions are the cause of their unemployment. This is not a case in which an employee's religious convictions serve to make him a nonproductive member of society. [Our] holding today is only that South Carolina may not constitutionally apply the eligibility provisions so as to constrain a worker to abandon his religious convictions respecting the day of rest.

The *Sherbert* case, as well as that involving the Amish in Wisconsin,[58] raises the question of whether the Constitution can be read as totally "religion-neutral" or "religion-blind." Professor Philip B. Kurland has suggested that one can find a unifying principle in the two religion clauses and that they ought to be "read as a single precept that government cannot utilize religion as a standard for action or inaction, because these clauses prohibit classification in terms of religion either to control a benefit or impose a burden."[59] The argument parallels the suggestion made by the first Justice Harlan that the Constitution is "color-blind,"[60] and like that argument, is manifestly incorrect.

Neither the Constitution nor the Court have been color-blind. Both the original Constitution and the Civil War amendments recognized that blacks stood in a position of decided inferiority to whites; the original Constitution tended to sustain this arrangement,[61] whereas the amendments sought to erase the prevailing discrimination. The Court that decided *Plessy* favored the post–Civil War South's efforts to recreate a dual society, whereas the Warren and Burger Courts sought to erase the badges of discrimination.

Similarly, neutrality in religious matters is more of an ideal than a reality in constitutional adjudication, and for the same reason. Very few issues that reach the Court can be resolved in simple ways; if the cases had been easy to resolve, the Court would not have heard them. Religion, like race, is a tangled skein and not amenable to simplistic solutions. The Court has recognized this, and from the absolutist decisions of the early Warren era, the Court has moved steadily toward a jurisprudence of balancing various considerations. We will see this balancing more fully in the Burger era, especially in the complex matter of public aid to religious schools.

CONSCIENTIOUS OBJECTORS

A final free exercise issue heard during the Warren years involved claims by those opposed to war in general, or specifically to American involvement in Vietnam. In this century Congress has shown a commendable sensitivity toward those with religious scruples against war, and in the World War I draft law it had provided an exemption for conscientious objectors. The Supreme Court had summarily rejected First Amendment objections to this exemption, holding it to be an appropriate exercise of legislative discretion.[62]

Following World War II, Congress revised the draft in the Universal Military Training and Service Act of 1948. Section 6(j) exempted persons from military service who conscientiously opposed participation in war in any form because of their "religious training and belief." The statute defined this clause as a "belief in a relation to a Supreme Being involving duties superior to those arising from any human relation, but [not including] essentially political, sociological, or philosophical views or a merely personal moral code." Critics attacked Section 6(j) on establishment, free exercise, and due process grounds, arguing that it did not exempt nonreligious conscientious objectors and that it discriminated among various forms of religious expression.

A number of challenges reached the courts in the early 1960s, as American involvement in Southeast Asia began to escalate, and in 1965 the Supreme Court heard three challenges decided together as *United States* v. *Seeger*.[63] The Court evaded the constitutional challenges by the simple expedient of reading the statute so broadly as to provide exemptions for all of the petitioners. Justice Clark declared that Congress, by using the phrase "Supreme Being" rather than "God," meant to "embrace all religions" and exclude only nonreligious objections to military participation. Therefore, the proper test would not be adherence to a particular denomination, but rather "whether a given belief that is sincere and meaningful occupies a place in the life of its possessor parallel to that filled by the orthodox belief in God of one who clearly qualifies for the exemption."

Whether the Congress that had passed the 1948 statute really meant this is impossible to determine, but two years later Congress ratified and in fact expanded the scope of the exemption by deleting the phrase "belief in a relation to a Supreme Being." The Warren Court, for all that it read the statute broadly, nonetheless evaded the First Amendment questions and also the more particular challenges of those opposed to the Vietnam War. In this, as in other areas, the Warren Court set out new interpretations in broad brush strokes and left the more difficult problems to its successor.

CONCLUSIONS

When the Warren Court began to hear Religion Clauses cases, it had a small body of precedent on which to rely. A nineteenth-century case had established the belief/action dichotomy, and in the 1940s two important rulings had been handed down, one declaring that the truth of a belief could not be questioned by the courts and the other incorporating the Religion Clauses and applying them to the states.

In the major cases, the justices took a strict view of what the First Amendment required, and time and again they quoted Thomas Jefferson's view that it called for a "wall of separation" between church and state. Here we find what will become a familiar pattern—the Court confronting new issues and striking out, at least initially, in an absolutist interpretation of what the Constitution required. The Court, in fact, could have gone much further than it did in some areas, such as the Sunday closing laws, where a majority attempted to accommodate the widespread belief in a mandatory day of rest on Sunday.

Many Americans, however, believed the Court had gone too far, and by the late 1960s critics of the religion cases had begun developing what would be termed a jurisprudence of original intent, in which they claimed that the Framers of the Constitution had never intended an absolute wall of separation. The First Amendment, they argued, did not bar all contacts and support by the state of religious affairs, but only prohibited the preference of one sect above the others. Conflict between the absolutist and accommodationist views marked the Burger Court's decisions on the Religion Clauses.

3

"As Winding as the Famous Serpentine Wall"

The Burger Court and the Religion Clauses

In religion cases, as in so many other areas, the perception of the Burger Court differs considerably from the reality. The Warren Court, as we have seen, dealt with the Religion Clauses almost as if they were a blank slate; as a result, its landmark cases on school prayer, Bible reading, evolution, and Sabbath observance captured public attention and struck many Americans, especially those who believed that religion belonged in schools, as wrong. Political and religious conservatives expected, indeed demanded, that the Burger Court reject these earlier rulings.[1] Some members of the Court appeared willing to do so and espoused an accommodationist view based on what came to be known as a jurisprudence of original intent. Especially in the latter years of Warren Burger's tenure, debate over original intent, and what the Religion Clauses actually meant, occupied a central place in both popular and academic debate over the Court.

THE FRAMERS AND ORIGINAL INTENT

Justice Black, in his majority ruling in *Everson* v. *Board of Education*, had expounded at length on the historical development of the Establishment Clause and had concluded that "in the words of [Thomas] Jefferson, the clause against establishment of religion by law was intended to erect 'a wall of separation between church and State.'"[2]

Black's opinion set the basis for all Establishment Clause cases for the next forty years and also opened the door to the flourishing debate over the original intent of the Framers in drafting not only the First Amendment but also the Constitution as a whole, and how justices today ought to interpret that document. The debate—in the courts, in law schools, and in the public—has gone under several names, "judicial restraint" vs. "activism" and "interpretivism" vs. "noninterpretivism," but the core issue is whether judges, in deciding constitutional issues, should confine themselves to norms that are either stated or clearly implicit in the written document (restraint and inter-pretivism) or whether they can go beyond the four corners of the written Constitution to discover evolving or implied standards (activism and non-interpretivism).[3]

Edwin Meese, who served as attorney general in the second Reagan administration, led the attack for a strict adherence to what he called a "juris-prudence of original intention," in which the courts would determine exactly what the Framers had meant and would interpret the Constitution accordingly:

> We know how the Founding Fathers lived, and much of what they read, thought, and believed. The disputes and compromises of the Constitu-tional Convention were carefully recorded. The minutes of the Convention are a matter of public record. Several of the most important participants— including James Madison, the "father" of the Constitution—wrote com-prehensive accounts of the Convention. Others, Federalists and Anti-Federalists alike, committed their arguments for and against ratifica-tion, as well as their understandings of the Constitution, to paper, so that their ideas and conclusions could be widely circulated, read, and under-stood. In short, the Constitution is not buried in the mists of time. . . .
>
> Where the language of the Constitution is specific, it must be obeyed. Where there is a demonstrable consensus among the Framers and ratifiers as to a principle stated or implied by the Constitution, it should be followed. Where there is ambiguity as to the precise meaning or reach of a constitutional provision, it should be interpreted and applied in a manner so as to at least not contradict the text of the Constitution itself.[4]

But what exactly did the Framers and ratifiers of the First Amendment Religion Clauses intend? Did they mean, as Justice Black argued, that the exact meaning of "Congress shall make *no* law" meant just that, that Congress (and through the Fourteenth Amendment the states) could not in any way, shape, or form do anything that might breach the "wall of separation"?[5] Or did they mean that while government could not prefer one sect over another, it might provide aid to all religions on an equal basis?[6] Or is the historical record not as clear as Meese and others would have us believe, so that the "original intent" of the Framers is either not available or irrelevant to contemporary jurisprudence?[7]

There is an argument to be made that the historic record is, at best, only a preliminary guide to interpreting what the Constitution means and that the record is often confused and contradictory.[8] Take, for example, the dispute that swirled around George Washington's 1793 Proclamation of Neutrality, which he issued without first consulting Congress. Alexander Hamilton defended the president's action in a series of articles signed "Pacificus" and expounded a sweeping interpretation of executive powers under Article II. James Madison, the "father" of the Constitution, penned several newspaper pieces under the pseudonym "Helvidius" in response to Hamilton, and he argued that the president had limited authority and could not act without approval by the Congress.[9] The three men—Washington, Hamilton, and Madison—had been at the Philadelphia Convention; the latter two wrote the most authoritative constitutional commentary we have, *The Federalist*. Yet within four years of the Constitution's ratification they stood diametrically opposed on interpreting a major provision![10]

At the core of the problem of interpreting what the Constitution means is one's view of the document and its role in American government. It is not just a framework for the visible aspects of that government, establishing two houses of Congress, two senators from every state, a president, and so forth; it is also the repository for the political soul of the nation, that is, for how we wish to be governed. Advocates of original intent believe that the vision of the Framers is as good today as 200 years ago and any deviation from that view is an abandonment of the ideals which have made this country free and great. Judges, they argue, should hew strictly to what the Framers intended, for they are not empowered to revise the Constitution through judicial fiat. If revisions are to be made, it must be through the amendment process.

Defenders of judicial activism agree that courts ought not to amend the Constitution, but they believe that for the document to remain true to the intent of the Framers, it must be interpreted in the light of two lamps: the spirit of the Framers and the realities of modern society. They believe that the founding generation never intended to put a straightjacket on succeeding generations; rather, the Framers set out a series of ideals, expressed through powers and limitations, and deliberately left details vague so that Americans who came after could apply those ideals to the world they lived in. As conditions changed, so too would the meaning of some sections of the Constitution; this view would apply not only to broad delegations of power, such as the Commerce Clause, but to more specific prohibitions as well, such as the Bill of Rights.

In regard to the Establishment Clause, for example, advocates of original intent argue that the Founders never intended a complete prohibition of aid to religion or to establish an impregnable wall. Rather, they meant that no single sect would be elevated above the others and government could aid religious agencies provided it did so on a nondiscriminatory basis. Therefore, state aid to parochial schools, nondenominational prayers, and public involvement in religious activities are not forbidden provided no particular religion is favored above the others.

The noninterpretationist response is that while this situation may or may not have been true in 1787, conditions have changed dramatically in the intervening two centuries; in fact, conditions were changing even in the latter part of the eighteenth century. The Framers sought language in the First Amendment that would reflect not so much their distaste of a single established church (that model was already passing from the scene) but rather their fears of church-state entanglement in general.[11] That accounts for the absolute prohibitions expressed in the First Amendment, and courts should, therefore, decide Establishment Clause cases to preserve inviolate a wall of separation between religion and the state.

The conflict between these two schools of thought can easily be seen in the Burger Court's decisions on state aid to parochial education.

AID TO EDUCATION—THE FIRST CASES

Even as the Warren Court was broadening the reach of the Establishment Clause, the Johnson administration raised new problems through its education programs. In January 1965, Lyndon Johnson proposed a massive aid-to-education program as part of the Great Society. The federal government would provide $1.5 billion in grants to the nation's schools—primary and secondary, public and private, secular and parochial. Recognizing that aid to religious schools would be challenged in the courts, the administration attempted to immunize the provision from judicial scrutiny and defeated an effort by Senator Sam Ervin that would have allowed taxpayer suits to challenge the constitutionality of the law.[12]

In *Flast* v. *Cohen*,[13] however, Chief Justice Warren differentiated between earlier cases, which barred taxpayer suits, and one in which First Amendment protections were at stake. By this decision, Warren ensured that the Court would have a significant voice in the national debate over educational policies. Most of these cases would not reach the Court until after Warren had retired, but there seemed little doubt that the issue would have to be adjudicated. Following the Elementary and Secondary Education Act of 1965, both Congress and the states passed dozens of educational-aid programs that benefited parochial schools.

The Warren Court itself heard only one of these cases, a challenge to a 1965 New York law mandating local school boards to furnish textbooks from a state-approved list to nonprofit private schools within their jurisdictions. Technically, the boards merely "loaned" the books and retained title to them; in fact, the books would remain in possession of the private schools until the school boards wrote them off for wear and tear. In *Board of Education* v. *Allen*[14] the Court upheld the law on what is known the pupil-benefit theory, which derived directly from Justice Black's opinion in *Everson*. The loan of the texts, according to Justice White, did not aid religion, but instead benefited the individual student, whether at a public or parochial school, and that, he claimed, had been the primary intent of the legislature. Given these facts, the Court found no violation of the Establishment Clause.

White's opinion drew strong protests from Black and Douglas and a partial dissent from Harlan. Black claimed that the New York arrangement represented exactly the type of involvement he had warned about in *Everson;* Douglas entered a lengthy opinion that argued the centrality of textbooks in education and the intrinsically sectarian nature of parochial schools. But White had not gone as far as the dissenters charged; in an opinion described as "laconic" and "cloudy," White left the door open for the Court to reverse itself without embarrassment. He handed down no grand rulings on the meaning or scope of the Establishment Clause, only narrow approval of a particular program.[15]

AID TO EDUCATION—FINDING A RULE

The Warren Court's decisions had made it clear that parochial schools could not expect state aid to teach religion, but *Allen* held out the hope that they might receive government money for teaching secular subjects. Under the pupil-benefit rule, the Court had upheld bus transportation and the loan of textbooks; might not this philosophy be extended to cover the actual costs of instruction in history, mathematics, or science? The launching of *Sputnik* in 1957 triggered an enormous public clamor for better education, and many parents, dissatisfied with the public schools, saw religious schools as an attractive alternative. Why shouldn't tax monies be used to support school systems that provided good education to children? The students, and not religious doctrine, would benefit. This argument commanded the support of a number of justices during the Burger years, and in some cases it found a majority.

The Warren Court had handed down two tests in Establishment Clause cases—legislation had to have a secular purpose and neither advance nor inhibit religion.[16] In *Walz* v. *Tax Commission* (1970),[17] the Court added a third. The case involved a challenge to the traditional real-estate tax exemptions granted by state and local governments to property used solely for religious purposes. Chief Justice Burger wrote for a near unanimous Court (only Justice Douglas dissented) and justified the exemption as an effort to promote free exercise by sparing religion a burden placed on private-profit institutions. In his opinion, though, Burger warned against "an excessive government entanglement with religion." One year later, the Chief Justice added the entanglement rule to devise the three-pronged test that governed all subsequent Establishment Clause cases.

Rhode Island had enacted legislation providing supplemental salary payments to parochial-school instructors who taught secular subjects; Pennsylvania had a somewhat different scheme in which the state "purchased" secular educational "services" from private and parochial schools. Both plans specifically prohibited payment for religious education and required use of state-approved texts for the secular subjects. The Court struck both plans down as violating the Establishment Clause in *Lemon* v. *Kurzman* (1971).[18]

Chief Justice Burger set out what became known as the *Lemon* test: "First, the statute must have a secular legislative purpose; second, its principal or primary effect must be one that neither advances nor inhibits religion; finally the statute must not foster an excessive government entanglement with religion." The Chief Justice's opinion could not have pleased strict separationists more, for in examining the two schemes he hit upon nearly every objection raised by those opposed to state aid, and his statement that "government is to be entirely excluded from the area of religious instruction and churches excluded from the affairs of government" seemed a solid buttress for the wall of separation. Moreover, in talking about the political divisiveness that might develop along religious lines, Burger echoed James Madison's views in the 1785 Memorial and Remonstrance.

In articulating the three-pronged test, the Chief Justice seemed to be sending several messages. First, proponents of the pupil-benefit theory should not rely on the limited application of that doctrine in *Everson* and *Allen* to justify further support. Second, he wanted to provide lower courts with a clear and easily applied constitutional rule that could be used in an anticipated flood of litigation resulting from hundreds of state and federal programs.

The Court, however, also indicated that it would apply the rule in a discretionary manner; on the same day it handed down *Lemon*, it also decided *Tilton* v. *Richardson*,[19] in which it approved federal construction grants to church-related colleges for buildings devoted exclusively to secular purposes. In somewhat questionable reasoning, a plurality of the Court held that religious indoctrination was not a substantial purpose of these schools and that college students were not as susceptible to religious teachings as were younger pupils. Applying the *Lemon* test, the Chief Justice did not find excessive entanglement, because only minimal inspection would be needed to ensure the secular usage of the buildings.

The Burger Court now had its rule—and one that could be used to either prohibit or approve state aid to religious schools. In cases over the next fifteen years, nearly every majority and minority opinion invoked the *Lemon* rule, often with strikingly opposite conclusions. Some of this unpredictability stemmed from shifting alignments among the justices, but by the early 1980s, one could find three fairly distinct groupings on the bench.

Justices Stevens, Brennan, and Marshall most strongly supported separation and believed the *Lemon* test too permissive. Stevens suggested abandoning the test altogether and resurrecting "the 'high and impregnable' wall between church and state constructed by the Framers of the First Amendment."[20] At the other extreme stood Justices White and Rehnquist, frequently

joined by the Chief Justice. White proved the most consistent supporter of aid
to parochial education and apparently had no qualms about public money
indirectly supporting religious instruction.[21] In the middle stood Justices
Blackmun, Powell, and Stewart,[22] who themselves often split on whether the
Lemon test had been violated or whether it was even applicable.[23]

A "SERPENTINE PATH"

One should note that although the Supreme Court has wide discretion
over which cases it chooses to accept, in a broader sense its agenda is set by
society. Growing pressure from advocacy groups seeking to strengthen parochial schools led sympathetic legislatures to enact laws providing that aid.
Following the 1971 cases, state governments tried a variety of measures either
to meet the *Lemon* criteria or to get around them. State aid constituted an issue
the Court could not avoid.

In the spring of 1972, with all four of the Nixon appointees on the bench,
the Court ruled on a variety of state efforts to aid religious education. In *Levitt*
v. *Committee for Public Education and Religious Liberty*,[24] Chief Justice Burger
spoke for an 8-1 Court in striking down a New York law designed to reimburse
nonpublic schools for services mandated by the state. One provision of the
statute allowed for the disbursement of $28 million on a per capita basis, with
no requirement that the schools account for the monies or show any relationship between the monies received and the actual costs. The Court had no
difficulty here, because New York had failed to establish any safeguards to
ensure that the services were in fact completely secular and fully divorced from
religious instruction.

Justice Lewis Powell delivered three other Establishment Clause decisions that came down the same day as *Levitt*. Powell had quickly established
himself as the Court's resident authority on education because of his extensive
experience on the Richmond city and Virginia state boards of education; he
also appreciated the legacy of two other Virginians, Madison and Jefferson,
regarding the separation of church and state.[25]

In the first case it appeared that Powell would join White as an
accommodationist, when he spoke for a 6-3 majority in upholding the South
Carolina Educational Facilities Authority Act in *Hunt* v. *McNair*.[26] The state
had created a bond authority, similar to that already in existence in many other
states, to help colleges finance badly needed construction. Under the scheme,
the Authority issued bonds to finance the project; the school would then
convey title to the Authority, which would hold it until the school had paid off
the indebtedness. Unlike some other states, however, South Carolina permitted the Authority to finance construction at church-related schools, but the

statute specifically prohibited support for buildings used for any form of sectarian instruction or religious services. In addition, the Authority's power to intervene in school management was strictly limited to ensuring that adequate financial arrangements existed to pay off the indebtedness. For the majority of the Court, these provisions met the *Lemon* test.[27]

Although Powell upheld the statute, and did so under *Lemon*, he refined the primary effect test to make the rule more precise. A program would now be considered to have a primary effect of advancing religion if the school receiving aid is so sectarian in nature that it would be impossible to isolate its secular functions. State aid to fund a primarily sectarian activity in an otherwise secular setting would also be considered a constitutional violation. Powell then used this analysis in *Committee for Public Education and Religious Liberty* v. *Nyquist*[28] to strike down all three sections of a New York law attempting to provide various forms of aid to parochial schools.

One provision provided $30–$40 per student per year to maintain and repair facilities of schools in low-income areas. Relying on *Tilton*, Powell ruled that if "the State may not erect buildings in which religious activities are to take place, it may not maintain or renovate them when they fall into disrepair." The second section provided tuition grants of $50–$100 per pupil for families with annual incomes under $5,000. Again, Powell ruled that the state may not do indirectly what it is forbidden to do directly. A state could not make outright grants to parochial schools; neither could it make indirect payments in the form of tuition assistance. The third provision allowed tax credits for families with annual incomes between $5,000 and $25,000, and Powell again looked past the form to the substance; tax credits, like the tuition grants, would aid institutions pervasively sectarian in nature and thus violate the *Lemon* test.[29]

Although separationists applauded this decision, they misunderstood Powell if they considered him as firmly in their camp. Previous cases did allow for some forms of public aid to sectarian institutions, and Powell believed that total separation was neither possible nor desirable:

> As a result of these decisions and opinions, it may no longer be said that the Religion Clauses are free of "entangling" precedents. Neither, however, may it be said that Jefferson's metaphoric "wall of separation" between Church and State has become "as winding as the famous serpentine wall" he designed at the University of Virginia.[30]

The basic premise remained intact, and the burden always rested upon the state to prove that excessive entanglement did not result from its aid. Neither Powell, nor the majority of the Burger Court, accepted the notion that Douglas and Black had espoused—that the First Amendment required a total separation. The Establishment Clause decisions do not satisfy the desire for a simple black-letter test; they are pragmatic efforts to find some way to permit limited aid without subverting the intent of the First Amendment. As a result, the Burger Court majority tended to state broad principles, such as the *Lemon* test, and then focus on the particular facts of the case.

In *Meek* v. *Pittenger* (1975),[31] for example, the Court dealt with another Pennsylvania effort to bypass the *Lemon* entanglement barrier. A new statute allowed public-school employees to provide an extensive range of services to students in private schools—services such as counseling, speech and hearing therapy, and testing for exceptional or disadvantaged pupils. The state, in addition, provided materials and equipment such as maps, overhead projectors, and laboratory supplies. Pennsylvania claimed that the new law did not entangle the state in the affairs of religion, because public-school employees would provide the services and the materials and equipment related entirely to secular subjects.

With Justice Stewart writing for the majority, the Court struck down all but one provision of the law. To observe the Establishment Clause requirements, the state would have to ensure that none of the public-school teachers taught religion, whether in math or history; therefore, there would be excessive entanglement if the state had to oversee its own people to make sure they remained religiously neutral. While Stewart certainly addressed the facts of the case, his reasoning appears more than a little sophistic. Public-school teachers are not supposed to teach religion in any event, so why would the state have to exercise any more, or any less, supervision of a math teacher to make sure he or she did not teach religious doctrine in St. Joseph's than in P.S. 35? The Court also struck down the materials aid, with the exception of textbook loans, which it upheld on the basis of *Allen*.

But the near unanimity of *Levitt* had been shattered. Stewart spoke for only a plurality of the Court in his decision; Brennan, Marshall, and Douglas joined those parts that struck down the aid but dissented at the approval of the textbook loans. Brennan called it a "pure fantasy" to believe that the loan program did not benefit the school. Chief Justice Burger and Justice Rehnquist joined White, who until then had been the chief, and often the lone, accommodationist on the bench, in strong dissent. Henceforth there would be at least three members of the Court willing to allow at least limited public support for religious schools. And at least two members of the majority, Blackmun and Powell, believed that aid in certain forms might not violate the Establishment Clause.[32]

Taking its cue from this decision, Ohio carefully crafted a plan whereby public-school personnel performed speech, hearing, and other diagnostic services on parochial-school premises, while providing remedial and therapeutic services off premises. In addition, the state provided textbooks for secular subjects, as well as funds to reimburse private schools for materials, equipment, and field trips. The state drew a parallel between the diagnostic services and other medical and welfare programs that it provided to all pupils in the state, and by moving the remedial services off parochial school grounds, it would avoid the entanglement problem.

A divided Court agreed in *Wollman* v. *Walter* (1977).[33] Teaching religion, a main fear in these cases, is less likely to take place in administering a standardized test or in diagnosing a learning problem. Any form of regular classroom activity, even in remedial programs or secular subjects, seemed to open the possibility of proselytizing. Powell, Blackmun, Stewart, and John Paul Stevens (who took Douglas's seat in 1975) accepted the state's argument that remedial services off the school grounds avoided the entanglement problem, and they were joined by the three accommodationists. Brennan and Marshall found a constitutional violation no matter where the state offered remedial services to parochial-school students, and only Brennan took a stict separationist stance that even denied the validity of the diagnostic services. The divisions on the Court confounded those who sought some simple rule; for many, the Court's decisions often seemed to rely on hairsplitting, its distinctions without any differences.

ACCOMMODATIONISM (APPARENTLY) TRIUMPHANT

Fundamentalist religious groups constituted a highly vocal part of the conservative coalition that carried Ronald Reagan into the White House in the 1980 election. Reagan shared the platform at fundamentalist Christian rallies with Jerry Falwell, called himself a "born-again Christian," and declared that "it is an incontrovertible fact that all the complex and horrendous questions confronting us at home and worldwide have their answer in that single book"— the Bible. Reagan also announced that he had "a great many questions" about evolution and believed the biblical version of creation, as well as Darwinian theory, ought to be taught in the schools. To Catholic groups, Reagan promised that as soon as elected, he would ask Congress for tuition tax-credit legislation.[34]

Once Reagan was in office, these issues took a back burner, but throughout his eight years he seemed more than willing to lend his support to fundamentalist demands, especially for a constitutional amendment to permit prayer in the school.[35] Reagan called for a return to "that old time religion and that old time Constitution" and charged that the First Amendment had been twisted "to the point that freedom of religion is in danger of becoming freedom from religion." In addition, the new president espoused what he called a "pro-religion" program that included financial support for religious schools. A proposal to provide tuition tax-credits, similar to the New York plan struck down by the Court in *Nyquist*, received vigorous endorsement from the Reagan administration.[36]

But despite the presence of an articulate accommodationist bloc, the Court's rulings from the time Warren Burger took the center chair in 1969 and throughout the 1970s had reinforced rather than repudiated the separationist doctrine that had been expounded during the Warren years. The government could not support religious practices or institutions; government had to be neutral in its dealings with religions; and in those secular programs that benefited pupils in religious schools, the government had to avoid excessive entanglement in the management or activities of those schools. This adherence to separation received confirmation in the first church-state case of the 1980s, *Stone* v. *Graham* (1980), in which the Court summarily voided a Kentucky statute requiring the posting of the Ten Commandments in all of the state's public schools.[37] Only Justice Rehnquist dissented, although Burger, Blackmun, and Stewart noted their dissatisfaction with the summary reversal of the state court decision, without, however, indicating their views on the merits of the case.

Mr. Dooley's old aphorism that the Court follows the election returns seemed to be sustained in a series of cases in the early 1980s, when the accommodationist wing of the Court apparently gained ascendency. In *Committee for Public Education and Religious Liberty* v. *Regan* (1980),[38] Justice White, who had been the only dissenter in the *Lemon* case, wrote for a 5-4 majority in upholding a New York statute authorizing reimbursement to private and religious schools for performing testing and reporting services required under state law. The law differed from the Ohio statute in that it provided direct cash payments to the schools. Justice White utilized the tripartite *Lemon* test and pronounced that the law met the standards. Four members of the Court disagreed, however, and Justice Blackmun called the majority opinion "a long step backwards in the inevitable controversy that emerges when a state legislature continues to insist on providing public aid to parochial schools."[39]

The following year the Court heard a speech case that had establishment ramifications. The University of Missouri at Kansas City refused to permit the use of its buildings for religious services or religious teaching. An evangelical Christian student club challenged the regulation on First Amendment and equal protection grounds, and the Court agreed. In *Widmar* v. *Vincent*, Justice Powell took a fairly standard First Amendment approach for an 8-1 majority.[40] Once the university allowed its buildings to serve as a forum in general, it could not prohibit their use on content grounds; the fact that the group in particular wanted to engage in religious speech did not matter.

The university had not been attempting to stifle religion but had been concerned that as a state agency, allowing religious activities on its premises would be construed as violating the separation of church and state. The Court ignored this concern, and Powell's opinion emphasized that the decision had been based on the First Amendment's speech and associational rights. But religious groups quickly saw the wedge they wanted. If they portrayed their religious activities as primarily speech in nature, then perhaps they would be able to introduce those activities into primary and secondary schools. Efforts to achieve this goal ran aground in the lower courts, which persisted in seeing the religious nature of such activities.[41] Fundamentalists won a partial victory in 1984, however, when Congress provided for limited "equal access" for religious clubs to hold meetings in public schools, even if those meetings frequently assumed the character of religious services.

A sympathetic Reagan administration increased its efforts to secure support for religious schools on the state level. The failure of the Burger Court to enunciate a firm standard led legislatures to seek some way to distinguish their forms of aid from those proscribed by the Court. In the *Nyquist* case, the Court had invalidated a New York law allowing tax credits for private and parochial school tuition, as well as tuition grants. Minnesota passed a law that provided for a deduction from state taxable income of up to $700 not only for parents with children in private schools but for those with children in public schools as well.[42]

The accommodationists on the Court upheld the Minnesota plan in *Mueller* v. *Allen* (1983).[43] Justice Rehnquist, who had dissented in the earlier *Nyquist* case, along with Burger and White, now had a majority; he was joined by the Court's newest member, Sandra Day O'Connor, and most surprisingly, by Justice Powell, who had written the *Nyquist* opinion. Rehnquist based his decision on the fact that the tuition exemption was available to all parents and was but one of many deductions allowed by state law; by extending these benefits to all groups, the state thus met the "effects" prong of the *Lemon* test, in that the law did not work to either advance or inhibit religion. Rehnquist casually dismissed the entanglement criterion, which had played so important a role in previous cases, and implied that it only mattered when direct financial subsidies were paid to parochial schools or their teachers.[44]

The accommodationists seemed to go from strength to strength in the next few terms. Chief Justice Burger, in *Marsh* v. *Chambers* (1983),[45] spoke for a 6-3 Court in holding that paid legislative chaplains and prayers at the start of each session of the Nebraska legislature did not violate the Establishment Clause. Just as Justice Black had elaborated a long historical analysis to justify his view of a wall of separation, so now Burger went back to show that the Framers of the First Amendment had been aware of such practices and had not objected to them and that opening prayers had been a staple of national, state, and local government since the founding of the Republic.

Although both the majority and dissenting opinions characterized the holding as "narrow . . . careful . . .[with] a limited rationale [that] should pose little threat" to the Establishment Clause, the Chief Justice's opinion could be read as implying that the same rationale might be applied in other areas. He compared the Nebraska practice with the Court's earlier Sunday closing decisions as "simply a tolerable acknowledgement of beliefs widely held among people of this country." If one took this reasoning, might it not as well be applied to school prayer and Bible reading, both practices that had even longer histories than opening legislative sessions with prayer? The First Amendment, and other parts of the Bill of Rights, had been adopted to protect minorities from majoritarian tyranny; the Burger opinion implied that the majority will should be given greater latitude.

Such a reading seemed more than justified the following term when the Court, by a 5-4 vote, upheld placing a crêche—the Christmas nativity scene—at public expense in front of the city hall in Pawtucket, Rhode Island. For many people, no matter what their faith or view on the First Amendment, there could hardly be a more religious symbol than a crêche. Nor could one imagine any activity more likely to run counter to all the values enunciated by the Court in regard to the Establishment Clause since 1947, or more likely to flunk all of the criteria of Burger's own *Lemon* test—it was not a secular activity, it advanced religious ideas, and it entangled the government in religion. Moreover, even if one took all of the arguments used by the accommodationists to justify previous decisions—free speech, secular benefits, historical exceptions—none of them applied to this case. Public monies were being expended to support an openly religious display.[46]

The majority opinion in *Lynch* v. *Donnelly* (1984)[47] must be recognized as the most extreme accommodationist position taken by the Burger Court, but also one that upset and dismayed legal scholars and laypersons alike. Burger's opinion stood more than three decades of Establishment Clause jurisprudence on its head when he claimed that the Constitution "affirmatively mandates" accommodation. He referred to his earlier decision in *Marsh* v. *Chambers* to prove that the Framers had intended there to be public support for some activities religious in nature, although he did not make clear the connection between a chaplain opening Congress with a prayer and the display of a crêche. Other activities that supported his view of an affirmative mandate included the Court's released-time decision in *Zorach* v. *Clauson*, coins that bore the motto "In God We Trust," the phrase "One Nation under God" in the Pledge of Allegiance, and paintings with religious messages on display in the National Gallery of Art in Washington!

Burger's application of the *Lemon* test was even more fanciful. He placed the crêche "in the context of the Christmas season" and thus found that it had a secular purpose in depicting "the historical origins of this traditional event long recognized as a National Holiday." Its primary effect did not benefit religion or Christianity, nor did the Court find any administrative entanglement in religious affairs. Since there had been no direct subsidy to a religious agency, the Court had no need to inquire into "potential political divisiveness."[48] In essence, Christmas, according to the opinion, should not be viewed as a religious holiday but as a secular festival.

As Justice Brennan noted in his dissent, acknowledging a deity in public ceremonies or on coins was a far different story than active endorsement of an event considered holy by Christians whatever their particular denomination. The exhibit of works of art that happened to have religious motifs could also hardly be considered as carrying government endorsement of religion. Brennan's opinion differed most significantly from that of the Chief Justice in its sensitivity to the meaning of the crèche. While it is true that the Christmas season has taken on a number of very secular attributes, especially the materialism of the shopping malls, its essence is the birth of Christ, and Brennan caught quite clearly the importance of such a symbol to Christian and non-Christian alike:

> The essence of the crèche's symbolic purpose and effect is to prompt the observer to experience a sense of simple awe and wonder appropriate to the contemplation of one of the central elements of Christian dogma—that God sent His son into the world to be Messiah. Contrary to the Court's suggestion, the crèche is far from a mere representation of a "particular historic religious event." It is, instead, best understood as a mystical re-creation of an event that lies at the heart of the Christian faith. To suggest, as the Court does, that such a symbol is merely "traditional" and therefore no different from Santa's house or reindeer is not only offensive to those for whom the crèche has profound significance, but insulting to those who insist for religious or personal reasons that the story of Christ is in no sense a part of "history" nor an unavoidable element of our national "heritage."[49]

The crèche decision carried a message which it is doubtful had been intended by the Chief Justice, namely, that those who did not subscribe to such "national" symbols, such as atheists, Muslims, Hindus, or Jews, did not belong to the community.[50] Many Christians who, like Justice Brennan, recognized the deep spiritual significance of the crèche, objected to the majority's debasing of the religious aspects of Christmas. A spokesperson for the National Council of Churches complained that the Court had put Christ "on the same level as Santa Claus and Rudolph the Red-Nosed Reindeer,"[51] and soon many cars sprouted bumper stickers to "Keep Christ in Christmas." For scholars, the decision seemed to constitute a major breach in the wall of separation, one that might not be repairable.[52] Reports of the wall's demise, however, proved premature.

SEPARATION REDIVIVUS

Separationists found little to cheer about during the early 1980s other than *Larkin* v. *Grendel's Den* (1982),[53] a silly decision that struck down a Massachusetts statute giving schools and churches power to veto applications for liquor licenses at sites within 500 feet of the church or school. Chief Justice Burger held that the law gave both real and symbolic benefit to churches, enmeshed churches in the affairs of government, and created potential divisiveness along religious lines, therefore violating the *Lemon* rule. In fact, as Justice Rehnquist (the lone dissenter) pointed out, Massachusetts had originally imposed an absolute ban on all taverns and then decided that its objective, maintaining neighborhood peace, might be better served if only those schools and churches that actually objected to having saloons as neighbors initiated the complaint.

While separationists approved of the *Larkin* decision, they viewed the apparent shift of Justice Powell to the accommodationist wing and the arrival of Justice O'Connor with dread. They were all the more surprised, then, when the Court handed down a series of decisions in the 1984 Term strongly reaffirming its commitment to a wall of separation.

The first case involved the highly emotional issue of school prayer. Fundamentalist groups had never accepted the Court's 1962 *Engel* v. *Vitale* ruling, and the resurgence of the religious right in the 1970s led to a number of efforts to overturn the decision by constitutional amendment or to bypass it statutorily.[54] In Alabama, the legislature passed a law in 1978 requiring elementary school classes to observe a period of silence "for meditation" at the beginning of the school day. Three years later it amended the law and called upon the teacher to announce "that a period of silence not to exceed one minute in duration shall be observed for meditation or voluntary prayer." The following year saw another change, this time authorizing any teacher or professor in any of the state's public educational institutions to lead "willing students" in a prescribed prayer that recognized "Almighty God" as the "Creator and Supreme Judge of the World."[55]

State Senator Donald G. Holmes made no secret either in the legislative debate or afterwards in the district court hearings of exactly what he had in mind in regard to the 1981 measure:

> Gentlemen, by passage of this bill by the Alabama Legislature our children in this state will have the opportunity of sharing in the spiritual heritage of this state and this country. The United States as well as the State of Alabama was founded by people who believe in God. *I believe this effort to return voluntary prayer* to our public schools for its return to us to the original position of the writers of the Constitution, this local philosophies and beliefs hundreds of Alabamians have urged my continuous support for permitting school prayer. Since coming to the Alabama Senate I have worked hard *on this legislation to accomplish the return of voluntary prayer to our public schools and return to the basic moral fiber.*[56]

Separationists challenged all three statutes, but the Supreme Court decided the merits of only the 1981 version, with its formula for either "meditation or voluntary prayer."[57] The original statute, with its "pure" moment of silence and no legislative mandate to teachers, could easily have been interpreted as having a secular intent. The alteration, with its direction that teachers should announce that the time could be spent in prayer, had been acknowledged by the sponsor and by the district court as having a religious motivation—to return "voluntary prayer to our public schools." This would certainly violate the first prong of the *Lemon* test, if that test still had any meaning after the Chief Justice's interpretation of it in the crêche case.

Speaking for a 6-3 majority, Justice Stevens struck down the Alabama statute in *Wallace* v. *Jaffree* (1985) and reaffirmed the vitality of the *Lemon* test, although over the separate objections of Burger, White, and Rehnquist. Had the case been decided a half-dozen years earlier, commentators would have given it little thought. It relied on *Engel* as precedent and imposed a fairly straightforward *Lemon* analysis. But given the accommodationist decisions of the previous terms, Stevens decided to reexamine some of the assumptions that had guided the Court since *Everson*.

The growing complexity of Establishment Clause cases, and the wide latitude in which the *Lemon* test could be applied, had led to dissatisfaction both in the academic community and within the Court. Justice O'Connor had raised these issues in her concurrence in *Lynch*, and Stevens now adopted some of her comments in redefining the "purpose" section of the *Lemon* test. The rule had previously been interpreted to ask whether there had been a secular or a religious purpose behind the bill. O'Connor had suggested that there might be *both* secular and religious purposes and that the existence of a secular purpose would not by itself be sufficient to turn away an establishment challenge. Stevens, quoting from O'Connor, now stated, "[I]t is appropriate to ask whether the government's actual purpose is to endorse or disapprove of religion."[58]

In another step away from accommodation, the majority held that the Court would look beyond the words of the statute and see what the actual practices or pronouncements of the state had been. This brought forth an angry dissent from Justice Rehnquist, who in essence said that the Court should accept the terms of the statute on its face value; if it said it had a secular purpose, then the Court should accept that the law had a secular purpose. The Chief Justice also dissented, and his ire was aimed at that part of Stevens's opinion which rejected the accommodationist view Burger had set forth in *Lynch*.

Perhaps most important, a majority of the Court rejected two basic challenges to post-*Everson* jurisprudence. Judge W. Brevard Hand in his district court opinion had held that the Constitution imposed no obstacle to Alabama's establishment of a state religion. Had this view been articulated in 1847, it would have been considered correct; to say it in the 1980s, however, struck most observers as a mental and judicial aberration. The incorporation of the protections guaranteed in the Bill of Rights and their application to the states had been going on for more than six decades and, with very few exceptions, had been accepted throughout the judicial, academic, and political communities. No one on the Court supported this view, and Stevens was probably responding to Rehnquist's long historical analysis which purported that the Establishment Clause did not create any wall of separation, but rather it allowed government to aid religion provided it did so on a nonpreferential basis.[59] Stevens provided the strongest opinion in support of the traditional jurisprudence that the Court had issued in a number of years.

At the very end of the 1984 Term, the Court handed down two important school-aid cases that apparently signaled a return to the stricter standards that had prevailed in the 1970s. In *Grand Rapids School District* v. *Ball*,[60] the Court examined the "shared-time" program, in which the city's public-school teachers offered remedial and enrichment reading and mathematics, as well as some art, music, and physical education courses, in forty-one private schools; of these, forty were religious schools. A related "community education" program offered a variety of academic and nonacademic courses in nonpublic schools, but at the end of the regular school day. Most of the faculty in the community program were on the staffs of the schools where the courses were offered, so most of them were religious-school teachers. *Aguilar* v. *Felton*[61] dealt with a federally funded New York program similar to the Grand Rapids shared-time scheme. New York, however, had a monitoring system that it claimed insulated the program from the religious inculcation that prevailed in the surrounding church schools.

The Court invalidated both shared-time programs by narrow 5-4 votes,[62] the Grand Rapids plan because in effect it advanced religion and the New York scheme because of excessive government entanglement. Chief Justice Burger and Justice O'Connor joined the majority in striking down the community education program. Justice Brennan spoke for the majority in both cases and found the rationale of *Meek* v. *Pittenger* still compelling. "Teachers in such an atmosphere may well subtly (or overtly) conform their instruction to the environment in which they teach," he declared in *Grand Rapids*, "while students will perceive the instruction provided in the context of the dominantly religious message of the institution, thus reinforcing the indoctrinating effect." The Court produced no new doctrine in these cases, but the return to the basic principles of *Lemon*, *Nyquist*, and earlier cases produced great relief among separationists.

THE FREE EXERCISE CASES

The majority of the religion cases before the Burger Court involved the Establishment Clause, but it decided several free exercise cases as well. Perhaps the most notable involved a challenge by the Old Order Amish to a state's compulsory education law in *Wisconsin* v. *Yoder* (1972).[63] The Amish objected to provisions of the state law requiring attendance past the eighth grade. They believed, and the state did not challenge the sincerity of their belief, that sending adolescent children to high school would endanger their spiritual salvation. Although the Court recognized that the Amish marched totally out of step with contemporary society, Chief Justice Burger affirmed their constitutional right to do so. Enforcement of the law would raise "a very real threat of undermining the Amish community and religious practices as they exist today; they must either abandon belief and be assimilated into society at large, or be forced to migrate to some other and more tolerant region." Given the small number of children involved, the state's interest in educating its citizens would not suffer if it granted the Amish an exception.[64]

Yoder appeals to most people because it seems to carry out the intent of the Free Exercise Clause. A small, powerless faction, wanting to be left free from state regulations that it believed impinged upon its religious beliefs, appealed to the highest court in the land, seeking protection of the First Amendment, and proved victorious. But it also raises the question, as did *Sherbert* v. *Verner* (1963) in the Warren era, of whether such findings impinge upon Establishment Clause values. By relieving the Amish of the secular obligation imposed by the school laws, did the Court impinge upon the command of the Establishment Clause, which bars any classification that would either impose a burden *or a benefit* on religion? Do *Sherbert* and *Yoder* represent the Free Exercise Clause version of accommodation, another breach in the wall of separation? Justice Harlan had suggested in *Sherbert* that government may, but need not, carve out exceptions from general rules when faced by religious scruples. But how far should the exceptions go? And if the government allows exceptions for one religious group, does that mean it must respond affirmatively to the demands of others?

The problem derives from the Court's criteria for Establishment Clause cases, namely, that a religious purpose alone—the first prong of the *Lemon* test—constitutes a First Amendment violation. The fact is that many practices in this country have a religious cast, and the Court has had to bend its criteria in order to sustain these practices. Yet in the free exercise decisions, the Court on several occasions permitted states to provide exemptions or, as in *Yoder*, required them to do so. As Jesse Choper succinctly put it:

> On the one hand, the Court has read the establishment clause as saying that if a law's purpose is to aid religion, it is unconstitutional. On the other hand, the Court has read the free exercise clause as saying that, under certain circumstances, the state must aid religion. Logically, the two theses are irreconcilable.[65]

In examining the Court's decisions in this area, this tension is apparent; less clear is whether the Court could have adopted a single standard to govern both clauses in a logically consistent manner.

In *Thomas* v. *Review Board* (1981), an 8-1 Court relied on *Sherbert* to strike down an Indiana ruling denying unemployment benefits to a Jehovah's Witness who had left his job in a munitions factory because of his religious objections to war. State law barred payment to an individual who "voluntarily left his employment without good cause in connection with the work," and the Indiana Supreme Court held that quitting a job because of religion did not constitute "good cause."[66] Chief Justice Burger disagreed; as in *Sherbert*,

> the employee was put to a choice between fidelity to religious belief or cessation of work; the coercive impact on Thomas is indistinguishable from Sherbert. [Where] the state conditions receipt of an important benefit upon conduct proscribed by a religious faith, or where it denies such a benefit because of conduct mandated by religious belief, thereby putting substantial pressure on an adherent to modify his behavior and to violate his beliefs, a burden upon religion exists. While the compulsion may be indirect, the infringement upon free exercise is nonetheless substantial.[67]

The fact that Sherbert had been fired by the employer, and that Thomas had left voluntarily, made no difference; in both cases, the Chief Justice explained, the termination had resulted because the employment became religiously objectionable. While conceding that the decision did provide a benefit based upon religion, and thus a potential violation of the Establishment Clause, Burger dismissed this as a minor consideration, reflecting "no more than the tension between the two Religion Clauses which the Court resolved in *Sherbert*."

Justice Rehnquist disagreed and accurately pointed out that the tension had not been resolved in *Sherbert*, and that the Court's decision in *Thomas* merely left it hanging for case-by-case adjudication in the future. Ironically, the Court's leading accommodationist in terms of the Establishment Clause and government aid to religion in general proved far stricter when it came to individual cases. He urged a return to the *Braunfeld* v. *Brown* rulings[68] and supported Harlan's dissent in *Sherbert*, where the decision of whether or not benefits would be granted would be left to the discretion of the state.[69]

Yoder and *Thomas* indicated the Burger Court's belief that the Free Exercise Clause required some exemptions from governmental regulations under certain circumstances, but the Court also made it clear that these circumstances were limited. In conscientious objector cases, for example, the Court continued a broad reading of Sec. 6(j) of the Military Service Act to include persons with "essentially political, sociological, or philosophical views or a merely personal moral code."[70] But in *Gillette* v. *United States* (1971),[71] the Court upheld congressional refusal to exempt selective conscientious objectors from the draft, namely, those who did not object to war in general but only to a particular war—in this case, American involvement in Vietnam. The Court

extended the logic of this case in *Johnson* v. *Robinson* (1974),[72] in which it upheld
a federal statute granting veterans' educational benefits to those who had served
in the armed forces but denying them to conscientious objectors who had
performed alternative service. The withholding of benefits, Justice Brennan
claimed, involved only an incidental burden on petitioners' free exercise rights
if, in fact, any burden existed at all.

At the same time that the Court handed down some of its most accom-
modating Establishment Clause cases, it tightened up its rulings on how far
employers and the government had to go to accommodate individual free
exercise. In *United States* v. *Lee* (1982),[73] the Court rejected an Old Order Amish
claim that paying Social Security taxes violated their religious scruples. Chief
Justice Burger asserted that a strict scrutiny standard existed, but that the
government had met that criterion, because "mandatory participation is indispensable to the fiscal vitality of the social security system."[74]

The following year, in a highly publicized case that broke no new
constitutional ground, the Court upheld the Internal Revenue Service's statutory authority to deny tax-exempt status to Bob Jones University and Golds-
boro Christian Schools. Both practiced racial discrimination, which they
claimed stemmed from their religious beliefs; to deny them tax-exempt status,
they charged, would restrict their free exercise of religion. The IRS, in turn,
responded that racially discriminatory policies ran "contrary to settled public
policy" and thus disqualified the schools as "charities." In *Bob Jones University*
v. *United States*,[75] the Court agreed. According to Chief Justice Burger, there
"can no longer be any doubt that racial discrimination in education violates
deeply and widely accepted views of elementary justice." The fact that the
schools based their discriminatory practices on religious beliefs made no
difference, and the Court dismissed the free exercise claim.[76]

The Court also refused to extend the *Sherbert–Thomas* reasoning to private
employers. Title VII of the 1964 Civil Rights Act required private employers
to make "reasonable accommodations" to the religious practices of their employees, a section deriving directly from *Sherbert*. Such statutory language
raises establishment problems in that it can be read as conferring benefits upon
particular religions, but in the first case it heard under Title VII, the Court
interpreted it as imposing only minimal burdens upon employers.[77]

A similar case resulted from a Connecticut law that had been designed to
preserve a day of rest for all employees and at the same time accommodate those
persons who observed a Sabbath. Under terms of the law, no employer could
require an employee to work on his or her Sabbath day or fire them for their
refusal to do so. Thornton, a manager of a retail chain store in Connecticut,
refused to work on Sunday, his Sabbath, and refused a transfer either to a
Massachusetts branch that did close on Sunday or to a nonsupervisory position
at a lower salary in another Connecticut store. After an involuntary transfer to
the latter position, he resigned, and a state administrative agency found the
employer in violation of the law.

In *Thornton* v. *Caldor, Inc.* (1985), a near unanimous Court, with only Justice Rehnquist dissenting, not only rejected the free exercise claim but also invalidated the statute as an impermissible establishment of religion. The state, according to the Chief Justice,

> has thus decreed that those who observe a Sabbath any day of the week as a matter of religious conviction must be relieved of the duty to work on that day, no matter what burden or inconvenience this imposes on the employer or fellow workers. The statute arms Sabbath observers with an absolute and unqualified right not to work on whatever day they designate as their Sabbath.[78]

In her concurrence, Justice O'Connor drew a useful distinction in evaluating Title VII requirements. The Connecticut statute failed because it had an absolutist religious orientation, requiring an employer to take unreasonable steps to satisfy employees' religious demands. The law had been designed, she explained, to prevent discrimination because of religion, and its emphasis had to be on avoiding bias rather than on imposing extensive affirmative obligations.

CONCLUSIONS

Despite its accommodationist stage in the early 1980s, the Burger Court for the most part extended the doctrines laid down by the Warren Court, and it did so in the face of growing and more sophisticated pressure from religious lobbies. If in fact a total and inflexible wall of separation is impossible and perhaps not even desirable, then where does one draw the line demarcating what is constitutionally permissible? Must it be, to use Justice Powell's analogy, a serpentine wall? The answer is probably yes, that such a wall will be somewhat erratic and objective tests unattainable except in a few circumstances. But one can certainly understand the confusion of Americans when they are told that compulsory Sunday closing laws, crèches on public property, secular books for parochial-school students, and paid chaplains for legislatures do not violate the First Amendment, whereas nondenominational prayers and Bible readings in school, as well as remedial courses for parochial-school students with learning disabilities, do.[79]

Justice Douglas, in his opinion in *Zorach*, claimed that Americans "are a religious people whose institutions presuppose a Supreme Being," and it is true that religious motifs do permeate our public life. Aside from a few extreme separationists, most Americans would not want to see "In God We Trust" struck from our coins, "One Nation under God" deleted from the Pledge of Allegiance, or legislatures deprived of prayer. At the same time, all but the most extreme fundamentalists would strenuously oppose the establishment of any particular religion, or even widespread government support to all religions

Between these extremes, however, one can find a wide range of views on what constitutes appropriate limits on state action, and the varying intensity of these views led legislatures in a number of states to enact programs that included some components to aid religion. The Court responded with a simple test and soon discovered the various parts of the *Lemon* test to be far more subjective than had been anticipated. Nonetheless, the basic criteria seem as valid today as when first enunciated in 1971—legislation must have a secular purpose, it must neither advance nor inhibit religion, and it must avoid government entanglement.

In applying this test, the Burger Court—despite some egregious exceptions—did not depart significantly from the line of decisions laid down by its predecessor. It prohibited school prayer, refused to bar evolution, kept required Bible reading out of the schools, and restricted the state from penalizing Sabbath observance. The Warren Court did not face the question of public aid to parochial schools except in a limited manner, yet the pupil-benefit theory it adopted in *Everson* and *Allen* informed most of the later decisions in this area. While strict separationists disapproved of the Court's decisions in the early 1980s, overall the Burger Court did not move that far from the path laid out in the 1960s.

4

"The Central Meaning of the First Amendment"

The Warren Court and Free Speech

T he hallmark of a free society is the ability of its citizens to express their opinions, on any number of topics and in a variety of ways, without fear of punishment by the state. Freedom of expression is the core value of democracy, the right valued above all others, "the matrix," in Justice Benjamin Cardozo's phrase, "the indispensable condition of nearly every other form of freedom."[1] Although speech cases arising under the First Amendment are a relatively recent development,[2] free expression issues have become a significant part of the Court's business.

For absolutists like Justices Black and Douglas, the clear wording of the First Amendment—"Congress shall make no law . . . abridging the freedom of speech, or of the press"—allowed only one interpretation: Congress, and by incorporation the states, could not in any way limit individual expression. For them the First Amendment rights constituted the cornerstone of American liberty and occupied a "preferred" position in the hierarchy of protected rights.[3] Other members of the Court, even while conceding the importance of speech, never accepted the Black/Douglas view of a constitutionally protected right to unlimited speech. The Court has thus wrestled with a number of issues, such as what constitutes speech, what restraints may be imposed in balancing freedom against order, and whether certain types of speech are more "valuable" and therefore deserving of special attention. Before examining specific issues, it may help to look briefly at some historical and philosophical developments underlying modern notions of free speech.

FREE SPEECH AND SOCIETY

When Sir William Blackstone wrote his *Commentaries* in the latter eighteenth century, he defined freedom of speech as the lack of prior restraint; that is, government could not prevent someone from saying or publishing what they believed, although such freedom did not extend to "blasphemous, immoral, treasonable, schismatical, seditious or scandalous" speech, and they could be punished afterwards for having uttered or printed forbidden speech.[4] The English, like the ancient Greeks, established legal restrictions on three types of speech—sedition, defamation, and blasphemy—each of which they called "libels."[5] Of these, the most politically important was seditious libel, because ruling elites believed that any criticism of government or its officials, *even if true*, subverted public order by undermining confidence in the government. The provocation itself, not the falsity of the charge, invited the punishment.

During the seventeenth and eighteenth centuries, the Crown prosecuted hundreds of cases of seditious libel and often imposed draconian penalties. When William Twyn published a book supporting the right of revolution, he was convicted of sedition and of "imagining the death of the king," and the court sentenced him to be hanged, emasculated, disemboweled, quartered, and beheaded. Given the possibility of such punishment *after* publication, the lack of prior restraint meant little, and English writers for the most part imposed a rigid self-censorship to avoid such penalties.[6]

English common law carried over to America, but there seems to have been a great discrepancy between theory and practice in the colonies. Assemblies passed a number of statutes regulating speech, but neither royal governors nor local courts seemed to have enforced them with any degree of regularity or stringency.[7] Then in the important case of John Peter Zenger, the colonists established truth as a defense to charges of seditious libel. One could still be charged if one criticized government officials, but now a defendant could present evidence of the truth of his statements, and it would be up to the jury to determine their validity.[8] Despite the infamy heaped upon the 1798 Sedition Act and its use by the Adams administration against Republican critics, the statute did embody truth as a defense.[9]

The Sedition Act raises the question of what the Framers of the First Amendment had intended, and there is no clear answer. James Madison and his colleagues in that first Congress knew their British history, in which the most prominent restrictions on speech had been licensing of printers and prosecution for seditious libel. Although licensing had been abandoned in England in 1694, it is possible that the Framers wanted to make sure that it would not be resurrected in America.[10] However, when Madison penned the Virginia Resolution against the 1798 Sedition Act, he paid little attention to the First Amendment and based his opposition on states' rights grounds. Following Jefferson's election, Congress allowed the Sedition Act to expire and, with the exception of a few Civil War regulations, did not attempt to limit speech or press until World War I. It is with the cases arising out of the Espionage Act of 1917 and the Sedition Act of 1918 that the debate, both within the Court and out, really begins over the meaning of free speech.

Zechariah Chafee, Jr., a professor at Harvard Law School and the scion of an old Rhode Island family, entered the lists in the wake of the World War I sedition prosecutions. In his influential book, *Free Speech in the United States*, first published in 1920, he argued that the Framers had more in mind than merely prohibiting licensing; instead, they "intended to wipe out the common law of sedition and make further prosecutions for criticism of the government, without any incitement to lawbreaking, forever impossible."[11] For Chafee, free speech served two purposes: *individual* interest (persons speaking on matters that are crucial to their own beliefs and desires) and *social* interest (matters that citizens must understand so that democratic government can function). The latter interest is by far the more important and can only be achieved by full and free discussion. Chafee criticized Holmes's clear and present danger test in *Schenck* v. *United States* (1919) because it failed to differentiate degrees of danger; for Chafee, speech could be limited only "when the interest in public safety is really endangered." While the defendants in *Schenck* may have posed a distant, abstract threat to society, no real danger existed. The value of free and unfettered speech to the democratic workings of society far outweighed the minor inconvenience that the Schencks of the world posed.[12]

While Chafee argued for nearly unlimited speech in the political arena, he did not suggest expanding the meaning of the First Amendment in regard to nonpolitical speech, such as the profane, the indecent, or the insulting. Such speech contributed nothing to the analysis of ideas and the search for truth, and it could be restricted in order to serve the greater social values of "order, morality, the training of the young, and the peace of mind of those who see and hear." The Supreme Court unanimously endorsed Chafee's view of the social uselessness and lack of First Amendment protection of obscenity, libel, and so-called fighting words in *Chaplinsky* v. *New Hampshire* (1942).[13]

One of the most influential theorists of free speech in this century happened to have been a man who taught Chafee when the latter was an undergraduate. Alexander Meiklejohn went even further than his former pupil in postulating an absolute protection for political speech, which he saw as essential to self-government. Meiklejohn used the analogy of a New England town meeting, where the voters are made wise by means of vigorous debate. In such a situation, he argued, it is not necessary that each person be heard but instead that "everything worth saying shall be said." Although there may be procedural rules to allow for orderly debate, there must be no fetters on *ideas*. "The freedom of ideas shall not be abridged."[14]

The protection of congressional speech in the Constitution (Art. I, Sec. 6) is designed to allow just that type of robust, unfettered discussion, and according to Meiklejohn, it is as essential for the people to enjoy that protection as it is for congressional representatives and senators, for both are engaged in the business of developing public policy. Where Chafee drew a limit on political speech when it created a real and imminent danger, Meiklejohn seemed to believe it totally untouchable, "beyond the reach of legislative limitation, beyond even the due process of law. . . . Congress has no negative powers whatever."[15]

Private speech, on the other hand, defined primarily as not involving political matters, enjoys only a limited protection. Chafee criticized Meiklejohn on this bifurcation between public and private speech, asserting that no historical evidence supports the view that the Founders had any such distinction in mind. Moreover, the line is not always sharp, and what may strike one person as "public" may seem "private" to another. Would a novel, for example, be considered a private expression if it dealt fictionally with important social matters? For Chafee, it would be far better to exclude clearly useless speech and to protect all other expression, be it private or public.[16]

The problem of line-drawing, or balancing, led Yale law professor Thomas Emerson to attempt a systematic exploration of free speech, in which he proposed the "expression/action" theory, a criterion reminiscent of the belief/action dichotomy utilized by the Court in religion cases.[17] For Emerson, freedom of expression is absolute, no matter what form it takes. People can express their views either through traditional speech or writing or by other means, such as music and art. Moreover, the right of free expression includes the right to hear the opinion of others, the right to inquire freely, and the right to associate with others of similar view. The benefits of this libertarian policy, Emerson argues, are individual self-fulfillment, discovering truth, democratic decision making, and the achievement of a more stable community.[18]

Emerson draws the line between the expression of ideas, no matter what form they take, and their manifestation as action, which may be controlled by other constitutional requirements. The problem, as he himself recognized, is that the distinction between expression and action is not always clear, especially in areas that Chafee delineated as outside the reach of First Amendment protection—obscenity, libel, and provocation. While Emerson's scheme is more systematic than that of Chafee or Meiklejohn, and provides judges with greater guidance in determining what is protected and what is not, in the end it too requires judges to make balancing decisions.

All of the distinctions—political/nonpolitical, public/private, expression/action—give members of the Court rational and systematic criteria by which to strike a balance between freedom of speech and social order. But the distinctions require balancing through subjective evaluation because the lines are rarely clear-cut, and as all of the philosophers concede, there are community concerns, such as the need to maintain peace and social order, which must also be considered.

Justices Black and Douglas opposed balancing and, in speech as in religion, adopted an absolutist position—the First Amendment allowed *no* abridgments of speech:

Without deviation, without exception, without any ifs, buts, or whereases, that freedom of speech means that government shall not do anything to people, or in the words of the Magna Carta, move against people, either for the views they have or the views they express or the words they speak or write.[19]

Even the clear and present danger test failed their standards, because it involved balancing and could therefore be used to punish advocacy of unpopular ideas. For Douglas, advocacy even for the purpose of incitement fell within the limits of constitutional protection, and he declared he could see "no place in the regime of the First Amendment for any 'clear and present danger' test."[20] The only time speech could be in any way restricted was when it involved, as he put it, "speech brigaded with action," and then the state could regulate the action that posed a threat to public order or safety.

Despite powerful advocacy of their position, Black and Douglas could never win over a majority away from balancing tests. Over the years the Court has adopted different strategies in trying to strike an appropriate balance. In some areas it has attempted to establish definitional categories to include or exclude certain types of speech. It has adopted absolute prohibitions against particular types of regulation. It has subjected all regulation of speech and press to "strict scrutiny," in which the burden of proof falls upon the state to show that it has compelling interests to justify limitations on speech. While members of the Court have disagreed among themselves on strategies and philosophic rationales, all of them agree that protected free expression is one of the greatest liberties incorporated in our constitutional system.

BURYING SEDITIOUS LIBEL

In the year that Earl Warren took the center chair, the country remained in the grip of anti-Communist hysteria, and security-related speech cases came before the Court throughout Warren's tenure. The worst aspects of the red scare manifested themselves most sharply in the demagoguery of Wisconsin Senator Joseph McCarthy, who exploited the fear of foreign ideologies that had played a major role in American politics since the Depression era. That fear found legislative expression in 1940, shortly after the fall of France, when Congress had passed an Alien Registration Act, commonly called the Smith Act. Its sedition sections specifically aimed to muzzle and punish anyone who attempted to create disloyalty in the military, advocated the forceful overthrow of the government, or conspired to violate any portion of the Act. Punishment ranged from a fine of up to $10,000 and/or ten years in jail, later increased to $20,000 and/or twenty years in jail.[21]

During the war the government had invoked the Smith Act only twice, but the most notorious prosecution came in 1948 when the Justice Department secured indictments against Eugene Dennis and ten other members of the American Communist Party Central Committee. In a trial that lasted six months and at times seemed a mockery of justice,[22] all of the defendants were indicted for advocating the forceful overthrow of the government and conspiring to spread this doctrine. The Court of Appeals upheld the conviction, and in *Dennis* v. *United States* (1951), the Supreme Court, by a 6-2 vote, affirmed the convictions.[23] The majority opinion, written by Chief Justice Vinson, seemed to ignore two decades of history in which the Court had expanded the concept of protected speech, and it took the very restrictive view that even if the words did not present a clear and present danger, they nonetheless represented a "bad tendency" that could prove subversive of the social order.[24]

Justices Black and Douglas dissented, in tones reminiscent of Holmes and Brandeis in the twenties. Both men had traveled quite a distance since their approval of the 1942 *Chaplinsky* decision, and they now articulated a belief in the nearly unfettered right of free expression under the First Amendment. Black claimed that the Smith Act conspiracy section violated constitutional bans against prior restraint, but that even if one believed that advocacy of the Communist party line might be dangerous, proof had never been introduced to show that it posed any clear and present danger to the government. Justice Douglas pointed out that the defendants were being punished for the "crime" of meeting together for the purpose of teaching themselves and others the doctrines of Marx and Lenin. Because in another setting this might be perfectly appropriate, their crime had to consist in their purpose for learning this information, and the First Amendment did not allow Congress to punish people for what they thought.[25]

Whatever philosophical test one wished to apply—Chafee, Meiklejohn, or Emerson—there seemed little justification for such a drastic restriction on speech, and *Dennis* has not stood the test of time. About the only justification one can find for *Dennis* and other Vinson Court security decisions is that the majority had been caught up in the hysteria of the times. One critic charged that "the McCarthy–McCarran era could scarcely roll the repression along fast enough to keep pace with the Vinson Court's approval of it," whereas another historian has termed the Vinson majority "pusillanimous" in its protection of free speech against congressional witch-hunting.[26]

As the red scare slowly receded following the exposure of McCarthy in the army hearings and Senate censure of him and the addition of Earl Warren, William Brennan, and John Marshall Harlan to the Court, a majority of the bench now stood ready to take a different tack on sedition trials. The three newcomers did not subscribe to the Black/Douglas view, which would have thrown out any conviction restricting speech, but neither would they go along with the timidity disguised as restraint that Justice Frankfurter preached.

Rather, they applied the same techniques used in the desegregation cases—vigorous statutory interpretation in which the words of the law could be used to achieve the ideals of the First Amendment, or as Paul Murphy phrased it, "By steering a middle course between the preferred freedoms activism of Black and Douglas and the self-restraint of Frankfurter, [the Warren Court] accomplished many of the goals of the former through the techniques of the latter."[27] Much of the credit goes to the political astuteness of Earl Warren and the lawyerly skills of John Harlan.

Thus, in three cases challenging the investigating authority of congressional committees in general and the techniques of the House Un-American Activities Committee in particular, Chief Justice Warren acknowledged the right of Congress to investigate as part of the legislative process. However, even this power had limits and could not be used to pry into "private affairs unrelated to a valid legislative purpose."[28] The following Term the Court struck a major blow against state versions of HUAC by ruling that in the Smith Act the federal government had preempted the field of subversive control, thus in one swoop invalidating all or part of sedition statutes in forty states.[29] Over the next few years the Court kept chipping away at the problem, finding one technicality after another to invalidate congressional contempt citations or actions of the Subversive Activities Control Board.[30]

During these years the Justice Department, following its victory in *Dennis*, had invoked the Smith Act against a number of lower-echelon Communist party officials, and in 1957 the Court heard the appeal of Oleta Yates and thirteen other "leaders" of the movement. With *Dennis* so recently decided and cold war fears still rampant, the Court no doubt believed it would have been impolitic to have summarily overturned that ruling. So Justice Harlan, speaking for the majority, danced around *Dennis* and took a narrow view of the meaning of "organize" and "advocate."[31] As Harry Kalven put it, "[A] more unlikely 'great' precedent would be hard to imagine; at first acquaintance it seems a sort of *Finnegans Wake* of impossibly nice distinctions."[32]

Harlan ruled that the lower court had erred in accepting the government's overly broad meaning of the term "organize," and that in fact the statute of limitations had run on any organizational crime.[33] The Court also struck an important note in rejecting the government's claim that the Smith Act applied especially to the Communist party; rules regarding speech, Harlan declared, must be general rules and must apply equally to all groups. In what we would term an "Emersonian" opinion, Harlan limited the applicability of *Dennis* to acts rather than speech. The Smith Act, he explained, proscribed advocacy "to do something, now or in the future, rather than merely to *believe* in something."

It is true that, as Justice Clark noted in his dissent, the Yates group could hardly be distinguished from the Dennis defendants—they "served in the same army and were engaged in the same mission." But it is unlikely that the Court that decided *Yates* would have decided *Dennis* as the Vinson Court had done.

While precedents are limiting, the Court in these cases showed itself responsive (in *Dennis* perhaps overresponsive) to popular sentiment. In the earlier case, a court influenced by cold war hysteria had affirmed the conviction of Communist leaders for advocating the overthrow of the government, although no proof existed that they had done more than engage in radical rhetoric; in the latter case, with the public climate changing against red-baiting, the court renewed an earlier commitment to rational and close examination of limits on speech.

That same day, June 17, 1957, the Court handed down three other decisions indicating that, as far as it was concerned, the cold war would no longer have the chilling effect on civil liberties that had existed during the McCarthy era. In *Watkins* v. *United States*[34] and *Sweezy* v. *New Hampshire*,[35] the Court put an end to some of the arbitrary abuses of the legislative investigating power by committees looking into subversion, and in *Service* v. *Dulles*[36] the justices overturned a dismissal finding in an infamous loyalty security case. Even though the Court had begun to look more critically at restrictions based on the need to combat subversion, it had not yet articulated a major doctrinal shift that would weight the First Amendment's protection of free expression more heavily than society's need to maintain order.

Although Harlan's opinion in *Yates* curtailed Smith Act prosecutions, the Court later upheld that part of the law which made membership in any organization advocating the overthrow of the government by force or violence a felony in *Scales* v. *United States*.[37] Yet on the same day in a companion case, Harlan invalidated just such a conviction on the grounds that the evidentiary test had not been met; the prosecution had failed to prove that the Communist party actually advocated forceful or violent overthrow of the government.[38]

A similar pattern of seeming to uphold the power to restrict speech while in fact strictly limiting the use of that power can be seen in the Court's handling of McCarran Act cases. Congress passed the Subversive Activities Control Law, commonly known as the McCarran Act, in the spring of 1950, and through a series of highly complex procedures tried to force the Communist party to register as a subversive organization. Had the party agreed to do so, of course, it would have forfeited nearly all of the rights that nonviolent political groups enjoy in the United States. President Truman had vetoed the measure, calling it "the greatest danger to freedom of speech, press, and assembly since the Sedition Act of 1798," but Congress, fearful of being considered "soft" on communism in an election year, overrode the veto by large margins in both houses.

In the first case testing the law, the Court sustained the registration provisions by a 5-4 vote, with Justice Frankfurter denying that the First Amendment prevented Congress from requiring membership lists of organizations "substantially dominated or controlled by that foreign power controlling the world Communist movement."[39] But if the Court, albeit by a hairbreadth margin, had affirmed the power in general, it then proceeded to make the exercise of that power impossible. It set aside convictions of Communists refusing to register on grounds that the Subversive Activities Control Board's orders were so worded as to constitute a violation of the Fifth Amendment's right against self-incrimination.[40] It also overturned the provisions denying passports to Communists and prohibiting them from working in defense facilities as overly broad and vague.[41]

The Court finally reached the position it had been searching for regarding "subversive speech" in the final Term of the Warren Court. In a per curiam decision, it did away with the last vestiges of seditious libel in *Brandenburg* v. *Ohio*.[42] The issue in *Brandenburg*, as it had been in all of these cases, is the problem of regulating speech that carries the risk of moving the audience to forbidden action—whether it be directed against one individual (a speaker urging the lynching of a prisoner in a local jail) or against the state (advocacy of rebellion). Long ago Oliver Wendell Holmes had noted that all ideas are incitement to action, and no doubt fringe groups as well as mainstream bodies hope that their words will move their listeners to particular actions—whether it be casting a vote in an election or joining a revolution.

In *Schenck* v. *United States* (1919),[43] the Court held that the First Amendment did not protect general advocacy of violence; starting with their dissent in *Abrams* v. *United States* that same year,[44] Holmes and Brandeis set out the argument that radical speech could only be curtailed by showing that it would provoke an imminent danger. During the early 1940s, the clear and present danger test, as articulated by Holmes and Brandeis, seemed to have gained ascent and was used to protect dissident speech in several cases.[45] Then in *Dennis*, the Court seemingly reformulated the test to make it an even more stringent limitation on speech, one that penalized thought as well. Between *Dennis* and *Brandenburg*, however, the country rid itself of the McCarthy mentality, and the Court itself engaged in an active examination of just what freedom of expression meant. The central meaning of the First Amendment, the Court agreed, was a core of free speech without which democracy cannot function.

In *Brandenburg*, the Court articulated what Justice Harlan intimated in *Yates*, that only "incitement to imminent lawless action" can justify restriction of free speech. The Ku Klux Klan had held a rally near Cincinnati and invited a local television station to cover the event. About a dozen members of the Klan, garbed in white sheets and hoods with some carrying arms, had burned a cross in an open field. Their leader then proceeded to mumble several antiblack and anti-Semitic remarks, called for the expulsion of blacks and Jews from the country, and declared that the Klan would resort to violent action if Congress and the Supreme Court did not stop denying true Americans their country. Brandenburg was arrested and convicted under the Ohio Criminal Syndicalism statute, fined $1,000, and sentenced to one to ten years in prison.

The Ohio law dated back to 1919, and in 1927, over a strenuous protest by Holmes and Brandeis, the Court had upheld a similar statute in *Whitney* v.

California.[46] The Court now validated Brandeis's eloquent opinion calling for full and unfettered speech and enunciated the rule that "the constitutional guarantees of free speech and free press do not permit a State to forbid or proscribe advocacy of the use of force or of law violation except where such advocacy is directed to inciting or producing imminent lawless action and is likely to incite or produce such action."[47]

Brandenburg remains the clearest statement of the Warren Court's understanding of the First Amendment's protection of political ideas. It concedes that if speech can incite imminent unlawful action, it may be restricted, but the burden of proof in all speech cases rests on the state to show that action will result, rather than on the defendant to show that it will not.[48] It does, of course, as do all First Amendment cases, retain an element of judicial balancing, a fact that upsets some who would prefer a completely objective test. In constitutional law, however, there are few completely objective rules; the judicial process is at heart a balancing of rights and interests, and all of the speech cases from 1919 on had involved the same process. There is a clear line from Holmes's classic dissent in *Abrams* through Brandeis's concurrence in *Whitney* to *Brandenburg*. The Court had slowly expanded the meaning of First Amendment rights. Although the extent of First Amendment protection had never before been stated so broadly, the Warren Court in fact did no more than develop the predcedents it had inherited. *Dennis*, although it cast such a huge shadow in the 1950s, may better be seen as an aberration, the last gasp of the older restrictive view of speech set forth in *Schenck* and the majority opinion in *Whitney*. The Warren Court recognized this anomaly and had moved quickly to disencumber itself of the *Dennis* ruling; when viewed in the fifty-year history of speech cases, there is little doubt as to the wisdom of that decision.

OBSCENITY

In its 1942 *Chaplinsky* decision, the Court stated explicitly that First Amendment protection did not cover obscene or libelous speech, a judgment that reflected not only contemporary thinking but historic legal tradition as well. The origin of obscene libel in English law dates to the medieval ecclesiastical courts, which until the early eighteenth century heard all cases involving charges of lewdness, profanity, heresy, and blasphemy. In 1708 the Queen's Bench dismissed a secular indictment against James Read for publishing *The Fifteen Plagues of a Maidenhead*, noting that while a "crime that shakes religion" was indictable, writing an obscene book was not, "but punishable only in the Spiritual Court."[49] Less than twenty years later, however, secular authorities indicted Edmund Curll for publishing *Venus in the Cloister, or the Nun in Her Smock*, a "dialogue" about lesbian love in a convent. Although the Court had the Read case as a precedent, it abandoned it and found Curll guilty, and obscene libel entered the common law.[50]

Originally, obscenity cases involved heresy, blasphemy, and antireligious tracts as much as sexually explicit material, but by the latter nineteenth century obscene libel prosecutions dealt almost entirely with sexually oriented literature. Parliament passed several antiobscenity acts, including one designed to keep French postcards out of the country. In 1857 it adopted Lord Campbell's Act, which empowered magistrates to seize books and prints that they considered obscene. In the initial case tried under Lord Campbell's Act, *Regina* v. *Hicklin* (1868), we get our first judicial test for determining whether a particular work is obscene. Lord Chief Justice Cockburn declared that obscenity could be determined on the basis of certain passages, which would have the tendency "to deprave and corrupt those whose minds are open to such immoral influences and into whose hands a publication of this sort may fall." In other words, the test was based on the effect the most explicit sexual passages would have on those particularly susceptible (such as children and young adults), and not on the work as a whole.[51]

The Hicklin test became the standard in the United States as well as in England, and most people assumed that government could ban material it deemed obscene under the police power. As a result, the Post Office compiled an ongoing list of allegedly obscene literature that could neither be imported into the United States nor handled by the mails. Unfortunately, new forms of literature often shocked the postal inspectors, who consigned works such as James Joyce's *Ulysses* to that list. In a famous 1933 case involving that book, Federal Judge John M. Woolsey relied on the testimony of literary experts to sustain the artistic value of the Joyce novel and ruled it was not obscene.[52] Woolsey's decision, however, still accepted the premise that obscene materials did not enjoy First Amendment protection, an assumption reinforced by Justice Murphy in his 1942 *Chaplinsky* opinion.

That case, however, did not involve obscenity, and the Court dealt with the substantive issues only tangentially over the next fifteen years.[53] It ducked the issue in *Doubleday & Co.* v. *New York* (1948), when by a 4-4 vote it affirmed, without opinion, a state court conviction for the publication of Edmund Wilson's *Memoirs of Hecate County*.[54] Aside from procedural issues, the Court may have been troubled by the prospect of having to review every work alleged to be obscene. State and lower federal courts did, however, begin to hear more censorship cases, and articles on the subject proliferated in the law journals. Moreover, local censors went after works such as James T. Farrell's *Studs Lonigan* trilogy, William Faulkner's *Sanctuary*, and Erskine Caldwell's *God's Little Acre*.

In 1957 the Warren Court faced the issue of censorship directly in *Butler* v. *Michigan* and overturned a state statute that made it a crime to "publish materials tending to the corruption of the morals of youth." The Court interpreted the statute to mean that the general adult public could not buy a book which state authorities considered unsuitable for impressionable children. A unanimous bench, speaking through Justice Frankfurter, held the statute violated the First Amendment, by arbitrarily curtailing "one of those liberties of the individual . . . that history has attested as the indispensable conditions for the maintenance and progress of a free society." The decision, however, still excluded obscene works from First Amendment protection; it merely said that material judged unsuitable for children could not on that criterion alone be labeled obscene. Otherwise, the law would "reduce the adult population of Michigan to reading only what is fit for children."[55]

The Court confronted the issue directly later that year in *Roth* v. *United States*.[56] Samuel Roth, at the time one of the nation's leading distributors of sexually oriented material, had been convicted of mailing obscene publications in violation of federal law. At his trial, Roth claimed the statute unconstitutionally restricted freedom of speech and press. The trial court denied the claim, as did the Court of Appeals, which noted that Supreme Court precedent clearly excluded obscene works from constitutional protection. In a concurring opinion, however, Judge Jerome Frank explored the legal and philosophical considerations of censorship and suggested that only material which posed a clear and present danger of inducing serious antisocial behavior should be proscribed.[57]

Judge Frank's comments directly addressed the dilemma faced by the high court. Over nearly five decades, both liberals and conservatives on the Court had utilized the clear and present danger test for evaluating restrictions on speech. To uphold the federal and state obscenity laws, which obviously restricted speech, the Court would have to point to some clear danger presented by dirty books. But what would that danger be? Putting aside the problem of the children's audience, the alleged evils of obscenity, according to First Amendment scholar Harry Kalven, are

> (i) The material will move the audience to anti-social sexual action; (ii) the material will offend the sensibilities of many in the audience; (iii) the material will advocate or endorse improper doctrines of sexual behavior; and (iv) the material will inflame the imagination and excite, albeit privately, a sexual response from the body.
>
> On analysis, these purported evils quickly reduce to a single one. The first, although still voiced by occasional politicians and "decency" lobbies, lacks scientific support. The second may pose a problem for captive audiences, but obscenity regulations have been largely aimed at willing, indeed all too willing, audiences. The third, thematic obscenity, falls within the consensus regarding false doctrine; unsound ideas about sex,

like unsound ideas about anything else, present an evil which we agree not
to use the law to reduce.[58]

This left the Court faced with upholding a restriction on speech because it
possibly posed a clear and present danger of exciting the sexual fantasies of
adults!

Speaking through Justice Brennan, the Court evaded the dilemma by
reverting to the *Chaplinsky* dictum that obscenity is not covered by the First
Amendment. But there had been too many lower federal and state court cases,
too many questions raised about how one determined if a work was indeed
obscene. Even granting that the state had the power to regulate or ban obscene
materials, did the judges have any constitutionally acceptable criteria with
which to validate or void these determinations? Brennan recognized that unless
the Court could fashion a judicially manageable definition of obscenity, *Roth*
would be only the first of a flood of cases. And so he tried.

"All ideas having even the slightest redeeming social importance—unor-
thodox ideas, controversial ideas, even ideas hateful to the prevailing climate
of opinion—have the full protection" of the First Amendment; but obscenity
did not. In the first major reformulation of what constituted obscenity since
Hicklin, Brennan established the new test: "Whether to the average person,
applying contemporary community standards, the dominant theme of the
material taken as a whole appeals to prurient interest."

There is no question that the *Roth* test, which reflected four decades of
growing liberalism and sophistication in American case law, is an improvement
over *Hicklin*. It takes the work as a whole, rather than the most salacious parts;
it applies to the average adult, not the susceptible child; it utilizes overall
community standards, not those of the self-styled keepers of purity; and it asks
whether the theme of the entire work appeals to prurient interests. It is,
however, still censorship; it still requires judges and juries to make subjective
judgments; and by conceding that work with "even the slightest redeeming
social importance," no matter how sexually explicit or disturbing, is entitled
to First Amendment protection, it issued an open invitation to every smut
peddler to show that he dealt, no matter how marginally, with matters of social
import. By shifting the focus of obscenity litigation away from the substantive
issue of First Amendment coverage, from the question of whether state interests justified restraint, to one of definition, the Court sank into a morass from
which it spent the next twenty years trying to extricate itself. In the following
decade the Court heard thirteen more obscenity cases, in which the justices
handed down fifty-five separate opinions. Shortly after his retirement, Chief
Justice Warren characterized obscenity as the Court's "most difficult area."[59]

The majority opinion in *Roth* expanded the two-tier strategy that had first
appeared in *Chaplinsky*. On one level can be found "important" speech, which
can be regulated only if the state can show that the utterance will pose a clear

and present danger to social order, the standard test used in the seditious libel cases. On another level is speech that is deemed unimportant and lacking in social utility, and this type of speech may be regulated. Obscenity can, by this strategy, be regulated not because it is dangerous but because it is worthless. By declaring obscenity in the second category, Justice Brennan did not have to confront the harder questions involved.

The dissenters in *Roth* did try, at least to some extent, to deal with the broader issue of whether the Constitution permitted regulation, and if so, under what conditions. Justice Harlan objected to the broad definition sketched in by Brennan, which he warned would undermine the "tight reins which state and federal courts should hold upon the enforcement of obscenity statutes." Second, he opposed lumping state and federal statutes together; he believed that the states, reflecting local community standards, had the power under the Constitution to control obscene materials, whereas the First Amendment denied a similar power to the national government.

Justice Douglas, joined by Justice Black, entered a short opinion reaffirming their belief in the absolute nature of the First Amendment's prohibition, which "was designed to preclude courts as well as legislatures from weighing the values of speech." Neither the states nor the federal government may control expression under the guise of protecting morality. As for the "community conscience" standard, Douglas pointedly asked whether such a standard would be constitutionally acceptable "if religion, economics, politics or philosophy were involved. How does it become a constitutional standard when literature treating with sex is concerned?" The Brennan opinion evaded these issues not by explanation but by assertion, and it failed to provide a rationale for why the state should be allowed to exercise censorship. The Douglas/Black view may have been simplistic, but it had the virtue of consistency, and had it been followed the Court might have avoided decades of frustration.

THE GRAPES OF *ROTH*

One year later, the New York Board of Regents withheld an exhibition license for the motion picture version of D. H. Lawrence's novel *Lady Chatterley's Lover*.[60] The regents acted under a 1954 statute that defined an immoral film as one "which portrays acts of sexual immorality, perversion or lewdness, or which expressly or impliedly presents such acts as desirable, acceptable or proper patterns of behavior." Chief Judge Albert Conway of the New York Court of Appeals upheld the regents, on the ground that the film depicted adultery as "proper behavior" and therefore fit the definition of the statute. But he did more than that. He tried to frame a rational constitutional standard to determine when sexually explicit films fell within the scope of obscenity regulation.[61]

The Supreme Court reversed in *Kingsley International Pictures Corp.* v. *Regents* (1959).[62] It did so on precisely the grounds set out by the New York court, but without any effort to establish judicially manageable standards. According to Justice Stewart, the regents had prevented exhibition of the film because it advocated an unpopular idea—that adultery might be proper behavior—and thus "the state, quite simply, has struck at the very heart of constitutionally protected liberty." Why the advocacy of adultery is protected, while other materials are not, is never explored in Stewart's opinion and invites the suggestion that all one has to do is present pornographic material in a matter that implies some sort of advocacy, and one can draw the constitutional mantle around the smut and its peddler. Does the literature deal with perverse sexual practices in an explicit manner? Yes it does, but it is explicit in order to make a point about how such behavior may at times be proper. That is an idea and therefore protected.

Kingsley Pictures opened the floodgates, and during the remaining decade of the Warren Court the justices struggled valiantly to deal with the pornography issue. It would take far too much of our time to examine each case in depth, but a brief summary of the major ones will illustrate the problems faced by the Court.[63]

In *Manual Enterprises* v. *Day* (1962),[64] the Court continued its trend toward defining obscenity in terms of hard-core erotica. The Post Office had excluded from the mails three magazines catering to homosexuals and featuring pictures of nude men. Justice Harlan had the onerous job of writing the Court's opinion, and he added the criterion of "patent offensiveness" to the *Roth* test of "prurient interest." Harlan, like Brennan, evaded the substantive issue while attempting to develop a clear test in an area that had become anything but clear. And, as had become the norm, the Court handed down multiple opinions.

The task of finding a workable definition returned to Justice Brennan in the next two cases. In *Jacobellis* v. *Ohio* (1964),[65] the Court overturned the conviction of an Ohio theater owner for showing the French film *Les Amants* (The Lovers). Brennan expanded the *Roth* test of "contemporary community standards" to mean national rather than local standards; otherwise, "the constitutional limitations of free expression in the Nation would vary with state lines." Moreover, Brennan made explicit what had been implicit in his *Roth* opinion, that the phrase "utterly without social importance" was part of the constitutional test.

Jacobellis is perhaps best remembered for Justice Stewart's concurring opinion, in which he pointed out that the Court's opinions since 1957 had pointed in the direction of a "hard-core only" test for obscene materials. As he noted, however, a definition of hard-core obscenity had evaded the Court and would probably continue to do so:

> I shall not today attempt to define the kinds of material I understand to be embraced within that shorthand definition; and perhaps I could never succeed in intelligibly doing so. But I know it when I see it and the motion picture involved in this case is not that.[66]

Although Stewart later complained that people only remembered his "I know it when I see it" test, in fact he had put his finger directly on the central problem of the obscenity issue. He knew what offended him, and this picture did not; it obviously had offended others. Obscenity, like beauty, is in the eye of the beholder, and so long as we have an open, tolerant, and pluralistic society, one will find an enormous range of opinion on the nature of sexually oriented material. Nonetheless, the Court continued doggedly to seek a workable definition.

Two years later the Court, again speaking through Justice Brennan, narrowed the requirements even further in *Memoirs* v. *Massachusetts* (1966).[67] The state had attempted to suppress sale of a book that had been the subject of one of the first American obscenity cases in 1821, John Cleland's *Memoirs of a Woman of Pleasure*, popularly known as *Fanny Hill*.[68] In overturning the state decision, Brennan elaborated the obscenity test as first enunciated in *Roth* and now refined by nearly a decade's experience:

> Three elements must coalesce: it must be established that (a) the dominant theme of the material taken as a whole appeals to a prurient interest in sex; (b) the material is patently offensive because it affronts contemporary community standards relating to the description or representation of sexual matters; and (c) the material is utterly without redeeming social value.[69]

The new tripartite test hardly commanded the full allegiance of the brethren. Only Chief Justice Warren and Justice Fortas joined Brennan's opinion, the former somewhat reluctantly. Justices Stewart, Black, and Douglas concurred in the result, but not the reasoning; Stewart would have cut through the morass and stated simply that only hard-core pornography remained outside First Amendment protection, whereas Black and Douglas remained consistent in their opposition to any form of censorship. Among the dissenters, Justice Harlan, as he had in *Roth*, would have left control of obscenity to state discretion; Justice White would have eliminated social value from Brennan's test, a point elaborated upon by Justice Clark.

If the majority had hoped to clarify the issue, it muddied the waters even more in two other opinions handed down the same day, in which the Court affirmed obscenity convictions. *Mishkin* v. *New York*[70] involved sadomasochistic materials and was the easier case because of the particularly brutal and revolting contents of the magazine. The publisher, however, took the interesting approach that the contents did not appeal to prurient interest, because they did not appeal to the average person's normal definition of sexual relations! The

Court dismissed this bit of sophistry and declared that the test would apply to the audience to which the magazines deliberately aimed.

The other case, *Ginzburg* v. *United States*,[71] involved a glossy, sophisticated magazine, *Eros*, which featured highly erotic articles and pictures. Whether it met the tripartite test is unclear, because the case centered on the prosecution's claim that the material had been promoted and marketed to appeal to the lascivious. The Court upheld the conviction and thus added the feature of "pandering" to the obscenity morass.

The decision is troubling and confusing, because there is a strong argument that the defendant had been denied due process; as the dissenters pointed out, the Court had rewritten the law so that it sustained Ginzburg's conviction on a different theory (pandering) than that which he had originally been tried upon (distributing obscene materials). Moreover, "pandering" is perhaps an even more obscure term than "obscene" and calls into question all sorts of subjective judgments. It has been suggested that the Court, concerned at the time by charges that it was "soft" on criminals and was fostering moral permissiveness by its obscenity decisions, wanted to show that convictions could be secured against pornographers.[72]

These three cases—*Memoirs, Mishkin,* and *Ginzburg*—reflect the ambivalence that marked the Warren Court's efforts to deal with obscenity and to determine how much freedom of expression is protected when it deals primarily with sexually oriented material. As Justice Black noted in dissent in *Ginzburg*, there had been fourteen separate opinions handed down that day in the three cases and "no person, not even the most learned judge much less a layman, is capable of knowing in advance of ultimate decision in his particular case by this Court whether certain material comes within the area of 'obscenity.' "[73]

Following these three cases, the Court seemed to abandon its effort to articulate a definition of obscenity and finally began to look at what it should have examined in the first place: whether sufficient state interests existed to regulate such material, and if so, under what rationale. In 1967 the Court in per curiam decisions reversed several obscenity convictions. The accompanying brief opinion noted that the seven justices who constituted the majority for reversal held four different theories to justify their views. But in none of the cases

> was there a claim that the statute in question reflected a specific and limited state concern for juveniles. . . . In none was there any suggestion of an assault upon individual privacy by publication in a manner so obtrusive as to make it impossible for an unwilling audience to avoid exposure to it. And in none was there evidence of the sort of "pandering" which the Court found significant in *Ginzburg* v. *United States*.[74]

The Court does not even mention the tripartite *Roth–Memoirs* test; in fact, it hardly mentions obscenity per se. Rather, it asks whether there have been intrusions into certain accepted areas where the state police power is acknowledged—protection of children and of captive audiences and prevention of pandering. The Court had finally gotten around to asking the right questions; the terseness of the memorandum, however, indicated that the Court had a long way to go until it found the right answers.

The following year, the Court upheld a New York statute forbidding the sale of material to minors deemed to be obscene to them. As Justice Brennan exclaimed, the courts had traditionally left the care of children to their parents, and so if parents wanted their children to read some of these materials, they could buy it for them. But the state also had a traditional interest in protecting the welfare of its minor citizens and under its police power may pass legislation to that effect. (Protection of children had been acknowledged in the *Redrup* v. *New York* memorandum as a justifiable grounds for regulation.) Because obscenity remained unprotected speech, Brennan invoked the two-tier strategy and asked: Did New York have a reasonable basis to conclude that children might suffer some harm from exposure to pornography? If the legislature believed this so, then the courts would not question the wisdom of that decision.[75]

The Court in some ways had to adopt a two-tiered approach, because nearly all of the major philosophers of free expression, from John Stuart Mill through Chafee, Meiklejohn, and Emerson, had dealt with political, as opposed to artistic, expression. The great dissenting opinions of Learned Hand, Oliver Wendell Holmes, and Louis D. Brandeis had similarly focused on the importance of robust political speech. Artistic expression just cannot be judged within those parameters and is moreover a highly personal experience. Critics at one time considered Marcel Duchamps's "Nude Descending a Staircase," James Joyce's *Ulysses,* and even Igor Stravinsky's "La Sacre du Printemps" as obscene; even today there are persons who object to Mark Twain. Justice Stewart's comment well summed up the Court's problem in its definitional approach, in that it tried to establish objective criteria for a subjective topic. Only when they began to explore what might be considered the artistic parallel to the clear and present danger test, the balance of state against individual interests, did the justices finally begin to make sense.

In its last term, the Court took another step in trying to define the legitimate interests of the state. In its final case dealing with obscenity, the Warren Court unanimously held that the mere possession of obscene material for private viewing in one's home could not be criminally punished.[76]

In the course of investigating alleged bookmaking activities, police had secured a warrant and searched Stanley's house. They found little evidence of illegal gambling but did uncover several reels of film, which upon later examination proved obscene. In the ensuing prosecution, both the state and the defense agreed that the films met the *Roth–Memoirs* definition of obscenity; the issue thus boiled down to whether the state had any justification in regulating what a person read or saw in the privacy of his or her own home. The state argued that just as it had an obligation to protect the physical well-being of its citizens, so it could protect their minds as well.

All nine members of the Court agreed on the reversal of Stanley's conviction. Stewart, Brennan, and White chose not to reach the First Amendment issues, believing that Stanley's Fourth Amendment rights had been violated. Justice Thurgood Marshall, who had replaced Tom Clark in 1967, finally did what the Court had failed to do earlier—examine what interests the state had in regulating obscene materials. Although he went to great trouble to claim that nothing in his opinion impaired the *Roth* holding that obscenity lay outside constitutional protection, the logic of *Stanley* did just that. If the state had no legitimate claim to interfere with what a person read or viewed privately, and if *Roth* remained intact, then a citizen of the United States had a constitutional right to possess obscene materials, but the person who provided those materials could be criminally prosecuted. The Court ignored this conundrum in *Stanley;* as in so many other areas, the Warren Court left the hard cases to its successor.[77]

In the area of obscenity as in seditious libel, the Warren Court left the law significantly altered from what it had found. In both areas, however, the Court undertook no massive restatement of doctrine but instead built upon precedents it inherited. But where it articulated a relatively clear philosophy of why political speech had to be protected, the Court failed to develop a coherent rationale for dealing with obscene materials. Instead, the justices foundered in trying to define obscenity, and only at the end of the Warren Court era did they finally begin to reexamine the key question of what state interests existed to justify regulation of obscene materials.

LIBEL AND PRIVACY

In *Chaplinsky* the Court had placed criminal libel, along with obscenity and provocation, outside the protection of the First Amendment. Under the common law, three general rules had developed in regard to defamatory statements. First, such statements were presumed false, which placed the burden upon the alleged defamer to prove the truth of the comments. In many situations, "truth" might be difficult to establish, especially if it involved subjective judgments. Second, if the statement were false, it did not matter whether it had been printed[78] through malice or negligence; one published at one's peril, and the common law presumed malice from the publication of false statements. Finally, the aggrieved party did not have to prove actual harm to reputation; the publication of false statements implied that general harm had occurred. Once a plaintiff proved that a libel had occurred, he or she was entitled to monetary damages; determination of these damages varied according to individual state law.[79]

The Supreme Court first heard a libel case ten years after *Chaplinsky*. During World War II several state legislatures, trying to prevent the rampant racism that marked Hitler's Germany, had enacted group libel statutes, which extended the rules of defamation against individuals to groups. Illinois passed such a law and under it prosecuted the president of a "White Circle League" for remarks directed against Negroes. Shortly after the Supreme Court had struck down the validity of restrictive covenants,[80] Beauharnais published an ad urging Chicago city officials to prevent blacks from moving into white neighborhoods, because they would bring "rapes, robberies, knives, guns and marijuana" with them.

On appeal, the Supreme Court upheld the conviction by a 5-4 vote.[81] Justice Frankfurter, writing for the majority, adopted the *Chaplinsky* comment that libel did not enjoy First Amendment protection and reasoned that if the state could establish laws on individual libel, it could do the same for group libel. Among the dissenters, Justices Black and Douglas entered strong and prescient dissents. Black declared that the decision "degrades First Amendment freedoms" and warned that "the same kind of state law that makes Beauharnais a criminal for advocating segregation in Illinois can be utilized to send people to jail in other states for advocating equality and nonsegregation."[82] Douglas labeled the majority opinion "a philosophy at war with the First Amendment" and warned that under group libel laws "tomorrow a Negro will be hauled before a court for denouncing lynch law in heated terms."[83] In fact, the Warren Court first dealt with the libel issue in the context of the great civil rights revolution of the 1960s.

The case arose following publication of an advertisement in the *New York Times* entitled "Heed Their Rising Voices," which detailed the difficulties Martin Luther King, Jr., and his associates faced in the South and which requested funds to aid in the civil rights struggle. Although L. B. Sullivan, the police commissioner of Montgomery, Alabama, had not been mentioned by name in the text, he sued the *Times* on the basis that the advertisement derogated his performance of his public duties. An Alabama court found the advertisement defamatory and disallowed the defense of truth because of several minor factual inaccuracies in the text. The jury awarded general damages of $500,000, and the Alabama Supreme Court affirmed the decision.

No doubt the case involved more than a bit of malice on the part of southerners directed against outside "interference" in the civil rights movement. But in fact, Alabama had made no new law on this subject; rather, the facts of the case merely showed how harsh the technical rules of criminal libel could be. When the Alabama trial court disallowed the defense of "fair comment" because of factual inaccuracies, it may have appeared vengeful, but in fact many other states had exactly the same rule.

The Court, which in *Brown* had triggered the civil rights struggle, obviously had "to rescue the *Times* and equally compelled by its role to seek high ground in justifying its result, arrived at some very high ground indeed."[84] Unlike its decisions on seditious libel and obscenity, here the Court did indeed chart a new path, and in *New York Times* v. *Sullivan* (1964)[85] it wrote an important chapter in the history of freedom of expression.

Justice William Brennan, who in his more than thirty years on the Court has helped shape a large part of American constitutional doctrine, spoke in his opinion to more than the archaic common law rules of libel. He addressed the larger issue of what limits constrain individuals and the press in a free society when they criticize the government or its officials. While Brennan has not been an absolutist on First Amendment rights (witness his opinions that obscenity remained outside constitutional protection), he had moved consistently to a Meiklejohnian view that political speech in any form must be completely protected. In this case he utilized what he termed "the central meaning of the First Amendment" to cut through centuries of accumulated restrictions on speech.[86]

Because of some minor factual errors[87] the defendant could not enter one of the traditional defenses against libel, that of "fair comment." Reporters may fairly comment on people or institutions that offer their work for public approval or in the public interest, provided that the criticism is fair, honest, and made without malice.[88] By adhering strictly to the requirement of accuracy in the factual recital, the Alabama trial court cut off this defense. As a result, it had a chilling effect on criticism of public officials, since newspapers would be very reluctant to offer any criticism if, because of a minor and even irrelevant factual error, they would be denied their defense against libel suits.

Although Sullivan had sued in his private capacity, and the suit had been tried under the law of criminal libel that governed defamation of individuals, in a broader sense the case involved seditious libel, the criticism of the government itself. Sullivan claimed that the advertisement derogated the official performance of his department, and if government officials could sue every time their official conduct came under critical scrutiny, one would be back to the status of the 1798 Sedition Act. Brennan realized this, and in his opinion noted specifically that

> [a]lthough the Sedition Act was never tested in this Court, the attack upon its validity has carried the day in the court of history. . . . The invalidity of the Act has also been assumed by Justices of this Court. . . . These views reflect a broad consensus that the Act, because of the restraint it imposed upon criticism of government and public officials, was inconsistent with the First Amendment.[89]

The old notion of seditious libel—that criticism of the government even if factually in error—could no longer be tolerated in a free society. The central meaning of the First Amendment is that seditious libel in any form cannot be tolerated, and the Alabama rule, with its demand for strict accuracy, had the effect of making seditious libel an offense. The penalties faced under the Sedition Act and the Alabama law differed only in degree; they both had the same objective, to stifle "uninhibited, robust and wide-open" debate on public issues.

At one point in his opinion, Brennan noted that in a 1959 case the Court had ruled that high-ranking government officials enjoyed immunity from libel suits when acting in their public capacity.[90] Certainly the same privilege should be extended to citizens when they perform their duties, namely, to scrutinize closely public policies. In a democracy, as Meiklejohn claimed, the citizen is the ruler and therefore the most important official of the government.

Justice Brennan realized that at times criticism could be harsh and might exceed the limits of good taste, perhaps even of truth—that it may, as he noted, "well include vehement, caustic, and sometimes unpleasantly sharp attacks on the government and public officials." While this might not be comfortable for the officials under attack, it constituted a necessary part of the mechanism of democracy, protected in all its vigor by the First Amendment. To allow, as Alabama did, transmutation of such criticism into the basis for personal suit would have a chilling effect on protected free expression, and that was constitutionally unacceptable.

There is no question that the decision in *New York Times* marked a major step in broadening the level of free expression protected under the First Amendment, but it did not go far enough to assuage at least two members of the Court, Justices Black and Douglas, who entered a concurrence expressing their belief in an "absolute, unconditional constitutional right to publish" criticisms of public officials. Although the majority opinion did not speak of balancing competing interests, the decision did not, as Black and Douglas realized, affirm an unconditional protection of political criticism.

The normal criteria for evaluating First Amendment protection, which are explicitly balancing tests, are not mentioned in *New York Times*. It is nonetheless balancing, although not of the ad hoc variety that marked the seditious libel cases. In this case and elsewhere Brennan tried to define protected speech, albeit more successfully than his efforts to define unprotected speech in the obscenity cases. Justice Powell later explained the need for such definitional rules. Case-by-case adjudication of competing interests—free speech versus reputational integrity—would produce "unpredictable results and uncertain expectations, and it would render our duty to supervise the lower courts unmanageable."[91] But definitions, as Black and Douglas well understood, would always involve including and excluding certain types of speech, a result they believed incompatible with the First Amendment mandate against any restriction on speech.[92] "The only sure way," Black declared,

> to protect speech and press against these threats is to recognize that libel laws are abridgements of speech and press and therefore barred in both federal and state courts by the First and Fourteenth Amendments. I repeat what I said in the *New York Times* case that "An unconditional right to say what one pleases about public affairs is what I consider to be the minimum guarantee of the First Amendment."[93]

New York Times did not, as Justice Black recognized, do away with libel law in its entirety. Rather, it set up a dividing line between two types of allegedly defamatory speech: that directed against public officials and personalities and that involving private persons. In general, criticism of public officials is now, with certain limited exceptions, protected under the First Amendment. The chief exception involves false information propagated with "actual malice"; that is, the person knows the material to be untrue and prints or says it anyway in order to harm the official.[94]

The Court did not find actual malice in the inconsequential errors in the *Times* advertisement, but later in the year it had the opportunity to develop this standard in *Garrison* v. *Louisiana*.[95] James Garrison, the flamboyant district attorney of Orleans Parish, Louisiana, got into a public shouting match with eight justices of the criminal district court when they denied him access to the fines and fees fund for money to conduct an investigation of commercial vice. He called a press conference and claimed that the judges' decision "raises interesting questions about the racketeer influences on our eight vacation-minded judges." The judges sued, and a Louisiana court tried and convicted Garrison of libel under the state Criminal Defamation Law. He appealed, and the Supreme Court unanimously reversed on the basis of the *New York Times* doctrine.

Honest although inaccurate statements always have the potential for furthering the search for truth, Justice Brennan exclaimed, and are to be protected:

> [I]t does not follow that the lie, knowingly and deliberately published about a public official, should enjoy a like immunity. . . . For the use of the known lie as a tool is at once at odds with the premises of democratic government and with the orderly manner in which economic, social, or political change is to be effected. . . . Hence the knowingly false statement and the false statement made with reckless disregard of the truth do not enjoy constitutional protection.[96]

Garrison's charges may have been reckless, but there had been no showing made, nor even required under existing Louisiana law, that there had been actual malice against the officials.[97]

Another refinement of the *Times* test came in two cases decided together in 1967: *Curtis Publishing Co.* v. *Butts* and *Associated Press* v. *Walker*.[98] The first case came out of a *Saturday Evening Post* article alleging that Wally Butts, a former coach and then University of Georgia athletic director, had fixed a football game. In the second case, Edwin Walker, a retired army general, sued the wire service following a story that he had led a violent crowd in opposing enforcement of a desegregation decree at the University of Mississippi.

Neither plaintiff held public office and therefore did not come under the public official category of the *Times* test. But as Chief Justice Warren explained, "[D]ifferentiation between 'public figures' and 'public officials' and adoption of separate standards of proof for each have no basis in law, logic, or First Amendment policy." Such public figures, by their reputation, have access to the press through which they may rebut allegations against them, a right enjoyed by public officials as well but denied to private citizens.

Although the Court did extend the *Times* doctrine, it also introduced the ideas of "reckless disregard" and "hot news" into the formula. In the Butts case, the magazine based its story on the questionable report of George Burnett, who allegedly overheard a telephone conversation because of an electronic error. As Justice Harlan explained in the 5-4 decision that upheld the libel award to Butts, the information provided by Burnett "was in no sense 'hot' news and the editors of the magazine recognized the need for a thorough investigation of the serious charges." They failed to do so, however, and this showed a reckless disregard for the facts and a gross failure to conform to normal standards for investigative journalism.

In the Walker case, however, a unanimous Court overturned the libel judgment because the news had been reported in the midst of riots on the Ole Miss campus. It was "hot" news that required immediate dissemination, from a reporter on the scene who gave every indication of trustworthiness and reliability. Under the pressure of events, such errors must be considered innocent and not a reckless disregard of truth.

The Butts and Walker cases marked the limit to which the Warren Court was willing to expand the *Times* doctrine, and four members of the bench—Harlan, Clark, Stewart, and Fortas—opposed that extension. In fact, only three members of the Court actually supported the public figure doctrine (Warren, Brennan, and White), and they prevailed because Black and Douglas supported a broader immunity.[99] The major innovation had been the *Times* decision, and while the Court had attempted to articulate manageable tests such as actual malice and reckless disregard, the cases involved had been fairly easy ones.

CONCLUSIONS

The Warren Court had undertaken the most serious review of speech-related issues in the Court's history. In some areas, such as seditious libel, it had taken a string of often contradictory precedents and had steered a middle course between the absolutist position of Black and Douglas on one hand and the deference to legislative policy advocated first by Frankfurter and then by Harlan on the other. In the end, in *Brandenburg*, it adopted a position more fully protective of political speech than any other Court had done and helped to articulate a fairly consistent jurisprudential theory for doing so. Moreover, and to its credit, the Court had gotten away from the red scare mentality of the Vinson years, and by very lawyerlike attention to detail, had erected procedural as well as some substantive barriers to the worst abuses of congressional red-baiting.

The Court had been far less successful in its cases on obscenity, where it had been unable to establish clear rules on what constituted obscene material or even a philosophical base to evaluate the rationale for legislative controls. The Court might have ducked the issue for a while, but in the end the changing climate of the country, with its growing permissiveness amd the reception of a younger generation to new ideas, would have forced a constitutional challenge to censorship statutes. It is unlikely that a later Court would have had any greater success with the issue.

The one decision that marks a significant change from past doctrine is that in *New York Times* v. *Sullivan*. Yet even here one can find doctrinal precedent, especially the rule against prior restraint, that coupled with Meiklejohn's view about the absolute protection of all politically related speech makes the decision look much less radical than it appeared at the time.

In all areas of free speech, the Warren Court opened a figurative Pandora's box of issues, many of which could not have emerged without these earlier rulings. The Burger Court would inherit these very difficult problems, none of which had easy solutions.

5

"*Free Speech Is Powerful Medicine*"
The Burger Court and Free Speech

The Warren Court, despite some notable decisions expanding freedom of expression, had never developed a comprehensive First Amendment jurisprudence. The Burger Court thus inherited a variety of precedents without the luxury, as it were, of a specific theory that it could either advance or reject. Thomas Emerson complained in 1970 that at various times the Court had used such diverse tests as bad tendency, clear and present danger, incitement, a variety of ad hoc balancings, vagueness, overbreadth, and prior restraint, but it "has totally failed to settle on any coherent approach."[1]

Academic commentators always bemoan this lack of consistency, but even if the Court adopts some sort of test, such as the tripartite *Lemon* scheme,[2] it does not follow that the Court will methodically apply that test or that it can develop specific rules which will be followed at all times. In trying to analyze the Court's decisions, especially in First Amendment areas, it must be remembered that some issues, such as the "intractable" obscenity problem, are not amenable to simple formulas.

The multiplicity of theories reflected not just changing views but also a serious effort by the Court to develop judicially manageable standards to govern First Amendment problems. The introduction and abandonment of particular ideas did not indicate a Court hostile to free speech so much as one attempting to confront difficult issues. The major issue confronting the Warren Court had been sedition, and there the justices had a string of precedents dating back to 1919, as well as extensive academic commentary, upon which to rely. The Burger Court did not have to deal with sedition, because that issue had been settled; but in other areas it did try to develop standards and rationales to guide lower courts. Its legacy is a mixed record of success and failure.

THE OVERBREADTH DOCTRINE

Of the various tests the Court tried, overbreadth has been one of the most important. Justice Harlan summarized the essential point when he declared that "a governmental purpose to control or prevent activities constitutionally subject to regulation may not be achieved by means which sweep unnecessarily broadly and thereby invade the area of protected freedoms."[3] In other words, even when the state imposes a legitimate and permissible means of regulation, it must do no more than is absolutely necessary to achieve its goal. To go further, the Court has held, would have a chilling effect on free speech.

Overbreadth analysis and litigation differ significantly from other forms of constitutional challenges. In most cases, a person claims that a law is unconstitutional as applied to him or her and is not allowed to raise the issue of how it would affect those not party to the suit. Because speech is involved, though, the Court does permit the challenger to raise the issue of third-party rights, and if the challenge is successful, the Court will strike down the legislation "on its face" or "as construed," not merely as it may have been applied in a particular situation. But although overbreadth rulings do favor the population in general and not just the litigants, they also appear to leave room for the legislature to correct the flaws in application if the original goal of the regulation is permissible. Overbreadth decisions rarely expound jurisprudential substance; they are concerned with pragmatic considerations. This may have been the aspect that appealed most to the pragmatism of the Burger majority.

Overbreadth analysis came into full flower toward the end of the Warren years and could be manipulated to appear as if the Court merely applied mechanistic rules rather than made value choices in balancing interests. In *United States* v. *Robel* (1967), Chief Justice Warren specifically denied that the Court had engaged in an ad hoc balancing test:

> It has been suggested that this case should be decided by "balancing" the governmental interest, expressed in [the statute] against the First Amendment rights asserted by the appellee. This we decline to do. . . . We have ruled only that the Constitution requires that the conflict between congressional power and individual rights be accommodated by legislation drawn more narrowly to avoid the conflict.[4]

Warren's claim did not persuade many commentators, and it recalled Justice Robert's equally unpersuasive dictum of forty years earlier that all the Court did was lay a challenged statute next to the Constitution to see if it squared.[5] One of the nation's leading constitutional scholars, Gerald Gunther, dismissed the Chief Justice's disclaimer and hoped that some day the Court "will be able to confront competing ultimate values, as it does here, without denying that it is doing so."[6]

In addition to *Robel*, the Warren Court resorted to the overbreadth technique in several other challenges to legislation that attempted to control alleged subversives through broad proscriptions. The State Department could not deny passports to Communists, because the regulation "too broadly and indiscriminately restricts the right to travel."[7] New York State could not dismiss faculty who refused to sign a loyalty oath, because the statutory scheme covered permissible as well as impermissible associations.[8] An overly broad statute not only regulated activities that did not enjoy constitutional protection but swept within its scope protected activities as well.[9]

A few cases early in the Burger era also utilized the overbreadth technique,[10] but criticism mounted that the courts used the device to impose their own values on policy matters. Even Justice Black, who had been unswerving in his devotion to free speech, warned lower courts to be sparing in their use of injunctive relief against state laws on the basis of an overbreadth claim. The federal judicial power, he noted, should be used to resolve "concrete disputes," and not be used in cases of potential abuses because of alleged overbreadth.[11] The new Nixon appointees also expressed unhappiness that convictions for speech under carefully and narrowly drawn statutes had been set aside for alleged vagueness.[12]

In 1973 the Court, its personnel significantly changed, refined the overbreadth doctrine in an effort to make it a more precise tool of judicial analysis. Chief Justice Burger, picking up on Justice Black's comments, had suggested that a narrower approach which would still safeguard legitimate speech would be "substantial overbreadth," and a majority of the Court adopted that suggestion in *Broadrick* v. *Oklahoma*.[13] The case involved a challenge to an Oklahoma law restricting the political activities of state workers. Justice White, who had been in the minority in several earlier overbreadth decisions, here spoke for the 5-4 majority, while Justice Brennan, who had authored several of those decisions, now spoke for the minority. White refused to apply the overbreadth doctrine, because, as he explained, the Court had normally not applied it to ordinary criminal law that might incidentally have an impact on expression. Moreover, "where conduct and not merely speech is involved, we believe that the overbreadth of a statute must not only be real, but substantial as well, judged in relation to the statute's plainly legitimate sweep."[14]

If the Court expected the new standard to be clearer than the old, its hopes never materialized. Justice Brennan complained in his dissent that the majority proposed treating deterrence of conduct differently from deterrence of speech, even if both were equally protected by the First Amendment. Moreover, the new test did not clarify what standards the Court would impose in those cases involving "speech plus," that is, speech accompanied by some form of conduct. Traditionally, pure speech had enjoyed greater protection than speech tied to action, but, as Justice Brennan pointed out, sometimes the activity itself may be protected.[15] In *Broadrick* the statute proscribed political activity so broadly that about all a state worker could do was vote. Yet in cases both before and after *Broadrick*, the Court held political *activity* protected under the First Amendment.[16] The dichotomy between "pure speech" and speech plus, or "expressive conduct," according to legal scholar Martin Redish, is "based solely on the most technical formalism, a ground entirely divorced from any rational first amendment policies or values." And, as he pointed out, the legal consequences of that dichotomy "are equally devoid of logic."[17]

In fact, the *Broadrick* dichotomy proved unusable in subsequent cases, but the newer justices felt uncomfortable with the bludgeon approach of overbreadth as it had been applied in the last years of the Warren era. Justice Stevens, for example, concurred in a speech case and explained that his

> reasons for avoiding overbreadth analysis in this case are more qualitative than quantitative. When we follow our traditional practice of adjudicating difficult and novel constitutional questions only in concrete factual situations, the adjudications tend to be crafted with greater wisdom. Hypothetical rulings are inherently treacherous and prone to lead us into unforeseen errors; they are qualitatively less reliable than the products of case-by-case adjudication.[18]

In another case, Stevens admitted that the criterion of substantial overbreadth "is not readily reduced to an exact definition."[19]

The Burger Court compiled a mixed record on overbreadth challenges. In some cases, the majority took a very narrow view of what constituted overbreadth. In *Arnett* v. *Kennedy*,[20] for example, Justice Rehnquist spoke for a 6-3 Court in sustaining a federal law providing for the dismissal of civil service employees for "such cause as will promote the efficiency of the service." Several employees had been dismissed for making derogatory comments about fellow workers. Rehnquist conceded that the law probably intended to allow dismissal for speech as well as other activity, but he construed the statute as not authorizing discharge for constitutionally protected speech and therefore not overbroad.

The Court did find overbreadth in a New Orleans city ordinance that made it unlawful "to curse or revile or to use obscene or opprobrious language toward or with reference to any member of the city police while in the actual performance of his duty." Justice Brennan's opinion for the majority termed words like "opprobrious" much too vague, and it could be applied to statements that would not incite a breach of the peace. Brennan did not even mention *Broadrick*.[21]

Nor did the Court refer to *Broadrick* in a case involving action as well as speech, even though Justice White authored both opinions. The Court struck down as overly broad an ordinance prohibiting door-to-door or on-street solicitation of contributions by charitable oganizations that did not use at least 75 percent of the receipts for "charitable purposes."[22] The Court apparently recognized some expressive conduct as protected in its own right, and the false dichotomy set up in *Broadrick* could not be sustained. Rather than continue to impose a rule that made little sense, the Court for the most part abandoned it. In the rare overbreadth cases that subsequently came up, the majority occasionally paid lip service to the notion of substantiality, but the doctrine remained, as it had in the Warren era, a broad and flexible if somewhat imprecise rule that can be evoked for want of a better one. Extensive discussion of overbreadth, however, did come in connection with that troubling subject, obscenity.

THE NEW OBSCENITY RULE

There had been some speculation following the Warren Court's ruling in *Stanley* v. *Georgia*[23] that if a person could not be prosecuted for possessing and viewing pornographic materials at home, then there could be no basis for any obscenity legislation. Although Justice Marshall had insisted that *Stanley* had not impaired *Roth*, some commentators and lower-court judges assumed that *Stanley* had in fact brought obscenity within the scope of First Amendment protection. After all, if one had a right to possess obscene materials, it seemed a logical corollary that someone else had a right to supply those items.[24] It was exactly this reasoning that a lower court used in ruling the federal mail obscenity statute unconstitutional: "If someone has a right to receive and possess" pornography, "then someone must have a right to deliver it to him."[25]

In an opinion by Justice White, a 6-3 Court in *United States* v. *Reidel* (1971)[26] reaffirmed the vitality of *Roth*. "To extrapolate from Stanley's right to have and peruse obscene material in the privacy of his own home a First Amendment right in Reidel to sell it to him would effectively scuttle Roth, the precise result that the Stanley opinion abjured." The Court had upheld First Amendment rights to read and think in one's own home; Reidel also had that right, but not the right to go out and sell the material. In case anyone missed the point, White reiterated that "*Roth* has squarely placed obscenity and its distribution outside the reach of the First Amendment and they remain there today. *Stanley* did not overrule [*Roth*]."[27]

Reidel, as Harry Kalven pointed out, was a transitional case between the Warren and Burger Courts. Not only did the two new members join Justice White's opinion, but so did Harlan, Stewart, and Brennan, while Marshall, the author of *Stanley*, concurred in the result. Only Black and Douglas dissented. After fifteen years of obscenity cases, the Court had reached the "threshhold of the conclusion" that the First Amendment prohibited regulation of obscene materials for consenting adults. But, Kalven noted, the Court "was not quite ready to take the final step across that threshold."[28]

It never did take that step, as the next two appointees helped form a new majority on the bench. Lewis Powell and William Rehnquist, along with Burger and Blackman, joined with Justice White, one of the dissenters in the *Memoirs* case. The five undertook what the Chief Justice called a "re-examination" of the issue in an effort to articulate a clearer definition of what constituted obscenity and how far First Amendment protection went. They also wanted to settle the question as quickly as possible, so that the high court could get out of the business of determining whether particular books or movies were pornographic.

There is no question but that all the members of the Court were, by this time, thoroughly tired of dealing with the issue. As Justice Brennan noted, "No other aspect of the First Amendment has, in recent years, demanded so substantial a commitment of our time, generated such disharmony of views, and remained so resistant to the formulation of stable and manageable standards."[29] The Court had also read the report of the U.S. Commission on Obscenity and Pornography (1970). The commission had been established by Congress in 1967 to investigate the impact of obscene materials on behavior. The majority of its members had concluded that erotica did not substantially alter patterns of sexual behavior and that existing studies had failed to establish any significant link between erotica and sex crimes or attitudes on sexuality and sexual morality. The majority also recommended repealing laws prohibiting the sale of sexually oriented materials to consenting adults, but retaining regulations regarding display of the materials and their sale to minors.[30] The Court's response to the report, as well as its own frustration in dealing with obscenity cases, surfaced in two cases handed down the same day in 1973.[31] The Court's majority there set out its rationale of why obscene materials could be regulated, as well as a new definition of what constituted obscenity.

In *Paris Adult Theatre I* v. *Slaton*,[32] Chief Justice Burger categorically rejected the rationale of both *Stanley* and the Obscenity and Pornography Commission's majority report that there should be no regulation in the case of consenting adults, or that obscene material acquired some sort of constitutional immunity when directed toward consenting adults. While people could read or do whatever they wanted in the privacy of their homes, the state had a right to protect the quality of life for the rest of its citizens. The fact that the commission had been unable to find any link between erotica and social behavior did not mean that a link did not exist. It might be unprovable, but

> from the beginning of civilized societies, legislators and judges have acted on various unprovable assumptions. . . . If we accept the unprovable assumption that a complete education requires certain books and the well nigh universal belief that good books, plays, and art lift the spirit, improve

the mind, enrich the human personality and develop character, can we then say that a state legislature may not act on the corollary assumption that commerce in obscene books, or public exhibitions focused on obscene conduct, have a tendency to exert a corrupting and debasing impact leading to antisocial behavior? . . . Nothing in the Constitution prohibits a State from reaching such a conclusion and acting on it legislatively because there is no conclusive evidence or empirical [data].[33]

Chief Justice Burger's opinion thus set out a twofold rationale for regulation, namely, that the state had a right to protect the quality of life from the debasing influence of obscene material and that such material did, as the commission's minority claimed, have a direct relation to antisocial behavior. He also reaffirmed that obscenity per se is unprotected by the First Amendment.

That left the problem of defining what constituted obscenity, and the Chief Justice turned to that task in the companion case of *Miller* v. *California*.[34] He believed the Court had gone astray in the *Memoirs* case when a majority had insisted that for the state to prove obscenity, it had to show that the material in question was *utterly* without redeeming social value, a "burden virtually impossible to discharge." Burger acknowledged the difficulty of articulating standards and warned that states could not use obscenity laws in a fashion that would impinge upon legitimate works of art dealing with sexual themes. The basic guidelines for the trier of fact are, he declared:

(a) whether the "average person, applying contemporary community standards" would find the work, taken as a whole, appeals to the prurient interest, (b) whether the work depicts or describes, in a patently offensive way, sexual conduct specifically defined by the applicable state law, and (c) whether the work, taken as a whole, lacks serious literary, artistic, political or scientific value.[35]

Miller thus reaffirmed the basic elements of the *Roth* test, first enunciated by the Warren Court sixteen years earlier, and in fact the first part of the new test came directly from *Roth*. The second prong was also not new, but reaffirmed the "patently offensive" standard of *Manual Enterprises* and *Jacobellis*, with the addition of a due process standard that the state had to be specific in its definitions. It also limited regulation to hard-core pornography, another reflection of earlier Warren Court decisions.

The major departure proved the definitional section, which rejected the *Memoirs* standard of "utterly without redeeming social value," a standard that had never had the support of more than three justices at any one time. As with all such tests, it is subjective and involves value judgments by the trier of fact, but it seemed to allow a wide scope for permissible regulation. Because local rather than national standards would apply, the danger existed of parochialism and of an administrative patchwork in which items deemed acceptable in one state might be found obscene in another. The Court tried to avert this problem by requiring very specific definitions in the state legislation, but obscenity is in the eye of the beholder, and it is difficult to define objective criteria in so subjective an area. As Justice Douglas noted in his *Miller* dissent, the justices "deal with highly emotional, not rational, questions. To many the Song of Solomon is obscene."[36]

The dissent of Justice Brennan in these two cases is worth examining, because he had been the author of the *Roth–Memoirs* test. Unlike Douglas and Black, who had consistently opposed any and all censorship as violations of the First Amendment, Brennan had begun his intellectual odyssey committed to the idea that obscenity did not enjoy First Amendment protection. During the Warren years he had tried to fashion a workable test that would protect legitimate artistic expression while excluding pornographic materials, and in *Miller* he admitted his failure. "I am convinced," he said, "that the approach initiated 16 years ago in *Roth* v. *United States*, and culminating in the Court's decision today, cannot bring stability to this area of the law without jeopardizing fundamental First Amendment values, and I have concluded that the time has come to make a significant departure from that approach."[37]

The majority opinion, Brennan argued, did not constitute a new approach but merely continued down the futile trail of trying to establish a workable definition of obscene material that would then be subject to regulation. Every effort at definition, he warned, would either be too vague for consistent application or so broad as to include clearly protected expression as well. He recommended adopting the proposals of the Commission on Obscenity and Pornography that would do away with all regulations with the exception of those dealing with minors and unwilling audiences, the two groups whose protection justified state intervention.

It should be noted that Brennan did not argue that obscenity enjoyed First Amendment protection or that the state had only a trivial interest in its regulation. Rather, his experience had convinced him that no way could be found to regulate obscenity for consenting adults without violating the First Amendment or creating an administrative and judicial morass.

OBSCENITY AFTER *MILLER*

If the majority in *Miller* hoped that it had resolved the "intractable" problem, it soon learned otherwise. The number of obscenity cases reviewed by the Court dropped significantly, but not because of the new standards. With the retirement of Justices Douglas and Stewart, the liberal wing often lacked the four votes necessary to grant certiorari, and the Court consequently heard fewer obscenity cases. Also, as states wrestled with the problem of defining offensive material—the second prong of the *Miller* test—they ran into exactly the kinds of problems Justice Brennan had warned of in his dissent. In some states, the practical results of their struggles led to very limited laws directed primarily at protecting children and unwilling audiences.

The community standards prong brought the first post-*Miller* case to the Court, *Jenkins* v. *Georgia* (1974).[38] A local jury had found the film *Carnal Knowledge* obscene, and the state appellate court had interpreted *Miller* to mean that if a jury found material obscene, then it had no power to review that finding. Not so, said Justice Rehnquist. *Miller* did no more than outline what juries might find offensive or appealing to the prurient, but it did not give them license to impinge on constitutionally protected expression. While the film did depict sexual acts,

> the camera does not focus on the bodies of the actors at such time. There is no exhibition whatever of the actors' genitals, lewd or otherwise, during these scenes. There are occasional scenes of nudity, but nudity alone is not enough to make material legally obscene under the *Miller* standards.[39]

Shades of Justice Stewart's "I know it when I see it"![40]

The Court had other problems with community standards, and its decisions have been less than consistent. In *Jenkins*, Justice Rehnquist seemed to say that local parochialism would have to give way to more cosmopolitan standards, although the Court refused to require that statewide standards apply in state prosecutions. But in a companion case decided the same day, *Hamling* v. *United States*,[41] the Court, by the same 5-4 vote, upheld local community standards rather than state or national criteria in a federal prosecution. Other cases showed similar inconsistency,[42] yet the *Miller* test specifically required states to spell out these criteria in order to preserve a due process standard.

The Court clearly agreed on the state's power of regulation over child pornography. From the beginning, the Court had viewed protection of children and unwilling audiences as legitimate exercises of the state's police power. In *New York* v. *Ferber* (1982),[43] a unanimous bench rejected a First Amendment challenge to a New York law prohibiting the distribution of material depicting children engaged in sexual conduct, whether the material as a whole is considered legally obscene or not. Justice White's opinion is refreshing in that he eschewed the definitional approach, and instead delivered a careful and persuasive exposition of society's interest in regulation. The state had always had a special obligation in safeguarding the physical and psychological well-being of minors. Distribution of child pornography, he claimed, also related to the problem of sexual abuse of children; in fact, the use of children as actors constituted a form of sexual abuse to which the state could respond. Here New York had carefully defined what it wanted to prohibit; it had a clear interest in protecting children; and the law did not impinge on constitutionally protected expression.[44]

Ferber, like *Chaplinsky*, assumed that certain forms of expression per se fall outside of First Amendment protection.[45] In the four decades between the two cases, however, the Court had come to realize that simple categorization by itself is insufficient in First Amendment jurisprudence. Justice White's opinion not only assumed that no constitutional protection existed; but he also went on to demonstrate why that was so and why the state had a valid reason to regulate this area.

The Warren Court's obscenity decisions had been highly criticized among both the general public and the scholarly community, although for different reasons. The Burger Court tightened up some of the procedural rules involved in obscenity litigation, but its overall record "actually reinforced rather than undercut Warren Court policy."[46] Even in its efforts to redefine what constituted obscenity, the *Miller* test for the most part followed the general guidelines of the earlier cases. One should recall that the Warren Court never brought obscene expression within the protection of the First Amendment; it did, however, grapple with the problem of what constituted obscenity and when material that deviated from normally accepted artistic or behavioral standards should be protected.[47] The Burger Court, for better or worse, never repudiated that definitional approach, and its efforts proved no more successful in establishing an objective obscenity test.

One might, perhaps, note the political prudence of the justices. They read the recommendations of the Commission on Obscenity and Pornography but also took into account the public reaction against some of its proposals. President Nixon had totally repudiated them, labeled the commission's report as "morally bankrupt," and urged every state in the union to enact antiobscenity legislation.[48] Rather than continue what every member of the Court considered an impossible task, the justices gave it one last try and then agreed to defer to local legislation except in egregious cases of censorship. One might wish that the Court had, as Justice Douglas suggested, declared all censorship laws unconstitutional and thus moot the whole issue. A majority of the American people, however, believe that government ought to control obscene publications; in the end, the Warren and Burger Courts differed less on the kind of legislation each would permit than on the degree of deference it would allow local sentiment. The Court's record in a closely related area shows a similar pattern.

OFFENSIVE SPEECH

Chaplinsky had placed obscenity, libel, and offensive speech outside the pale of constitutional protection. In the latter category, Justice Murphy spoke of words "which by their very utterance inflict injury" and whose suppression may be justified by society's interest in order and morality. Murphy thus included not only "fighting words" that might provoke a breach of the peace but also speech that offended moral sensibilities. The question of offensive speech did not arise during the Warren years; the early Burger Court dealt with the issue in several cases but carefully avoided the definitional approach it used in the obscenity cases. Instead, the justices followed the more traditional balancing evaluation, comparing the First Amendment values of free speech to state interests in restraint.

The first case to come before the Court arose from the Vietnam War protests, with the arrest and conviction of Paul Cohen for wearing a jacket with the slogan "Fuck the Draft" in the corridors of a Los Angeles courthouse. The California Court of Appeals upheld the conviction, on grounds that the law[49] had a legitimate purpose in trying to prevent violence and that it was "reasonably foreseeable" that others might be provoked to such action by these words. The Supreme Court disagreed and by a 5-4 vote reversed the conviction. Justice Harlan's majority opinion is a skilled and lawyerly piece of work, in which precedent is maintained while First Amendment coverage is expanded.[50]

Harlan began by reaffirming the *Chaplinsky* rule that fighting words lack First Amendment protection, but he drew a distinction between the *content* of the message and its *manner* of delivery. The content, in this case Cohen's views on the morality of the draft, stood beyond the reach of government sanction. While Cohen chose a four-letter word that "is not uncommonly employed in a personally provocative fashion," in this instance the message had not been aimed at any particular person or group. "No individual actually or likely to be present could reasonably have regarded the words on appellant's jacket as a direct personal insult."[51]

Part of the problem with the fighting words category is the presence of a captive audience—people who have no desire to hear the speaker yet may be moved to violent action in response to what is said. The Court has had to balance the legitimate right of the state to protect captive audiences and maintain order against the right of the speaker to be free from the so-called heckler's veto, in which the potential reaction by the audience is used to limit otherwise protected speech. Harlan acknowledged that at times speech may be limited to protect a captive audience, but that in order to do so, the state must show that the speaker has invaded a "substantial privacy interest" in an "essentially intolerable manner." That had not happened here, because anyone who did not like the message on Cohen's jacket could have avoided it by the simple expedient of looking away. The real issue, Harlan explained, is whether the state could excise "one particular scurrilous epithet from the public discourse," because some people found the word offensive. Such censorship, he concluded, could not be tolerated under the Constitution; censorship of words was but a short step from censorship of ideas. Harlan thus reaffirmed *Chaplinsky* while limiting it to personal insults directed at a person or persons likely to respond in a violent manner. That the words chosen might offend one person's sense of propriety or another's moral sensibilities was irrelevant; only an invasion of privacy in "an essentially intolerable manner" could justify censorship.[52]

The following year the Court summarily vacated and remanded three convictions for use of offensive language.[53] In two of the cases the Court referenced *Cohen*, and in all three referred the lower courts to the overbreadth rule in *Gooding* v. *Wilson*. In all three cases the defendants had used obscene and offensive language at public meetings and had been convicted under breach of peace or indecent language statutes; the majority in each case believed that the language, while offensive, did not constitute the fighting words proscribed by *Chaplinsky*. Chief Justice Burger, along with Justices Blackmun and Rehnquist, dissented in all three cases and took a broader view of both abusive language and its connection to possible retaliation. "When we undermine the general belief that the law will give protection against fighting words and profane and abusive language," the Chief Justice declared, "we take steps to return to the law of the jungle." The fact that violence had not been immediately triggered did not preclude the possibility that someone in the audience, justifiably outraged at what had been said, would seek retaliation afterward.

The issue of profane or offensive speech raised different questions than did either obscene language or deliberately provocative words, which remain unprotected by the First Amendment. But what if obscene language is used to express political sentiments? For example, Justice Powell's concurrence in one of the cases, *Brown* v. *Oklahoma*, noted that the Black Panther leader had been specifically invited to present that group's viewpoint, and "in these circumstances language of the character charged might well have been anticipated by the audience."[54] Given the recognition, if not approval, by the Court and the general public that profane language had become widespread by the 1970s, the *Chaplinsky* rule against words that "by their very utterance inflict injury" may well have passed into disuse. In the obscenity cases, the Court majority openly acknowledged the state's interest in preserving a moral and decent environment, and it appeared willing to allow "community standards" to determine those values. In the offensive speech cases, however, it recognized often competing values, and the issue became one of balancing the rights of the speaker against the sensibilities of the audience, some of whom might be offended by the speech.

Related to offensive speech is what may be called offensive displays, and the Court dealt with that problem in *Erznoznik* v. *Jacksonville* in 1975.[55] A local ordinance prohibited drive-in movies with screens visible from public streets from showing films containing nude scenes. The prohibition applied to admittedly nonobscene as well as obscene films, and the city claimed that it could protect its citizens "against unwilling exposure to materials that may be offensive."

Justice Powell's majority opinion, striking down the ordinance on over-breadth grounds, developed the argument that Justice Harlan had set out in *Cohen:* that allegedly offensive speech can be restricted only if it invades the privacy of the listener in an intolerable manner. In deciding these cases, Powell said:

> Some general principles have emerged. A State or municipality may protect individual privacy by enacting reasonable time, place, and manner regulations applicable to all speech irrespective of content. But when the government, acting as censor, undertakes selectively to shield the public from some kinds of speech on the ground that they are more offensive than others, the First Amendment strictly limits its power. Such selective restrictions have been upheld only when the speaker intrudes on the privacy of the home or the degree of captivity makes it impractical for the unwilling viewer or auditor to avoid exposure. The plain, if at times disquieting, truth is that in our pluralistic society [with] constantly prolif-erating new and ingenious forms of expression, "we are inescapably captive audiences for many purposes." Much that we encounter offends our esthetic, if not our political and moral, sensibilities. Nevertheless, the Constitution does not permit government to decide which types of other-wise protected speech are sufficiently offensive to require protection for the unwilling listener or viewer.[56]

SPEECH OF LESSER VALUE

Justice Powell's reference to content regulation leads us to a key element of First Amendment jurisprudence: that in areas of protected expression, the government cannot tie regulation to the content of the speech. It cannot, for example, bar speakers in a public park who advocate communism but permit those who champion capitalism. This analysis, however, assumes that all speech falls into one of two categories—protected or unprotected—and that the former is fully shielded against any and all government regulation aside from neutral time, place, and manner rules. Soon after *Erznoznik*, the Court indi-cated its willingness to distinguish among varieties of protected speech, assign-ing to some a higher value than to others.

Young v. *American Mini Theatres* (1976)[57] upheld a Detroit zoning ordi-nance controlling the sale or display of sexually explicit, although not neces-sarily obscene, materials. The city had tried to combat urban decay by prohibiting so-called adult movie houses, those that showed sexually explicit films, in certain areas of the city. The ordinance had been challenged as a form of content regulation, because it did not control the location of theaters that did not show sexually explicit films. In his plurality opinion,[58] Justice Stevens put forward a theory that different levels of speech warranted different levels of protection. Political speech constituted the core of First Amendment values and received the highest level of protection. But, he claimed, the Court had never held that all expressions of ideas are fully protected. The Court's previous statements had to be read in the context of specific facts, and "whether speech is, or is not, protected by the First Amendment often depends on the content of the speech. . . . Even within the area of protected speech, a difference in content may require a different governmental approach."

The Court had held that the state had the right to protect juveniles and unwilling adults from exposure to obscene materials, and that constituted a form of content regulation. If the material passed the *Miller* test and had some redeeming social value, it still had less value than the expression of political ideas had. "Even though the First Amendment protects communication in this area from total suppression, we hold that the State may legitimately use the content of these materials as the basis for placing them in a different classification from other motion pictures." The only issue at stake was the location of film houses, not their suppression. The city had carefully drawn its ordinance to avoid overbreadth problems and to meet a narrowly defined and legitimate purpose.

Justice Stevens expanded on this theory two years later in *FCC* v. *Pacifica Foundation.*[59] The Federal Communications Commission had received a complaint about the airing on WBAI (New York) of a twelve-minute monologue by comedian George Carlin, which included a list of seven words he claimed (correctly) one could not say on the public airwaves. The commission issued a ruling describing the monologue as "patently offensive" and banning it except for possible late-night broadcast. The FCC dismissed any question as to whether it met the literary, artistic, political, or scientific value test of *Miller.* The agency declared the words themselves, no matter how used, as offensive, and it put news organizations on alert to edit them out of broadcasts. Pacifica, the owner of WBAI, appealed, and the Court of Appeals ruled in favor of the station. The FCC, which rarely lost in the D.C. Circuit, and which was under heavy political pressure to control gratuitous sex and violence on television, appealed to the Supreme Court.[60]

In a 5-4 decision, the Court found in favor of the FCC, and that part of the decision which interests us is Part IV, in which Justice Stevens dealt with the central First Amendment issue. If all content regulation were forbidden, then the FCC rule could not stand, but "our past cases demonstrate, however, that no such absolute rule is mandated by the Constitution." Patently offensive words ordinarily received little First Amendment protection, but even if one accepted the argument that the Carlin monologue would be protected in other contexts, "nonetheless, the constitutional protection accorded to a communication containing such patently offensive sexual and excretory language need not be the same in every context." The majority opinion accepted the FCC's rationale that material on the airwaves went into people's homes and that, unlike the *Cohen* situation, persons, including children, unaware of what was being broadcast could not avert their eyes or ears but had to suffer an unwanted invasion of their privacy.

Once again, Stevens had spoken for only a plurality of the Court, and once again Justice Powell, joined by Justice Blackmun, concurred in the result, but without accepting Stevens's two-tier theory. This led Justice Brennan to note that for the second time in two years

> the Court refuses to accept the notion, completely antithetical to basic First Amendment values, that the degree of protection the First Amendment affords protected speech varies with the social value ascribed to that speech by five Members of this Court. . . . [Yet despite] our unanimous agreement that the Carlin monologue is protected speech, a majority of the Court nevertheless finds that, on the face of this case, the FCC is not constitutionally barred from imposing sanctions on Pacifica.[61]

The effort to assess the value of speech has, on the face of it, a certain common-sense logic. We distinguish good novels from bad, fine plays from the ordinary, compelling cinema from the merely entertaining, and challenging essays from the mediocre. While we may, in theory, grant total freedom to artists or politicians to express their ideas, we do not feel compelled to treat all ideas, all art, or all expression as equal. The Court had already excluded certain types of speech, such as the obscene and the provocative, from First Amendment protection and had identified political ideas as the core value the Framers intended to protect. Why not, then, draw further distinctions between types of speech? Why not say that the merely entertaining is less valuable than political expression, or that comedy, even political satire, is less valuable than tragedy?

The problem, as several members of the Court recognized, is that this type of evaluation is highly subjective and, like the efforts to define obscenity, doomed to failure. As Justice Harlan noted in *Cohen*, one man's vulgarity is another's lyric. But beyond that, as he explained so eloquently,

> [t]he constitutional right of free speech is powerful medicine in a society as diverse and populous as ours. It is designed and intended to remove governmental restraints from the arena of public discourse, putting the decision as to what views shall be voiced largely into the hands of each of us, in the hope that use of such freedom will ultimately produce a more capable citizenry and more perfect polity and in the belief that no other approach would comport with the premise of individual dignity and choice upon which our political system rests.
>
> To many, the immediate consequence of this freedom may often appear to be only verbal tumult, discord, and even offensive utterance. . . . That

the air may sometimes be filled with verbal cacophony is, in this sense, not a sign of weakness but of strength. We cannot lose sight of the fact that, in what otherwise might seem a trifling and annoying instance of individual distasteful abuse of a privilege, these fundamental societal values are truly implicated.[62]

Justice Harlan did not hold all speech as equal in value; rather, in a free society speech had to be treated equally by the government and not be hampered in its efforts to compete in the intellectual marketplace. Once the government could ascribe greater or lesser value to particular types of speech on the basis of content, then censorship of "less valuable" speech became inevitable. With censorship would come the loss of that freedom which makes our democratic society work.

A majority of the Court, it should be noted, never subscribed to Stevens's two-tier theory and within a short time abandoned the concept. In *Consolidated Edison* v. *Public Service Commission* (1980),[63] the Court struck down a PSC order that prohibited an electric company from including, with the monthly utility bill, inserts explaining the firm's position on controversial public issues, such as atomic power. Justice Powell, who had objected to the two-tier theory in both previous cases, declared:

> The First Amendment's hostility to content-based regulation extends not only to restrictions on particular viewpoints, but also to prohibition of public discussion of an entire topic. To allow a government the choice of permissible subjects for public debate would be to allow government control over the search for political truth.[64]

As for the invasion of privacy, the unwilling audience had a simple solution comparable to those who averted their eyes from Cohen—they could throw the inserts away.[65]

An even more forceful rejection of *Pacifica* came a few years later when the Court struck down a federal law banning the mailing of unsolicited advertisements for contraceptives. The government's argument that it had the power to protect unwilling recipients from offense brought a quick retort from the bench: "[We] have never held that [government] can shut off the flow of mailings to protect those recipients who might potentially be offended."[66]

The Court also limited the holding in *American Mini Theatres* when the small New Jersey borough of Mount Ephraim passed a zoning ordinance prohibiting live entertainment anywhere in the town. The challenge to the regulation came from the owner of an adult bookstore who had installed a coin-operated device that allowed customers to watch a nude woman dance behind a glass window. Justice White's opinion employed a classic overbreadth analysis, as he distinguished between the Detroit ordinance, which had been narrowly drawn and which had only an incidental effect on speech, and the

New Jersey regulation that swept away all forms of live entertainment, regardless of form or content. At no point did he invoke the two-tier theory that had been at the heart of the earlier ruling.[67]

In the area of offensive speech, the Burger Court moved a long way from the simple exclusion of *Chaplinsky*. The earlier Court had written in a more genteel time and had assumed, as Justice Murphy noted, that some words "by their very utterance inflict injury" in that they offend moral sensibility. The Court in the seventies may have regretted the passing of a more polite era, but it had to deal with a public discourse in which, as Justice Harlan noted, "words are often chosen as much for their emotive as their cognitive force."[68]

The Court extended First Amendment protection to offensive speech provided the speaker did not invade "substantial privacy interests . . . in an essentially intolerable manner." That some invasion of privacy takes place in modern society is unavoidable, and the Court refused to allow the abstract concept of an unwilling audience to limit free expression; the reluctant viewer could avert his or her eyes or throw unwelcome material in the wastebasket.

Nor do *American Mini Theatres* and *Pacifica* detract from the Burger Court's record in this area. One has to see the latter case in the broader context of the judiciary's general deference to the FCC resulting from earlier decisions that the broadcast media did not enjoy the same First Amendment protection as print journalism did. The entire reasoning in *Pacifica* falls apart if one were to replace the "radio" with "newspaper" or "magazine."[69] *American Mini Theatres* is best understood through the concurring opinion of Justice Powell, a classic example of traditional First Amendment balancing. This case abjured the two-tier theory promoted by Justice Stevens as well as the absolutist view of the minority, and it also pointed the way toward the Burger Court's most significant contribution to First Amendment jurisprudence, the interpretation of speech as a property right.

SPEECH AND PROPERTY

In 1983 Professor Norman Dorsen, one of the nation's leading authorities on freedom of speech and president of the American Civil Liberties Union, surveyed the Burger Court's record in that area and noted the "bewildering variety of seemingly disharmonious decisions," some of which expanded earlier rulings, some of which contracted them, "and in some instances dramatically chart new ground." In attempting to make sense of the Burger Court record, Dorsen suggested that property provided the key:

> With few exceptions, the key to whether free speech will receive protection
> depends on an underlying property interest, either private or governmen-
> tal. In other words, throughout the past decade the values of the First

Amendment have been protected, it appears, mainly when they have coincided with property interests; conversely, free expression has received diminished protection when First Amendment claims have appeared to clash with property interests.[70]

Whether or not this trend is expansive or restrictive of free speech claims is not clear,[71] but Dorsen's analysis seems to hold up in cases where speech has been pitted directly against property rights, be they of an individual or of a corporation. Perhaps the most dramatic example is the reversal of a Warren Court ruling relating to shopping centers. First Amendment jurisprudence had long held that citizens wishing to express particular viewpoints have a right to so-called public forums, such as parks, streets, and municipal facilities, with the state permitted only to impose reasonable, content-neutral time, place, and manner restrictions. In 1946 the Court had upheld the claim of Jehovah's Witnesses to distribute religious literature in a company-owned town, on the grounds that although private property, the town served a public function.[72]

In 1968, at the end of the Warren era, a narrow 5-4 majority extended this logic in *Amalgamated Food Employees* v. *Logan Valley Plaza*.[73] Justice Marshall ruled that a state trespass law could not be invoked to ban the peaceful union picketing of a supermarket in a privately owned shopping center. The center, he explained, "is clearly the functional equivalent of the business district." The narrowness of the vote led to a reevaluation of the holding twice in the Burger era. In *Lloyd Corporation* v. *Tanner* (1972),[74] a 5-4 majority ruled that no right existed to distribute antiwar handbills in a privately owned shopping center. Justice Powell distinguished the two cases in that in *Logan Valley* the picketing had been directed against a particular store located in the center, with no other reasonable opportunities available to convey the union's message. In *Tanner* the message bore no relation to the stores in the shopping center. Moreover, patrons had to cross public streets to get into the center, and the handbills could be conveniently distributed from those streets. Most importantly, Justice Powell ruled that the First Amendment protects speech against state action and not against the owners of private property. "This Court has never held," he pointed out, "that a trespasser or an uninvited guest may exercise general rights of free speech on property privately owned."[75]

Although the majority claimed at the time to distinguish *Lloyd* from *Logan Valley*, four years later the Court in *Hudgens* v. *NLRB*[76] declared that in fact it had overruled the earlier case. Justice Stewart held that employees of a warehouse maintained by a store owner at a location outside the shopping center had no constitutional right to picket the store within the center:

> If a large self-contained shopping center *is* the functional equivalent of a municipality, as Logan Valley held, then the [First Amendment] would not permit control of speech within such a center to depend upon the speech's content. [It] conversely follows, therefore, that if the respondent

in the Lloyd case did not have a First Amendment right to distribute handbills concerning Vietnam, then the respondents in the present case did not have a First Amendment right to enter this shopping center for the purpose of advertising their strike.[77]

The shopping center cases certainly seem to set property rights above expressive values, but rather than looking at them primarily as speech cases, one might also consider them in the broader context of state action doctrine.

The modern Court had begun to expand the concept of state action in the 1940s, beginning with *Marsh* v. *Alabama*, in which it had set out the "public function" analysis. Where private property served an essentially public function, it would be subject to the same constitutional limitations as applied to public property. Most of the state action cases over the next two decades related primarily to racial discrimination, and the leading decision remains *Shelley* v. *Kraemer* (1948),[78] in which the Court struck down state court enforcement of restrictive covenants in private-housing contracts. This constituted the so-called nexus strand of state action analysis, whether there was direct involvement between the state and private discrimination; if so, the fact that private individuals, acting on private property, engaged in discrimination did not immunize them from constitutional prohibitions.

The Warren Court attempted to extend the public function analysis beyond company towns to shopping centers and private parks,[79] but the analysis never commanded a strong majority of the Court. Moreover, it seemed that even the Warren Court did not consider the state action analysis limitless, and its failure to articulate clear principles meant that at some time a reevaluation of the reach of the doctrine would be in order. The Burger Court undertook that reevaluation in connection with the shopping center cases, and in two nonspeech cases also indicated that it did not care to extend the reach of the public function analysis.[80]

COMMERCIAL AND POLITICAL SPEECH

If the Burger Court favored property over speech in the shopping center cases, it proved very sympathetic to speech related to property and expanded First Amendment coverage to areas previously considered unprotected, such as commercial speech, or advertising.

Years earlier, the Court had, in what Justice Douglas later called a "casual, almost offhand" manner, stated that the First Amendment imposed no "restraint on government as respects purely commercial advertising."[81] In *Valentine* v. *Chestensen* (1942), the Court viewed advertising as a function of business rather than of speech and thus subject only to the rational basis test applied to economic regulation.[82]

This ruling did not mean that First Amendment protection evaporated in the presence of a commercial motive; the Warren Court in *New York Times* v. *Sullivan* had specifically rejected that claim. But the distinction between commercial and noncommercial remained significant for thirty years after *Valentine*, and a 5-4 Court relied on it in *Pittsburgh Press Co.* v. *Human Relations Commission* in 1973.[83] Speaking for the majority, Justice Powell sustained a local regulation prohibiting newspapers from listing advertisements for jobs covered by a sex discrimination ordinance in sex-designated help-wanted columns. He termed the ads "classic examples of commercial speech" outside the First Amendment's protection.

In 1975, however, the Court dramatically changed direction. In *Bigelow* v. *Virginia*,[84] the Court struck down a state statute making it a misdemeanor to publicize how one could secure an abortion. The Court did not totally abandon the *Valentine* doctrine but noted that the ads, while "simply propos[ing] a commercial transaction . . . contained factual material of clear 'public interest.' " Thus one could infer that commercial information on important issues might be differentiated from advertisements for cars or deodorants.[85]

The following year, in the landmark case of *Virginia Pharmacy Board* v. *Virginia Consumer Council*,[86] the Court squarely faced the commercial speech issue. Virginia law held pharmacists guilty of unprofessional conduct if they advertised the prices of prescription drugs. Because only pharmacists could dispense these drugs, nearly all of which were prepared by the manufacturers rather than the pharmacists themselves, the ruling in effect prevented consumers from securing any price information prior to having a prescription actually filled. The challenge to the law came not from the pharmacists but instead from a consumer advocacy group that claimed a First Amendment right to drug price information.

Justice Blackmun, speaking for seven members of the Court,[87] agreed. First Amendment protection covered the communication, "to its source and to its recipient both." Plainly the content here was not of the type previously considered within constitutional protection:

> Our pharmacist does not wish to editorialize on any subject, cultural, philosophical, or political. He does not wish to report any particularly newsworthy fact, or to make generalized observations even about commercial matters. The "idea" he wishes to communicate is simply this: "I will sell you the X prescription drug at the Y price." Our question, then, is whether this communication is wholly outside the protection of the First Amendment.[88]

The state had justified the regulation on the need to maintain high standards within the pharmacy profession, and while a laudable goal, it had chosen the device of suppressing information. The regulation thus conflicted with the First Amendment, which prohibited states from banning not only the flow of political messages but also of commercial information. Commercial speech, therefore, with some exceptions (such as false or deceptive advertising)[89] enjoyed the same protection as did other varieties of speech.

The decision did not make clear whether the holding applied only to pharmacists or to advertising by other professions as well. The Court resolved this ambiguity in 1977 when, by a 5-4 vote, it held that states could not prohibit lawyers from advertising prices of routine legal services.[90] Three years later, Justice Powell put forward a four-part test for commercial speech that reflected traditional First Amendment balancing:

> At the outset, we must determine whether the expression is protected by the First Amendment. For commercial speech to come within that provision, it at least must concern lawful activity and not be misleading. Next, we ask whether the asserted governmental interest is substantial. If both inquiries yield positive answers, we must determine whether the regulation directly advances the governmental interest asserted, and whether it is not more extensive than is necessary to serve that purpose.[91]

The elevation of commercial speech raised a number of questions as to why, as Justice Rehnquist noted in his dissent in *Virginia Pharmacy Board*, "commercial intercourse between a seller hawking his wares and a buyer seeking to strike a bargain [is elevated] to the same plane as has been previously reserved for the free marketplace of ideas."[92] The classical rationales of Chafee, Emerson, and Meiklejohn regarding representative government and individual fulfillment do not seem to apply. Some commentators have suggested that the Court relied not on traditional First Amendment rationales but rather on maxims of economic liberty—the need for an efficient marketplace and the opportunity for individual buyers and sellers to maximize their own economic utility. These considerations added up to a form of economic due process that impeded legislative control of the marketplace under the rubric of free speech.[93]

The speech and property decisions of the Burger Court are not that easily categorized, however, and one can discern several strands in this area. In regard to normal commercial advertising, the Court extended protection comparable to more traditional forms of speech. The state may not regulate its content except for compelling purposes, which include the prevention of false or deceptive material, although it may impose neutral time, place, and manner restrictions.[94] Two other areas are worth examining, one because it involves more traditional political speech and the other because private property is in fact the determining consideration.

In 1978 the Court by a 5-4 vote struck down a Massachusetts criminal law prohibiting banks and business corporations from making certain types of expenditures to influence the vote on referendum proposals, other than questions "materially affecting any of the property, business or assets of the corporation." The law specifically excluded taxation questions from this category. In *First National Bank of Boston* v. *Bellotti*,[95] several companies challenged the law in connection with a referendum on a graduated income tax. The Supreme Judicial Court of Massachusetts had upheld the law in an opinion that gave narrower rights to corporate speech than to individual speech, claiming that businesses could only assert a "property" right rather than a "liberty" interest. In effect, the state court adopted the type of two-tier approach Justice Stevens had proposed, and because corporations (economic interests) were affected, the court deferred to the legislative judgment.

Justice Powell rejected this analysis and declared that to begin the analysis with the extent of corporate speech posed "the wrong question. . . . The proper question [is] not whether corporations 'have' First Amendment rights and, if so, whether they are coextensive with those of natural persons. Instead, the question must be whether [the Massachusetts law] abridges expression that the First Amendment was meant to protect. We hold that it does." In shifting the focus from the speaker to the content, Powell directed the analysis toward more familiar ground. As he pointed out, if instead of a bank an individual had expressed views on the referendum, there would be no question but that it "is the type of speech indispensable to decision making in a democracy," and "no one would suggest that the State could silence their proposed speech." Thus, as the Court had held in a number of speech cases, the content itself, especially when related to the core value of the First Amendment, the political process, acquires protection regardless of who or what the speaker may be.

The dissenting opinion of Justice White, joined by Justices Brennan and Marshall (Justice Rehnquist dissented on separate grounds), also rejected the lower-court analysis, but it raised some unique First Amendment questions. The minority did not dispute that if an individual had spoken on this topic, he or she would have been protected. But it had been a corporation, and corporations controlled assets normally unavailable to individuals. The state, in attempting to regulate corporate participation in the political process, had not done so to limit the First Amendment but rather to protect the free marketplace of ideas from domination by wealthy business interests. The government's interest in regulating corporate comments on the electoral process is significantly different from any effort to limit individual speech. Corporations "control vast amounts of economic power which may, if not regulated, dominate not only the economy but also the very heart of our democracy, the electoral process."

The majority and minority views both expressed concern for the integrity of the political process, the one by protecting all political speech regardless of the speaker, the latter by claiming for the state the right to ensure fairness in that process. But if one conceded that the state had the right to restrict corporate speech so that economic power would not affect the political process unfairly, then would not the same reasoning apply to restrictions on the very wealthy? That question had, in fact, come before the Burger Court two years earlier in a challenge to the Federal Elections Campaign Act of 1971 and its 1974 revision.

In *Buckley* v. *Valeo*, a highly divided Court sustained some parts of the law and struck down others.[96]

Shifting majorities of the Court sustained those parts of the law that (1) limited individual political *contributions* to $1,000 per candidate per election, with an overall annual limit of $25,000 per individual contributor; (2) stipulated disclosure and reporting requirements; and (3) established public financing of presidential campaigns. They struck down limitations on (1) campaign *expenditures* by candidates; (2) campaign expenditures by individuals or groups to $1,000 annually per candidate; and (3) expenditures by candidates from their personal funds.

The reasoning of the Court—its distinction between a campaign expenditure (speech and therefore protected) and a campaign contribution (not speech and therefore not protected)—elicited a great deal of critical comment in the law journals.[97] Yet the logic of *Buckley* is of a piece with that of *Bellotti*, in its view of expressive freedom. The person who contributes to a campaign is supporting political ideas, but in an indirect manner; he or she has no control over how that money will be spent. On the other hand, the person who spends money is making a direct political expression; he or she is controlling the manner and content of the paid message. The campaign spender in *Buckley* and the corporate spender in *Bellotti* and their messages are thus protected, because they are engaged in the core value of First Amendment protection: expression specifically related to the political debate.

The issues raised by Justice White in his dissent related directly to *Buckley*, where a majority had agreed that the government did have a legitimate interest in protecting the integrity of the process from corruption. Because a contributor does not speak for himself or herself as a spender does, the Court there reasoned that potential harm from large donors could be restricted by limiting the amounts given. But in 1981 the Court struck down a Berkeley, California, ordinance imposing a $250 limit on individual contributions to committees formed to support or oppose ballot referenda, on grounds that it violated both freedom of expression and of association guaranteed by the First Amendment.[98] As Justice White noted in his dissent, the ordinance had been tailored to meet the "odd measurements of *Buckley* and *Bellotti*," in that it limited contributions but not expenditures and restricted individuals but not corporations. The majority opinion by Chief Justice Burger seemed even odder; it drew the distinction between campaigns for candidates (*Buckley*) and for ballot measures (*Bellotti*), and restrictions could only be imposed on the former!

CONCLUSIONS

On the whole, the charge leveled by Thomas Emerson at the beginning of this chapter that the Burger Court failed to settle on any coherent approach on speech issues is probably true. One explanation, however, is that the Court in the seventies had to deal with new and difficult problems in a moral climate that had changed considerably in recent years. The older notion that certain forms of speech per se fell outside of First Amendment protection no longer commanded wide support within judicial, academic, or social circles. Whether this marked an increase in tolerance or a decline in civility is questionable, but the Court recognized that as society changed its views of acceptable discourse, so judges would have to adapt older views of permissible communication.

The Burger Court's greatest failures came in its inability to define judicially manageable standards to cover obscenity and offensive speech. Both remained questions of highly subjective taste, and efforts to establish objective criteria may have been beyond the ability not only of the Burger Court justices but of anyone; as Justice Harlan noted, one man's vulgarity is another's lyric. The status of constitutional law regarding obscenity changed little during the Burger years; in essence, the majority slightly modified the Warren standards, announced the problem solved, and refused to grant certiorari in obscenity appeals.

The Warren Court had paid relatively little attention to property rights in general, because the general view since the Roosevelt years had been to defer to the legislature in matters of economic regulation. The Burger Court justices as a group had a greater sensitivity to property and, for whatever reasons, certainly expanded the meaning of free expression in its commercial speech rulings. While no one on the Court claimed that advertisements constituted the core value of the First Amendment, the idea of more speech rather than less has been valued by liberals for many decades.

Somewhat troublesome is the connection between wealth and speech. Although corporations have enjoyed the status of "persons" under the Fourteenth Amendment for over a century, there is a difference between political expression made by an individual and a corporation. Even if one takes the view that political speech is the core value of the First Amendment, does this mean that large and wealthy companies are to be considered equivalent to average flesh-and-blood citizens in discussing, and affecting, basic political decisions? In the abstract, the argument makes sense that speech which could not be regulated if uttered by a person ought to be as protected if made by a corporation. But questions about the resources available to large corporations to affect public policy are legitimate concerns in a democracy. There is no question, however, that the legacy of the Burger Court, like that of the Warren Court, is larger freedom of speech.

6

"A Press That Is Alert, Aware, and Free"

The Press Clause in the Court

In 1979, a little more than halfway through the Burger era, the president of the American Newspaper Publishers Association urged his colleagues to "fight to rescue, defend and uphold the First Amendment" from an "imperial judiciary" that had created an "atmosphere of intimidation" for the press.[1] In a symposium on the Burger Court a few years later, writer Sidney Zion spoke of the "awesome trashing" First Amendment press rights had taken "at the hands of the statists who controlled the Supreme Court during the Chief Justiceship of Warren E. Burger."[2] When the Court handed down a "pro-press" decision in 1984 that did little more than reaffirm rules of long standing,[3] the press treated it as a great victory.

Was the Burger Court's record in regard to the press so bad as to justify such charges, and how far did it stray from the precedents handed down by earlier courts? Or did the press overreact?[4] Once again, perception and reality of what the Court has done, or failed to do, may often differ.

A THEORY OF PRESS FREEDOM

The First Amendment declares that Congress shall make no law "abridging freedom of speech, or of the press." That the press enjoys protection is clear, but the real question is the extent and nature of that protection. Does the press enjoy only that protection afforded to other types of speakers, or is there some additional level which can be justified on the basis that the Framers specifically mentioned "press" as well as "speech"?[5] In his concurrence in *First National Bank of Boston* v. *Bellotti*, Chief Justice Burger explored this question and concluded:

> Because the First Amendment was meant to guarantee freedom to express
> and to communicate ideas, I can see no difference between the right of those
> who seek to disseminate ideas by way of a newspaper and those who give
> lectures or speeches that seek to enlarge the audience by publication and
> wide dissemination.[6]

The Framers, he believed, had not intended any "special" or "institutional"
status to the press, and prior to 1789 people had used the phrases "freedom of
the press" and "freedom of speech" interchangeably. The addition of the Press
Clause, he claimed, had resulted from the fact that restrictions on speech in
England and in the colonies had often taken the form of restrictions on the
press.[7]

The Chief Justice's view that Press Clause cases ought to be judged by
the same criteria as other speech cases reflected the general refusal of the Court
in this century to read any special privileges or protections into the Press
Clause. Only one justice has, in fact, attempted to explicate a special constitutional role for the press. Potter Stewart saw the press as serving a structural
role in society, helping to expose corruption and thus keeping the political
process honest:

> The Free Press guarantee is, in essence, a *structural* provision of the
> Constitution. Most of the other provisions in the Bill of Rights protect
> specific liberties or specific rights of individuals. . . . In contrast, the Free
> Press Clause extends protection to an institution.[8]

This "institutional" view has never been accepted by a majority of the Court,
but particular members have utilized Stewart's argument from time to time.
Justice Douglas, for example, in his dissent in *Branzburg* v. *Hayes* (1972),
argued that the press enjoyed a preferred constitutional position in order "to
bring fulfillment to the public's right to know. The right to know is crucial to
the governing process of the people, to paraphrase Alexander Meiklejohn."[9]

Even while denying the press a special status, the Burger Court did in
fact recognize that the press had a critical role to play in the democratic process,
and if the Court refused to grant additional rights, it ensured that the press did
not suffer special disabilities. In examining the Burger Court cases, it appears
that those decisions which the press applauded as well as those it criticized
derived directly from the same line of precedents.

PRIOR RESTRAINT: THE KEY DOCTRINE

Modern Press Clause jurisprudence begins with the landmark case of
Near v. *Minnesota* in 1931,[10] which in many ways reiterated the traditional
views of free speech going back through Holmes and Blackstone to Milton,

who protested against the British system of licensing the press. The 5-4 decision might well have gone the other way had it been argued earlier, when William Howard Taft still occupied the center chair. But between the time the Court accepted the case and heard oral argument, Taft had died, and the new Chief Justice, Charles Evans Hughes, had greater sympathy toward the idea of a free press.

Minnesota had authorized abatement, as a public nuisance, of any "malicious, scandalous or defamatory" publication, a law aimed at *The Saturday Press*, a Minneapolis tabloid that in addition to exploiting rumors had uncovered some embarrassing facts about local political and business figures.[11] The state courts gladly "abated" the *Press*, which appealed to the Supreme Court claiming that its First Amendment rights had been violated. The Court's decision extended the reach of the Press Clause to the states, and established as the key element of press protection freedom from prior restraint, that is, from having the government censor materials before their publication. Chief Justice Hughes quoted approvingly from Blackstone that the liberty of the press "consists in laying no *previous* restraints upon publication, and not in freedom from censure for criminal matter when published."

In a passage that the government would later invoke in alleged national security cases, Hughes noted that the rule against prior restraint had some very narrow exceptions. No one would question, he asserted, "that a government might prevent actual obstructon to its recruiting service or the publication of the sailing days of transports or the number and location of troops."[12]

The early prior-restraint cases following *Near* often dealt with censorship of motion pictures, which the Court did not equate with press publications. In 1961, for example, the Warren Court ruled against the notion that "the public exhibition of motion pictures must be allowed under any circumstances."[13] In 1965, however, the Court struck down a Maryland censorship scheme and imposed such a high standard for procedural safeguards that it did, in effect, wipe out state film censorship.[14]

Prior restraint, however, means only that the state cannot censor publications; it does not mean that the press is free to print anything it wants without fear of reprisal. In *Near*, Chief Justice Hughes had noted that certain types of expression which did not enjoy First Amendment protection, such as obscene materials, did not come within the rule against prior restraint. The publication of obscene and libelous works can also bring criminal and civil sanctions, and the Court on one occasion did permit a special scheme of prior restraint in regard to allegedly obscene publications.[15]

Within recent years there has been a lively academic debate over the rationale for the prior restraint rule. The scholar Frederic Schauer, for example, claims that the doctrine "focuses on the largely irrelevant *timing* of the restraint," rather than on the material that is the actual source of the objection.[16] Martin Redish suggests that the real issue ought to be whether there is a full and fair judicial hearing. An arbitrary administrative licensing scheme would be disfavored, but one that ensured a rapid and final judicial determination would not, in his view, violate constitutional protection.[17] Whatever the academic debate, the fact remains, as the Court noted, that "any system of prior restraints of expression comes to this Court bearing a heavy presumption against its constitutional validity."[18]

THE BURGER COURT, PRIOR RESTRAINT, AND THE PENTAGON PAPERS

The most famous press case of the Burger era involved the so-called Pentagon papers. In 1967 Secretary of Defense Robert S. McNamara ordered a full-scale evaluation of how the United States became involved in the Vietnam War. The study team of thirty-six persons took more than a year to compile the report, which ran to forty-seven volumes, with some 4,000 pages of documentary evidence and 3,000 pages of analysis. Daniel Ellsberg, a former Defense Department economist who had grown disillusioned with the war, copied major portions of the study and then turned them over to the press.

On Sunday, June 13, 1971, the *New York Times* began publication of the papers with that part of the analysis dealing with clandestine South Vietnamese raids against North Vietnam in early 1964. The study concluded that these raids had been carried out with U.S. knowledge and support and with the goal of provoking a North Vietnamese response that could then be used to justify greater U.S. involvement. The *Times* announced that it would continue publication of the Pentagon papers in daily installments.[19]

The following day, Attorney General John Mitchell sent a telegram to Arthur O. Sulzberger, the publisher of the *New York Times*, requesting him to cease publication of the series on the grounds that it would cause "irreparable injury to the defense interests of the United States." Mitchell threatened court action under the Espionage Act if the paper did not comply voluntarily and asked that the documents be turned over to the government. The paper refused both requests, and that day it published the second installment, dealing with the Johnson administration's early decision to escalate the war.

On Tuesday, June 15, the government went into U.S. District Court in New York and secured a temporary injunction to prevent further publication of the Pentagon papers, pending a full hearing. Judge Murray Gurfein scheduled the hearing for that Friday, June 18. Although the *Times* had already appeared with the third article, it obeyed the injunction and did not publish further documents. It refused, however, to turn over the documents to the government, although it did provide a list of them.

On Friday, the day of the *Times* hearing in New York, the *Washington Post* began publishing articles based on the purloined documents. The administration immediately sought a restraining order, but Judge Gerhard Gesell of the District Court for the District of Columbia refused to grant even a temporary injunction. The next day, Judge Gurfein denied the government's request for an injunction, a decision anticipated by the administration, which immediately appealed the ruling. Judge Irving Kaufman of the Second Circuit Court of Appeals immediately blocked further publication, and on Monday, a three-judge panel of the Second Circuit extended the prohibition and announced that in a case of such magnitude, the entire court would hear the issue.[20]

In the meantime, the District of Columbia Circuit Court ordered Judge Gesell to hold a hearing on the government's request for an injunction and issued a temporary restraining order pending that hearing. Judge Gesell heard the government's argument and again refused to issue an injunction. The government appealed, and the entire circuit decided to hear the case en banc.

On Tuesday, June 22, the *Boston Globe* became the third paper to begin publication—and to be restrained from doing so. That same day, the District of Columbia Circuit upheld the *Post*'s right to publish the materials but continued the restraining order to allow the government to appeal. In New York, the Second Circuit also said the *Times* could resume publication, but not those documents the administration deemed sensitive to national security interests. All of the parties announced they would appeal to the United States Supreme Court.

On Thursday, June 24, 1971, the Court received the appeals but did not announce whether it would take the case. In the meantime, a number of other newspapers around the country began publication, and the Nixon administration did not take legal action against them. On Friday, the Court announced it would take the case on an expedited basis and then took the extraordinary step of scheduling oral arguments the next day, a Saturday. Justices Black, Brennan, Douglas, and Marshall dissented, on the grounds that the lower-court orders constituted a prior restraint and should be dissolved immediately without any hearing.

The Court heard oral arguments on Saturday morning and by a 6-3 vote rejected the government's request that the courtroom be closed to the public during the hearing. Four days later, on June 30, seventeen days after the *Times* had begun publication of the Pentagon papers, the Court handed down its decision. By a 6-3 vote, it upheld the three newspapers' right to publish the materials, and the following day papers all across the nation carried excerpts from the documents.

The chronology is important to this case for several reasons. For one, it is unique for the speed with which the issue moved through the lower courts and then on to the Supreme Court; not even in wartime had the Court ever acted so swiftly.[21] Second, nearly all of the justices commented upon the speed of the proceedings in their decision, and some complained about the "haste" in which they had been forced to act. Perhaps that haste prevented a majority from forming around any single opinion. Instead, the Court announced a brief three-paragraph per curiam decision. The first paragraph, consisting of one sentence, stated that the Court had granted certiorari in cases in which the government sought to prevent publication of a classified study. The second paragraph explained that the state always bears a heavy burden in seeking to impose prior restraint, and the Court agreed with the Court of Appeals for the District of Columbia that the government had not met that burden. In the final paragraph, the Court vacated all stays against publication.[22]

Justices Black, Douglas, and Brennan concurred in the judgment but believed the injunctions should never have been issued, because they clearly constituted a prior restraint on the press. Justices White, Marshall, and Stewart concurred on different grounds. White made it a point that the decision rested solely on the question of prior restraint, but "I do not say that in no circumstances would the First Amendment permit an injunction against publishing information about government plans or operations."[23] Moreover he, like some of the other justices, noted the absence of any statutory scheme to govern the case. Stewart anticipated some of his later ideas about the structural role of the press, noting that the

> only effective restraint upon executive policy and power in the areas of national defense and international affairs may lie in an enlightened citizenry. . . . [A] press that is alert, aware, and free most vitally serves the basic purpose of the First Amendment.[24]

The Chief Justice along with Justices Harlan and Blackmun all dissented. Harlan declared that "the Court has been almost irresponsibly feverish in dealing with these cases," a sentiment echoed by Burger, who noted the "unseemly haste" of the proceedings. "We literally do not know what we are acting on."[25] Nonetheless, Burger took special pains to answer one of the issues raised by the newspapers, and seemingly endorsed by Potter Stewart, namely, that the Press Clause implied a right to know on the part of the public and that it was the special obligation of the press to provide the public with such information.

The entire rationale behind the pilfering of the Pentagon documents and then providing copies to the press had been to inform the public of the double dealing and lying that the U.S. government had engaged in regarding the Vietnam War. The people had a right to know what its government had done.[26] General Maxwell Taylor, who had been ambassador to South Vietnam during the early stages of the war, condemned this idea. A citizen's right to know, he declared, is limited "to those things he needs to know to be a good citizen and discharge his functions, but not to . . . secrets that damage his government and indirectly the citizen himself."[27]

The Chief Justice, in noting the newspaper claim that under the First Amendment the public had a "right to know," ridiculed the idea that the press served as the trustee of that alleged right. Along with five other justices, Burger believed that the government might well have the authority to prosecute publishers of classified information for criminal violation of security statutes *after* publication. The *Times*, which he characterized as a great newspaper, had other and far clearer obligations:

> To me it is hardly believable that a newspaper long regarded as a great institution in American life would fail to perform one of the basic and simple duties of every citizen with respect to the discovery or possession of stolen property or secret government documents. That duty, I had thought—perhaps naively—was to report forthwith, to responsible public officers. This duty rests on taxi drivers, Justices and the *New York Times*.[28]

Despite the dissenting justices' complaint about the haste of the proceedings, and the disagreement among the entire bench on the limits, if any, of prior restraint, the fact remains that all of the justices believed that the general rule mitigated against prior restraint. In fact, in a speech to the American Bar Association a week later, Warren Burger described the opinions in the case as "actually unanimous."[29] In many ways, this was true. All of the justices did believe in the basic doctrine of no prior restraints, and with the sole exception of Black and Douglas, who took an absolutist stance, they all believed that circumstances might exist in which the government could, in fact, suppress certain types of information, provided an appropriate procedural mechanism existed to meet constitutional requirements.[30]

Although the Burger Court decided several "national security" cases, only one other involved the issue of prior restraint. The Central Intelligence Agency had long required its employees to sign an agreement to submit any proposed writings, even after they left the service, for review before publication. Frank W. Snepp, a former CIA agent, published a book about the CIA's involvement in Vietnam without clearing the manuscript. The Court of Appeals for the Fourth Circuit ruled that Snepp could be subject to punitive damages, but it refused to impose a constructive trust to deprive him of any profits from the book. The Supreme Court, in a per curiam decision without briefs or oral argument, reversed on the question of the remedy (it prohibited punitive damages but imposed the constructive trust).[31]

The only reference to the First Amendment came in a footnote. The Court's prior cases made clear that "even in the absence of an express agreement, the CIA could have acted to protect substantial government interests by imposing reasonable restrictions . . . that in other contexts might be protected by the First Amendment."[32] Justices Stevens, Brennan, and Marshall decried what they termed the Court's fashioning of a "drastic new remedy to enforce a species of prior restraint on a citizen's right to criticize his government."

While critics saw *Snepp* as one more example of the Court deferring to arbitrary state power,[33] other considerations most certainly played a role in the majority's decision. Although the CIA did not claim that Snepp's book, *Decent*

Interval, contained any classified information, obviously the whole purpose of the agreement had been to prevent publication of classified or damaging materials. If the CIA could not enforce the agreement with Snepp, then it would be unable to enforce similar contracts in the future, when more sensitive, rather than merely embarrassing, material might be involved. With the exception of the absolutists, few people saw the *Snepp* case as undermining the doctrine of prior restraint.[34]

PRIOR RESTRAINT AND FAIR TRIAL

The question of prior restraint came before the Court again, this time in the context of a so-called gag order, issued by a trial judge in an effort to secure a fair trial. In *Nebraska Press Association* v. *Stuart* (1976),[35] we see a problem that often comes before the Court, a conflict between rights, in this case the First Amendment freedom of the press and the Sixth Amendment guarantee of a fair trial.

In the small town of Sutherland, Nebraska (pop. 850), an unemployed handyman had been charged with raping a ten-year-old child, murdering her and five members of her family, and then sexually assaulting some of the dead children. It would have been a sensational trial any place, but in a small town, the trial judge decided that only a gag order, prohibiting the press from printing reports about the crime, would make it possible to get an unbiased jury.

In this case the Court did not deal with questions of power claimed by another branch of government, but instead dealt with the traditional authority trial judges had always exercised in their courtrooms to ensure fair trials. The press objected to the total ban imposed, which they claimed made no sense; they could not even report on statements made in open court at the pretrial hearing. People in the audience could discuss what had been said, but the press could not report it. All the members of the Court except Justice Rehnquist believed that the trial judge had gone too far, because alternative methods existed to prevent contamination of the jury process without resorting to prior restraint, methods which the trial judge had not utilized.

The real division came not on whether this particular ban had been ill-advised but instead on whether there should be a total prohibition against gag rules. Chief Justice Burger's majority opinion took a strong First Amendment stance, holding that "prior restraints on speech and publication are the most serious and least tolerable infringement on First Amendment rights."[36] But while striking down the Nebraska ban, Burger did not want to go further in the Court's first case in this area; the law, he believed, ought to develop slowly and incrementally. Moreover, only a minority of the brethren had ever held First Amendment rights absolute; there might be circumstances in which gag orders would be appropriate.

Justice Brennan's concurrence, prepared in anticipation of the Chief Justice's opinion,[37] called for a total ban on gag orders, a position that had evidently been supported by at least five members of the Court at conference. Justices Marshall and Stewart joined Brennan's opinion fully; Justice Stevens said he subscribed to "most" of Brennan's points "and if ever required to face the issue squarely, may well accept his ultimate conclusion."[38] Justice White added a brief one-paragraph concurrence doubting if gag orders would ever be justified.

It should be noted that *Nebraska Press Association*, while effectively banning gag orders under the prior restraint doctrine, did not proscribe all limitations on press coverage of trials.[39] Implicit in the majority opinion is the idea that some circumstances might call for restraints on the press. Justice Powell's concurrence made the case explicitly:

> [A] prior restraint properly may issue only when it is shown to be necessary to prevent the dissemination of prejudicial publicity that otherwise poses a high likelihood of preventing, directly and irreparably, the impaneling of a jury meeting the Sixth Amendment's requirement of impartiality. This requires a showing that (i) there is a clear threat to the fairness of the trial, (ii) such a threat is posed by the actual publicity to be restrained, and (iii) no less restrictive alternatives are available.[40]

Powell, in fact, delivered the majority opinion in a subsequent case upholding a state protective order prohibiting a newspaper from using information procured through discovery for any purpose other than the trial of the case.[41] The newspaper claimed that the state rule, which was modeled on the Federal Rules of Civil Procedure, constituted an impermissible prior restraint. Justice Powell noted that if the newspaper could get that information from another source, the trial judge could not bar publication. But the state had a substantial interest in securing fair trials, in which some suppression of expression was incidental, and therefore the Court did not need to invoke any "heightened First Amendment scrutiny."[42]

Although a majority of the Court had eschewed inferring a "right to know" from the Press Clause, the *Nebraska Press Association* decision may be seen as the first step on the road to recognizing a variation of that idea, a right of access. The various speech theories utilized to explicate the First Amendment all agreed that political speech occupied the highest rung of the ladder. The people and the press could not be limited in their discussion and publication of political issues, because intelligent discussion by the body politic constituted the core of democratic government.

But for the citizenry to carry on intelligent discussion, they had to be informed about the issues, and obviously 200 million people could not descend on a presidential press conference or research the small print in Pentagon contracts. Here the press served as the surrogate for the people, securing the information that made intelligent discussion possible. As the surrogate, the argument ran, the press had a constitutionally protected right of access to places and documents relevant to the news.

The basic reasoning of this argument is that if some kinds of information are important to the discussion underlying the democratic process, then there must be some "right" to get that information. But the corollary argument, that the press had an unlimited right of access as surrogate for the people, did not necessarily follow. Certainly nothing could be found in either the Press Clause or prior cases to justify this view. In the flush of *New York Times* v. *Sullivan*, however, the press itself began to expound theories of access, of a "right to gather the news" so that the people could enjoy their "right to know." Before long, the press had generated a self-image of "a constitutionally endowed public-service institution" and believed that the Constitution "formally confirmed its function as a conduit of governmentally generated information."[43]

But if one grounds such a right in the Constitution, then it is subject to interpretation by the courts, which, as in libel cases, may place restraints on the press as well as grant it wider freedom. Moreover, if one subscribes to the idea that the public has a right to know, then what are the obligations of the press when it has possession of information that the government believes it needs for a public purpose? Much of the press furor over the Burger Court decisions can be found in its unwillingness to accept the Court's view of press responsibility as the price for expanded freedom.

PRESS RESPONSIBILITY

About one year after Chief Justice Burger lectured the *Times* that it had the same responsibility as taxi drivers in obeying the law, the Court ruled that reporters had an affirmative obligation to provide information about a crime to the government, if the government requested the information in a proper manner. The bitter reaction of the press to the decision arose because it involved the so-called journalists' privilege, the claimed right not to divulge the names of confidential news sources.[44] The issue arose when Paul Branzburg, a Louisville reporter who had written a series of articles about drug activities, refused to identify to a grand jury persons he had seen using marijuana and preparing hashish.[45]

The common law had long recognized certain privileges, which protected the confidentiality of communications between priest and penitent, lawyer and client, husband and wife, and doctor and patient. The common law had never, however, recognized a similar privilege for reporters, and because one had not been claimed in the eighteenth century, it could hardly be considered as part of the Press Clause. Some two dozen states do have "shield laws," which statutorily grant reporters the privilege to keep news sources confidential.[46]

The argument for the press privilege stemmed directly from the idea of a public right to know. For reporters to ferret out information, they claimed they had to be able to promise anonymity to their sources. While this admittedly might interfere with governmental activities such as grand jury investigations, that was a small price to pay for the public's access to information. The government's case took a different tack but also relied on the people's right to know. However, its argument was that the people's own representatives, in the government, could force disclosure of privately held information to serve the public good.

Both the majority and the minority opinions in *Branzburg* v. *Hayes* (1972)[47] discussed the public's right to know. Justice White, writing for the 5-4 majority, put the matter succinctly:

> Of course, the press has the right to abide by its agreement not to publish all the information it has, but the right to withhold news is not equivalent to a First Amendment exemption from the ordinary duty of all other citizens to furnish relevant information to a grand jury performing an important public function.[48]

The public, he concluded, acting through the grand jury, has a right to every person's evidence.

The dissenters, especially Justice Stewart, grounded their opinions on the same alleged public right to know:

> A reporter's right to protect his source is bottomed on the constitutional guarantee of a full flow of information to the public. A newsman's personal First Amendment rights or the associational rights of the newsman and the source are subsumed under that broad societal interest protected by the First Amendment.[49]

This right exists, Stewart claimed, not for the benefit of the press but for the benefit of the public.

Given the fact that only a theoretical rather than a jurisprudential basis existed for the reporter's privilege, it is hardly surprising that the majority decided as it did.[50] But one needs to note that although Justice White denied this particular privilege, his opinion acknowledged that a "right to gather news" existed and that it enjoyed some First Amendment protection. Moreover, Justice Powell's concurrence seemed to imply a willingness to go further than White in granting press protection, depending upon the particular fact situation. The minority jumped on these concessions, calling the right to gather news the corollary of the right to publish. But again, the extent of that right remained to be spelled out.

Justice White wrote the majority opinion in another case denying the press special protection, this time against ex parte warrants authorizing searches of newsrooms. Following violent student demonstrations at Stanford

University, a state court authorized search of the campus newspaper office for photographs that might be used to identify leaders of the protest. Although the student paper tried to make a First Amendment claim, the majority opinion focused almost entirely on whether the search procedures had violated the Fourth Amendment. White made only one passing reference to the First Amendment, to the effect that courts should "apply the warrant requirements with particular exactitude when First Amendment interests would be endangered by the search."[51] Although Justice Powell's concurrence, like that in *Branzburg*, took a more sympathetic view toward the press, he too believed it did not have any special right to withhold information; he did urge, however, that magistrates issuing warrants be very careful in this area and "should consider the values of a free press as well as the societal interests in enforcing the criminal law."[52]

DEVELOPMENT OF A RIGHT TO ACCESS

While the press could complain about certain practical and negative effects of the Court's rulings in *Branzburg* and *Stanford Daily*, the fact remains that the Court did not take away anything the press already enjoyed in terms of constitutional or legal protection; it simply refused to extend those rights or to create new ones. However, in reaching these and other decisions the Court began to explore for the first time what rights actually fell within the scope of the Press Clause and slowly developed what came to be called a right of access.

One of the continuing debates in a free society is the extent to which the government may withhold information. The arrogance of General Maxwell Taylor is one end of the spectrum and is as unacceptable as demands that the government withhold nothing. Even strong defenders of the First Amendment agree on the necessity of governmental agencies keeping certain types of material hidden from public scrutiny. But where should the line be drawn between legitimate needs, such as privacy and national security, and illegitimate reasons, such as efforts to hide corruption or incompetence? And what role, and what rights, does the press enjoy in seeking out this information? Prior to the 1970s, little in the way of case law can be found to answer these questions.

The Court first dealt with press demands for access in two companion cases decided in 1974, *Pell* v. *Procunier*[53] and *Saxbe* v. *Washington Post Co.*[54] In *Pell*, the Court upheld a California rule barring press interviews with specific individual inmates in the state prisons, while *Saxbe* rejected an attack on a similar federal rule. Justice Stewart, who had been the chief champion of the press in previous cases and who had attacked what he termed the majority's "crabbed" view of the First Amendment in *Branzburg*, spoke for the Court in both cases. He found no First Amendment violations, because the regulations did not "deny the press access to sources of information available to members of the general public." The government may not interfere with normal news-gathering and publication, but "it is quite another thing to suggest that the Constitution imposes upon government the affirmative duty to make available to journalists sources of information not available to members of the public generally."[55] In other words, the press had the same right of access as the public—but no more.

Where Justice Powell had voted in the majority in *Branzburg* and *Stanford Daily*, here he dissented, and his opinions are noteworthy for they pointed the way the Court would go within a few years. He found the Stewart analysis unduly simplistic and believed the absolute ban on interviews "impermissibly restrains the ability of the press to perform its *constitutionally established function* of informing the people of the conduct of their government."[56] In *Saxbe* Powell spelled out a view of the press as surrogate that must have warmed the heart of every reporter in America:

> For most citizens the prospect of personal familiarity with newsworthy events is hopelessly unrealistic. In seeking out the news the press therefore acts as the agent of the public at large. It is the means by which the people receive that free flow of information and ideas essential to intelligent self-government. The underlying right is the right of the public generally. The press is the necessary representative of the public's interest in this context and the instrumentality which effects the public's right.[57]

Four years later, in an unusual 3-1-3 vote, the Court sustained a part of press claims for access to jails in *Houchins* v. *KQED, Inc.*, but did so by distinguishing the situation from *Pell*, rather than establishing any new right.[58] The following year, in *Gannett Co.* v. *DePasquale*, a majority specifically rejected a newspaper's attack on a court order barring the public, including the press, from a pretrial hearing on suppression of evidence in a murder case.[59]

Nearly all of the opinions focused on the question of what the Sixth Amendment required in its guarantee of a "public trial" and whether this guarantee applied to the defendant, the public, or both. In this case the judge, the prosecution, and the defense had all agreed to close the pretrial hearing in order to ensure a fair trial. Justice Stewart's somewhat ambiguous majority opinion found no historical evidence to support the idea that the public, rather than the accused, had the constitutional right to insist on a public trial. Moreover, he found no independent First Amendment right to attend trials.

Justice Powell's concurring opinion undertook a fuller First Amendment analysis of the issue and how the First and Sixth Amendments intersected. The public had a right to know whether the criminal justice system operated effectively, and because only a limited number of people could attend a trial, the press would serve as the public's surrogate. In a vigorous dissenting opinion

Justice Blackmun, joined by Brennan, White, and Marshall, argued that the Sixth Amendment did provide for public access and the accused could not exclude the public (including the press) unless it could be shown that there existed "a substantial probability that irreparable damage" would impair the chance of a fair trial and no satisfactory alternatives to closure existed.

In the year following this decision, an estimated 270 efforts occurred attempting to close various parts of criminal trials, of which half were granted, most relying on the holding in *Gannett*.[60] Yet this did not seem to be what the justices had meant. The four dissenters, as well as the Chief Justice (who had distinguished between pretrial hearings and the trial itself) and Justice Powell all believed in some degree of public access to trial, and if the public had access, then the press also did. Only Justice Rehnquist believed that neither the First nor the Sixth Amendment granted access to trials, and in the summer of 1979 several of the justices made public comments that *Gannett* did not confer blanket authority on trial judges to close their courtrooms to the public, even if all of the parties agreed.

The new majority view emerged in a 7-1 decision in the landmark case of *Richmond Newspapers, Inc.* v. *Virginia* (1980),[61] which held that absent some overriding interest, the trial of a criminal case must always be open to the public. The case arose in regard to the trial of John Paul Stevenson for the stabbing death of a hotel manager in 1975. The first trial had been overturned by the Virginia Supreme Court because of the improper admission of certain evidence; the second trial ended in a mistrial, as did the third. When the fourth trial began, the defense requested that the courtroom be closed, so as to make sure this trial proceeded properly. The judge, who had presided over two of the previous trials, asked the prosecution if it had any objections, and when the prosecutor agreed to abide by whatever decision the judge made, he ordered the court cleared of everyone except the parties and witnesses. In the audience were two reporters, and their motion for admittance initiated the series of appeals that led to the high court.

The Chief Justice delivered the Court's opinion, but he was joined only by Justices White and Stevens, mainly because he framed the opinion in as narrow a manner as possible. He distinguished the circumstances from *Gannett*, which dealt with a pretrial hearing, rather than, as here, with the trial itself. Burger's historical inquiry concluded that at the time the Sixth Amendment had been adopted, it had been the practice both in this country and in England for criminal trials to be open. But while the Sixth Amendment provided the basis for an open trial, the right to attend a trial was rooted in the First Amendment. There were few things more important to the people than the proper conduct of criminal trials, and the First Amendment protects the right of everyone to attend trials. As for press attendance, it made little difference, the Chief Justice declared, if one spoke of a right to gather news or a right of access, "the explicit, guaranteed rights to speak and to publish concerning what takes place at a trial would lose much meaning if access to observe the trial could [be] foreclosed arbitrarily."[62]

Six of the seven justices who supported the result entered a separate opinion, differing in the main on the degree of First Amendment protection involved in the opinion. Justice Stevens, for example, held that for the first time the Court accorded constitutional protection to the acquisition of news-worthy material. Justice Brennan developed a lengthy structural analysis of First Amendment values, but he, like the other justices, did not see the grant of access as endowing the press with any special rights. The right of access to criminal trial belonged to the public, and the press had the same right, not a greater one.

Although a majority of the Court had seemingly agreed on a principle, the failure of five members to agree on the criteria and scope of the holding meant the Court would have to deal with those issues before very long.[63] In 1982 the Court heard arguments on a Massachusetts law that excluded the public and the press during the testimony of a minor who allegedly had been the victim of a sex offense. The state justified the law on grounds of protecting the physical and psychological well-being of minor victims of sexual assault from further trauma and embarrassment and, by holding out the promise of privacy, encouraging such victims to come forward and provide testimony against their assailants. The *Boston Globe* challenged its exclusion from the trial of a man charged with the rape of three teenage girls, and the state's highest court construed the law as not just permitting but requiring exclusion of press and public during such testimony.

In *Globe Newspaper Co.* v. *Superior Court* (1982),[64] Justice Brennan spoke for six members of the Court in striking down the Massachusetts law for requiring closure. While Brennan found the first of the state's two reasons for closure—protecting the victims from further trauma—"compelling," he found no empirical support for the second—that it would encourage other victims to come forward. The state could accomplish its first goal by narrow and more flexible means; the trial judge could make a determination on a case-by-case basis, and close the court only when necessary. To allow otherwise would be to violate the First Amendment right of access to criminal trials.

Aware of the problems involved in sexual assault cases, especially with minor victims, Brennan emphasized the narrowness of the ruling and the fact that the states could close such trials, provided they drew flexible guidelines rather than mandatory closure schemes. The important part of the opinion, however, lay in its broad application of *Richmond Newspapers*. Even Chief Justice Burger, who dissented here, adopted essentially the majority reasoning two years later in *Press-Enterprise Co.* v. *Superior Court*.[65] A state court had closed the voir dire examination of prospective jurors in a case involving the rape and murder of a teenage girl. Again, the Court did not hold that a trial judge could never close all or part of the proceedings, but to do so it had to be shown that other less restrictive means would not accomplish the same purpose. Here, other ways existed to save prospective jurors embarrassment than by closing the court.

By 1984, then, the Court had agreed that the public had a right of access to certain types of information and that the press had as great a right, because it often served as a surrogate for the citizenry in securing important information. The Court had, however, resisted granting the press any greater rights than the public or treating it in some special way.[66] We will return to the question of whether the press should in fact be treated differently, but first we need to look at two final areas in our assessment of the Burger Court: the electronic media and libel law.

BROADCASTING IS DIFFERENT

While there has been general agreement that the press enjoys First Amendment protection, that protection is not granted to the entire press in an equal manner. While we may think of both Bob Woodward and Mike Wallace as reporters, they work in different media, Woodward for a newspaper and Wallace for television. One of the anomalies of First Amendment jurisprudence is that the courts have treated broadcast media as an inferior form of the press, and therefore subject to the type of regulation that would never be countenanced if applied to newspapers or magazines. One cannot imagine a court sustaining an injunction to prevent the *New York Times* or the *Chicago Sun* from printing a transcript of George Carlin's "Seven Words You Can't Say on the Air."[67] For the part the Burger Court continued the tradition of dealing with broadcast media differently, although in one of its later opinions it took a small step toward eliminating the distinction.

The rationale for regulating broadcast media arose in the early days of radio, when it was believed that only a finite number of radio frequencies existed. Therefore, in order to ensure fair distribution of such a scarce but precious commodity, the government would license and control radio and later television stations. Moreover, because most early radio and television programs provided entertainment rather than news, it was assumed that the broadcast media did not enjoy any First Amendment protections.[68]

The Supreme Court first endorsed these views in *NBC* v. *United States* in 1943.[69] In a 5-3 opinion, Justice Frankfurter essentially ignored any First Amendment considerations and treated the issue of FCC regulation of radio networks as a form of economic legislation, which, after the constitutional crisis of the 1930s, received great deference from the courts. The issue came before the high court again a quarter-century later in *Red Lion Broadcasting* v. *FCC* (1969),[70] one of the last of the Warren Court cases. This time Justice White, speaking for a unanimous bench, upheld the FCC's fairness doctrine, which required broadcast licensees to grant equal time to opposing political views, and also the personal attack rule, which required stations to give people whom it had criticized equal time to respond. As for First Amendment arguments, Justice White claimed that the rules would enhance rather than abridge freedom of speech, by ensuring opportunity for differing opinions to be aired.

In essence, White had adopted a "right-to-know" model as opposed to the "debate" model of Meiklejohn, which had animated the *New York Times* v. *Sullivan* decision. In that case the Court in essence had said that it would remove a stumbling block to free expression so that all ideas, even if tainted with some error, could engage in robust debate, with the citizenry determining the winner. The *Red Lion* majority believed that insofar as broadcast media were concerned, the "debate" model would not work. The marketplace of ideas needed intervention by an outside agency, such as the FCC, to ensure fairness and the flow of correct information.[71]

To see just how differently broadcast and print media are treated, one need look only at the Burger Court's decision in *Miami Herald Publishing Co.* v. *Tornillo* (1974).[72] The newspaper had severely criticized a candidate for the state assembly, and he invoked an old 1913 statute that required any newspaper attacking a public official or a candidate for public office to print that person's reply free of charge. Although rarely invoked, the statute constitutes the functional equivalent of the FCC fairness doctrine, and if one applied Justice White's reasoning in *Red Lion*, it should have been sustained as enhancing free speech, by assuring the public its right to know both sides of the debate.73 Instead, a unanimous Court, speaking through Chief Justice Burger, struck the law down as a violation of the First Amendment and declared there is no right of access to the press.

It is possible that *Red Lion* itself might have gone another way had it come before the Court a few years later, after it had begun to cast a more skeptical eye at federal regulatory bodies. The Burger Court, in fact, began to narrow the holding in *CBS, Inc.* v. *Democratic National Committee* (1973).[74] The case arose after the FCC supported the network's refusal to take paid editorial advertisements from the committee and from some antiwar groups. A circuit court condemned the ban as a violation of the First Amendment.

The Supreme Court reversed, and held that *Red Lion* did not stand for any generalized right of access to the media, but where *Red Lion* had been decided by a unanimous bench, the *CBS* case showed deep divisions within the Court. Chief Justice Burger delivered the decision of the Court, with the bulk of his opinion rebutting the idea of a right of access; only Justice Rehnquist joined him fully. Justice Stewart concurred with parts of the opinion, and he entered an extensive opinion. There were brief partial concurrences by Justices White and Blackmun, the latter joined by Justice Powell. Justice Brennan entered a lengthy dissent, joined by Justice Marshall, in which he applied traditional First Amendment balancing and concluded that free speech interests had suffered from the FCC-approved ban. Perhaps the most interesting opinion was the opinion of Justice Douglas, who while joining in the result did so for a most unusual reason: "My conclusion is that TV and radio stand in the same protected position under the First Amendment as do newspapers and magazines." Just as one could not force the print media to accept advertising or even carry rejoinders, one could not force the broadcast media to do so either.[75]

If no generalized right of access to the broadcast media existed, Congress created a particular right for candidates in the Federal Election Campaign Act of 1971. The law allows the FCC to revoke a broadcast license for

> willful or repeated failure to allow reasonable access to or to permit
> purchase of reasonable amounts of time for the use of a broadcasting station
> by a legally qualified candidate for federal elective office on behalf of his
> candidacy.[76]

The first test of what this new provision meant came when the Carter–Mondale Presidential Committee requested that the three networks make available thirty minutes of prime time during early December 1979 for a program highlighting the accomplishments of the Carter administration and timed as a boost to Carter's announcement of his intention to seek reelection. All three networks declined, saying it was far too early to start airing advertisements for the 1980 presidential campaign. The committee appealed to the FCC, which found that the networks' reason for refusal was "deficient" and that they had violated the law by failing to provide "reasonable access."

Chief Justice Burger, who in the earlier CBS case had argued that *Red Lion* did not support any First Amendment right of access, now agreed with the FCC that the 1971 statute did and that the FCC's broad reading of what § 312(a)(7) meant did not interfere with the broadcasters' First Amendment rights. The First Amendment rights of the candidates and the voters, he claimed, are implicated, and the new rule makes "a significant contribution to freedom of expression by enhancing the ability of the candidates to present, and the public to receive, information necessary for the effective operation of the democratic process."[77] Once again, the Court upheld restrictions that would have been unthinkable if applied to print media, but in doing so it only continued a long tradition.

There has been growing criticism of the distinction between print and broadcast journalism, a distinction that makes little sense in terms of fact or law. Technological developments such as cable television have completely undercut the old idea of limited airwaves.[78] A large number of Americans, perhaps even a majority, get their news from radio or television, not from the newspapers, while major news events, such as presidential press conferences and candidate debates, are pitched at television audiences. The Burger Court did not invent the distinction, and although it still clings to it, there are signs that its strength has eroded somewhat.

A hopeful, albeit small, sign was the Court's decision in *FCC* v. *League of Women Voters of California* in 1984.[79] Congress had prohibited "editorializing" by noncommercial educational broadcasting stations that received funds from the tax-supported Corporation for Public Broadcasting. A 5-4 Court speaking through Justice Brennan struck down 47 U.S.C. § 399 as an impermissible content regulation, but because this was broadcast and not print media, Justice Brennan conceded that a lower standard of scrutiny applied. However, he did not invoke the by-now traditional claim of airwave scarcity; restrictions would be upheld, he argued, when the Court is satisfied "that the restriction is narrowly tailored to further a substantial governmental interest, such as ensuring adequate and balanced coverage of public issues."[80] There is still a long way to go until the Court, and the law, catch up with reality.

LIBEL

One case, more than any other, led the press to believe that the Warren Court was its friend, and that was the 1964 landmark decision in *New York Times* v. *Sullivan*. In striking down the old rules of libel, the Court reaffirmed a central meaning of the First Amendment in the democratic process; free expression constituted how the people kept tabs on their governors. The decision seemingly invited the press to join with the public in the "uninhibited, robust and wide open . . . debate on public issues."

Problems inhered in the opinion from the start—problems that few people noticed in the heady atmosphere of the late sixties. As the opinion's author explained, the decision rested on a Meiklejohnian view that free expression was bound up with sovereignty and was as part of the "governmental responsibility . . . a public power." The Constitution protected the press so that it could participate in the governing responsibility through reporting and criticism.[81]

As Lyle Denniston, *The Baltimore Sun*'s Supreme Court correspondent, suggests, this view is troublesome for two reasons. First, it establishes a variable measure for press freedom; more freedom is attached to those press activities that have high social value because they contribute to the political debate. Second, it requires public accountability as a regulatory device; otherwise, the press could abuse its power and distort the political process.[82] The first prong did not bother the press, because it believed that its normal journalistic endeavors, if unhindered, easily satisfied the criterion of social usefulness. The second prong, that of accountability, also did not seem to bother journalists, because their professional rhetoric already spoke to the idea of meeting high standards. What they were not prepared to accept was the possibility of others, such as the courts, judging their social usefulness and imposing standards of accountability.

As Denniston noted:

> Without bothering to analyze critically what it believed, the press proceeded upon the assumption that it enjoyed its rights as a matter of institutional autonomy for its organizations, and personal autonomy for its individual practitioners. The internal inconsistency of a private industry serving a public right, yet doing so under an ill-defined and probably indefinable code of private ethics, apparently never troubled the press, which failed to appreciate that, in any ultimate constitutional reckoning over its performance, public law would prevail over industry self-restraint. The "public's right to know" would be too important to be left to journalists.[83]

The reckoning actually began with *Sullivan*, because in granting the press freedom to criticize, it also imbued that criticism with an element of public accountability. As such, the standards by which criticism would be judged would not be the professional ethics taught in journalism schools or adopted by trade groups, but standards of law. In fact, the Warren Court set out the first standard, actual malice, in *Sullivan*, and in subsequent cases added other criteria even as it seemed to expand freedom of the press. The process continued into the early years of the Burger regime, with the justices allowing almost any connection to the *public* interest to justify hitherto restricted press behavior.[84] Then in *Gertz* v. *Robert Welch, Inc.*,[85] Justice Powell led the Court in shifting its analysis to public figures as against private figures, even when their activities might be somehow construed as public. The Court refused to grant exemption to the press in cases involving private persons in divorce proceedings, receiving public funds, or even convicted of crime.[86]

Journalists in the late 1970s and early 1980s might well be excused if they suffered from legal schizophrenia. On the one hand, the Court seemed to be establishing a critical new right of access and grounding it solidly in the First Amendment. On the other hand, the Court not only refused to expand *Sullivan* but also opened up internal editorial processes to scrutiny in libel cases. In *Herbert* v. *Lando*, arising from a CBS "60 Minutes" segment on army atrocities in Vietnam, the Court ruled that what went on in the various stages of the story's preparation might reveal the state of mind of the journalists involved, and this might reveal whether the story had been tainted by actual malice.[87]

The press greeted this decision with horror, as well they might, for it opened up what had hitherto been a closed area of journalism: editorial decision making regarding what stories to pursue, what approach to take, and how the material would be presented. Now editors and reporters, as well as the publishers and their lawyers, would have to worry about what might be said, even in jest, should the subject of their stories seek to sue. Yet even here, the result in *Lando* came right out of *Sullivan's* "actual malice" standard. How else could a plaintiff determine if malice existed than to query the defendants about what and how they thought at the time they prepared the story? A more serious criticism is that the Court "rushed" to take the case. At some point the issue would have come before the high court, but in *Lando* the Court reviewed an interlocutory discovery ruling, a matter it rarely accepts.[88]

The *Sullivan* decision, moreover, had never said public figures could not sue; it merely made it far more difficult for them to win, especially if the news stories dealt reasonably accurately with legitimate issues of public concern. In the early eighties, though, press reputation slipped badly, and the public was treated to several so-called celebrity lawsuits, most notably General William Westmoreland's suit against CBS-TV and Israeli General Ariel Sharon's against *Time*. Neither plaintiff won, but the lengthy suits cost the defendants hundreds of thousands of dollars in litigation costs. While CBS and *Time* could absorb such costs, smaller newspapers and radio stations could not, and even the threat of a costly suit, according to press commentators, put a chill on the investigative journalism that had been popularized during the Watergate era.

The Supreme Court "encouraged" this type of press-bashing, according to critics, in decisions which, while not overturning *Sullivan*, seemed to crab its spirit. In *Keeton* v. *Hustler* (1984),[89] the Court reaffirmed the traditional view that state libel laws served a legitimate function in protecting reputation even of public figures. Moreover, false stories harm "both the subject of the falsehood and the readers of the statement," a view of value and accountability fully in keeping with *Sullivan*.

From the press point of view, probably the nadir of Burger Court opinions came in what many people considered an obscure case over an unimportant issue. A credit service, Dun & Bradstreet, had sent routine notices to five of its subscribers that a building company in their area had filed for voluntary bankruptcy. The owner of the company first learned of this totally erroneous report when he went to conduct some business with his banker. Dun & Bradstreet eventually sent out a correction but refused to inform the builder who had gotten the false report. He sued for libel and damages, and a Vermont jury awarded him $350,000.

The Court, speaking through Justice Powell, ruled that First Amendment protection, as explicated in *Sullivan*, did not apply in libel suits where the subject matter involved "no issue of public concern." One should recall that Justice Powell had been the chief architect in bringing commercial speech within the fold of the First Amendment, yet he declared that speech on matters of purely private, as opposed to public, concern enjoyed less protection. Here the libel laws held sway, because

> there is no threat to the free and robust debate of public issues; there is no potential interference with a meaningful dialogue of ideas concerning

self-government; and there is no threat of liability causing a reaction of self-censorship by the press.[90]

Even Justice Brennan, who dissented from the decision, agreed that in libel cases speech on commercial matters enjoyed a lesser constitutional protection because it did not directly implicate "the central meaning of the First Amendment" and was "not at the essence of self-government." A year later, in the Burger Court's last press decision, the justices removed any doubt about the emphasis on subject matter rather than person when they held that media defendants would be entitled to constitutional protection against having to prove the truth of stories when those stories dealt with matters of public concern.[91]

With these cases, the Court seemed to have gone from an emphasis on subject matter to the question of the public/private nature of the figure back to subject matter. The press, for the most part, viewed the Burger Court libel decisions as an abandonment of the Warren Court's liberalism as expressed in *Sullivan*. Yet a close reading of the cases would indicate that while it had difficulty in defining the exact nature of First Amendment protection in this area, the Burger Court did not transform the constitutional dogmas of *Sullivan*. The basic principles and fundamental political theory remained intact. "Rather, the Court simply let what was always implicit in *Sullivan* come to fruition. . . . [T]he decision certainly did not mean [press] liberation."[92]

CONCLUSIONS

There are several ways to look at the Burger Court and its decisions affecting freedom of the press. One view is that the Burger Court abandoned the commitment to open and robust journalism espoused in the Warren years and instead took what Justice Stewart called a "crabbed view" of the Press Clause. Others might claim that the press was not only no worse off in 1986 than in 1969 but in fact enjoyed greater constitutional privileges, especially in matters of access. There is no clear answer, and how one views the record depends on one's personal philosophy.

One can argue that journalists complain more about what the Court did not do than what it did—it did not, for example, grant the reporter's privilege; it did not grant the press greater access to government agencies and information than regular citizens enjoyed; it did not immunize the press completely from libel suits; it did not eradicate the distinction between print and broadcast journalism; it did not adopt the view that the tort of libel imposes intolerable burdens on free expression. In short, the Burger Court did not animate the Press Clause to give journalists a specially protected place within the constitutional scheme.[93]

Whether the Burger Court should have gone further is also debatable. Thomas Emerson, one of the strongest advocates of free expression, questions whether the press ought to be given a special status greater than that accorded everyone else. While the courts need to be sensitive to certain problems raised by the nature of newsgathering, Emerson believes that freedom of expression in general and of the press in particular is best served by treating the press as one feature of "an integrated system of freedom of expression." In denying the press unique privileges, Emerson concludes, the Burger Court had been "entirely correct."[94]

That the Burger Court had been hostile to press claims in general is a debatable proposition. Advocates of free speech and press argue that by refusing to take a pro-press position, the Court in effect encouraged press-bashing and punitive litigation that chilled First Amendment rights. Yet in terms of the question that is being asked throughout this study—did the Burger Court depart radically from the positions of the Warren Court?—the answer must be that it did not. The Warren Court did not decide that many press cases, and its reputation for championing freedom of the press rests almost entirely on *Sullivan* and the few cases decided in its wake.

As in other areas, one might also suggest that the Warren Court had the easy case—that while *Sullivan* certainly is a landmark decision, it took the high ground and never dealt with the more complicated issues that it generated. The Burger Court had to face the question of whether all libel law should be proscribed by the First Amendment, and it decided against this proposition. Libel laws serve a useful function, one of which is to keep the press within certain bounds of propriety. We have come a long way from old English law where merely the speaking of a critical statement could be punished. That we tolerate a high level of often scurrilous comment, and grant it First Amendment protection, would seem to indicate that the press is far from cowed, as Burger Court critics would infer. Certainly one of the early decisions of the Rehnquist Court, whose composition is not that different from the Burger Court of the eighties, would seem to indicate that the First Amendment, and the *Sullivan* decision, are alive and well. How else to explain the *unanimous* decision reversing the libel judgment against *Hustler Magazine* for its parody that had the Reverend Jerry Falwell talking about incest with his mother in an outhouse![95]

Perhaps the most balanced assessment comes from lawyer Floyd Abrams, who fought many of the speech battles. He believes that in most areas the "battle" between the courts and the press is over. Prior restraint was resolved in the Pentagon papers case, and is not likely to be a major issue in the future. The question of closed courtrooms has also been settled—in favor of the press. The *Zurcher* decision, allowing ex parte warrants, has been overturned by act of Congress.

The matter of press confidentiality will probably generate more cases, but despite *Branzburg*, the press seems to be winning this battle as well, either through state shield laws or in sympathetic lower courts where judges have found both First Amendment and non–First Amendment grounds to protect press source confidentiality. A "dour" perception of the Burger Court's attitude toward the press is not unwarranted, Abrams concludes, but "in many areas, however, freedom of expression has triumphed under the Burger Court and is likely to again." If the press has not gotten everything it demanded, it has gotten a great deal. "This is, in part, to the credit of the Burger Court and, in part, notwithstanding that Court."[96]

III

RIGHTS OF THE ACCUSED

AMENDMENT IV

The right of the people to be secure in their persons, houses, papers, and effects, against unreasonable searches and seizures, shall not be violated, and no Warrant shall issue, but upon probable cause, supported by Oath or affirmation, and particularly describing the place to be searched, and the persons or things to be seized.

AMENDMENT V

No person shall be held to answer for a capital, or otherwise infamous crime, unless on a presentment or indictment of a Grand Jury, except in cases arising in the land or naval forces, or in the Militia, when in actual service in time of War or public danger; nor shall any person be subject for the same offence to be twice put in jeopardy of life or limb; nor shall be compelled in any criminal case to be a witness against himself, nor be deprived of life, liberty, or property, without due process of law; nor shall private property be taken for public use, without just compensation.

AMENDMENT VI

In all criminal prosecutions, the accused shall enjoy the right to a speedy and public trial, by an impartial jury of the State and district wherein the crime shall have been committed, which district shall have been previously ascertained by law, and to be informed of the nature and cause of the accusation; to be confronted with the witnesses against him; to have compulsory process for obtaining Witnesses in his favor, and to have the Assistance of Counsel for his defence.

AMENDMENT VIII

Excessive bail shall not be required, nor excessive fines imposed, nor cruel and unusual punishments inflicted.

7

" . . . In No Way Creates a Constitutional Straightjacket"

The Warren Court and Criminal Procedure

Winston Churchill once said that "the quality of a nation's civilization can be largely measured by the methods it uses in the enforcement of its criminal law."[1] Compared to England, the colonies from the beginning had far more humane criminal laws with only a few capital crimes, but they highly valued the English idea of due process and the notion that an accused person should be considered innocent until proven guilty. Several grievances in the Declaration of Independence complained about the king's alleged infringements on due process, and the postwar state and federal constitutions established procedural safeguards to prevent arbitrary actions by the state as well as to ensure a fair trial.

The Fourth, Fifth, Sixth, and Eighth Amendments comprise the bundle of rights afforded to persons accused of crime. The Fourth Amendment protects the security of persons both personally and in their homes against search and seizure without proper authorization and proscribes the issuance of warrants without probable cause. Americans had had enough of general search warrants since the days of the writs of assistance.

The Fifth Amendment requires grand jury indictment and prohibits double jeopardy. Its most famous provision is a bar against forcing a person to testify against himself or herself. It also includes the guarantee that no one shall be deprived of life, liberty, or property without due process of law.

The Sixth Amendment guarantees a speedy and public local trial, thus preventing the state from keeping an accused person incarcerated indefinitely or trying him or her in secret or at a place where the accused would face a jury of strangers. This amendment also derives from the colonial experience, especially the efforts of the Crown to deal with smuggling and revenue collection. In order to ensure a fair trial, the Sixth Amendment guarantees the accused the right to know the charges, to confront his or her accusers, to compel witnesses to appear to testify, and most important, to have the assistance of counsel.

The Eighth Amendment prohibits the infliction of cruel or unusual punishment or the imposition of excessive bail or fines.[2]

These four amendments, and the rights they encompass, are not only interrelated in their goal of protecting the rights of accused persons but also in how they go about reaching that goal. The right to a fair trial often depends on whether the police acted within their prescribed limits or whether the accused had access to a lawyer at an appropriate stage in the proceedings. The Framers of the Bill of Rights wrote with memory still fresh of an overbearing royal authority, which the colonists had seen as encroaching on these rights. They also wrote in the context of the late eighteenth century, a simpler period than our own, with far simpler crimes as well as a relatively limited system of criminal justice. Not until the twentieth century did the courts begin to deal with how and to whom these rights applied in the context of modern communications, an established police and court system, and a society whose criminals as well as statesmen functioned in national and global terms.

CRIMINAL PROCEDURE AND INCORPORATION

The average, law-abiding citizen will probably never have occasion to learn how the criminal justice system deals with offenders. But if in 1960 he or she were to consider what would happen if they were charged with a noncapital felony, they would probably have assumed that the Constitution required that they be accorded the assistance of counsel, a jury trial, confrontation of witnesses against them, and protection against double jeopardy—all guarantees listed in the Bill of Rights. They would have been wrong.

In 1833 the Supreme Court ruled that the Bill of Rights applied only against the federal government,[3] and this remained the accepted interpretation until after the Civil War. In the *Slaughter-House Cases* (1873),[4] a bare majority of the Court read the Fourteenth Amendment's Due Process and Equal Protection Clauses very narrowly. The minority, however, suggested that these clauses had been intended to change relations between the states and the federal government and thus expand the constitutionally protected rights of individuals. When the Court adopted the doctrine of substantive due process in 1897, it extended the constitutional mantle to protect economic rights against arbitrary state interference but failed to resolve whether this same doctrine affected noneconomic rights.

In 1884 the Court held that a state could indict through information rather than through the grand jury procedure called for in the Fifth Amendment,[5] and nearly a quarter-century later ruled that the Self-Incrimination

Clause did not apply to the states.[6] Not until 1932 did the Court apply any of the criminal procedure guarantees against the states; in that year, in the infamous Scottsboro case, the Court found that denial of counsel in a capital case denied defendants the due process of law.[7]

The incorporation of defendants' rights has proceeded in a more difficult and irregular pattern than have the protections of the First Amendment. Once the Court agreed that the Fourteenth Amendment incorporated freedom of speech, the debate ended; cases afterwards dealt with whether particular actions constituted an impermissible infringement of expression. Similarly, once the Religion Clauses applied to the states, subsequent cases took the fact of incorporation as a given, and the justices looked to see whether the state had violated the Establishment Clause or restricted free exercise.[8]

But the Fourth, Fifth, Sixth, and Eighth Amendments cover a number of rights, and one of the major constitutional debates of this century has centered on which of those rights the Fourteenth Amendment applies to the states. The debate began with Justice Cardozo's opinion in *Palko* v. *Connecticut* (1937), upholding the right of a state to take an appeal from a "not guilty" verdict and secure a second trial. The majority held that granting the state the same right as the accused enjoyed did not violate the double jeopardy provision of the Fifth Amendment. Cardozo faced squarely the issue of whether the Fourteenth Amendment "absorbed" the entire Bill of Rights and concluded that it did not. Only those "implicit in the concept of ordered liberty" applied to the states through the Fourteenth Amendment, and the stricture on double jeopardy did not meet that definition.[9]

Ten years later, the question of self-incrimination came up again in *Adamson* v. *California*.[10] Justice Frankfurter, writing for the majority, expanded upon Cardozo's *Palko* opinion and urged a "selective incorporation" of the Bill of Rights. Not all rights are "implicit in the concept of ordered liberty," and the Court would be the arbiter of which rights met the test of "fundamental fairness" and which did not. Justice Black, who a decade earlier had agreed with Cardozo, had in the meantime grown increasingly uncomfortable with the idea that only some of the rights in the first eight amendments, but not others, applied to the states. In a dissent joined by Justice Douglas, Black set out the idea of "total incorporation" and argued that the Fourteenth Amendment prevented the states from denying its citizens *any* of the protections of the Bill of Rights. Black also objected to what he termed the "natural law" approach of *Palko*, which he claimed invited the Court to add rights not found in the Constitution if a majority thought such rights met the "fundamental fairness" standard.[11]

The debate between the Cardozo/Frankfurter view of selective incorporation and the Black argument for total incorporation went on into the early 1960s. During the term of Chief Justice Vinson and the early years of Earl Warren, Frankfurter's jurisprudential view prevailed, and the Court, preoccupied with racial segregation, barely touched questions of criminal procedure.

Beginning in the early 1960s, however, a significant change took place, caused only in part by Frankfurter's retirement from the bench in 1962. Justice Harlan developed his own ideas regarding what constituted fundamental fairness. One looked to the Bill of Rights for a start, but courts had to remember that due process is a flexible concept. If the right is in fact fundamental, then the states are bound by it; but states may choose a variety of ways to apply the right, provided the methods they choose are themselves fair. This approach allowed the establishment of national norms but still permitted the states to experiment within certain parameters. The Warren Court continued to use the language of "fundamental fairness" but incorporated more and more of the rights in the Fourth, Fifth, and Sixth Amendments. The Court also insisted that, once incorporated, the rights applied with equal vigor to the states as to the federal government.

The story of the Warren Court in this area is, therefore, revolutionary in some aspects, in that it took guarantees once applied only to the federal government and required the states to live up to the same standards. Beyond that, the Warren Court had to interpret what these eighteenth-century protections meant in the twentieth century. Its responses triggered some of the most vehement criticism of judicial activism in this century. We will turn to that criticism after we see exactly what the Warren Court did, and although the various issues are often interconnected, our survey will be easier if we look at the specific constitutional guarantees one at a time.

THE FOURTH AMENDMENT AND SEARCH WARRANTS

The right of people to be secure in their home and person is the heart of the Fourth Amendment. Simply stated, it prohibits the state from arbitrarily searching one's home, office, or person or taking someone into custody without reason. For the police to search premises or arrest a suspect, they need—with certain exceptions[12]—to convince a magistrate that they have reasonable suspicions that specific evidence can be found in a distinct place or that a certain person did commit a particular crime.

The wording of the Fourth Amendment is ambiguous, however, and thus open to conflicting interpretations that can be used to expand or limit its protection. For example, the amendment refers to the right of the *people*, not of individuals, and this has led some commentators to suggest that the courts ought to focus on general rules to regulate police conduct rather than on rectifying particular misdeeds.[13] The Court did, in fact, deal with both the individual and the regulatory aspects of this language, and its most controversial decisions, concerning the exclusionary rule, addressed the regulatory problem.

The Fourth Amendment also includes words that are at best subjective and therefore open to a wide range of interpretation. What is an "unreasonable" search? What constitutes "probable" cause sufficient to secure a warrant? If a warrant issues, does that fact by itself make the search "reasonable"? The word "unreasonable" apparently modifies "search," but does it also provide a standard for the issuance of warrants? Furthermore, the language does not indicate against whom the right applies. It does not say the people shall be secure against police searches, but against searches, and the courts have interpreted this to mean all forms of governmental investigation. Finally, it should be noted that the Fourth Amendment appears to make no distinction between people and things, although the courts, applying common sense, have distinguished between the two. However, the language raises problems over nonintrusive techniques such as electronic eavesdropping. Is a wiretap a search, and if so, of persons or of objects?

The Warren Court in the area of search warrants, as in so many other areas, did not write on a blank slate. The Cardozo/Frankfurter/Black debate had been under way for nearly two decades before Earl Warren joined the Court, and in that time the Court had handed down a number of Fourth Amendment decisions.[14] Several of these decisions had to do with the requirements police had to meet to secure a search warrant.

Prior to 1933 all a policeman had to do to get a warrant was intone a formula, "I have cause to suspect and I do believe that. . . " While courts normally assume that a policeman is telling the truth, the Supreme Court held that the Fourth Amendment required some proof to secure a warrant—that the magistrate needed facts, not just opinion, to justify the search.[15] In *Harris* v. *United States* (1947),[16] the Vinson Court ruled 5-4 that where police had a valid arrest warrant, they did not need a separate search warrant to make a valid search. The following year the Court held invalid a warrantless search that preceded an arrest.[17]

The Warren Court heard its first warrant case in 1958, and in essence did little more than reaffirm the old rule. A federal agent had sworn to the magistrate that Veto Giordenello had received and concealed narcotics, but he offered no facts to support this conclusion. The Court voided the conviction and noted that a warrant could not issue unless the police could show some proof that the evidence sought would be in the place they wanted to search.[18]

All of these cases involved the federal government, but in 1961 the Supreme Court extended Fourth Amendment guarantees to the states in *Mapp* v. *Ohio*.[19] Three years later it heard its first major state warrant case, *Aguilar* v. *Texas*.[20] In the application for a search warrant, local police had stated that they had received reliable information from credible persons that narcotics were being stored in a certain place and that they had believed this information to be true. They offered no facts in support of their application, and the Court, relying on past cases, voided the conviction. The Warren Court made no new law in this case, but it did try to give police, magistrates, and lower courts some guidelines as to what the Constitution required. The police needed to provide (1) facts to justify probable cause and (2) reasons that the magistrate should believe that probable cause existed.

If this had been all, few people would have been upset by the course of developing Fourth Amendment jurisprudence. The Court really said little more than that the Constitution requires a warrant prior to a search; that although some searches are valid even without a warrant (such as search incident to arrest), it is always better for the police to get a warrant; and that a valid warrant requires some factual proof, not just the officer's opinion, to support the magistrate's decision that probable cause exists. Only the most zealous law-and-order advocate could complain that this interpretation of the Fourth Amendment crippled police work; without these basic safeguards, the Warrant Clause would mean very little.

Then came two cases in the final Term of the Warren Court that seemed to many people to be carrying the warrant requirements beyond reason. The FBI had been investigating the activities of William Spinelli, a known book-maker, for suspected illegal gambling activities. Agent Robert L. Bender had followed Spinelli for several days and believed that Spinelli had a telephone bank operating out of an apartment rented by his girlfriend. The affidavit Bender filed to secure a warrant to search that apartment listed in detail the number of times Spinelli had been observed driving from his home in East St. Louis, Illinois, to his girlfriend's apartment in St. Louis, Missouri, and the quantity and numbers of the phones in that apartment. The final two paragraphs read as follows:

> William Spinelli is known to this affiant and to federal law enforcement agents and local law enforcement agents as a bookmaker, an associate of bookmakers, a gambler, and an associate of gamblers.
>
> The Federal Bureau of Investigation has been informed by a confidential reliable informant that William Spinelli is operating a handbook and accepting wagering information by means of the telephones [in the apartment].

The affidavit seemed to meet the *Aguilar* criteria, but the Court, speaking through Justice Harlan, said no. It boiled down to assertions that Spinelli often drove back and forth from his own apartment to that of his girlfriend, that she had two phones in her apartment, and that an informant said that Spinelli operated a book out of that apartment. The facts did not support probable cause, because in and of themselves they could be entirely innocent. The whole application rested on the assertion that Spinelli had a prior reputation and that an unknown informant claimed Spinelli was engaged in illegal gambling. This constituted nothing more than hearsay, and the magistrate had to have real evidence, if not of actual gambling then at least about the informant's reliability. The police need not disclose an informant's identity, but the magistrate at least has to know if there had been a prior relationship to support credibility.[21]

Police screamed over the *Spinelli* case, interpreting it to say that in order to get a warrant, they would have to present the type of evidence that would stand up in court, whereas they had always assumed that "probable cause" in an investigation required a lower level of evidence. As Justice Black noted in his dissent, the *Aguilar* and *Spinelli* decisions seemed to elevate the magistrate's hearing for a warrant to "a full-fledged trial." The FBI had tailed Spinelli, had seen him engage in suspicious behavior that conformed to his reputation as a gambler, and had reliable information that Spinelli had been taking bets on the phones in his girlfriend's apartment. This had been good investigative work. What more could the Court want?

Part of the problem is Justice Harlan's opinion—for him an unusually poorly written one—that gave neither the police nor the magistrates guidance as to what the Court expected. Yet the opinion contained a simple two-prong test. First, the magistrate must evaluate the truthfulness of the source of information, whether it comes from a police officer or an informant, and second, he or she must evaluate the adequacy of the facts to support probable cause.[22] The Court had not denied police the use of reputational evidence but merely required them in some way to corroborate it so that the magistrate could believe its truthfulness. As a practical matter, *Spinelli* would force police to tighten up their procedures in securing a warrant.

On the day Earl Warren retired from the bench, the Court imposed a warrant requirement in situations previously considered legitimate warrantless searches incident to an arrest. California police went to the house of Ted Chimel, a coin dealer, with an arrest warrant relating to the burglary of a coin shop. After arresting him, they asked to look around and, when he objected, told him that on the basis of a lawful arrest, they had the right to conduct a search. Chimel's wife then accompanied the officers around the house, and they confiscated a number of coins and other items that they believed had been stolen.

In *Chimel* v. *California*,[23] Justice Stewart wrote for a 6-2 Court in holding that police had exceeded the limits of a search incident to arrest. Stewart examined the historic reasons for such a search and held that they had been primarily for two reasons: (1) to remove any weapons that the suspect might have on him or within his reach and (2) to seize evidence related to a crime that might be on a suspect, such as the proceeds of a robbery. Once police had satisfied themselves that the suspect had neither weapon nor evidence on his person or within immediate grasp, they needed a warrant to search further.[24]

As CBS legal correspondent Fred Graham noted, "Under the best of circumstances, this ruling could be expected to run headlong into resistance in many states where search warrants have been oddities."[25] In this and in other cases, however, the Court had done little more than lay down certain rules for police procedure, in order to bring some sense out of the ambiguities in the Fourth Amendment. To make the constitutional guarantees meaningful, the Court declared that a search warrant would always be the preferred means of police investigation of premises; that to secure a warrant, the police would have to present real facts, not just suspicions, and convince the magistrate of the truthfulness of their assertions; and that in terms of searching persons and places, the Court placed greater protection about persons.

These requirements all appear to be fairly common-sensical, if one is to give any credence to the Fourth Amendment. The outcry that greeted these decisions must be seen in its historical context, namely, that state and local police had hardly bothered with warrants prior to the 1960s, and if they had (because required by some state constitutions to do so), they had been able to secure warrants from friendly magistrates with little more than an avowal of their suspicions. Earlier Courts had indeed taken a somewhat erratic course during the 1940s as to what the Fourth Amendment required, but those cases had for the most part been ignored at the state and local levels. The Warren Court had not only attempted to determine consistent Fourth Amendment rules but, more importantly, to apply them to the states as well.

The preceding cases would seem to imply that all of the Warren Court's decisions tended to limit police, and that is far from true. In *McCray* v. *Illinois* (1967),[26] the Court ruled that police could withhold the identity of a confidential informant, so long as they could convince the magistrate that their information was reliable. That same year, Justice Brennan wrote the majority opinion in *Warden* v. *Hayden*,[27] which allowed police wide discretion in the type of evidence they gathered in a search subsequent to a "hot pursuit." Both of these cases took a hard and common-sensical look at what the police had to do in their line of work and upheld standard police practice. One of the most "pro-police" decisions of the Warren Court took this same approach, but it is often overlooked by those who charge that the Court did nothing but coddle criminals.

Officer Martin McFadden, dressed in plain clothes, was patrolling a section of downtown Cleveland one afternoon when he noticed two men who "didn't look right to me at the time." The two men, John Terry and Richard Chilton, kept walking up and down past a certain store, and he suspected them of "casing" the store. When a third man joined the other two, McFadden decided to investigate further; he approached the three men, identified himself as a police officer, and asked their names. When Terry "mumbled something" in response, McFadden grabbed him, spun him around between himself and the other two men, and patted down his outer clothing. He felt a pistol on Terry, and later one on Chilton, seized their weapons, and arrested them.

The defendants tried to suppress evidence of the guns, because they claimed that Officer McFadden had not taken them in a search incident to an arrest and that he had no probable cause to stop them. But the trial court and the Supreme Court both upheld McFadden's actions. He had been a policeman for thirty-nine years, a detective for thirty-five, and during that time he had built up instincts and habits based on experience. To deny the public the benefit of that experience would be foolish, declared the Chief Justice, and would hamper the police in their work.[28]

The "stop-and-frisk" decision is a good indication of the Warren Court's philosophy. In situations involving private quarters or immobilized vehicles, where the evidence could not "walk away," the Court insisted that the police comply with regular warrant procedures. In on-the-street situations, or when the police were in hot pursuit of a suspect, rigid application of constitutional rules could not be expected. In the *Terry* case the Court adopted what might be called a "rule of reason," which allowed police wide discretion provided they had some reasonable basis to support their action.

THE FOURTH AMENDMENT AND WIRETAPPING

In 1928 the Court began to deal with how modern technology affected the Fourth Amendment, when it ruled that wiretapping did not constitute an unauthorized search. In a highly formalistic opinion, Chief Justice Taft ignored the intent of the amendment and claimed that there had been no actual entry, merely the use by police of an enhanced sense of hearing. To pay too much attention to "nice ethical conduct by government officials," he said, "would make society suffer and give criminals greater immunity than has been known heretofore."[29] The opinion brought dissents by Justices Pierce Butler, Oliver Wendell Holmes, Jr. (who called wiretapping "a dirty business"), and especially from Louis D. Brandeis. The Brandeis opinion not only set forth the idea of a constitutionally protected right to privacy but also warned against "government law-breaking."

Taft had noted in his opinion that Congress could make wiretap evidence inadmissible in federal courts, and Congress did just that in Section 605 of the 1934 Federal Communications Act. Early cases interpreted the statute to cover all federal officials, although as late as 1952 the Vinson Court held that state officials could use such evidence in state courts.[30] In 1942 the Court ruled that eavesdropping by placing a detectaphone next to an office wall to hear conversations did not violate the Fourth Amendment, because there had been no trespass, and a decade later upheld wiring an undercover agent to pick up what the defendant thought would be a private conversation.[31]

One of the first decisions in this area by the Warren Court barred the use in federal courts of state-gathered wiretap evidence.[32] Finally, in 1961 the Court unanimously overruled *Olmstead* and vindicated Brandeis's view. In *Silverman* v. *United States*, federal agents had slipped a spike with a microphone under a baseboard and against a heating duct, so that they could hear conversations throughout the house. Justice Stewart dismissed as an irrelevant technicality the issue of whether an actual trespass had occurred; the decision "is based upon the reality of an intrusion into a constitutionally protected area."[33]

In the 1960s the Court decided a number of cases dealing with undercover agents wired for sound or who had lured suspects into a location wired for sound. Justice Stewart labored with the problem of a "constitutionally protected area" as the technology for eavesdropping became ever more sophisticated. At least in the early part of the decade, a majority of the Court sustained the use of such devices by law enforcement agents, and often the deciding factor was the technicality of whether a trespass had taken place.[34] A few of the justices raised the question of whether a warrant should have been secured, but the majority recognized that undercover work had little connection to the type of investigation normally covered by warrants.

The justices, however, were becoming aware of the pervasiveness of electronic surveillance as well as the scientific advances in the devices used. In 1928 Brandeis's law clerk had objected to the justice suggesting that in the future it would be possible to listen to conversations through walls and from far off. Less than thirty years later, a leading student of the subject warned that "modern technology has breached at vital points the physical limits that once guarded individual and group privacy."[35] Physical trespass no longer made any sense as a demarcation between permissible and impermissible electronic surveillance, and the Court acknowledged this in 1967.

A New York statute authorized warrants for wiretapping and eavesdropping, and as part of their investigation into alleged bribery of state liquor-license officials, police had secured a warrant to place a recording device in the office of Ralph Berger. Within two weeks police had uncovered a conspiracy, and transcripts of recorded conversations helped secure Berger's conviction. The Court, speaking through Justice Clark, found the statute defective, because it did not require that a particular crime be named to secure a warrant. This in effect made it a general warrant, the very thing proscribed by the Fourth Amendment. Clark admitted that it might be difficult to draft a statute that would be specific enough to meet the warrant criteria yet flexible enough to permit the type of surveillance police wanted to use.[36]

The opinion left obscure a number of issues, including the criteria that courts might apply to electronic surveillance. Part of the majority opinion would seem to indicate that police may listen only to particular conversations that relate to the suspected crime, obviously an impossibility. Justice Douglas's dissent hit the mark when he invoked historic precedent to argue that the Fourth Amendment barred all searches for mere evidence and limited the government to seizing contraband or fruits of crime. A wiretap is an open-ended type of general warrant, but the Court recognized that it could not deprive law enforcement officials of modern weapons while criminals availed themselves of the latest technological advances. So they left the issue to be resolved in future cases.

The next Term the Court handed down its strongest decision yet in regard to wiretapping. FBI agents had planted an electronic listening and recording device outside a public phone booth from which a known gambler normally placed his bets, and the evidence they obtained helped convict him of violating a federal statute prohibiting interstate transmission of wagering information. The lower court upheld the conviction, because there had been no physical intrusion into the phone booth. In a 7-1 decision, the Court voided the conviction, and Justice Stewart's opinion merged many of the Fourth Amendment ideas the Court had been developing for over a decade with its recently announced right to privacy.[37]

Stewart admitted that the phrase "constitutionally protected area" failed to define the meaning and reach of the Fourth Amendment. In a notable phrase, he declared that "the Fourth Amendment protects people, not places." Where an action took place mattered less than whether a general expectation of privacy existed; if so, then the individual's privacy would be protected there.

By this time, the anti-Court forces had been gaining strength for nearly fifteen years, and much of the discontent generated by the desegregation, reapportionment, and First Amendment decisions seemed to focus on the alleged impact of the Court's criminal procedure decisions. When President Johnson called for progressive anticrime legislation, the law-and-order advocates in Congress went to work with a vengeance, and the Omnibus Crime Control and Safe Streets Act of 1968 had a decided animus against the judiciary. The law specifically attempted to overturn or modify several of the Court's major decisions, and Title III dealt with wiretapping and eavesdropping. The Crime Act authorized judge-approved taps that could monitor a wide range of activities, and it allowed any law officer, or indeed any person obtaining information in conformity with the process, to disclose or use that information as appropriate.[38] What impact, if any, that law would have on Fourth Amendment adjudication would be a question to be answered in the Burger Court.

THE FOURTH AMENDMENT AND THE EXCLUSIONARY RULE

If the constitutional guarantee against unreasonable and unlawful searches is to have any significance, evidence seized in violation of the Fourth Amendment should be excluded from trial; otherwise, it is a guarantee without meaning. Yet no criminal procedure decisions have been so bitterly complained about as the exclusionary rule, which gives teeth to the Fourth Amendment. The complaints stem from the fact that the amendment itself provides no clue as to what remedies are available when it is violated; the exclusionary rule has been, from the start, a judge-made rule, and critics condemn it as judicial activism at its worst, with judges making policy rather than interpreting the law.

For a century after the adoption of the Bill of Rights, victims of illegal searches had only civil remedies available to them, either suits in trespass for damages or suits in replevin for return of the goods, and neither proved particularly effective. The Court first articulated the exclusionary rule in *Weeks* v. *United States* (1914), and Justice Day made as strong a case for the rule as one can find:

> If letters and private documents can thus be [illegally] seized and held and used in evidence against a citizen accused of an offense, the protection of the Fourth Amendment declaring his right to be secure against such searches and seizures is of no value, and, so far as those thus placed are concerned, might as well be stricken from the Constitution. The efforts of the courts and their officials to bring the guilty to punishment, praiseworthy as they are, are not to be aided by the sacrifice of those great principles established by years of endeavor and suffering which have resulted in their embodiment in the fundamental law of the land.[39]

A few years later, the Court prohibited the use of copies of illegally seized documents as a basis to secure a warrant for the originals. Justice Holmes declared that the "essence" of the Fourth Amendment protection is not merely that "evidence so acquired shall not be used before the Court but that it shall not be used at all."[40]

The Court had explicitly declared in *Weeks* that the rule did not apply to the states, so in the next thirty years state and federal authorities colluded in what came to be known as the "silver platter doctrine." Evidence obtained by state authorities in a manner that would be illegal if engaged in by federal agents could be admitted in federal court so long as there had been no federal participation in the search. In 1949 the Vinson Court took a small step toward reining in warrantless state searches in *Wolf* v. *Colorado*,[41] when Justice Frankfurter spoke for the majority in holding that unreasonable state searches and seizures violated the Fourteenth Amendment's Due Process Clause. Frankfurter, however, avoided the issue of remedies and in fact allowed that evidence so seized could be used in a state trial for a state crime. As Justice Murphy wrote in dissent, "[T]he conclusion is inescapable that but one remedy exists to deter violations of the search and seizure clause. That is the rule which excludes illegally obtained evidence."[42]

In 1961 what appeared to be a First Amendment case came to the Court. Police officers attempted to gain entrance to the home of Dollree Mapp, because they had information that a person wanted in connection with a bombing was hiding there. She initially refused to allow them in without a warrant; three hours later they forced a door, waved a piece of paper they claimed was a warrant, but refused to let her read it. She grabbed the paper, and in the ensuing scuffle police manhandled and handcuffed her for, as Justice Clark noted in the Court's opinion, resisting the policemen's "official rescue of the 'warrant' from her person."[43] After subduing her, police searched her house and in a trunk in the basement found a cache of pornographic items. They arrested her for possession of obscene materials. The state courts conceded that there had probably never been a warrant, but the prosecution correctly claimed that under existing law, it could use evidence obtained by a warrantless, unreasonable search.

Although neither the state nor the appellant briefed or argued the exclusionary rule, the Court overruled *Wolf* 6-3 and held that the Fourteenth Amendment incorporated the Fourth Amendment and applied it to the states. It also applied the exclusionary rule remedy. Both the majority and the minority in *Mapp* agreed that the police had acted egregiously, but the three dissenters—Harlan, Frankfurter, and Whittaker—objected to imposing a federal judge-made rule on the states. The majority argued, however, as had Justice Day a half-century earlier, that the only remedy to violation of the Fourth Amendment—the only way to ensure that police did not act as they did in Dollree Mapp's home—was to deprive them of the fruits of an illegal search.[44]

There is general agreement that for the Fourth Amendment to be effective, there has to be some remedy for its violation.[45] This seemingly obvious conclusion is clouded, however, by the public's failure to understand why evidence that clearly establishes guilt cannot be used, and, as Justice Benjamin Cardozo once said, "the criminal is to go free because the constable has blundered."[46]

The exclusionary rule rests on several considerations. In *Mapp* the Court spelled out one of them, namely, that the only way to deter police from illegal searches is to deprive them of the evidence they obtain. Another has been described by Chief Justice Warren Burger as "the 'sporting contest' thesis that the government must 'play the game fairly' and cannot be allowed to profit from its own illegal acts."[47] Perhaps Justice Brandeis said it best in his dissent in the wiretapping case:

> Decency, security, and liberty alike demand that government officials shall be subject to the same rules of conduct that are commands to the citizen. Our government is the potent, the omnipresent teacher. For good or ill, it teaches the whole people by its example. If the government becomes a lawbreaker, it breeds contempt for the law; it invites every man to become a law unto himself; it invites anarchy.[48]

The exclusionary rule does limit police investigations, and it may make it more difficult to obtain proof and convict criminals, although evidence on this claim is inconclusive.[49] But as Justice Clark noted, "[N]othing can destroy a government more quickly than its failure to observe its own laws, or worse, its disregard of the charter of its own existence."[50]

THE SIXTH AMENDMENT AND THE RIGHT TO COUNSEL

We will temporarily put aside the Fifth Amendment, because in order to understand the Warren Court's interpretation of the right against self-incrimination, we must first examine its views on the right to counsel embedded in the Sixth Amendment.

At the time of the American Revolution, English common law gave an accused person the right to counsel in misdemeanor but not felony cases; that right did not come until 1836. In practice, however, it appears that English courts, even in the absence of an acknowledged right, permitted counsel to appear and to argue points of law and assist in the defense.[51] By the adoption of the Constitution, twelve of the original thirteen states had rejected the English practice and established a right to counsel in all criminal cases. They applied this right to the federal government in the Sixth Amendment, which provides that "in all criminal prosecutions, the accused shall enjoy the right . . . to have the Assistance of Counsel for his defence."

Even before ratification of the Bill of Rights, Congress began to implement this right. Section 35 of the Judiciary Act of 1789 provided that in all federal courts "the parties may plead and manage their own causes personally or by the assistance of such counsel or attorneys at law." The wording indicates a privilege extended to the parties, and not a requirement that counsel be appointed. The following year, however, in the Federal Crimes Act of 1790, Congress imposed a duty on federal courts to assign counsel in capital cases, and over the years the custom developed in most federal courts to appoint counsel for indigents in all serious cases.

In 1938 the Supreme Court held that the Sixth Amendment required counsel in all federal criminal proceedings, unless the defendant waived this right.[52] Whether a right to counsel existed in state courts depended for the most part on state law, although as a result of the infamous Scottsboro trial in 1931, the Court held that failure to provide effective counsel to indigents in capital cases violated their due process rights.[53] By relying on due process, the Court avoided the question of whether the Fourteenth Amendment incorporated the Sixth.

The Court faced this question directly a decade later in *Betts* v. *Brady* (1942), and by a divided vote decided that counsel for indigents did not constitute a fundamental right "implicit in the concept of ordered liberty" nor an essential element of a fair trial. The accused, according to the Court, "was not helpless, but was a man forty-three years old, of ordinary intelligence, and ability to take care of his own interests" at the trial.[54] The Court endorsed a case-by-case review with an emphasis on the totality of the circumstances. In situations involving illiterate defendants or complex legal questions, then due process required an attorney.

This approach proved enormously time-consuming, and despite hearing dozens of cases over the next two decades, the Court never established clear criteria to guide state judges in determining when counsel had to be provided. Moreover, it found special circumstances present in so many instances that by 1962 it had for all practical purposes eroded the *Betts* rule.[55] Finally, the justices decided to review the situation and accepted an appeal filed by an indigent, Clarence Earl Gideon, who had requested and been denied counsel in a Florida breaking-and-entering case. The Court named as his attorney an influential Washington lawyer and future member of the Court, Abe Fortas, and specifically requested both sides to argue whether *Betts* should be overruled.[56]

Not only had the *Betts* rule come under increasing criticism over the years, but also a number of states had voluntarily adopted the federal standard of providing counsel to indigents accused in felony trials. By 1962 forty-five states provided counsel for all or nearly all indigent felony defendants. Only five states—Alabama, Florida, Mississippi, North Carolina, and South Carolina—did not, and even there some cities and counties assigned attorneys to poor persons charged with serious crimes.[57] As the Court prepared to hear the Gideon case, only two states backed the Florida position that the Court ought to leave the rule alone; twenty-two states filed amicus briefs condemning *Betts* as "an anachronism when handed down" and asking that it be overruled.

The Court agreed, and Justice Black, who twenty years earlier had dissented in *Betts,* spoke for a unanimous bench in declaring that *Betts* had been wrongly decided.[58] Numerous cases in the intervening years had proven conclusively that one could not have a fair trial without assistance of counsel and that it therefore was "implicit in the concept of ordered liberty." The importance of counsel meant that the Fourteenth Amendment's Due Process Clause incorporated the Sixth Amendment right and applied it to the states. Moreover, the Court took the unusual step of applying *Gideon* retroactively, so that states which had originally not supplied counsel in felony cases now either had to retry the defendants properly or, as it often happened, with witnesses dispersed and evidence grown cold, let them go.[59]

Gideon applied only to felony cases; not until 1972 did the Burger Court extend the right to misdemeanor cases as well.[60] The Warren Court, however, did expand the right to counsel in two 1967 cases. In response to growing criticism over shoddy and unreliable police identification methods, the Court extended the right to counsel back to the lineup. As Justice Brennan explained, the Sixth Amendment requires counsel from the time the police shift their investigation from a general sifting of facts to accusing a particular person.[61] By this time Brennan could say that the Court had developed a set of precedents which agreed on the fact that the Sixth Amendment came into play at "critical" stages of criminal proceedings. In response to critics who claimed the Court had distorted the meaning of the right, he noted:

> When the Bill of Rights was adopted, there were no organized police forces as we know them today. The accused confronted the prosecutor and the witnesses against him, and the evidence was marshalled, largely at the trial itself. In contrast, today's law enforcement machinery involves critical confrontations of the accused by the prosecution at pretrial proceedings where the results might well settle the accused's fate and reduce the trial itself to a mere formality. . . . The plain wording of this guarantee [of counsel] thus encompasses counsel's assistance whenever necessary to assure a meaningful "defense."[62]

In other words, the Court would apply the spirit of the Sixth Amendment to ensure a comparable level of protection intended by the Framers in differing circumstances. That same Term the Court applied this reasoning to extend the right in the other direction, past the determination of guilt to the sentencing phase of a trial in *Mempa* v. *Rhay*.[63]

In the one case it heard dealing with right of counsel on appeal, the Warren Court decided the matter on equal protection rather than Sixth Amendment grounds. In California, convicted persons had one appeal as a matter of right, but the state did not provide counsel to indigents for appeal. The Court viewed denial of counsel on the basis of status, namely indigency, as discrimination violating the Fourteenth Amendment.[64] This reasoning followed the Court's logic in an earlier case, *Griffin* v. *Illinois* (1956),[65] in which it had ruled that the appeals process cannot be denied to convicted defendants because they have no money to purchase copies of the trial transcript.

THE FIFTH AMENDMENT AND THE GREAT PRIVILEGE

The Court's concern over providing accused persons with effective counsel at all critical stages of the proceedings carried over into its Fifth Amendment decisions. The right against compulsory self-incrimination had been established as a tenet of English common law by the end of the seventeenth century. The origins of the privilege are somewhat murky, but in English common law "the initially vague maxim that no man is bound to accuse himself had come to mean that he was not required to answer against himself in any criminal cause or to any interrogatories that might tend to expose him to persecution."[66] At about the same time, a rule also developed that forced confessions could not be used against a defendant because of their unreliability.

The colonists prized this right greatly, and by 1652 Massachusetts, Connecticut, and Virginia had provisions against the use of torture to force confessions. Following the Revolution, the patriot leader George Mason wrote into Virginia's Declaration of Rights that a man cannot "be compelled to give evidence against himself." Eight other states followed suit, and it later found its way into the federal Bill of Rights. The provision that no person "shall be compelled in any criminal case to be a witness against himself" is lodged in a miscellany of rights in the Fifth Amendment that bar double jeopardy, guarantee due process, and require just compensation for the taking of land. There has thus been a controversy over the original intent of the Framers, whether the privilege extends to just the accused, or to witnesses as well, and to what portions of the criminal proceedings.[67] As with so many other provisions of the Constitution and the Bill of Rights, the early records shed little light on precisely what the Framers intended. The few contemporary references seem to view it as a shield against torture.

The Fifth Amendment came into some disrepute during congressional hearings in the 1950s, in which witnesses suspected of Communist or criminal affiliations refused to answer and "took the Fifth." Aside from professional patriots who objected to people who might or might not be Communists availing themselves of constitutional protection, serious commentators also questioned the propriety of the rule. Judge Henry Friendly, a former Brandeis law clerk and certainly no reactionary, noted that the theory of the privilege seemed to run against everything that we taught our children, namely, that a clean breast of a misdeed is the best policy. "Every hour of the day people are being asked to explain their conduct to parents, employers and teachers." He believed that nearly all of the reasons used to justify the right, such as protection of the innocent, deterrence of perjury and improper police conduct, and privacy, could not be supported by the privilege or could be managed in a more effective manner.[68]

Despite such criticism, the Supreme Court from the beginning has interpreted the privilege broadly. In *Boyd* v. *United States* (1886),[69] the Court found the subpoenaing of business records to be equivalent to forcing a person to be a witness against himself. A few years later, the Court reaffirmed this broad view by holding that the privilege extended to grand jury investigations.[70]

The Fifth Amendment has never been interpreted to mean that the police have to make their case without any help from the accused. The defendant may not have to talk to police or to testify at his or her case, but he or she is required to give physical evidence, such as fingerprints or blood samples. Moreover, if a person wants to confess to a crime, or testify on their own behalf, they have a right to do so. The rule is that they cannot be coerced into giving oral evidence.

Although there are a number of facets to Fifth Amendment cases,[71] the question of confession caught the public's attention, and the Warren Court's most famous (or infamous) criminal procedure decisions came in this area. The essential issue in confession cases has always been whether confessions are truly voluntary, and therefore admissible as evidence, or if they have been coerced in violation of the defendant's rights.

From 1936 to 1964, the Court dealt with the issue of coercion on the basis of the Due Process Clauses of the Fifth and Fourteenth Amendments. In its first major case, the Court summarily reversed convictions in a state court based on confessions obtained through whippings.[72] The Court decided thirty-five confession cases between 1936 and 1964, and moved from the easy-to-resolve cases where confessions had been induced through physical coercion to the much harder issue of psychological coercion. The justices attempted to define appropriate limits on police behavior through a case-by-case process. In some of its early cases, the Warren Court showed its sensitivity to such factors as illiteracy[73] or limited education,[74] mental retardation[75] or incompetence,[76] or unnecessary delay in bringing a suspect before a magistrate,[77] all leading to a "totality of the circumstances" test to determine whether the confession had been voluntary and thus admissible.[78]

Some members of the Court found the case-by-case approach as unsatisfactory in Fifth Amendment confession cases as they had in the post-*Betts* counsel cases, and they believed that the voluntariness standard did not give police and lower courts sufficient guidance. The totality-of-the-circumstances standard appeared very subjective and caused confusion among trial and lower appellate court judges. In 1959 four members of the Warren Court pointed to the next phase of the evolving standard on confessions.

Vincent Spano had been arrested for murder, and although he repeatedly asked to see his attorney, who was in the police station, police refused his request and continued to interrogate him until he confessed. The Court unanimously threw out the confession as involuntary, on the grounds that his will had been "overborne by official pressure." Justice Douglas, joined by Justices Black, Brennan, and Stewart, concurred in the result, but suggested that the real issue had been that Spano had been unable to see his attorney, and raised the question of whether any confession given without proper legal advice could be considered voluntary.[79]

The question of counsel had been raised in a number of confession cases, mainly in relation to whether the accused knew or understood his rights. In one case, the Court sustained the conviction of a former law student, because he knew of his constitutional right to remain silent. Justice Douglas dissented, joined by Warren, Black, and Brennan, and claimed that

> [t]he mischief and abuse of the the third degree will continue as long as an accused can be denied the right to counsel at this the most critical period

of his ordeal. For what takes place in the secret confines of the police station may be more critical than what takes place at the trial.[80]

In 1964 the Court moved away from the due process totality-of-the-circumstances approach to confession and emphasized in its place the Sixth Amendment right to counsel. The shift occurred in *Massiah* v. *United States*,[81] a confusing case that some commentators believe to have been wrongly decided.

Winston Massiah, a merchant seaman, had been indicted along with Jesse Colson for attempting to smuggle cocaine into the United States. Massiah retained a lawyer and pleaded not guilty. Colson decided to cooperate with federal agents and agreed to have a radio transmitter placed in his car. He and Massiah subsequently had a long conversation in the car, which an agent monitored. The prosecution later used a number of incriminating statements made in that conversation against Massiah at his trial. Justice Stewart, for a 6-3 Court, held that use of the defendant's statements, obtained in a surreptitious manner *after* his indictment and retention of a lawyer, violated his Fifth Amendment rights against self-incrimination. Justice White, joined by Clark and Harlan, dissented, saying that the Court had no reason to scrap the voluntary/involuntary test and had not substituted another test in its place.[82]

Although nominally a Fifth Amendment case, *Massiah* is the intersection between the Court's developing Fifth and Sixth Amendment doctrines. Just as the various First Amendment guarantees cannot always be neatly differentiated, so the bundle of rights granted to accused persons are also closely interwoven. *Massiah* applied to the states as well as to the federal government, but what did it mean other than that the police could not utilize a defendant's statements "after indictment and in the absence of counsel"? Was the timing at all important? Why should it matter if police surveillance secured incriminating statements before or after indictment? The Court did not, in fact, indicate when it considered a defendant formally charged.

A little later in the Term, the Court decided a case that, unlike *Massiah*, clearly involved abusive and illegal behavior by the Chicago police. Danny Escobedo had been taken into custody and interrogated about the fatal shooting of his brother-in-law. He repeatedly asked to see his attorney, who was in the station house, and the attorney repeatedly asked to see his client. The police refused to allow the two to meet until after Escobedo had made statements incriminating himself in the shooting. The police charged him and only then allowed him access to his attorney.

In *Massiah*, the Court had not given a clear indication of when a defendant is considered formally charged and in custody and thus within the protective reach of the Fifth Amendment. In *Escobedo* v. *Illinois* (1964),[83] the Court rejected the state's claim that a person must be formally charged before he or she can avail themselves of counsel. In this case, Justice Goldberg noted that when Escobedo "requested, and was denied, an opportunity to consult with his lawyer, the investigation had ceased to be a general investigation of an 'unsolved crime.' Petitioner had become the accused." The fact that there had been no formal charge made no difference; once a suspect is treated as if accused, then he or she must have all the rights afforded to accused persons. Goldberg anticipated much of the criticism that the decision aroused, and his response indicates the emphasis the Warren Court placed on protection of rights and fairness in the criminal justice system:

> It is argued that if the right to counsel is afforded prior to indictment, the number of confessions obtained by the police will diminish significantly, because most confessions are obtained during the period between arrest and indictment, [and] "any lawyer worth his salt will tell the suspect in no uncertain terms to make no statement to police under any circumstances." . . . This argument, of course, cuts two ways. The fact that many confessions are obtained during this period points up its critical nature as a "stage when legal aid and advice" are surely needed. The right to counsel would indeed be hollow if it began at a period when few confessions were obtained. There is necessarily a direct relationship between the importance of a stage to the police in their quest for a confession and the criticalness of that stage to the accused in his need for legal advice. Our Constitution, unlike some others, strikes the balance in favor of the right of the accused to be advised by his lawyer of his privilege against self-incrimination.[84]

Most of this rationale dealt with the right to counsel, a Sixth Amendment right, and only at the end did Justice Goldberg mention the Fifth Amendment right against self-incrimination. The Court had gradually come to see the close connection between the two and realized that accused persons, often confused after police took them into custody, needed legal advice in order to exercise their Fifth Amendment right. Confessions need not be extracted by physical coercion to be involuntary; modern psychological methods could be just as effective in overbearing one's will.

Despite the sweeping language just quoted, the actual holding in *Escobedo* proved fairly narrow.[85] When police took a person into custody for interrogation about a particular crime, and the suspect requested counsel, then counsel had to be provided and given access to the client, or else statements taken in the interrogation could not be used against the suspect.[86] But what if the suspect were illiterate, or did not know his or her rights, or had become confused by the stationhouse procedures and failed to ask for counsel? These considerations did not appear to bother the dissenters in *Escobedo*—Justices Harlan, Stewart (author of the majority opinion in *Massiah*), Clark, and White. Their emphasis seemed to be that so long as the government did not use physical coercion and in the end allowed people to choose what to do, it could discourage people from exercising their rights. The majority of the Court took a different view—that the government had an obligation to nurture constitutional rights and to encourage its citizens to exercise those rights.

Law enforcement officials reacted predictably to *Escobedo*. The police chief of Los Angeles declared that "allegations that modern criminal investigation can compensate for the lack of a confession or admission in every criminal case are totally absurd!" Michael Murphy, the former New York City police chief, complained that "what the Court is doing is akin to requiring one boxer to fight by the Marquis of Queensbury rules while permitting the other to butt, gouge and bite." Prosecutors, however, seemed far less alarmed. The Los Angeles district attorney said that the apparently "restrictive" decisions would actually make police more professional, efficient, and effective. As for charges that the Court decisions coddled criminals and encouraged crime, David C. Acheson, the assistant secretary of the treasury in charge of the Secret Service and Bureau of Narcotics, said that "changes in court decisions and prosecution procedure would have about the same effect on the crime rate as an aspirin would have on a tumor of the brain."[87]

That same Term, the Court ruled that the Fifth Amendment right against self-incrimination is applicable to the states through the Fourteenth Amendment.[88] The Court had now moved from the due process concept of voluntariness as the standard for confessions to the belief that presence of counsel at the accusatory stage determined whether a confession had been properly obtained. All of these decisions, however, lacked precision; they lacked a bright-line test that would tell police, prosecutors, and trial and appellate judges whether constitutional standards had been violated or observed. What if police suspected a person and bore down heavily in their preliminary questioning, eliciting incriminating statements that they then used as a basis for indictment? The police always had an advantage in such situations and could deliberately confuse a person and trick him or her into confessing, before the suspect realized or knew that a lawyer ought to be there. Where did one draw the line between good police investigation and improper procedures?

The Warren Court tried to answer these questions and provide a simple standard in its most vilified criminal procedure case, *Miranda* v. *Arizona* (1966).[89] Although the final holding, expressed in the famous "*Miranda* warnings," was clear, Chief Justice Warren's majority opinion rambled all over the constitutional landscape, occasionally lapsing into specifics but for the most part getting lost in generalities. His opinion made an all too easy target for critics, a "self-inflicted wound" in Fred Graham's phrase.

In essence, the *Miranda* majority identified coercion in any form as the chief problem in determining the validity of confessions. Rather than proceed on a case-by-case basis attempting to evaluate the totality of the circumstances, the Court handed down definite rules to guide police and lower courts. If the rules had been obeyed and the suspect confessed, then that confession would be admissible as evidence. If police failed to obey the rules, then the confession would be thrown out.

The police had to inform a person in clear and unequivocal terms that he or she had a right to remain silent; that anything said could be used in court; that the accused had a right to a lawyer; and that if he or she had no money, the state would provide a lawyer. If the interrogation continued without the presence of an attorney, "a heavy burden rests on the Government to demonstrate that the defendant knowingly and intelligently waives his privilege against self-incrimination and the right to counsel."[90]

Miranda, despite the objections of the four dissenting members, is a logical culmination of the Warren Court's journey in search of a workable method to deal with the issue of forced confessions. It started out with the premise of earlier courts—that physical coercion could not be allowed and that an evaluation of the totality of the circumstances would determine whether due process had been violated. At the same time, the Court had been developing a broader interpretation of the Sixth Amendment right to counsel, and these doctrines coalesced in the *Massiah* and *Escobedo* rulings that if suspects asked for but had been denied counsel, then confessions under such circumstances had to be considered involuntary because they had been coerced. In *Miranda* these various strands came together in the belief that for rights to be meaningful, a suspect must know about them *before* interrogation begins, a process in which the physical and psychological advantage resides with the police. As Warren explained, police custody and interrogation contain "inherently compelling pressures which work to undermine the individual's will to resist and to compel him to speak where he would not do so freely."[91]

Because *Miranda* merged self-incrimination and confession law, and tied them to the right to counsel, it did depart from the due process analytical framework that had been the norm until the mid-1960s. Many critics, including the dissenters, characterized this as a radical departure from accepted doctrine. But the earlier due process, totality-of-the-circumstances rulings had never been all that clear, and one can certainly chart the seeds of *Miranda* in decisions reaching back nearly eight decades.[92]

In *Miranda* the Court tried to do two separate things. First, it wanted to establish a prophylactic rule to aid judicial review. While it is still possible to have a tainted confession even if the warning is given, the failure to inform suspects of their rights is a clear indicator that the confession should not be admitted. Some state and local police departments, who had never paid scrupulous attention to constitutional protection, did run into methodological problems following the decision.[93] Once they adopted the *Miranda* warning as part of their standard procedures, they discovered that it did not undermine their effectiveness; in many cases, the accused wanted to confess and could hardly wait for the police to finish reading them their rights.[94]

The second aspect of the decision reflected the Warren majority's view that in a democracy, with rights embedded in a written Constitution, all people had to be aware of those rights so that, if faced by police interrogation, they could make voluntary and intelligent choices. One should recall that few secondary school systems taught much in the way of law prior to 1966, and not many people knew what rights they had. This situation has changed considerably in the last two decades, with nearly all states adopting Constitution and law segments in their public school social-studies guidelines.

The Chief Justice no doubt anticipated that the *Miranda* decision would evoke strong criticism, and he tried to point out that the states remained free to experiment with how they implemented the basic procedural safeguards the Court now required. "Our decision in no way creates a constitutional straight-jacket," he declared. "We encourage Congress and the states to continue their laudable search for increasingly effective ways of protecting the rights of the individual while promoting efficient enforcement of our criminal law."[95]

The level of response had been anticipated in Justice White's dissent that the new rule would have the effect of "returning a killer, a rapist, or other criminal to the streets to repeat his crime whenever it pleases him."[96] Herman Talmadge of Georgia rose on the Senate floor to charge that the ruling virtually banned "effective police interrogation." In Senate hearings later in the year, Sam Irvin declared that the Court had "stressed individual rights" at the expense of public safety, and he introduced a constitutional amendment to overrule the *Miranda* decision and to withdraw from Supreme Court review all rulings of trial judges, state or federal, admitting confessions into evidence. The uproar over *Miranda* continued for the remainder of Earl Warren's tenure, affected provisions of the 1968 Omnibus Crime Control Act, and played a role in that year's presidential election.[97]

CONCLUSIONS

The Warren Court's criminal procedure decisions have often been described as "revolutionary." In terms of incorporation, it applied to the states the Fourth Amendment rules on search and seizure;[98] the Fifth Amendment's guarantees on double jeopardy[99] and self-incrimination;[100] Sixth Amendment provisions on a speedy trial,[101] a jury trial in criminal cases,[102] confrontation of witnesses,[103] compulsory process to secure witnesses,[104] and assistance of counsel;[105] and the Eighth Amendment ban against cruel and unusual punishment.[106] Although the debate over incorporation had been going on for several decades, the Warren Court not only greatly expanded the application of the Bill of Rights, but by adopting strict rules on search warrants, electronic surveillance, illegally seized evidence, assistance of counsel, and police interrogation, it put teeth into these guarantees as well. As Archibald Cox noted,

"Never has there been such a thorough-going reform of criminal procedure within so short a time. Nearly all the changes benefit the accused."[107]

Yet to charge the Warren Court with coddling criminals and ignoring society's needs for effective police work is to distort the meaning of the Constitution and to ignore the fact that the Court more often than not took a common-sensical approach in striking a balance between individual rights and public order. One should not forget that Earl Warren had begun his political career as a district attorney and then attorney general of California; he knew, more than many of the justices, the problems of law enforcement.[108] Despite the many cries that police would be hampered in their work, all the empirical studies of the effect of the exclusionary rule, warrant requirements, and the *Miranda* warnings indicate that investigation and prosecution have not suffered, as police have become more efficient and professional.[109]

Beyond that, one can point to specific cases that either supported the police or modified some of the broader strokes in the better known rulings. Although the Court overruled *Olmstead* and held wiretapping to violate the Fourth Amendment, it did not ban all electronic surveillance. Rather, it did little more than require police to justify a warrant for an electronic search of the home in the same way they had to for a physical search. Moreover, in an opinion handed down a few months before *Katz*, the Court modified the longstanding proscription against the police gathering "mere evidence" as opposed to specific material.[110] Although the *Berger* ruling struck down a state wiretap law, the Court in *Katz* cleared the way for the states and the federal government to establish warrant procedures for electronic surveillance.

While the Court imposed the exclusionary rule on the states in *Mapp* (1961), seven years later in *Terry* it made a significant exception by approving the widespread police practice of stopping and frisking people without a warrant, for no other reason than that they looked suspicious. The exclusionary rule, the Court admitted, "has its limitations . . . as a tool of judicial control."[111] As criminal law specialist Yale Kamisar suggests, had this decision been delayed a few years, it would have been deemed as solid evidence of a changing judicial philosophy, hailed by opponents of the Warren Court and lamented by its admirers.[112]

To take another example, the Court ruled that just citing an unnamed informant as a source did not provide sufficient cause for a warrant, but it upheld the government's privilege to withhold the identity of an informant, even when this seemed to violate the Sixth Amendment's Confrontation Clause.[113] Moreover, by failing to establish clear standards on the use of informants, the Court compromised some of the strict rules it had established governing the issuance of warrants.

Even in regard to *Miranda*, the most vilified of the Warren Court decisions in this area, the Court never intended, as its critics claimed, to kill off confessions. It did set up a prophylactic rule, but it still left police a great deal of leeway. For example, custody alone did not trigger the *Miranda* warning, and so long as the police did not initiate questioning, they could use a variety of psychological devices, such as the long ride to the station house, to hear and act upon "voluntary" confessions. Had the Court been serious in its desire to have all persons fully cognizable of their rights, it would have required that a suspect either have a lawyer present or have consulted with one before any statement could be deemed voluntary.

Sometimes, it would seem, change does not come in a gradual, evolutionary process, but in fits and starts, a sort of Hegelian series of advances, retreats, and then syntheses that move on ahead. The Warren Court's major decisions greatly expanded the reach of the Bill of Rights, and despite continued criticism by conservatives that the Fourteenth Amendment does not incorporate those guarantees, it is unlikely that those decisions will be reversed. As for the implementation of rights, the judicial rules that the Court expounded would of necessity be open to change. In some instances the Court made too sweeping a statement, and even before 1969 it began to modify and draw back. We now turn to whether the Burger Court rejected these rules or continued the modification process already begun by its predecessor.

8

"The Time Has Come to Modify the . . . Rule"

The Burger Court and Criminal Procedure

By 1968, public opinion polls indicated a growing resentment against the supposedly pro-criminal, anti-police rulings of the Warren Court, and Title II of the Omnibus Crime Control Act of that year specifically attempted to limit a number of those decisions.[1] The Republican candidate for the presidency, Richard M. Nixon, attacked the Court's alleged activism and charged that "some of our judges have gone too far in assuming unto themselves a mandate which is not there, and that is, to put their social and economic ideas into their decisions." To southerners who still smarted over the Court's civil rights decisions, and to law-and-order advocates who believed Warren & Co. coddled criminals, Nixon promised to name "strict constructionists" to the bench.[2]

The new chief whom Nixon appointed had been a critic of Warren Court activism, and especially of its decisions in criminal procedure. In a 1967 speech, then Circuit Court Judge Warren Burger complained that criminal trials took too long with subsequent execution of justice delayed by too many appeals, retrials, and other procedures devised by the courts. The American criminal justice system tilted toward the criminal, and that had to be remedied.[3] The addition of the three other Nixon appointees in the next few years all pointed to a significant shift away from the Warren Court's concern for the rights of the accused.

THE "THREE" BURGER COURTS

Yale Kamisar, writing in 1982, distinguished at least two Burger Courts. The "first" one "gutted the Warren Court's 'lineup decisions,' soon dealt heavy blows to the Fourth Amendment, appeared to be stalking the exclusionary rule, and seemed to be laying the groundwork to overrule *Miranda*." The later

Burger Court reinvigorated many Warren Court rules, and as Kamisar (a self-described Warren Court supporter) concluded, "the fears that the Burger Court would dismantle the work of the Warren Court (or the Bill of Rights itself) . . . seem to have been considerably exaggerated."[4] Then, with the retirement of Justice Potter Stewart in 1981 and his replacement by Sandra Day O'Connor, a "third" Burger Court emerged which, in legal scholar Wayne LaFave's words, "was hell-bent to seize any available opportunity to define more expansively the constitutional authority of law enforcement officials."[5]

Each Term the Burger Court heard many cases involving criminal procedure (in the 1972 Term it handed down ten opinions, 5.6 percent of the total, on Fourth Amendment issues alone), and it would be impossible to track every decision over seventeen years. So we must look at a few key issues to see whether the Burger Court trifurcated itself and whether, at the end of its tenure, the rights of the accused had been significantly reduced from the level established by the Warren Court. To do this, we can begin with the categories mentioned by Kamisar as particular targets of the Burger Court majority—line-ups, the Fourth Amendment, the exclusionary rule, and *Miranda*.

IDENTIFICATION PROCEDURES

There had been little protest when the Warren Court handed down its landmark decision in *Gideon* v. *Wainwright*, extending the right to counsel to indigents in state court proceedings. Nearly half of the states already provided counsel, and legislatures in the remaining states responded quickly with public defender laws and other necessary measures. When the Court extended the right to counsel in both federal and state proceedings to pretrial hearings, appeals, and juvenile proceedings, Congress and the state legislatures complied with little protest.[6]

The Warren Court, as it demonstrated in a number of cases, wanted to make counsel available in criminal cases as early as possible, so that persons accused of crimes could exercise their constitutional right at key points in the process. As the Court pointed out, lack of counsel in the accusatory stage of the investigation could well determine what happened at the trial. In 1967 the Court addressed one of these critical stages in *United States* v. *Wade*[7] and *Gilbert* v. *California*[8] and by a 5-4 vote extended the right to counsel back to lineups.

Lineups, in which victims and eyewitnesses to events are asked to identify one suspect from a group, have long been a staple in police investigation, as has been the practice of showing witnesses pictures of suspects. The problem is that, as the Court noted in *Wade*, "the vagaries of eyewitness identification are well-known; the annals of criminal law are rife with instances of mistaken identification."[9] While identifying a criminal is an important part of police investigation, reliance upon eyewitness testimony is considered by many criminologists the least reliable method of identification. Long ago Felix Frankfurter summed up the case when he declared that "the identification of strangers is proverbially untrustworthy. The hazards of such testimony are established by a formidable number of instances in the records of English and American trials."[10]

While in earlier cases the Warren Court had addressed problems of unjust procedures, such as forced confessions, in *Wade* and *Gilbert* the justices confronted this problem of unreliability. They did so with practically no prior case law on the subject, and it may well be the Warren Court's most flagrant example of "making law" in the area of criminal procedure. While the majority decisions are, as Fred Graham noted, "riddled with inconsistencies and easily debunked," he predicted the cases might well prove the Court's "most successful excursion into the criminal law." Graham, who wrote in 1970, was far from a fan of the Warren Court's criminal decisions, yet he believed:

> The new rules have cost almost nothing in terms of law-enforcement efficiency, yet they could eventually generate a long-overdue review of the faulty methods of identification that are in common use in the United States. They could become one of the most successful examples of the Supreme Court as Teacher, for it could encourage the law-enforcement establishment and the legal profession to reduce avoidable errors that contribute to that most tragic of all malfunctions of justice—the conviction of innocent men.[11]

Although some police departments moved quickly to adopt new procedures, others saw this as but one more example of the Warren Court's "pro-criminal" attitude. When the Senate held hearings on the nomination of Abe Fortas to be Chief Justice, several senators pointed out *Wade* and *Gilbert* as evidence of the Court's hampering of the police.[12]

The Warren Court decisions seemed to establish a per se rule that at any lineup counsel had to be present. Even in cases that appear to establish major rules, however, further adjudication is necessary to fill in details. This gives the Court an opportunity to make adjustments, correct misunderstandings, or if it desires, to cut back on too expansive a reading of its holding. Because *Wade* and *Gilbert* had come near the end of Earl Warren's tenure, cases testing the limits of pretrial right to counsel did not reach the Court until the 1971 Term, by which time the four Nixon appointees had taken their seats.

In *Kirby* v. *Illinois* (1972),[13] Justice Stewart (who had partially dissented in the earlier cases) spoke for a 5-4 Court in holding that the right to counsel only applied to lineups after a defendant had been indicted or otherwise formally charged. Police could utilize lineups without counsel present at an investigatory stage, a lineup which the Court did not consider a "critical stage" in the criminal justice system. Stewart spoke for himself, Chief Justice Burger, and Justices Blackmun and Rehnquist. He got his majority when Justice Powell concurred in the result, solely on the grounds that he did not want to "extend the *Wade–Gilbert* per se exclusionary rule."

The decision brought forth a strong dissent by Justice Brennan, joined by Douglas and Marshall, who pointed out that the earlier cases had not been governed by the question of timing but rather by the general unreliability of lineup identification. Justice White, who had also partially dissented in *Wade* and *Gilbert*, dissented here on the basis of stare decisis and believed those decisions should govern.

The plurality opinion did not fare well among academic commentators. One wrote that it could not be squared with *Wade* and *Gilbert*, "at least in any principled way."[14] Another condemned it as "wrong from every perspective. The opinion reads precedent so badly that it appears intellectually dishonest."[15] The lineups in *Wade* and *Gilbert* had taken place after indictment, and the Court's opinion had mentioned it, but neither the majority nor the dissenters had considered that a decisive feature.

Timing in some cases may be critical in triggering a constitutional right, and in fact a year earlier the Burger Court had ruled that the right to a speedy trial did not begin until the defendant had been accused, either by formal charges or by arrest.[16] How the Court could then decide that the right to counsel began at a different time is inexplicable. Moreover, the unreliability of lineups, the key consideration in the Warren Court decisions, remains the same whether they take place before or after indictment. *Kirby* allowed police to manipulate the early accusatory stages so that they could arrange lineups without counsel for suspects they already intended to charge. The ruling also signaled lower-court judges, many of whom disagreed with the general tenor of the Warren Court decisions, that they could cut back on rights accorded to the accused.

Later in the Term the Court also signaled a greater tolerance for suggestive procedures in witness identification. A suggestive procedure is one in which the witness or victim is shown only one suspect or one picture, leading him or her to believe that that person is the culprit. The Warren Court had considered such procedures in *Stovall* v. *Denno*,[17] a decision handed down the same day as *Wade* and *Gilbert*, and while it upheld Stovall's conviction, declared that suggestive identification procedures violated due process rights.

The Burger Court first faced the question in *Neil* v. *Biggers* (1972),[18] where the defendant had been convicted of rape after the victim identified him both out of the court and later at the trial. Archie Biggers claimed the earlier identification had been suggestive and violated his due process rights. Following the rape, the victim had looked at pictures and viewed lineups for seven months without identifying her assailant. One day the police arrested Biggers on a different charge and, because he fit the general description of the rapist, arranged for the victim to view another lineup. However, they could find no one of similar physique in either the city jail or the juvenile home, so they brought him in alone, walked him past the woman, and had him utter certain words. The victim identified him as the man who had raped her.

In his opinion for the Court, Justice Powell summed up the previous identification cases as holding "that the primary evil to be avoided is 'a very substantial likelihood of irreparable misidentification.' " He then went on to ask whether unnecessary suggestiveness by itself required exclusion of evidence, but avoided answering it, by noting that the only purpose of an affirmative answer "would be to deter the police from using a less reliable procedure where a more reliable one may be available."[19] Powell ignored two of the basic premises of the earlier cases: the general unreliability of eyewitness identifications and the need to balance the government's need for procedures that would prompt witness memories against the risks of those procedures. Here the Court assumed that the victim had been a good eyewitness and therefore had made a reliable identification. Powell ignored the thread that ran throughout the earlier cases, the worry that even good eyewitnesses do not make good identifications.

A year later, in *United States* v. *Ash*, the Court ruled that photographic identification can take place without defense counsel's participation, either before or after formal charging, and whether or not a suspect could have appeared in person at a lineup.[20] The problem in not having counsel present at photographic sessions is that the police may use suggestive procedures which would lead a confused witness or victim to identify a person the police already suspect. But Justice Blackmun described the right to counsel as a defendant's right to have a spokesperson or advisor, and because the accused is not present at the photographic sessions, then a spokesperson or advisor is not required.

Although the Court remanded the case for further consideration, Blackmun's opinion paid practically no attention to the dangers of misidentification or suggestive procedure considered in the earlier cases. The Court in *Kirby*, *Biggers*, and *Ash* shifted the emphasis away from the *Wade–Gilbert* desire to ensure the reliability of identification procedures, and in its place erected a vague totality-of-circumstances due process standard aimed at eliminating only the worst kind of suggestiveness.

This shift became clearer in a 1977 case, *Manson* v. *Brathwaite*.[21] There Justice Blackmun noted that the Courts of Appeal had adopted two different approaches to suggestive and unnecessary identification procedures. The Second Circuit had adopted a per se rule, excluding any identification evidence, regardless of reliability, if it had been obtained using unnecessarily suggestive procedures. Other circuits had adopted a more lenient attitude that judged the totality of the circumstances and allowed in evidence identifications that could be considered reliable despite suggestiveness. While Blackmun conceded that many reputable scholars, as well as the ALI Model Code of Pre-Arraignment Procedures (1975), frowned upon single-photo suggestive procedures, the

Court believed the ad hoc balancing test better and "that reliability is the linchpin in determining the admissibility of identification testimony." Trial courts should balance

> the opportunity of the witness to view the criminal at the time of the crime, the witness' degree of attention, the accuracy of his prior description of the criminal, the level of certainty demonstrated at the confrontation, and the time between the crime and the confrontation. Against these factors is to be weighed the corrupting effect of the suggestive identification itself.[22]

The Burger Court thus completed its narrowing or, as some would prefer, its dismantling of the Warren Court's efforts to deal with the generally recognized problem of unreliable identifications. While postindictment lineups are still governed by the *Wade–Gilbert* rule,[23] preindictment lineups are not, and police are free to arrange this stage of their investigation to avoid the per se rule. Counsel need not be present at photo sessions, which are judged only by an ad hoc evaluation of fairness in the totality of the circumstances but with no specific rules regarding avoidance of suggestiveness. *Manson* abandoned the outright ban against suggestiveness in *Stovall*, and replaced it with an ad hoc reliability standard. Thus many of the earlier procedural safeguards have been discarded, if the prosecution can show that the witness made a reliable identification without undue suggestiveness from the police. Nearly all criminologists condemn the unreliability of such identifications, so it is not surprising to find Yale Kamisar lamenting these decisions as "the saddest chapter in modern American criminal procedure."[24]

EXTENDING THE RIGHT OF COUNSEL

One has to be careful, however, in drawing such a blanket indictment. The lineup cases are part of the Court's interpretation of the Sixth Amendment right to counsel, as is a decision denying the right to court-appointed counsel in discretionary appeals.[25] On the other hand, the Burger Court in several cases has extended the right to counsel. In 1970, using the "critical stages" analysis introduced by the Warren Court, the Court held that a preliminary hearing (in which a magistrate determines whether there is sufficient evidence against an accused to present to a grand jury and to fix bail) constituted a critical stage and required appointment of counsel.[26] Two years later in *Argersinger* v. *Hamlin*, all the members of the Court agreed that counsel had to be provided in misdemeanor cases when the punishment involved imprisonment. In a plurality opinion, Justice Douglas set out a clear rule: "Absent a knowing and intelligent waiver, no person may be imprisoned for any offense, whether classified as petty, misdemeanor, or felony, unless he was represented by counsel at his trial."[27]

Argersinger left open the question of whether counsel would be required in cases where imprisonment for an offense may be authorized by statute, but not actually imposed on the defendant. In *Scott* v. *Illinois* (1979),[28] Justice Rehnquist, for a 5-4 majority, held that counsel need not be appointed in cases in which imprisonment would not be imposed. Where courts had discretion over the penalty, a decision not to provide counsel precluded a jail sentence as punishment. The majority took the view that the nature of the punishment triggered the right to counsel; the minority of Justices Brennan, Marshall, Stevens, and Blackmun believed the key issue was not punishment but the fairness of a trial, which could only be assured by the presence of counsel.

The Court, in its role as overseer of the nation's courts, fine-tuned the Sixth Amendment right to counsel in a number of cases that often involved technical questions. In *Faretta* v. *California* (1975),[29] the Court overruled a trial court decision that a defendant had no constitutional right to conduct his own defense and, over the defendant's objections, appointed an attorney to represent him. Provided a person can make a voluntary, intelligent, and knowing decision, the high court ruled, he or she may choose to waive counsel.

Three years later the Court dealt with a related issue, the right to *effective* counsel. Not only must a person entitled to an attorney have access to counsel, but the lawyer must also provide an acceptable level of legal assistance. In *Holloway* v. *Arkansas*,[30] a court-appointed attorney for three co-defendants in a rape and robbery case asked the judge, before the trial began, to appoint separate counsel for each defendant because of a possible conflict of interest resulting from information he had received from one of the defendants. The judge refused without making any effort to determine whether the potential conflict might affect the fairness of the trial. The attorney renewed his request at the trial, and again the judged denied the request. As a result, two of the defendants gave unguided direct testimony without the benefit of questioning by their own attorney. The Supreme Court reversed the convictions and remanded the case for a new trial, with Chief Justice Burger admonishing the trial judge for depriving the defendants of their Sixth Amendment right to the effective assistance of counsel.

The question of effective assistance of counsel arose again in *United States* v. *Cronic*[31] in 1984, a period in the Burger Court history when it supposedly adopted a tougher, antidefendant stance. Harrison Cronic and two others had been indicted on mail fraud charges resulting from a four-year investigation by the Justice Department. Shortly before the trial began, the attorney Cronic had retained withdrew, and the court appointed a young lawyer with a real estate practice to defend him and gave him twenty-five days for pretrial preparation. The two co-defendants testified for the government, and the jury found Cronic guilty on eleven of thirteen counts.

The Court of Appeals reversed without citing any specific errors of the counsel or making any claim that he failed to exercise proper judgment or diligence in defending his client. The court assumed that no such evidence is required "when circumstances hamper a given lawyer's preparation of a defendant's case."[32] Speaking for a unanimous bench, Justice Stevens agreed, and his opinion recited the history of the Court's interpretation of the Sixth Amendment to ensure fair trials through adequate representation. The mere presence of a lawyer was not enough, a rule that went back to the Court's earliest decisions in this area, notably *Powell* v. *Alabama*, the Scottsboro case in 1932.[33] Stevens's review of the Burger Court's record showed the importance it had attached to effective counsel:

> The special value of the right to the assistance of counsel explains why "[i]t has long been recognized that the right to counsel is the right to the effective assistance of counsel." *McMann* v. *Richardson* (1970). The text of the Sixth Amendment itself suggests as much. The Amendment requires not merely the provision of counsel to the accused, but "Assistance," which is to be "for his defense." Thus, "the core purpose of the counsel guarantee was to assure 'Assistance' at trial, when the accused was confronted with both the intricacies of the law and the advocacy of the public prosecutor." *United States* v. *Ash* (1973). If no actual "Assistance" "for" the accused's "defense" is provided, then the constitutional guarantee has been violated. . . .
>
> Thus, in *McMann* the Court indicated that the accused is entitled to "a reasonably competent attorney," whose advice is "within the range of competence demanded of attorneys in criminal cases." In *Cuyler* v. *Sullivan* (1980), we held that the Constitution guarantees an accused "adequate legal assistance." And in *Engle* v. *Isaac* (1982), the Court referred to the criminal defendant's constitutional guarantee of "a fair trial and a competent attorney."[34]

The Court had declined to be overly specific in defining what is meant by "effective assistance,"[35] but as the cases cited by Stevens showed, it had been concerned about the role attorneys played in ensuring fair trials. The emphasis on fairness at the trial stage may explain in part the apparent discrepancy between those Burger Court decisions on counsel in which it showed as much solicitude for Sixth Amendment rights as did its predecessor and those in which it restricted the right to counsel, especially in lineups and in discretionary appeals.

Legal theorist Herbert Packer described two competing models of law enforcement. The Due Process Model emphasizes procedural rights with a focus on the trial; the Crime Control Model emphasizes the efficient processing of cases, so that criminals, once apprehended, are brought to trial promptly, their cases heard in a timely manner, and if found guilty, their sentences executed forthwith. "If the Crime Control Model resembles an assembly line," Packer noted, "the Due Process Model looks very much like an obstacle course."[36] Prior to the 1960s, state criminal justice systems overwhelmingly favored the Crime Control Model, usually at the expense of individual rights. One way to understand the Warren Court is to concede that it went well over to the Due Process Model in an effort to mitigate the manifold abuses in the system.

The Burger Court did not abandon the Due Process Model but rather sought a balance between the two models. For the Burger Court, the essence of constitutional protection lay in the trial stage, beginning with the preliminary hearing and concluding with the first right of appeal. Here the accused had to be accorded the full range of rights guaranteed in the Fifth and Sixth Amendments, and the Court proved zealous in its insistence on trial courts carrying out the spirit as well as the letter of the law.

But the Burger Court viewed pre- and post-trial procedures in a different light. In accord with then-Judge Burger's views that too many of the Warren Court decisions favored the criminal's interests over those of society, he and his colleagues tended to give police more leeway in their investigative work, to shift the balance somewhat back toward the Crime Control Model. Police ought to be able to carry out as extensive an investigation as possible, so that at the trial the state would have the opportunity to make the strongest case it could, while the defendant would be equally prepared and equipped to argue his or her innocence. We can see this effort to "rebalance" the scales in the Burger Court's Fourth Amendment and exclusionary rule decisions.

SEARCH AND SEIZURE

While police learned to live with some of the Warren Court's prophylactic rules, they continued to object to what they saw as the Court's overly rigid requirements for securing a warrant as well as the limits on what they could search. As Potter Stewart once noted, the Court's rules on evidence could be restricted one of two ways: either the scope of the constitutional protection could be shrunk, or the circumstances surrounding search and seizure could be interpreted more liberally to give police greater leeway.[37] Because it is politically difficult for any court to shrink constitutional protections once announced, the most feasible way for the Burger Court to rein in the supposed excesses of the Warren Court was to reinterpret Fourth Amendment issues.

Where the Warren Court had preferred per se rules, the Burger majority from the start favored a "totality of the circumstances" approach in which it overlooked or forgave particular transgressions of the Fourth Amendment if, after taking all factors into account, the defendant had not been unduly prejudiced. The totality-of-the-circumstances approach does not, of course, always work against the accused, but it certainly gives the police and prosecution more leeway than they would enjoy under strict per se rules.

A recurring Fourth Amendment issue is the legitimacy of the search warrant: Have the police met all of the procedural rules and provided sufficient evidence to justify issuance of a warrant on probable cause? In the *Aguilar* and *Spinelli* decisions, the Warren Court had erected rigid criteria for evaluating warrant applications.[38] From the beginning, the Burger Court tended to take a more flexible approach, as in *United States* v. *Harris* (1971).[39] In this transitional period, Burger and Blackmun joined with Black, Stewart, and White to relax the *Spinelli* rule against uncorroborated hearsay, providing the magistrate, employing common sense, believed sufficient cause existed to issue the warrant. As the Chief Justice wrote, "The issue in warrant proceedings is not guilt beyond reasonable doubt but probable cause for believing the occurrence of a crime and the secreting of evidence in specific premises."[40]

In terms of specific doctrine, *Harris* hardly repudiated *Spinelli* and in fact addressed only one issue, that of reputation evidence. It is difficult to determine if the majority agreed totally on what it had decided, because the four justices who joined with Burger each filed a separate concurring opinion setting forth different reasons for their conclusions. Harlan, along with Douglas, Brennan, and Marshall, filed a powerful dissent that made a far better logical argument than did that of the Chief Justice. He pointed out that under the majority view, the magistrate had little to guide him or her in evaluating hearsay evidence. Perhaps, as Stephen Saltzburg notes, "to the extent that Supreme Court opinions have symbolic value above and beyond their value as statements of the law to those most directly affected by them, *Harris* must have soothed some of the nerves frayed by *Spinelli*."[41] The lesson of *Harris* to the police seemed to be that if you tell the magistrate what you know, where you got your information, and why the magistrate should trust you, you can probably get a warrant.

One should also recall that the Warren Court, while it did hand down a number of rules, never attempted to cripple police investigatory procedures. It upheld stop-and-frisk and the use of informants, among other practices, and in more areas than not, failed to establish criteria equivalent to an exclusionary rule or *Miranda* warning. The Burger Court also failed to establish clear-cut rules in many areas, and if we take a brief look at the Fourth Amendment cases it decided, there is little discernible doctrinal pattern. The Burger majority took what Yale Kamisar called a "crabbed view of what constitutes a 'search' or 'seizure,' "[42] and in doing so certainly evidenced a willingness to allow the police greater leeway in their investigative work.

■   *Vale* v. *Louisiana* (1970) held that an arrest on the street did not justify a warrantless search of the suspect's house as either a search incident to arrest or under exigent circumstances.[43]

■   *Chambers* v. *Maroney* (1970) continued the doctrine first enunciated in *Carroll* v. *United States* (1925)[44] that automobiles are exceptions to the warrant requirement.

In *Chambers* the police seized the automobile after an arrest, took it to a police station, and there searched it without a warrant.[45]

- *Coolidge* v. *New Hampshire* (1971) invalidated a search warrant issued by an attorney general as failing to meet the neutrality requirement and also held that a warrantless search of an automobile parked in defendant's driveway and under control of the police violated the Fourth Amendment.[46]

- *United States* v. *United States District Court* (1972). A unanimous Court held that neither the 1968 federal electronic surveillance law nor the president's inherent powers to protect against domestic subversion "justify departure [from] the customary Fourth Amendment requirement of judicial approval prior to the initiation or a search or surveillance."[47]

- *Schneckloth* v. *Bustamonte* (1973) broadened the interpretation of what constitutes consent in a warrantless search and required proof only that the police did not employ duress or coercion to secure the consent.[48]

- *United States* v. *Robinson* (1973) admitted into evidence narcotics seized in a warrantless search incident to Robinson's arrest for operating a car without a valid license. The ruling expanded the scope of search incident to arrest from a mere frisk for weapons to a full body search and relied on the arresting officer's on-site judgment of how extensive a search was needed.[49]

- *United States* v. *Edwards* (1974) held that taking and searching clothing without a warrant from a person lawfully arrested while he was in jail did not violate the Fourth Amendment. A search incident to an arrest may be made either at the time of arrest or when the suspect is in full police custody.[50]

- *United States* v. *Matlock* (1974) loosened up requirements for consent from a third party to search premises occupied by a suspect in a robbery.[51]

- *Andresen* v. *Maryland* (1976) held that police searching an attorney's office with a valid warrant directed at specific evidence could take away files, search through them at the police station, and then return nonrelevant materials.[52]

- *South Dakota* v. *Opperman* (1976) held valid a warrantless search of an automobile taken to a police compound, on the basis of the automobile exception, even though police had no fear that evidence would disappear and could have secured a warrant.[53]

- *United States* v. *Miller* (1976) held that bank depositors have no expectation of privacy in their checking accounts and that police may subpoena bank records without meeting the warrant requirements for a regular search.[54]

- *United States* v. *Chadwick* (1977). Police officers arrested Chadwick and two others on suspicion of transporting narcotics and took into possession a locked foot-locker, which they later opened and searched without a warrant. The Court held that even though the police had removed the footlocker from an automobile trunk, the fact that it had been locked indicated an expectation of privacy. Because the police had it in possession, no danger existed of the evidence disappearing, and so they should have secured a warrant.[55]

■ *Smith* v. *Maryland* (1979). Relying on *Miller*, the Court held that police could use a pen register to record the numbers dialed from a particular phone without securing a warrant.[56]

■ *Payton* v. *New York* (1980) held that police could not enter a private residence without a warrant and without consent in order to make a routine felony arrest.[57]

■ *New York* v. *Belton* (1981) expanded police authority to search the entire interior of a car following the lawful arrest of its occupants. The police could even open closed containers, such as the glove compartment, within the passenger compartment.[58]

■ *Illinois* v. *Gates* (1983) supported the issuance of a warrant following an anonymous tip, because police pursued an extensive investigation following the tip that did yield the necessary probable cause. In this case, the Court formally abandoned the specific two-pronged test of *Aguilar* and *Spinelli*, and in its place "reaffirm[ed] the totality-of-the-circumstances analysis that traditionally has informed probable cause determinations."[59]

■ *Illinois* v. *Lafayette* (1983) admitted into evidence amphetamines discovered during a routine inventory search (without a warrant) of a shoulder bag at a police station following the arrest of the defendant for disturbing the peace. The Court viewed inventory searches as exceptions to the warrant requirement, a variety of search incident to arrest.[60]

■ *United States* v. *Knotts* (1983) held that monitoring a suspect by means of an electronic beeper attached to his car until the car reached its destination is neither a search nor a seizure.[61]

■ *Oliver* v. *United States* (1984) upheld the "open fields" exception to the warrant requirement, on the basis that happenings and articles in open fields do not enjoy an expectation of privacy.[62]

■ *Hudson* v. *Palmer* (1984) held that Fourth Amendment rights against search and seizure do not apply to prison cells and that destruction of a prisoner's private property can be remedied by adequate state civil procedures.[63]

■ *United States* v. *Karo* (1984) held that monitoring a beeper in a private residence not open to visual inspection does constitute a search.[64]

■ *New Jersey* v. *T.L.O.* (1985) established a school exception to the Warrant Clause, allowing school officials, on reasonable suspicion, to search student belongings for drugs or other proscribed articles.[65]

■ *California* v. *Ciraolo* (1986). In one of the last opinions handed down before Chief Justice Burger's retirement, a sharply divided Court held that aerial surveillance of a person's backyard did not constitute a search, even if police in the airplane photographed marijuana under cultivation and then secured a warrant for an on-ground search.[66]

What can one make of this line of decisions? There were certainly some departures from Warren Court precedents, such as the abandonment of the *Aguilar–Spinelli* two-pronged test and the reinstatement of the totality-of-the-circumstances evaluation. One also finds a narrow view of what constitutes an area of assumed privacy; most people would probably think their checking accounts and the telephone numbers they call, as well as their backyards, should be safe from warrantless snooping by the police. The Burger Court, especially in the opinions written by Justice Rehnquist, seemed far more willing than its predecessor to give police greater leeway in determining what constituted probable cause or the scope of a search incident to an arrest.

Whether this string of cases justified hand-wringing over the death of the Fourth Amendment, however, is debatable. One can argue that the Burger majority took far too narrow a view of privacy and the protection afforded by the Warrant Clause. At the same time, one need not be a law-and-order fanatic to believe that some balancing is necessary between the rights afforded to accused persons and the leeway necessary for police to carry out their legitimate duties. While it is true that much of police investigation is plain hard work in tracking down leads, there is also an element of intuition, of reliance on anonymous tips, of evaluating a particular situation in the light of past experience. The Warren Court had recognized this in *Terry* v. *Ohio*, the stop-and-frisk case; the Burger Court proved itself more willing to defer to police judgment, yet as the cases show, in the end its decisions still supported the general rule that except in exigent situations, police needed a warrant, and to get that warrant, they had to show sufficient proof to meet the probable cause standard.

The problem is that there is no clear standard that can at the same time establish a prophylactic rule that is always applicable, while allowing police some discretion. The Warren Court leaned toward a rigid standard at the expense of discretion, and the Burger majority leaned in the opposite direction. The issue is whether the steps taken by the Burger majority will lead its successors away from any insistence on standards.

THE EXCLUSIONARY RULE

How effective a right is often depends upon the remedy available if the right is violated. The Warren Court, following its tendency to establish rules, had applied the exclusionary rule to the states in *Mapp* v. *Ohio* (1961), and had stated the basic principle that "all evidence obtained by searches and seizures in violation of the Constitution is, by that same authority, inadmissible in a state court."[67] Although the decision had generated a great deal of controversy,[68] it did appear to many people a logical—indeed, the only—remedy that fit the abuse. If you wanted the police to obey the Fourth Amendment, then prohibit the use of evidence seized in violation of its strictures on search and seizure.[69] Moreover, aside from any deterrent effect, the rule stood for the proposition that a government under a written constitution had to play by its rules, that it had to obey the law. "Nothing can destroy a government more quickly," Justice Clark declared, "than its failure to observe its own laws, or worse, its disregard of the charter of its own existence."[70] Nonetheless, the *Mapp* decision generated an ongoing debate whether the exclusionary rule in fact deters police violation of constitutionally protected rights.[71]

As much as any Warren Court doctrine, the exclusionary rule promised to be a prime target of the Nixon justices. The new Chief Justice believed the rule ineffective and costly and led to "the release of countless guilty criminals."[72] Burger also made the valid point that the rule directly affected police behavior only minimally—rather, the prosecutor bore the penalty for police noncompliance—that by the time of the suppression hearing, any effect on police action has evaporated.[73] However, Burger ignored the fact that there is a potent *indirect* effect on the police if prosecutors are constantly deprived of evidence because of slipshod police work. The word does get down to the ranks, and throughout the 1970s the number of cases being dismissed for Fourth Amendment violations declined dramatically as police learned to do their job right.

One has to be careful, however, not to draw a portrait using only black and white paint. At no time did the Burger Court ever hold that police could act without any restrictions, that they could search on whim or ignore the warrant requirements. Rather, the majority believed that a rigid application of the exclusionary rule placed an unjustified burden on the police; the deterrent effect could be achieved without coming down so hard on every transgression. In its decisions on this subject, the Burger Court attempted to set up a balancing test between the alleged violation of rights and the severity of the penalty. Some commentators have disparaged this "cost-benefit" analysis, and their comments indicate a major difference between how the Warren and Burger majorities view the exclusionary rule.

In *United States* v. *Calandra* (1974),[74] the Court ruled that a grand jury witness could not refuse to answer questions because the questions derived from illegally seized evidence. Justice Powell's majority opinion first put forward the balancing test, weighing the deterrent effect of the rule against the disruption of an investigation and finding the deterrent effect here to be only marginal. Powell, however, did not answer the obvious question that arose from the opinion: If as a result of using illegally seized evidence, the grand jury can gather all the evidence the government can find, will that evidence be suppressed at trial? If yes, then the inconvenience of allowing witnesses to challenge grand jury questions is far outweighed by having untainted evidence at trial. If no, then *Calandra* could be seen as a first step in abolishing the exclusionary rule.

In his opinion, Justice Powell described the rule as "a judicially created remedy designed to safeguard Fourth Amendment rights generally through its deterrent effect" rather than "a personal constitutional right of the party aggrieved." Whether courts should apply the exclusionary rule in particular instances thus became a question "not of rights but of remedies," and the answer depended on the likely costs of the rule as against the likely benefits.[75]

Two years later, in *Stone* v. *Powell*, the Court addressed the question of whether state prisoners could secure habeas corpus relief on the federal claim that the evidence which had led to their convictions had been illegally obtained. In his decision, Justice Powell rejected the notion that the exclusionary rule relied on the notion of "judicial integrity." "The primary justification for the exclusionary rule," he declared, "is the deterrence of police conduct that violates Fourth Amendment rights."[76] So long as the state had provided "full and fair litigation" of a Fourth Amendment claim, he ruled, a state prisoner could not secure habeas corpus relief on those grounds. Because habeas corpus exists to protect against the abuse of substantive rights, by viewing the exclusionary rule as a remedy rather than a *right*, the Court in effect narrowed the scope of cases that violations might affect. This proved insufficient for the Chief Justice, who in his concurrence argued that "the time has come to modify the reach of the exclusionary rule, even if it is retained for a small and limited category of cases."[77]

That same year, the Court took a major step in restricting the reach of the rule by holding that evidence illegally obtained by state police could be used in federal civil tax proceedings, a resurrection of the old "silver platter" doctrine that had been so abused in the 1920s and 1930s.[78] Over the next few years the Court continued to expand its cost-benefit analysis while chipping away at the exclusionary rule.[79]

In 1984 the Court decided two cases that focused on just the type of police behavior that critics of the Warren Court opinions said should not be penalized by a rigid application of the exclusionary rule. A confidential informant "of unproven reliability" tipped off police to a drug ring operating in Burbank, California. Local police and federal drug enforcement officials then began an extensive investigation of Alberto Leon and others, many of whom had previously been convicted of drug-related offenses. After gathering evidence, Officer Cyril Rombach, "an experienced and well-trained narcotics investigator," prepared an "extensive" application for a search warrant, which several deputy district attorneys reviewed. A state judge issued a warrant, and in the ensuing search police located and seized large quantities of cocaine. At the trial in federal district court, the judge granted the defense motion that the application for the warrant had failed to establish probable cause, and he suppressed some of this evidence as illegally seized. The government appealed on the grounds that evidence seized by police officers acting on good faith that they had a legitimate warrant should not be suppressed.[80]

Justice White, for a 6-3 Court, agreed with the government's contention and ruled that the exclusionary rule "can be modified somewhat without jeopardizing its ability to perform its intended functions."[81] In this case, the magistrate had erred, in that he found probable cause in an application that failed to meet constitutional criteria. But the exclusionary rule is aimed against police conduct. Here the police had conducted an extensive investigation; they had filed a warrant application that had been checked by the district attorney's office; they had secured what they believed to be a lawful warrant; and on the basis of that warrant had conducted a search that had turned up just the evidence they had claimed to exist in the place they claimed it would be. The police had done nothing wrong, and to penalize them because the magistrate had failed to apply the appropriate test would not deter illegal police activity in the future. As Justice White concluded, "[T]he officers' reliance on the magistrate's determination of probable cause was objectively reasonable, and application of the extreme sanction of exclusion is inappropriate."[82]

On the same day that *Leon* was decided, the Court handed down its decision in *Massachusetts* v. *Sheppard*,[83] another case in which the police acted in good faith reliance on what they believed to be a lawful warrant. A young woman had been beaten to death and her body burned in the Roxbury district of Boston. The police investigation led them to suspect Osborne Sheppard, one of the victim's boyfriends, and they sought a warrant to search Sheppard's apartment. The affidavit set forth in detail what they wished to search for and the reasons they had supporting probable cause. Detective Peter O'Malley prepared the affidavit and had it checked by his sergeant, the district attorney, and the D.A.'s first assistant, all of whom agreed that it met the requirements for probable cause.

But on a Sunday, with the local court closed, police could not find an appropriate warrant application form. Finally they located one from the nearby Dorchester district designed for drug searches. Detective O'Malley went through the form and changed "Dorchester" to "Roxbury" and crossed out the words "controlled substance" in the title but not the text of the form. He then went to the residence of a judge, and in his presentation informed the judge that he knew he had the wrong form and that he had made changes to conform the application to the circumstances of the present case. The judge understood what O'Malley had done, and when he signed it made some additional changes to ensure its applicability. With the warrant in hand, police searched Sheppard's residence and found the incriminating evidence which led to his conviction for first-degree murder. At the pretrial hearing, the trial judge concluded that the warrant failed to conform to Fourth Amendment requirements but that the evidence could be admitted because police had acted in good faith in executing what they believed to be a valid warrant. The Massachusetts

Supreme Judicial Court agreed with the findings of the trial judge but felt compelled to reverse the conviction because the United States Supreme Court had not recognized a good faith exception to the exclusionary rule.[84]

Relying on the *Leon* rationale, Justice White spoke for a 7-2 Court[85] in extending the good faith exception to cover a technically imperfect warrant. Here the police had done everything that could be expected of them; they had not tried to hide the fact that they did not have the correct form, but tried to perfect it; the magistrate had been informed of this problem; he had taken additional steps to make sure it conformed and assured the police officer that it now applied. "At this point, a reasonable police officer would have concluded, as O'Malley did, that the warrant authorized a search for the materials outlined in the affidavit."

The two cases, although decided the same day and both ostensibly about good faith, do have a significant difference. In *Leon*, police evidently failed to meet the probable cause criterion for a warrant, but because the magistrate issued it anyway, they had every reason to believe it valid. In *Sheppard*, the police knew they had the wrong form, took every step possible to correct the problem, and easily met the other criteria, including probable cause. If one looks at the exclusionary rule simply as a deterrent to police misconduct, then the Court majority made the right decisions, because in both cases the police had checked with legal authorities and had every reason to believe they acted lawfully. There could be no deterrent effect in deciding the other way. Moreover, in applying a cost-benefit analysis, the costs here in terms of law enforcement and police morale would be very high, and benefits practically nonexistent, because there could be no change in future police practice.

If, however, one believes that the exclusionary rule is designed primarily to promote the integrity of the criminal justice system, and especially of the judiciary, then one could argue that *Leon* should have been decided differently. Although the police did not err, the magistrate did, and in terms of constitutional rights, it matters little to the victim whether the police or the magistrate violated those rights.[86] At the same time, only a rigid purist would complain about the *Sheppard* ruling. Police and magistrate had taken every possible measure to ensure that the spirit of the warrant requirement had been met; the police had described in detail what they wanted to search for, and their reasons for doing so, and had made a convincing case that probable cause existed. If the right form had been available it would have been used, and there is a common-sense attitude in this decision that is quite convincing.

Only if one places *Sheppard* in a context of an ongoing assault against the exclusionary rule does it appear to be anything else than what it purports to be. That the Burger majority objected to the rule as applied in the Warren era cases is undeniable, but it did not call for its eradication. In fact, Justice White dissented strongly in the third case handed down that day, *INS* v. *Lopez-Mendosa* (1984),[87] in which Justice O'Connor spoke for a majority holding the exclusionary rule essentially a criminal justice remedy that should not be applied in civil deportation hearings. For White, a Fourth Amendment violation deprived citizens of their rights whether in a criminal or civil context, and the good faith exception should only apply where one could make out a case that police had acted in a reasonable belief that they had met legal requirements.

The cases did carve some exceptions out of the exclusionary rule but came nowhere close to overturning it or even seriously undermining its applicability. Because of the emphasis the Warren Court put on warrant requirements, most jurisdictions adopted procedures to meet those criteria. Recent studies indicate that the exclusionary rule has had little impact on prosecutions. One survey showed that evidence had been excluded because of Fourth Amendment violations in only 1.3 percent of cases and that prosecutions had been dropped in less than 0.5 percent of cases because of search and seizure problems. The police learned that securing a proper warrant at the beginning avoids problems later, and at no time did the Burger Court ever suggest that the police could act in disregard of the Fourth Amendment.

THE *MIRANDA* WARNING

One can discern a similar pattern in the Burger majority's handling of the most controversial of the Warren Court criminal procedure cases, the *Miranda* v. *Arizona* decision.[88] In a series of decisions in the early 1970s, the "first" Burger Court seemed determined to curtail *Miranda* if not to do away with it entirely; later decisions, however, reaffirmed the vitality of *Miranda* within somewhat better defined parameters.

For all that *Miranda* has been praised and damned, the actual holding was never as far-reaching as critics claimed. Police did not, under the ruling, have to read a person the warning before arresting or questioning him or her. Neither custody nor questioning alone triggered the warning; police could arrest someone, and if they did not care to question him or her, did not have to read the card; nor did they have to inform a person of his or her rights if they wished to question without arresting. The Warren majority addressed the condition of "custodial police interrogation," when police question someone they have arrested, with all the pressures that such a situation generates. Moreover, the Court never prohibited suspects from talking to the police or confessing; it required only that before they did so they be informed of their rights and that if they chose to waive those rights, they did so in a knowing and voluntary manner, either with or without an attorney present.[89]

The *Miranda* decision had been one of the chief targets of Richard Nixon during his attack on the Court during the 1968 campaign.[90] Views of the impact of the decision varied enormously. Four members of the President's Crime Commission, including future Justice Lewis F. Powell, believed that if *Miranda* "is implemented in its full sweep, it could mean the virtual elimination of pretrial interrogation of suspects."[91] Specific studies of *Miranda*, however, indicated minimal impact, with prosecutors losing essential confessions in very few cases as a result of police failing to inform suspects of their rights.[92] Nonetheless, the *Miranda* warnings, like the exclusionary rule, remained a bugaboo of law-and-order advocates and their continuing complaint about the Warren Court and its "softness" on crime.

The Burger Court began its attack on *Miranda* in *Harris* v. *New York* (1971).[93] Vivan Harris had been arrested after selling heroin to an undercover narcotics officer, and at the time of his arrest had not been informed of his rights. At the trial he took the stand in his own defense, and the prosecutor in cross-examination asked Harris if he had made statements to the police at the time of his arrest that contradicted his direct testimony. Over the objections of Justices Black, Douglas, Brennan, and Marshall, Chief Justice Burger held that such statements, which could not be used as direct evidence, could be used for the purpose of impeaching the defendant's credibility. While the *Miranda* decision had not talked about impeachment, the Chief Justice had to distort the earlier holding in order to limit its applicability. The original decision had not been aimed at specific applications as much as at the idea that people should not be put in jeopardy of life or freedom because they might say something unaware of their rights.[94]

The Court then used *Harris* to make further inroads a few years later in *Oregon* v. *Haas* (1975).[95] Here the defendant had been given his full *Miranda* warnings, and had said that he wanted to talk to a lawyer. The police told him he could not telephone an attorney until they reached the police station. On the ride to the station, Haas made some inculpatory statements before police allowed him to call a lawyer. Here, unlike *Harris* in which the police had given a defective warning, Haas had been read his rights and had chosen to exercise his right to counsel, and then the police had refused to honor his request and continued to question him. Nonetheless, a 6-2 majority held that the statements could be used for impeachment purposes, but not in the case-in-chief (the prosecution's main presentation of evidence).

Although *Harris* received greater publicity, as the first case in which the new Nixon appointees would roll back the Warren decisions, *Haas* struck a greater blow at *Miranda*. In many instances, suspects are ready to confess, and one of the deterrent effects of *Miranda* is that such confessions cannot be used if the arresting procedure, including notification of rights, is tainted. *Harris* told police that confessions obtained through faulty arrest procedures would be good only for impeachment, a relatively unimportant function because a majority of defendants do not take the stand. It would be better, therefore, for police to do the job right and use the evidence as part of the main case.

Haas seemed to say that after you give the *Miranda* warnings, you can then ignore them and get what you can. While *Haas* still did not allow such confessions to be used in the case-in-chief, it implied that the courts would take a far more lenient view of police practices in interrogating suspects. One could interpret the majority opinion as hinting that if police at least went through the formality of reading the *Miranda* card, they could then put as much pressure on a suspect as they wanted, whether he or she chose to exercise those rights.

In between the two impeachment cases, the Court added further support to the view that it did not consider the *Miranda* warnings an essential aspect of constitutional protection. In a minor case, *Michigan* v. *Tucker* (1974),[96] Justice Rehnquist termed the *Miranda* warnings "not themselves rights protected by the Constitution" but only "prophylactic standards" to safeguard or provide practical reinforcement for the privilege against self-incrimination. Moreover, Rehnquist implied that the test for compulsion was not the absence of *Miranda* warnings but rather a totality-of-the-circumstances approach, exactly what the *Miranda* Court had rejected as insufficient to protect constitutionally guaranteed rights.

Following these cases, however, the Burger Court entered what Yale Kamisar called its second phase, and *Miranda* showed a new vitality. The first sign came in another impeachment case, *Doyle* v. *Ohio* (1976),[97] in which the defendant had been read his rights at the time of arrest and had chosen to remain silent. At the trial he took the stand and told an exculpatory story he had not previously told to the police. In cross-examination, the prosecutor used the defendant's earlier silence in an attempt to impeach his credibility. In a 6-3 decision, the Court held that using a defendant's exercise of the constitutionally protected right to remain silent for impeachment violated the Fourteenth Amendment's Due Process Clause. The right to remain silent would have little value if it became a sword in the hands of the state instead of the shield its Framers had intended.[98]

Then came the Burger Court's most controversial criminal case, *Brewer* v. *Williams* (1977).[99] Robert Williams, an escaped mental patient, had allegedly abducted and then murdered a ten-year-old girl on Christmas eve in Des Moines, Iowa. Two days later he called his attorney from Davenport and, upon the lawyer's advice, surrendered to the Davenport police. The attorney also told Williams not to talk to the police until he arrived back in Des Moines, where the lawyer would be present. The Des Moines police promised the lawyer they would not interrogate Williams on the 160-mile trip back from Davenport. At the start of the trip, Williams again expressed his intent to remain silent. Nonetheless, the two police officers, aware of his religious beliefs, engaged him in discussions about religious questions and addressed him as "Reverend." It had started to snow, and the police pointed out that it would be difficult to find the little girl's body and give her "a Christian burial," a point they made several times. Williams eventually led them to the body.

By a 5-4 vote,[100] the Court, speaking through Justice Stewart, upheld the lower-court ruling that the evidence had been obtained improperly, because the two police officers, after agreeing to the suspect's request that he have counsel present before questioning, had interrogated him without benefit of that counsel. The Court remanded for a second trial, in which a jury again found Williams guilty. He appealed, but the Court ruled that the tainted evidence had not prejudiced the defense, because the body would have inevitably been found.[101]

Next the Court gave the term "interrogation" a broad meaning in *Rhode Island* v. *Innes* (1980).[102] Thomas Innes had been arrested for armed robbery and murder and had been read his rights not only by the arresting officer but also by superiors who arrived on the scene. He said that he wanted to speak to his lawyer, and the police captain told the three patrolmen who were to take Innes to the station not to question him. As the car passed a school for disabled children, one of the policemen expressed concern that a child might find the missing weapon, a shotgun, and be injured. Innes then offered to lead the police to where he had hidden the gun. The police returned to the scene of the arrest, where the captain again read Innes his rights. Innes said he understood his rights but insisted on taking the police to the shotgun because of the children. The Rhode Island Supreme Court had ruled that the gun, as well as the testimony of the officers, had to be excluded because it constituted custodial interrogation in violation of *Miranda*.

The Supreme Court reversed but did so in a manner to reinforce rather than weaken the *Miranda* ruling. Innes had not been charged with a crime, had no mental problems, and understood the *Miranda* warnings; he had voluntarily agreed to lead police to the weapon. Justice Stewart distinguished between "casual questioning," which would be allowed, and "custodial interrogation," which would not. *Miranda* safeguards come into play when police engage in express questioning or its "functional equivalent," which includes "any words or actions on the part of police that the police should know are reasonably likely to elicit an incriminating response from the suspect."[103] The wording of the opinion also brought police conduct, such as confronting a suspect with physical evidence or an accomplice, within the definition of custodial interrogation.

The most interesting statement in the decision is in Chief Justice Burger's concurrence, in which he declared that he "would neither overrule *Miranda*, disparage it, nor extend it at this late date."[104] The following Term the Court reinforced the view that it had accepted the basic premises of *Miranda* in *Edwards* v. *Arizona* (1981).[105] The majority held that when a suspect asserts his or her right to counsel (as opposed to the right to remain silent), police must cease their interrogation until a lawyer arrives, unless the suspect initiates further conversation.[106]

Then came several cases at the end of the Burger years, one of which could be explained as simple common sense, but the others might be interpreted as a renewed attack on *Miranda*. In *New York* v. *Quarles* (1984),[107] the Court created a "public safety" exception to the *Miranda* rule. Two policemen on patrol in Queens, New York, came across a young woman who informed them she had just been raped. She described her assailant and said she had seen him enter a nearby supermarket; she also told the police that the man carried a gun. The police went into the store and immediately spotted a person fitting the description; on seeing the officers, the man, Benjamin Quarles, ran toward the rear of the store, and one of the policemen, Frank Kraft, pursued him with a drawn gun, finally cornering him. Quarles surrendered without a struggle, but on searching him, police found his shoulder holster empty. Kraft handcuffed him, and without reading the *Miranda* rights, asked him where the gun was; Quarles nodded in the direction of some empty cartons and said, "The gun is over there." Kraft found the .38 caliber revolver, formally arrested Quarles, and then read him his rights. Quarles told Kraft he would be willing to answer questions and admitted owning the gun.

After conviction for criminal possession of a weapon (the rape charge was not implicated in this case), Quarles appealed and two New York appellate courts held that his rights had been violated, because he was in custody at the time Officer Kraft asked him the whereabouts of the gun and therefore was subject to *Miranda* protection. The Supreme Court, speaking through Justice Rehnquist, agreed that on the facts of the case, the lower courts had been correct in holding Quarles to have been in custody. But Rehnquist then carved out a "public safety" exception:

> In a kaleidoscopic situation such as the one confronting these officers, where spontaneity rather than adherence to a police manual is necessarily the order of the day, the application of the exception which we recognize today should not be made to depend on *post hoc* findings at a suppression hearing concerning the subjective motivation of the arresting officer. Undoubtedly most police officers, if placed in Officer Kraft's position, would act out of a host of different, instinctive, and largely unverifiable motives—their own safety, the safety of others, and perhaps as well the desire to obtain incriminating evidence from the suspect.
>
> Whatever the motivation of individual officers in such a situation, we do not believe that the doctrinal underpinnings of *Miranda* require that it be applied in all its rigor to a situation in which police officers ask questions reasonably prompted by a concern for the public safety.[108]

The next Term, the Court heard the case of Michael Elstad, an eighteen-year-old convicted of burglary. Following a tip police came to arrest Elstad, and without advising him of his rights, one of the officers told Elstad that he believed Elstad was involved in the burglary; Elstad responded, "Yes, I was there." The police then took Elstad to the station and read him his rights; he waived his rights and made a full confession. Following his conviction, Elstad appealed on the basis that his second confession had been "tainted" by his earlier remarks, which police had extracted without informing him of his rights.

Had the Court remained consistent with its decisions in *Williams* and *Innes*, it would have voided Elstad's conviction, for there is little doubt that police had him in "custody" at the time he initially admitted, "Yes, I was there." Instead, Justice O'Connor, for a 6-3 majority, went back to the Rehnquist opinion a decade earlier in *Michigan* v. *Tucker* (which she cited frequently) and denied that the failure to give *Miranda* warnings did not, by itself, violate the Fifth Amendment. "Absent deliberately coercive or improper tactics in obtaining the initial statement, the mere fact that a suspect has made an unwarned admission does not warrant a presumption of compulsion."[109]

The logic of this decision, if pursued by the Rehnquist Court, could seriously undermine or even reverse *Miranda*, because it treats the warnings as mere prophylaxis as opposed to a protected right. It says that suspects do have constitutional rights to an attorney, to remain silent, and so on, but no constitutional right to be informed of those other rights. If this view is accepted, then one is back, as Justice Rehnquist earlier proposed, to a totality-of-the-circumstances approach in which police need not inform suspects of their rights and need only be careful to avoid obvious strong-arm tactics. While these implications do exist, one must note that even this third-stage Burger Court did not totally reject *Miranda*.

During its last Term, the Burger Court heard a case in which police had picked up Brian Burbine for questioning on a burglary and learned that he might also have been involved in a murder. His sister, learning that he had been taken into custody on the burglary charge, called the public defender's office; an attorney called the station and received assurances that no interrogation would take place until the next day. In fact, police from the neighboring township where the murder had occurred had arrived at the station, and they began to question Burbine that evening. After a valid waiver of his rights, he confessed to the crime. In *Moran* v. *Burbine* (1986),[110] the Court, again speaking through Justice O'Connor, held that police conduct, as well as the suspect's ignorance of the attorney's efforts, did not taint the confession sufficiently to exclude it from evidence.

Six justices joined the opinion, which included the statement that *Miranda* "embodies a carefully crafted balance designed to fully protect *both* the defendants' and society's interests."[111] Moreover, these six justices included Burger, Rehnquist, White, Blackmun, and, of course, O'Connor, who had not previously been considered "friendly" to *Miranda*. The idea of seeing the rules as a device to balance interests, according to Yale Kamisar, is the way *Miranda's* defenders—not its critics—have talked about the case for the past twenty years. Although it is too early to tell, the Court's view of *Miranda* as a serious effort to strike a proper "balance" . . . may turn out to be more important than its specific ruling.[112]

And so after seventeen years and dozens of cases, two of the most attacked doctrines connected with the Warren Court, the exclusionary rule and the *Miranda* warnings, remained primarily intact. In both instances Justice Rehnquist, the leading ideologue of the Burger majority, had suggested doing away with what he termed judge-made, prophylactic rules. In both instances, the majority had handed down decisions which hinted that it might be willing to follow Rehnquist's lead. And in both instances, the Court came around to reaffirming the rules, albeit in somewhat more proscribed fashion. While one could claim that the rights of persons suspected of crimes had been reduced, one could also argue that the basic protections erected by the Warren Court had remained intact.

CAPITAL PUNISHMENT

The Warren Court, in its decisions on criminal procedure, had occasionally touched on the issue of capital punishment, but only at the fringes, such as in procedural cases affecting jury selection.[113] Nonetheless, the Supreme Court had played a significant role in reducing the annual number of executions in the United States from a peak of 199 in 1935 to zero in 1968. The reason is twofold. First, by expanding the right of habeas corpus, the Court allowed convicted prisoners to attack their state trials on federal grounds. As the Warren Court expanded the meaning of the Fourth, Fifth, and Sixth Amendments, more and more prisoners seized on flaws in their trials to file collateral attacks, and a state could not execute a prisoner while a court entertained his or her appeal.[114] Second, by 1968 everyone recognized that the Court stood ready to decide the core issue of whether the death penalty violated the Eighth Amendment ban on cruel and unusual punishment.

The issue had become a marginal topic of interest within the Court in 1963 following the appointment of Arthur Goldberg to the bench. Later in the year, Goldberg, joined by Brennan and Douglas, dissented from a denial of certiorari in a case that would have raised a fundamental constitutional challenge to the death penalty.[115] Seven years later a 6-3 majority of the Court voted to strike down the Arkansas capital punishment statute in *Maxwell* v. *Bishop*, because it failed to separate the guilt determination stage from a separate finding regarding the appropriate punishment. Warren assigned the case to Douglas, who wrote such a sweeping opinion that Harlan switched sides; then Fortas resigned, and the 6-3 vote became a 4-4 deadlock. Then Warren retired, and Burger voted to affirm the law, which now had a 5-3 majority in its favor. At Harlan's insistence, the justices put the case over until it could be heard by a full bench. With the appointment of Harry Blackmun, the Court stood 6-3 in support of the Arkansas statute, which it affirmed in 1970.[116]

The following year, the Burger Court decided in *McGautha* v. *California*[117] that a state did not violate due process if a jury had complete discretion in deciding whether to impose the death penalty. In a companion case the Court also held that states did not have to have a bifurcated proceeding, in which the jury determined guilt and punishment separately.[118] Following these decisions, the Court decided to take several representative cases from the hundreds of death sentence appeals awaiting action. In January 1972 the Court heard oral argument on these cases and then stunned the nation the following June when in a totally unexpected decision, it vacated the death sentences of approximately 600 inmates in prisons across the country. The Court split 5-4, and even the majority could not agree on the grounds to sustain the decision. So the Court issued a one-paragraph per curiam opinion:

> The Court holds that the imposition and carrying out of the death penalty in these cases constitutes cruel and unusual punishment in violation of the Eighth and Fourteenth Amendments. The judgment in each case is therefore reversed insofar as it leaves undisturbed the death sentence imposed, and the cases are remanded for further proceedings.[119]

This was followed by nine separate individual opinions. Justices Douglas, Stewart, and White emphasized the arbitrary and often capricious manner in which the penalty had been imposed, especially on black defendants. Brennan and Marshall alone believed that the death penalty by itself was unconstitutional, a minority position they clung to steadfastly for the remainder of the Burger years. The Chief Justice, Blackmun, Powell, and Rehnquist dissented in separate opinions.

Over the next few years, much to the dismay of abolitionists who had counted on a Supreme Court ruling to turn the tide, every one of the thirty-seven states that had previously imposed the death penalty reenacted a capital punishment statute to meet the criteria suggested in the concurring opinions: The statute should have clear guidelines to judge and jury when the death penalty would be appropriate; list the aggravating as well as mitigating factors that should be considered; bifurcate the guilt from the penalty determination; and provide for automatic review by an appellate court to ensure against excessive or disproportionate punishment. In 1976 the Court began reviewing the new statutes, and upheld the first of them in *Gregg* v. *Georgia*.[120] Justices Stewart, Powell, and Stevens announced the judgment of the Court, with the Chief Justice and Justices Rehnquist, White, and Blackmun concurring. While the seven members of the majority differed on a number of points, they all agreed that capital punishment per se did not violate the Constitution. Over the next ten years the Burger Court handed down several other decisions clarifying its views on particular issues raised by state laws.[121]

Given the supposedly anticriminal orientation of the Nixon appointees, one would not have expected them to be in the majority striking down the death sentence, and, in fact, all four of them—Burger, Blackmun, Powell, and Rehnquist—dissented in *Furman*. Yet in the next few years they too could be found writing opinions striking down particular statutes—with little protest from the public on an alleged "softness" for criminals.

The wide variety of capital punishment schemes, the arbitrary and often discriminatory application of the death sentence (blacks received the death sentence far more frequently than did whites, while the state hardly ever executed women convicted of capital crimes), and a lack of consistent standards led to a fair amount of support for the original 1972 decision. People understood that the Court had not abolished capital punishment but merely its unfair and inconsistent application. One wonders whether public response would have been so understanding had the decision come down earlier in the Warren Court.

CONCLUSIONS

The American Civil Liberties report for 1984, entitled *Our Endangered Rights*, concluded that the record of the Burger Court on criminal justice, "while regressive, is not totally negative. Warren Court precedents have been limited, but rarely directly overruled; on a few occasions, the current Court has reaffirmed constitutional principles."[122] Yale Kamisar, perhaps the country's leading authority on criminal procedure, had been a frequent critic of the Burger Court but noted that its path had been far from consistent and that the Chief Justice announced his retirement "just when the so-called Burger Court seemed to have hit its pro-police stride at last."[123] Herman Schwartz, another critic of the Burger Court, described its criminal procedure record as "much good, much bad, and on balance, probably beneficial."[124]

Any assessment of the Burger years would have to conclude that the dismantling of the Warren Court's criminal justice decisions failed to materialize. The Warren Court's efforts to erect simple rules failed because of the murky nature of the criminal world and the need for police to rely on intuitive responses, a need acknowledged by Warren in the stop-and-frisk case and more openly accepted by Burger and his colleagues. The Burger majority could certainly be characterized as pro-police, but not in the way that rabid law-and-order enthusiasts had demanded. Rather, in cases where police procedure did not seem patently unfair or coercive, the Burger Court appeared willing to strike a balance that gave police the benefit of the doubt. At no time, however, did the majority offer to write police a blank check or free them from constitutional constraints. The exclusionary rule still stood, as did the *Miranda* warnings, and procedures in capital punishment cases seemed far fairer and more consistent than in 1969. If liberals believed the Burger Court circumscribed the rights of accused persons too severely, conservatives believed it did not circumscribe them enough.

IV

EQUAL PROTECTION OF THE LAWS

AMENDMENT XIV

Section 1. *All persons born or naturalized in the United States and subject to the jurisdiction thereof, are citizens of the United States and of the State wherein they reside. No State shall make or enforce any law which shall abridge the privileges or immunities of citizens of the United States; nor shall any State deprive any person of life, liberty, or property, without due process of law, nor deny any person within its jurisdiction the equal protection of the laws.*

Section 5. *The Congress shall have power to enforce by appropriate legislation, the provisions of this article.*

9

"People, Not Land or Trees or Pastures Vote"

The Warren Court and Equal Protection

S ection 1 of the Fourteenth Amendment provides that no state shall "deny to any person within its jurisdiction the equal protection of the laws." In its first interpretation of that clause, the Supreme Court indicated that it applied only to racial concerns. "We doubt very much," said Justice Samuel Miller in the *Slaughter-House Cases* (1873), "whether any action of a State not directed by way of discrimination against the Negroes as a class, or on account of their race, will ever be held to come within the purview of this provision."[1] However, in the decades that followed, the Court approved a variety of state measures designed to segregate the former slaves, so that the Equal Protection Clause became in effect a dead letter. In the 1920s, Justice Holmes referred to it as "the usual last resort of constitutional arguments."[2]

The Warren Court revived equal protection in the most significant cases of this century, those calling for the desegregation of schools and other public facilities. Although most of the Warren Court's equal protection cases dealt with race, there are some tantalizing hints that the justices might have been willing to extend equal protection analysis to other groups. It would be the Burger Court, however, that actually dealt with nonracial issues.

Whether one sees the desegregation decisions as radical is a matter of judgment; for blacks and other supporters of civil rights, *Brown* v. *Board of Education* and its progeny finally corrected seven decades of constitutional error and secured the reading of the Equal Protection Clause that its Framers had intended. Critics of the Court, however, have seen these same cases as judicial policy making of the worst sort, grounded only in the predilections of the justices and not in the Constitution itself.

FROM *PLESSY* TO *BROWN*

Before looking at the Warren Court's desegregation decisions, one has to note, at least briefly, prior decisions in the area of race. A strong case can be made that *Brown* merely carried forward a line of reasoning that had been building within the Court for nearly two decades.

Following the Civil War the Court, as noted previously, initially saw the Due Process and Equal Protection Clauses of the Fourteenth Amendment solely in the light of protecting the freedmen from discrimination by the states. When Congress, however, tried to pass legislation to protect the freedmen's rights, the Court took an extremely cramped view of the enforcement provisions of the Thirteenth and Fourteenth Amendments, and in the *Civil Rights Cases* (1883), it denied Congress any affirmative powers to prevent discrimination. Only if a state restricted black rights could Congress act to remedy the injustice. Moreover, Justice Joseph Bradley held, if a state by inaction tolerated discrimination—such as exclusion from hotels, restaurants, and clubs—Congress lacked authority to interfere. By this one decision, the Court nullified nearly all congressional power under the Reconstruction Amendments to protect the freedmen and left their fate to the states.[3]

By the time of the segregation cases in the 1890s, both Court and Congress had essentially washed their hands of the racial problem. In the best known of these cases, *Plessy* v. *Ferguson* (1896), Justice Henry Brown held that distinctions based on race ran afoul of neither the Thirteenth nor Fourteenth Amendments. In the nature of things, he declared, the Fourteenth Amendment "could not have been intended to abolish distinctions based upon color, or to enforce social, as distinguished from political, equality, or a commingling of the two races unsatisfactory to either."[4] Although nowhere in the opinion can the phrase "separate but equal" be found, the Court's ruling approved racial segregation provided the law did not make facilities for blacks inferior to those for whites.[5]

Between 1900 and 1920, Jim Crow—the legal and systematic segregation of the races—triumphed throughout the former slave states. Signs marked "Whites Only" and "Colored" showed up everywhere, and hundreds of laws appeared on the statute books establishing and enforcing segregation. The statutes themselves, however, are not a fair index of the extent of racial discrimination; the laws set minima, and in practice segregation normally went beyond what the laws required. Institutionalized segregation bred hatred and distrust among both whites and blacks, and it fostered deeply ingrained attitudes that would not easily be changed after 1954.

Beginning in 1914, however, the Court slowly but surely began to unravel the fabric of discrimination it had helped weave in the latter nineteenth century. In the landmark case of *Buchanan* v. *Warley* (1917), the Court unanimously struck down residential segregation ordinances as violating the Fourteenth Amendment's protection of property rights on the basis of color.[6]

The Court did not hear another major race case until 1938.[7] By then the southern states had for many years ignored the "equal" part of the *Plessy* formula and were shocked when Chief Justice Charles Evans Hughes insisted that if the South wanted to maintain segregation, it had to provide truly equal facilities.[8] That same year, in an otherwise insignificant case, Justice Harlan Fiske Stone wrote what is undoubtedly the most famous footnote in American constitutional history. While describing the deference the courts should pay to legislative policy decisions and the simple "rational basis" test that would be applied to economic legislation, Stone inserted a footnote indicating that the Court would apply a higher standard of scrutiny when legislation affected rights protected within the Constitution or threatened the integrity of the political process.[9] This idea of a stricter standard became the basis for subsequent equal protection analysis.

The war and Hitler's racist persecution of the Jews, leading to the slaughter of 6 million innocent people, made many Americans extremely uncomfortable with segregation, which bore a striking resemblance to the Nazi program.[10] This unease in the late 1940s and early 1950s, along with legal challenges to segregation coordinated by the NAACP's Legal Defense Fund, led to a serious reconsideration of the *Plessy* doctrine. When Oklahoma refused to admit Ada Sipuel to the state's only law school, the Court unanimously ordered the state to provide her with a legal education "in conformity with the equal protection clause of the Fourteenth Amendment and to provide it as soon as it does for applicants of any other group."[11] A few years later the Court came down even harder on Oklahoma when, after reluctantly admitting a 68-year-old black man to its graduate school, it required him to sit in the corridors outside the classrooms or in separate roped-off areas. Chief Justice Vinson spoke for a unanimous Court in holding that such rules violated the Equal Protection Clause.[12]

The Court also struck down state enforcement of restrictive covenants, a device adopted in many areas following the 1917 invalidation of segregated zoning. Although the courts had long held that the Fourteenth Amendment did not reach private discrimination, if private individuals utilized state courts to enforce the restrictive covenants, then state action existed that violated the Equal Protection Clause.[13] But the Court had so far not indicated any willingness to question the basic premise of separate but equal, nor had the NAACP directly attacked the doctrine. Thurgood Marshall and his colleagues at the Legal Defense Fund kept attacking the failure of southern states to provide equal facilities, and in doing so they established a basis for the argument that separate accommodations could never be equal.[14]

The Court hinted that it might be willing to consider that argument in its ruling in *Sweatt* v. *Painter* (1950).[15] After the University of Texas refused to admit a black man into its law school, a lower court had ordered the state to provide a law school for blacks. The makeshift law school hastily created at the all-black Prairie View University certainly did not measure up to the prestigious white school in Austin, and if anything, the justices knew what made a good law school. For a unanimous Court, Chief Justice Vinson ordered Sweatt admitted to the University of Texas Law School—the first time the Court had ever ordered a black student admitted to a previously all-white institution. For many observers, the Court's opinion marked the end of *Plessy;* for Thurgood Marshall, the opinion was "replete with road markings telling us where to go next."[16]

The NAACP now altered its strategy to launch a direct attack on segregation. In the 1952 Term, it brought up challenges to various state segregation statutes in Delaware, Virginia, South Carolina, and Kansas, as well as the District of Columbia. The justices heard the cases that fall, but unable to reach agreement, they asked counsel to reargue the cases the following Term. Specifically, they wanted both sides to discuss whether Congress in proposing, and the states in adopting, the Fourteenth Amendment, had intended to ban racial segregation in schools. For the first time in more than fifty years, the Court would examine the root premise of the *Plessy* decision. One month before the Court convened for the October 1953 Term, Fred Vinson died of a heart attack. To replace him, President Eisenhower named the popular Republican governor of California, Earl Warren. When Warren arrived in Washington to take up the center chair, he found the school cases at the top of the Court's agenda.

BROWN V. BOARD OF EDUCATION

The story of *Brown* is by now very familiar,[17] but one needs to look at the decision both in terms of its alleged radical departure from precedent and as the basis it provided for future equal protection jurisprudence. The decision itself is deceptively simple; the Court, after all, had few cases it could refer to for guidance, and while they led away from *Plessy*, none had directly rejected the underlying premise of separate but equal. The Court, as an amicus brief from the Justice Department pointed out, had several options. It could avoid overruling *Plessy* by the simple expedient of finding the colored schools unequal, and then ordering either integration or another remedy. The justices could meet the issue head-on and condemn segregation as violating equal protection, but determine the particular remedy at a later date and then leave its implementation to the lower courts. Or, of course, they could affirm segregation, as former Solicitor General John W. Davis, representing South Carolina, proposed in oral argument in December: "To every principle comes a moment of repose when it has been so often announced, so confidently relied upon, so long continued, that it passes the limits of judicial discretion and disturbance."[18]

The Court, speaking through Chief Justice Warren, announced its decision at 12:51 P.M. on Monday, May 17, 1954. The history of the Fourteenth Amendment and its relation to education, which the Court had asked both sides to argue, had been "inconclusive," because public education in the South in 1868 had been so primitive that no one had bothered to think about it. There may, in fact, have been more guidance in history than Warren admitted,[19] but the Court was examining the problem in the middle of the twentieth century, and "in approaching this problem, we cannot turn the clock back to 1868 when the Amendment was adopted, or even to 1896 when *Plessy* v. *Ferguson* was written."[20] In 1954 public education played a far more central role in the nation's life than it had at the end of the Civil War.

Warren had read through two-thirds of the eleven-page opinion when he finally reached the crucial issue: "Does segregation of children in public schools solely on the basis of race . . . deprive the children of the minority group of equal educational opportunities?" Pausing for a moment, Warren then reaffirmed the eloquent dissent of the first Justice John Marshall Harlan in *Plessy*, that separate could never be equal. To segregate black schoolchildren

> from others of similar age and qualifications solely because of their race generates a feeling of inferiority as to their status in the community that may affect their hearts and minds in a way unlikely ever to be undone. . . . Segregation with the sanction of law, therefore, has a tendency to retard the educational and mental development of Negro children.[21]

As a result, Warren concluded, "in the field of public education the doctrine of 'separate but equal' has no place. Separate educational facilities are inherently unequal."

The last paragraph of the opinion showed Warren's famed political skill. Noting the wide applicability of the decisions and the complexity of deriving an appropriate solution, he invited the parties to return to the Court that fall to assist the Court in fashioning a proper remedy. The phrase "wide applicability" indicated that legal segregation, either in the North or the South, in rural or urban areas, would henceforth be unconstitutional. The reference to complexity signaled the South that the justices recognized the emotional and political distress that the decision would cause, and the delay in implementation would allow the states to accustom themselves and their citizens to the necessity for change. By inviting the parties to help fashion the remedy, the Court hoped that the Jim Crow states would cooperate in order to avoid potentially harsher solutions. Finally, Warren had framed the opinion to apply to only one area—the segregation by race of children in primary and secondary schools, a group most likely to win public sympathy as victims of racism. The Court did not even mention the many other facets of Jim Crow, and while one could hardly expect segregation to be struck down in one area and not in others, for the moment at least, the Court concerned itself only with education.

Is the *Brown* decision radical? Does it represent naked judicial policy making? Is it grounded in the rule of law? How one answers these questions depends in large measure on how one views racial segregation. If it offended one—if one believed that in a democratic society people should not be penalized and treated as inferiors because of the accident of skin color—then the Court's decision represented nothing more than "simple justice," and it freed not only black persons, but also the white South and the Court itself, from the weight of history. If one believed segregation to be not only constitutional but morally and socially right as well, then *Brown* was a disaster, pure and simple. We need not go into either of these arguments because, thirty-five years after the decision, an overwhelming body of public opinion opposes legal discrimination based on race. Moreover, without *Brown*, it is unlikely that Congress or the southern states would have voluntarily done away with racial segregation.[22]

The question remains, however, whether the decision is good jurisprudence, and that is a separate matter from either politics or morality. Ideally, one can agree with William Blackstone that law represents what is right and good, but we know that often law is not a choice between good and evil; rather, it is a choice between two competing goods or the lesser of two evils. Law is valued in society because it provides stability; it anchors society with a set of knowable rules so that people can act accordingly. If these rules are wrong, then it is up to the legislature to change them; that is a policy decision, reposed by the Constitution in the Congress. When courts make policy, even "good" policy, there is a danger of upsetting the delicate constitutional balance of powers.

There is much to be said for this reasoning, and people who by no stretch of the imagination can be described as racist have been uncomfortable with the *Brown* decision because it seems to rely less on legal reasoning than on moral intuition, less on legal precedent than on questionable social science findings. If one goes back to the conclusion in *Brown* quoted earlier, one finds a powerful assertion that segregation is harmful to children. The basis for this claim cannot be found in law reports; that segregation damages schoolchildren, wrote Warren, "is amply supported by modern authority." At this point the Chief Justice inserted the famous—or infamous—footnote 11 citing, among others, social psychologist Kenneth B. Clark's controversial study of children's reactions to dolls. Black children between the ages of six and nine attending segregated schools had been shown drawings of otherwise identical black and white dolls. When asked to select the "nice" doll, a majority had chosen the white doll, which Clark claimed showed that school segregation implanted in blacks a negative image of themselves at an early age.[23]

This is, of course, a simplified view of Clark's study, but one has to recall the limited ability of social scientists to measure the effect of discrimination in the 1940s and 1950s. There has been an ongoing debate as to the accuracy of social science studies and whether courts should rely on them in reaching legal decisions,[24] and one can hardly quibble with law professor Edmund Cahn's assertion that "I would not have the constitutional rights of Negroes—or of any other Americans—rest on such flimsy foundation as some of the scientific demonstrations in these [trial] records."[25] To Cahn, and others, one did not need questionable studies to see the obvious; the sources in footnote 11 did not strengthen the decision, but in fact gave critics an opening to attack it without invoking a straightforward racism.

For some, the Court had turned "over the making of law to social science opinion and the writers of books on psychology."[26] Former associate justice and now governor of South Carolina James F. Byrnes and Mississippi senator James O. Eastland attacked the social science sources as Communist inspired. The Georgia attorney general zeroed in on the citation of Gunnar Myrdal's classic study of racism, *An American Dilemma* (1944). The black radical W. E. B. DuBois had been one of Myrdal's teachers, he claimed, and DuBois had "sent a message of condolence on the death of Stalin."[27] And, of course, the South had produced dozens of social scientists of its own over the decades—men untainted by foreign ideologies—who had proven conclusively the inferiority of the Negro.[28]

A more serious attack came from someone who not only opposed segregation but also had been an active foe of racial discrimination and in fact had advised the NAACP on several cases, including *Brown*. Columbia University Professor Herbert Wechsler did not object to the fact that the high court had departed from precedent nor to the fact that it insisted on viewing the Fourteenth Amendment in the light of current conditions rather than those that governed at the time of its adoption. Rather, the justices had reached the conclusion that separate schools, because "inherently unequal," were unconstitutional. But how did they get there? What reasoning, what rules of constitutional interpretation, had the Court used to get from A (separate schools) to B (are inherently unequal) to C (and therefore unconstitutional)? Would all laws that segregated one group from another (such as men from women) be unconstitutional? Would all conditions that created inequality (such as poverty) be subject to constitutional remedy? The Court had failed, Wechsler claimed, to ground its conclusions in "neutral principles." Decisions must rest "on reasons with respect to all the issues in the case . . . that in their generality and neutrality transcend any immediate result that is involved." Only if society could see that such far-reaching decisions as *Brown* had, in fact, been reached through a rational and explainable method of legal reasoning would society be willing to accept the changes imposed by those decisions. The integrity of the judicial process outweighed any particular results.[29]

Is process enough? Is justice or society served if the courts only concern themselves with neutral principles? What about right results? For many, the "rightness" of *Brown* was sufficient. Professor Edward Beiser defended *Brown* as properly decided "because racial segregation was a grievous evil. Were this not so, the Supreme Court's decision would have been unjustified." Another legal scholar, Paul Bender, agreed that *Brown* had not been "tightly reasoned," but so what? The opinion had been "right," and if the Court had waited until it could write an "airtight opinion . . . it would have sadly failed the country and the Constitution."[30]

This debate between process and result is neither new nor concluded. Throughout the Burger years, as well as during the Warren era, critics of particular decisions claimed that the Court had abandoned its responsibility to judicial process and had exercised raw, unprincipled power.[31] Certainly society has a right to expect that its judiciary, constitutionally protected and insulated from emotionalism and politics, will act in a principled manner—that there will be articulatable standards by which to judge decisions. At the same time, society also expects its law to be morally acceptable, and in the United States particularly, people look to the courts to correct many perceived societal wrongs. Centuries ago, when the law proved so rigid that people saw it as ofttimes immoral, English kings established and then expanded the powers of the chancellor, the "keeper of the king's conscience," so that justice could be served by equity in those instances when law proved inadequate. Over the centuries the common law has responded to changing social conditions, and when necessary, common law judges have struck out in new directions, despite the contrary holdings of previous decisions. In the United States, the Constitution wiped out the barriers between law and equity, and if one accepts the premise that racial segregation is harmful and unfair, not just in broad terms but within the type of equality guaranteed under the Constitution, then Chief Justice Warren's opinion, while admittedly weak in legal reasoning, is nonetheless a powerful statement of the moral grandeur of the law. Whatever its flaws, according to J. Harvie Wilkinson, now a federal circuit judge, *Brown* "was humane, among the most humane moments in all our history. It was, with the pardonable exception of a footnote, a great political achievement, both in its uniting of the Court and in the steady way it addressed the nation."[32]

IMPLEMENTING THE DECISION

While one can lavish praise on *Brown*, the Court's ruling the following year in *Brown II* [33] on how desegregation should take place disappointed nearly everyone. Chief Justice Warren had assumed that during the year's grace period the southern states would come to accept the Court's decision, and the initial reaction to *Brown* in the South had seemed fairly moderate. The governor of Virginia, Thomas Stanley, called for "cool heads, calm study, and sound judgment." The respected Louisville *Courier-Journal* assured its readers that "the end of the world has not come for the South or for the nation. The Supreme Court's ruling is not itself a revolution. It is rather acceptance of a process that has been going on a long time." The editors endorsed the Court's example of moderation, advice akin to that of the *Atlanta Constitution*, which called on Georgians "to think clearly."[34]

Some southern communities did not wait for the Court to hand down its implementation decree but instead began desegregating their schools by the time the new academic year began in September 1954. Baltimore adopted a freedom of choice plan, which enabled 3,000 young blacks to attend previously all-white schools that fall. Louisville changed over its school system within a semester, whereas St. Louis initiated a two-year conversion plan. Counties in West Virginia, junior colleges in Texas, and public schools in Washington, D.C., and Wilmington, Delaware, all enrolled blacks in previously segregated schools. But the vast majority of southern school districts remained segregated, waiting to see what the Court would require.

The justices heard arguments on proposed remedies that winter and again in April. Aside from the controversial nature of the problem itself, the Court also had to decide whether to abandon in this instance its traditional policy of ruling only on the case before it. Normally, if someone raises a valid claim that his or her constitutional rights have been violated, the decree provides relief only for the petitioner; other persons suffering from the same infringement do not immediately benefit from the decision. Lower courts then take notice of the ruling and apply it prospectively to future petitioners raising the same issue. In the school cases, however, this would have meant that every black child wishing to attend a previously all-white school would have had to seek a court order to enjoy the same rights as Linda Brown now enjoyed in Topeka. Determined states and localities could tie up the desegregation process for years by litigating every single black child's efforts to secure a desegregated education.

Moreover, the Court usually takes little notice of practical problems in implementation. If a constitutional right exists, it has to be available to the citizenry, regardless of institutional dislocations. But circumstances across the South and in the border states varied enormously, and the Court recognized that in some schools desegregation would mean a few blacks sitting in predominantly white classrooms, and in other schools just the opposite—and this made a difference. How long should the South have? Too precipitate an order could trigger widescale resistance, even violence. On the other hand, every day black children remained in segregated and therefore inferior classrooms, they suffered deprivation of their constitutional rights.

The NAACP pushed for full integration,[35] while southern states urged the Court to face the "reality" of racial differences. Virginia offered statistical proof on the inferiority of blacks, while a poll in Florida showed that only one police officer in seven would enforce attendance at racially mixed schools. The federal government urged a middle position between "integration now" and "segregation forever."

On May 31, 1955, Chief Justice Warren, again for a unanimous Court, read the seven-paragraph implementing decision. *Brown II* called for the end of segregation everywhere but recognized that different localities would face different problems. Local school districts must "make a prompt and reasonable start toward full compliance." Oversight would be lodged in the federal district courts, whose judges would exercise the "practical flexibility" traditionally associated with equity. Delay and noncompliance should not be contemplated, and desegregation of the nation's public schools should proceed "with all deliberate speed."

The Court did not fix a date for the end of segregation nor even require, as the Justice Department had suggested, that the initial plans be filed within ninety days. The decision, in fact, gave the South far more than it had expected. Segregationists believed that implementation could be postponed indefinitely, because assignment of primary responsibility to the local federal courts meant southerners would decide what had to be done. Lieutenant Governor Ernest Vandiver of Georgia rejoiced when he heard the news. District judges, he declared, "are steeped in the same traditions that I am. . . . A 'reasonable time' can be construed as one year or two hundred. . . . Thank God we've got good Federal judges."[36]

As it turned out, federal judges in the South made it clear that they took their oaths to support the Constitution seriously.[37] By January 1956, decisions had been rendered in nineteen cases, and in every one district judges had reaffirmed the Supreme Court's holding that segregation denied equal protection of the laws. Then the South dug in its heels; it would be another decade before the former slave states finally bowed to the *Brown* rulings, and another decade after that before one could claim that legally enforced segregation had ended.[38]

Why the delay? Why did the Court, after the magisterial moral statement of the first *Brown* case, back off so dramatically in *Brown II*? The phrase "all deliberate speed" seemed to invite delay, and southern states did all they could to evade the rulings, from dragging out litigation to imposing alleged health and welfare criteria to actually closing schools in some areas. "There is not one way, but many," John Temple Graves of Alabama proclaimed. "The South proposes to use all of them that make for resistance. The decision tortured the Constitution—the South will torture the decision."[39]

As has often been noted, the Supreme Court has the power neither of sword nor purse and can rely for obedience to its decisions only on the moral authority it commands or on the aid of Congress and the President. In the years immediately following the two *Brown* decisions, the South refused to recognize any moral authority in the Court, and neither the White House nor Congress appeared willing to sign on to the decision. Dwight Eisenhower lamented the appointment of Warren as "the biggest damn fool mistake I ever made"[40] and denounced the decision as setting back racial progress in the South by fifteen years. Yet Eisenhower refused to use the moral authority of the presidency to lead the South away from intransigence. When officials at the University of Alabama defied a court order to admit a black student, Eisenhower refused to intervene, and the university remained segregated another seven years. Then came Little Rock, and a reluctant chief executive finally acted.

THE TIDE SHIFTS

In the fall of 1957, the Little Rock, Arkansas, school board agreed to a court order to admit nine black students to Central High School. Governor Orville Faubus, previously considered a moderate, called out the national guard to block the students from enrolling. He then withdrew the militia following another court order, but when mobs attacked black students trying to attend Central, he recalled the guard. In essence, the governor of a state was using the state militia to block enforcement of a federal court order, and Eisenhower could no longer sit back and watch federal authority flouted. He ordered a thousand paratroopers into Little Rock and federalized 10,000 Arkansas guardsmen to maintain order and protect the black students.[41]

The Court, which had been silent on school desegregation since *Brown II*, now spoke out in a case arising out of the Little Rock turmoil, *Cooper v. Aaron* (1958).[42] The justices not only reaffirmed the *Brown* ruling but also, in an unusual opinion signed by each of them, reasserted the Court's authority as the ultimate interpreter of the Constitution, the position first enunciated by Chief Justice John Marshall in *Marbury* v. *Madison* in 1803.[43]

Arkansas officials claimed they were not "bound" by the original *Brown* ruling because the state had not been a party to those suits. The later lower-court decision, which Faubus had tried to evade, had ordered the Little Rock school board to desegregate, and the high court could have contented itself with a sharp reminder that states have no power to nullify federal court orders. But the nine justices went on to affirm

> that the federal judiciary is supreme in the exposition of the law of the Constitution. . . . It follows that the interpretation of the Fourteenth Amendment enunciated by this Court in the Brown case is the supreme law of the land, and Art. VI of the Constitution makes it of binding effect on the States "any Thing in the Constitution or Laws of any State to the Contrary notwithstanding." Every state legislator and executive and judicial officer is solemnly committed by oath . . . "to support this Constitution."[44]

There has been some discussion as to whether the Warren Court merely reiterated Marshall's dictum in *Marbury* or went beyond it to assert an exclusive power that had not been claimed before.[45] The debate over the Court's power has been going on practically from the time the Court began to hear cases in 1790, and it is not likely to end so long as Americans insist on litigating every major public policy question. It is equally clear that while federal, state, and local officials are theoretically bound to obey the Constitution, unless there is a final arbiter of what that Constitution means we will have a legal morass that will undermine social stability. Once the Court had declared that the Equal Protection Clause forbade segregation, it had little choice but to invalidate any and all state and local interpretations to the contrary.

A good part of the problem, though, derived from the Court's miscalculation in *Brown II*. In trying to accommodate the South in the hope that reason would prevail, the Court gave segregationists an opening they aggressively exploited. And so long as neither the executive nor legislative branches would support the moral authority of the Court, it could do very little. Beginning with the Little Rock decision, however, the pendulum began to swing the other way.

First the justices began to state openly that the phrase "all deliberate speed" did not mean indefinite delay. "There has been entirely too much deliberation," declared Justice Hugo Black of Alabama, "and not enough speed."[46] The growing impatience of the Court resulted, at least in part, from recognition of its own prior miscalculations and from the mounting criticism it faced both in academic and civil rights circles. *Brown II*, designed to allow the better elements in the South to work out a peaceful solution, wound up permitting the most bigoted and violent segments of society to prevail.

Yet the very disgust generated by racist elements in the deep South finally moved the executive and legislative branches, as well as public opinion, to back the Court's ruling that segregation had to be ended. In 1957 Congress passed the first civil rights law since Reconstruction. Although this law had limited scope, it set the stage for further legislation that would eventually bring to bear the full power of the federal government to protect the civil rights of minority groups. While Dwight Eisenhower never showed much enthusiasm for the cause, the Kennedy and Johnson administrations put civil rights near the top of their domestic agendas. Despite continued violence in the South and grandstand defiance by governors Ross Barnett of Mississippi and George Wallace of Alabama, there could be no mistaking the trend. The 1963 march on Washington, and Lyndon Johnson's eloquent promise that "we shall overcome," set the civil rights agenda for the 1960s. And with that shift, the Court resumed its role as the chief exponent of constitutionally protected rights.

THE COURT MOVES AHEAD

After remaining largely silent in the late 1950s, the Court began accepting more segregation cases and, in one unanimous ruling after another, added to the growing national consensus that the time had come to act. It not only reaffirmed the basic premise that segregation violated the Fourteenth Amendment, but addressed itself to specifics as well.

In *Goss* v. *Board of Education* (1963),[47] the Court struck down a transfer plan that would have allowed white students to reestablish one-race schools. The following year, the justices attacked massive resistance in *Griffin* v. *County School Board*.[48] They told school officials in Prince Edward County, Virginia, to reopen the public schools that had been closed for five years to evade desegregation. Justice Black also warned the South to stop its delaying tactics; ten years had been long enough for southerners to reconcile themselves to *Brown*.

In 1968 the Court decided its last "easy" school desegregation case, one in which the justices took a significant new step in interpreting the constitutional mandate. *Green* v. *County School Board*[49] involved a "freedom of choice" plan that supposedly allowed students of either race to attend the school of their choice. Local officials in predominantly rural New Kent County, Virginia, defended the plan as a good faith effort to comply with *Brown*, but critics charged that it discouraged blacks from attending white schools and had little overall effect. After three years, not one white child had chosen to attend a formerly black school, and 85 percent of the black students still went to all-black schools.

Speaking for the Court, Justice Brennan declared that henceforth results, not good intentions, would be the mark of an acceptable plan, and the Court took the unusual step of indicating specific proposals that would be acceptable, such as dividing the county geographically, with all students living in each half attending the schools in that half.

Green was "easy" in the sense that it marked the last case in which black students had been segregated on the basis of law or of easily perceived racial discrimination. The freedom of choice plan that had been struck down in this case, and which lower courts overturned in similar situations, had been patently designed to avoid the *Brown* mandate. The case also marked the end of what might be called the first phase of school desegregation, in which the Court, following its initial pronouncements, had shown a willingness to allow the states and localities to work things out, to accept tokens of good faith in the hope that a gradualist approach would, in the end, work.

No doubt a gradualist approach had been necessary, and for all that the *Brown II* formula of "all deliberate speed" proved a failure, there is a lingering sense that if the Court, without the support of the other branches of government, had pushed for greater desegregation sooner, the reaction might have been even bloodier and more violent. The Court could, however, have provided greater leadership; it could have, as the Justice Department had urged, required school districts to submit plans with specific timetables. It could have taken more cases on appeal to give the lower courts and the nation more guidance. From *Brown* to *Griffin* the Court said practically nothing. After setting in motion one of the great social upheavals of the century, the Court retreated into silence. Given the deep-seated prejudice in the South, perhaps little more could have been expected.

Yet in other areas the Court's pronouncements had a significant impact. Even while NAACP lawyers continued their attack on segregation in public schools, they picked up on the unavoidable logic of *Brown:* If separating persons in school on the basis of race violated the Equal Protection Clause, then so did racial segregation elsewhere in public life. Civil rights litigants initiated a flurry of lawsuits aimed at racial segregation in public facilities.

Typically, a local federal judge would rule that the old *Plessy* doctrine of separate-but-equal no longer applied after *Brown,* and that segregation in a particular public facility violated the Fourteenth Amendment. An appeal to the Supreme Court invariably resulted in a per curiam affirmation of the lower-court ruling. In those few cases where district judges sustained segregation, the high court remanded with directions to proceed in a manner "not inconsistent with *Brown.*" These one- and two-sentence rulings ended decades of segregation on public beaches,[50] buses,[51] golf courses,[52] and parks.[53] In *Johnson* v. *Virginia* (1963), the Court reversed a contempt conviction imposed upon a black man for refusing to move to a section of the courtroom reserved for blacks. "Such a conviction cannot stand, for it is no longer open to question that a State may not constitutionally require segregation of public facilities."[54]

A more complicated issue faced the Court in the question of segregation in private facilities. Ever since the *Civil Rights Cases* in 1883, private discrimination had been considered beyond the reach of the Fourteenth Amendment. In *Shelley* v. *Kraemer* (1948), the Vinson Court had ruled that state enforcement of private restrictive covenants had in effect been state action and therefore prohibited. Using this idea of state action, the Warren Court struck down exclusion of blacks from a private theater located in a state park,[55] from private restaurants in a courthouse,[56] and from a municipally owned and operated parking garage.[57] In modern times there is very little private business that cannot be made to appear to have some real or imagined nexus to state authority, but as Justice Clark warned, the state action doctrine did have limits. The state, he said, had to be involved "to some significant extent," and over the next two decades a number of cases would test what constituted a "significant extent."[58]

The Court also struck down a series of state laws that regulated private conduct on the basis of race. Nearly all southern states, for example, had antimiscegenation laws on the books, some of them dating back to colonial times, which prohibited sexual relations, marriage, or cohabitation between members of different races. In 1883 the Court had sustained a state law imposing higher penalties upon partners in interracial fornication than those of the same race, on the grounds that the higher penalty applied equally to members of both races.[59] At first the Court had avoided taking the anti-miscegenation laws, because the justices recognized that interracial sexual relations remained one of the great fears in the South. In 1964, however, the Court invalidated a Florida criminal statute prohibiting cohabitation by inter-racial married couples as a violation of the Equal Protection Clause. As Justice Stewart noted in his concurrence, "[I]t is simply not possible for a state law to be valid under our Constitution which makes the criminality of an act depend upon the race of the actor."[60]

Challenges to laws prohibiting interracial marriages had been carried to the high court in 1955 and 1956, but the justices had hidden behind technical-ities to avoid deciding the question.[61] A dozen years after *Brown*, however, sixteen states still had such laws on their statute books, and after the Florida case, the Court could evade the issue no longer. In *Loving* v. *Virginia* (1967), Chief Justice Warren spoke for a unanimous Court in invalidating the anti-miscegenation laws. "Restricting the freedom to marry solely because of racial classification," he declared, "violates the central meaning of the Equal Protec-tion Clause."[62]

Some members of the Warren Court suggested that there ought to be a per se rule invalidating any legislative distinctions based on racial classification, but a majority of the Court never went that far. Rather, the Warren Court expanded on the suggestion Justice Stone had put forward in his *Carolene Products* footnote that certain categories required closer scrutiny by the courts. In all cases involving racial classification, the Court since *Brown* has applied a "strict scrutiny" standard, in which the state has the heavy burden of proving that a compelling governmental interest requires such classification. It is a difficult standard to meet, but in a few instances states have been able to show a legitimate, nondiscriminatory reason. In *Tancil* v. *Woods* (1964),[63] the Court upheld a requirement that divorce decrees indicate the race of the parties for record-keeping purposes, and in *Lee* v. *Washington* (1968),[64] it allowed prison authorities "acting in good faith, and in particularized circumstances," to take racial hostility into account to maintain order and, if necessary, to separate black and white prisoners.

THE SIT-IN CASES

The segregation, state action, and racial classification cases proved fairly easy for the Court once it had adopted the general rule of *Brown*. But in the early sixties a series of cases broke the unanimity that otherwise governed the Warren Court's handling of civil rights cases. In February 1960, four neatly dressed students from the all-black Agricultural and Technical College in

Greensboro, North Carolina, had sat down at the segregated lunch counter in Woolworth's and asked for a cup of coffee. When they were refused service, they remained in their seats until arrested. Black youths quickly took up the sit-in technique, and by the end of the year had desegregated lunch counters in 126 cities. Blacks then adapted this new weapon to protest other areas of discrimination, and the public began reading about "wade-ins" at public pools and "kneel-ins" at churches.

Prior to passage of the 1964 Civil Rights Act, restaurants had been considered private and, in the absence of a state law requiring segregation, had been considered free to choose whom they wished to serve or not serve. A protester sitting in at a segregated lunch counter or restaurant violated the owner's property rights and could be arrested for trespass. Although a majority of the Court obviously sympathized with the activist students, they could not agree on a rule to cover the situation.

Justice Douglas alone seemed willing to eliminate totally the distinction between state action and private discrimination, but others on the Court believed that in a free society, one had to tolerate some forms of private discrimination. Under the First Amendment people have the right of free association, which means they can choose not to associate with certain groups; private clubs, therefore, can elect to keep out Jews, blacks, women, or any other group that a majority of the members finds distasteful.[65] The only constitutional bar prevented the use of state resources to enforce that discrimination.

Douglas won more support when he suggested that restaurants and hotels not be seen as purely private property but instead as a type of public activity, a property "affected with a public interest," and therefore subject to legal prohibitions against discrimination. Under common law, for example, common carriers had to offer their services on a nondiscriminatory basis. If the Court had wanted to remain doctrinally consistent, it might have expanded the state action doctrine. In *Shelley* the Court had refused to allow state power to enforce private housing restrictions; why not bar the use of trespass to enforce discriminatory practices?

In the end, the Court seized upon technical reasons to set aside all of the sit-in convictions without citing *Shelley*, a sign that the majority felt state action had to be more than just evenhanded enforcement of private property rights.[66] In only one case did six of the justices reach the broader issue, and they divided evenly. The case arose from convictions of civil rights protesters under Maryland's criminal trespass law. After their conviction, the state had passed a public accommodations law forbidding restaurants and hotels from refusing service on the basis of race. Justice Brennan then vacated the conviction and remanded for further consideration by the state court in consideration of the new law, an easy way to avoid a doctrinal decision.[67]

Justice Douglas concurred in the result but entered a lengthy opinion joined by Goldberg and Warren. In it he argued that restaurants constituted businesses affected with public interest and therefore came within the *Shelley* doctrine. Justice Black, joined by Harlan and White, took the opposite view, arguing that the Fourteenth Amendment did not prohibit property owners from discriminating as to whom they would allow on their property. Bigots as well as saints had the right to call upon the state to protect their legitimate property rights. What is interesting about both opinions is that Douglas and Black cited the same historical sources, often even the same passages, to support their completely contradictory conclusions.

The justices had evaded a doctrinal ruling in the sit-in cases in the hope that Congress would act on the matter. President Kennedy had proposed legislation that would, in effect, have adopted Justice Douglas's reasoning and precluded discrimination in public accommodations. The bill stalled under southern pressure, but following Kennedy's assassination, Lyndon Johnson declared passage of the measure a top priority as well as a tribute to the fallen Kennedy. Under heavy pressure from the White House as well as civil rights groups, Congress enacted the 1964 Civil Rights Act. Within six months a unanimous Court had upheld the key provisions of the bill, the Title II restrictions against discrimination in public accommodations.

In *Heart of Atlanta Motel* v. *United States*,[68] the Court sustained the powers of Congress under the Commerce Clause as well as the Equal Protection Clause to declare racial discrimination a burden on interstate commerce. Seventy-five percent of the motel's guests came from out of state, and its business therefore clearly came within the reach of congressional power to regulate interstate commerce. In the companion case, *Katzenbach* v. *McClung*,[69] the Court, also unanimously, upheld the law as it applied to restaurants. With these cases, the Court could note that Congress and the executive branch had finally taken the path it had blazed a dozen years earlier in *Brown*. For the first time, all three branches stood agreed that the Fourteenth Amendment not only banned racial discrimination but also gave the federal government extensive affirmative powers to protect the civil rights of its minority citizens.

VOTING RIGHTS AND SUSPECT CLASSIFICATION

The Fifteenth Amendment had prohibited the denial of suffrage on account of race, but southern states had worked out a variety of stratagems to deny blacks an effective franchise. In Alabama, for example, Negroes made up about half the population but only 1 percent of the registered voters. To protest that situation, Martin Luther King, Jr., organized a march from Selma to the state capitol in Montgomery in March 1965. Governor George Wallace forbade the march, and when King went ahead, state troopers attacked unarmed men, women, and children using bullwhips, clubs, and tear gas as television broadcast the sickening spectacle to the nation and the world. President Johnson immediately federalized the Alabama national guard to protect the demonstrators and then asked Congress for legislation to guard the right to vote against the ingenious devices employed by southern officials.

The 1965 Voting Rights Act authorized the attorney general to send federal registrars into any county that he or she suspected of discrimination, in particular those counties where 50 percent or more of the voting age population had failed to register. Local voting regulations and procedures could be suspended, as could literacy tests and any other devices used to prevent otherwise eligible persons from exercising their right to vote. The attorney general, Nicholas Katzenbach, soon afterward issued a proclamation identifying Alabama, Alaska, Georgia, Louisiana, Mississippi, South Carolina, Virginia, thirty-four counties in North Carolina, and isolated counties in Arizona, Hawaii, and Idaho as meeting the statutory criteria. For the first time, federal law would be used to protect the integrity of registration and voting processes in the South, and unlike the first Reconstruction, this time all three branches of the federal government stood united in their determination to protect black voting rights.

Southern states quickly challenged the Voting Rights Act, and to expedite the matter so that another election would not go by with blacks still disenfranchised, the Court took *South Carolina* v. *Katzenbach*[70] on original jurisdiction. There is no question that, whatever technical difficulties may have existed,[71] the justices wanted to settle the constitutionality of this law as quickly as possible. After watching the southern states flout the desegregation ruling for more than a decade, they wanted to hand down their opinion so a sympathetic administration could enforce the law.

South Carolina's long and convoluted brief boiled down to three major challenges. First, the state claimed that Section 2 of the Fifteenth Amendment[72] spoke only in general terms; specific remedies to voting rights violations belonged to the judiciary, not to the legislature. Second, the formula for determining which parts of the country fell within the act's coverage violated the constitutional guarantee that all states be treated equally. Finally, a provision barring court review of administrative findings constituted a bill of attainder and infringed on the separation of powers.[73]

A nearly unanimous Court (Justice Black dissented on a minor point),[74] speaking through the Chief Justice, dismissed all of the state's challenges in upholding the law. Reciting a long line of cases reaching back to the Marshall era, Warren held that Congress could choose from a full range of means in carrying out a legitimate end. Congress had studied the problem at length and had noted information supplied by both the Justice Department and the Civil

Rights Commission. It could therefore rationally decide that resources and remedies should be targeted toward those areas in which one found the greatest discrimination. In the specific remedies, Warren concluded, Congress had chosen "appropriate means of combatting the evil."[75]

Shortly afterward, the Court overturned the use of poll taxes in state elections in *Harper* v. *Virginia Board of Elections* (1966).[76] The Twenty-fourth Amendment, ratified in January 1964, had abolished the poll tax in federal elections, and Justice Douglas, for a 6-3 Court, invoked the Equal Protection Clause to inter the state tax as well. Douglas's opinion utilized two different equal protection analyses, "fundamental interests" and "suspect classification." The Constitution, he conceded, nowhere specifically mentioned a right to vote in state elections, but voting constituted such a basic right of free citizens that any effort to restrict it ran into a strong presumption of unconstitutionality. To limit the right to vote on the basis of wealth, moreover, created a classification that could not withstand equal protection analysis. "Wealth, like race, creed, or color, is not germane to one's ability to participate intelligently in the electoral process. Lines drawn on the basis of wealth or property, like those of race, are traditionally disfavored."[77]

Douglas's opinion is one of his boldest, and also one of the most activist of the Warren Court era, and it brought forth impassioned dissents from Black and Harlan (joined by Stewart). While Black stood willing to expand the reach of the Bill of Rights through the Fourteenth Amendment, both he and Harlan took a fairly conservative approach in requiring some textual basis for establishing a constitutionally protected right. They attacked the majority opinion as akin to earlier courts' use of due process to strike down economic legislation that the justices had not liked; they also objected to the idea that the meaning of the Constitution changed over time.

Douglas had argued that the meaning of the Equal Protection Clause "is not shackled to the political theory of a particular era. . . . Notions of what constitute equal treatment for purposes of the Equal Protection Clause *do* change."[78] To conservatives, this argument smacked of heresy, for in their eyes it deprived the Constitution of fixed meaning and left it subject to the passing whims of changing judicial personnel. Equal protection, due process, all had to *mean* something, and that meaning had to be stable so that people could rely on it. But a fixed and rigid interpretation, as Douglas recognized, would be just as bad, because it would preclude the Constitution from ever having a contemporary meaning.

Beyond that, Douglas seemed willing to open up the range of suspect classifications to include wealth, an approach that horrified conservatives and appalled many constitutional scholars. There is a significant difference between a constitutional promise of equal treatment before the law and a promise of full economic as well as political and legal equality. One can find a textual basis in the Constitution to prohibit classification by race or religion, but it would be stretching the common sense of the document to suggest that it seeks to abolish economic inequity.

Efforts to bring wealth (or more accurately, poverty) in as a suspect classification have been raised periodically, but with very limited success. The Court has held that absence of money cannot be used to deny a basic right. In *Griffin* v. *Illinois* (1956),[79] for example, the Court ruled that a state had to provide a trial transcript to an indigent appealing a criminal conviction, because the inability to pay for a transcript would deny the defendant any appeal. A few years later the Court held that a state could not deny an indigent counsel on appeal,[80] and at the end of the Warren era, the Court struck down durational residence requirements for welfare payments as violating equal protection.[81] Comments in Justice Brennan's opinion in this last case prompted much speculation regarding the future of fundamental interest analysis. If one adopted the view, as Brennan implied, of food, housing, and education as fundamental in establishing a decent life, then could one utilize the Equal Protection Clause to force government to provide those items to all, or institute a wide-ranging redistribution of wealth? How did one determine what constituted fundamental interests? Who made the determination?

In this area, at least, the Warren Court left a legacy of ambivalence, and while advocates of the poor argued for the inclusion of poverty as a suspect classification, the Burger Court proved unwilling to go down that route.[82] In fact, the Warren Court itself applied this fundamental interest analysis only to voting, criminal appeals, and interstate travel. Douglas in *Harper* and Brennan in *Shapiro* suggested that this analysis could be taken much further, but how far it could have gone is questionable. Douglas and Brennan had put forward a very open-ended view, one amenable to reinterpretation in the light of changing social standards, but do the courts have the institutional competence to force the type of legislation that a judicial attack on poverty would have necessitated? And the sparse comments in both cases hardly qualify as a full-blown doctrinal explication of why poverty could or should be attacked through use of the Equal Protection Clause.[83]

THE APPORTIONMENT CASES

Douglas's suggestions in *Harper* regarding poverty never developed into a mature doctrinal statement, but his comments on fundamental interests became a standard form of equal protection analysis. For the Warren Court, as for so many of its predecessors, the right to vote constituted the basic interest, because without it a citizenry could neither control its government nor act to redress grievances. Given this view, as well as the Court's acknowledged activism, its decisions in the apportionment cases should have come as no surprise. Yet in a way that did not apply to any other group of decisions, including the desegregation cases, the apportionment rulings constituted perhaps the most radical of all the Warren Court's actions.

The Constitution assigns to each state two senators and a number of representatives proportional to its population, but does not specify how these seats are to be allocated within each state. James Madison had implied that the arrangement should be equitable, and many states had constitutional provisions designed to ensure at least a rough equality between congressional districts as well as among the seats in the state assemblies. During the 1950s, in fact, three-fifths of all the states reapportioned one or both of their legislative chambers.

Twelve states, however, had not redrawn their district lines for more than thirty years, despite major population shifts. Tennessee and Alabama had not redrawn their lines since 1901, and Delaware since 1897. Within some states discrepancies of enormous magnitude existed; in Vermont, for example, the most populous assembly district had 33,000 persons, and the smallest had 238, yet each had one seat. Distortions also appeared in many state senates, which often followed geographical boundaries. In California, the senatorial district comprising Los Angeles had 6 million people, whereas a more sparsely populated district had only 14,000. In all of the states that had not reapportioned, as well as in many which reapportioned but not along strict population criteria, the results magnified the power of the older rural areas while undervaluing the ballot of the new urban and suburban districts. Needless to say, the rural minorities who controlled the state houses had no incentive to reform, because that would have dissipated their power.

Prior to the Warren era the Court had steadfastly refused to accept cases challenging state apportionment formulas. The Court described the issue as "nonjusticiable," that is, either it did not appear amenable to judicial resolution or it involved an issue so political in nature that the judiciary should not interfere. The "political question doctrine" was first enunciated by Chief Justice Roger Taney in *Luther* v. *Borden* (1849),[84] a case that grew out of the political revolt in Rhode Island known as the Dorr Rebellion.[85] There are essentially two rationales for the court invoking this doctrine; one is that responsibility is clearly committed either to another branch of the federal government or to the states, and the other is that the court cannot fashion a judicially manageable solution.

The first constitutional attack against malapportionment arose under the Guarantee Clause of the Constitution (Art. IV, Sec. 4), which states: "The United States shall guarantee to every State a Republican Form of Government." For the most part, the Supreme Court over the decades had refused to assign any greater meaning to that clause other than that the federal government would protect states against foreign invasion or domestic rebellion. Challengers of congressional districting in Illinois claimed that districts had to be approximately equal in population in order not to violate the Constitution.

Justice Frankfurter, speaking for only a plurality of the seven justices who heard *Colgrove* v. *Green*, declared that

> the petitioners ask of this Court what is beyond its competence to grant. . . . Effective working of our government revealed this issue to be of a peculiarly political nature and therefore not meet for judicial determination. This controversy concerns matters that bring courts into immediate and active relations with party contests. From the determination of such issues this Court has traditionally remained aloof. It is hostile to a democratic system to involve the judiciary in the politics of the people. Due regard for the Constitution as a viable system precludes judicial correction. Authority for dealing with such problems resides elsewhere. The short of it is that the Constitution has conferred upon Congress exclusive authority to secure fair representation by the States in the popular [House]. Courts ought not to enter this political thicket.[86]

Frankfurter spoke only for himself, Reed, and Burton and got a plurality when Justice Rutledge concurred in the result. But three members of the Court—Black, Douglas, and Murphy—dissented, and believed that the complaint did, in fact, present a justiciable case and controversy. Four years later the Vinson Court again refused to enter the "political thicket," turning aside a challenge to Georgia's county unit system, which heavily weighted the electoral process in favor of rural areas.[87]

Ironically, the first hint of change came in an opinion written by Frankfurter, who nonetheless continued to insist that courts should stay out of this political morass. In 1960 the high court struck down a flagrant gerrymandering scheme in Tuskegee, Alabama, which effectively disenfranchised nearly all of the city's blacks. Frankfurter's opinion relied entirely on the Fifteenth Amendment, and he carefully avoided any intimation that the ruling might apply to other districting imbalances.[88] Whatever Frankfurter's intentions, reformers believed they now had a foot in the courthouse door; two years later, over Frankfurter's objections, the Court accepted a suit brought by urban voters in Tennessee, where there had been no redistricting in sixty years.

Baker v. *Carr*,[89] handed down later in 1962, took the Court away from the position Frankfurter had so vigorously defended in *Colgrove*. Justice Brennan, speaking for a 6-2 majority, ruled only that issues such as alleged malapportionment could be litigated in federal court. He prescribed no particular solution but sent the case back to district court for a full hearing; the high court would not deal with a remedy until the matter had been fully litigated and a final decree entered.

Brennan's opinion did not flatly reject the political question doctrine; it had often served the Court well as a safety valve, allowing the justices to evade, when they chose, issues whose decision, one way or the other, might damage the Court.[90] Nor did he challenge the traditional interpretation of the Guarantee Clause, which had very little precedential value in this case. Rather, he noted (correctly) that even in *Colgrove* a majority of the Court had thought the issue justiciable, and in *Gomillion*, it had specifically asserted judicial power to remedy the problem. Brennan justified his conclusion by drawing a distinction between recognized political questions, in which the Constitution demonstrably assigned responsibility to another branch of government, and apportionment, which he claimed could be resolved through "judicially discoverable and manageable standards." Malapportionment, he believed, violated the Equal Protection Clause.

Despite strenuous and predictable dissents from Justices Harlan and Frankfurter, both of whom urged judicial restraint and deference to the political process, it is easy to see why the majority of the Court agreed to consider the apportionment cases. Frankfurter's dissent, as a matter of fact, gives us a clear understanding of exactly what the majority had in mind. He accused the majority of risking the Court's prestige in an area that should be left to the political process. "In a democratic society like ours, relief must come through an aroused popular conscience that sears the conscience of the people's representatives."[91] While Harlan thought the system might be better, he found nothing in the Constitution to prevent a state "acting not irrationally, from choosing any electoral structure it thinks best suited to the interests, tempers and customs of the people."[92]

Both men ignored the heart of the issue—the political process had been stymied and perverted, so that the majority of the people could not adopt that system "best suited" to their needs because an entrenched minority blocked any and all change. The Court on a number of occasions had declared that not all issues could be resolved through litigation and that, in questions of public policy, change would have to come through the political process and not through the courts. In those cases, however, there had always been an assumption that the process would be amenable to majoritarian decision making—that all voters would have a say in the matter.

The Warren Court and the Burger Court both placed a high value on the integrity of the political process, because for all the debate about judicial activism and policy making, the Court always looked to that process to resolve most of the public questions of the day. The whole rationale for judicial restraint and deference to the legislative will had been based on the belief that the legislature truly and accurately reflected the will of the people. For the majority of the Warren Court, depriving a person of the full value of his or her ballot deprived them of the equal protection of the law, whether that deprivation came about because of race, poverty, or residence in an urban area.

Despite the dire warnings that the Court would do immeasurable harm to itself through entanglement in the "political thicket," in the end the Court found not only a clear standard but also one that quickly won the support of a majority of Americans. Following *Baker* v. *Carr*, the Court handed down decisions invalidating the Georgia county unit system[93] as well as the state's congressional districting plan.[94] In the first case, which technically dealt with voting rights rather than apportionment, Justice Douglas applied an equal protection analysis and then came up with the formula that not only provided judicial guidance but also caught the popular imagination—"one man, one vote." Who could object to assuring every person that his or her vote counted equally with those of others? Support of the formula equated with support of democracy and the Constitution; opposition seemed undemocratic and petty.

Following *Baker* many legislatures had voluntarily redistricted one or both of their legislative chambers, but they did not know exactly what criteria the Court would apply to measure the fairness of their plans. In some states rural minorities blocked any effort at reform, and in Colorado the electorate, by a 2-1 margin, approved a plan that apportioned the lower house on a population basis but gave rural areas additional, although not a controlling, weight in the upper house. In states where reapportionment had occurred as well as in states where it had been blocked, reformers launched dozens of suits seeking redress under the Equal Protection Clause.

In June 1964 Chief Justice Warren handed down the Court's decision in six representative cases. The leading suit attacked malapportionment of the Alabama legislature, which, despite a constitutional requirement for representation based on population and a decennial reapportionment, remained based on the 1900 census. Lower courts had found this scheme, as well as two proposed "reforms," violative of the Equal Protection Clause and had ordered a temporary reapportionment plan that combined features from the new proposals. Both sides in the lower court case then appealed. In *Reynolds* v. *Sims* (1964), Warren built upon the analyses in the two Georgia cases and adopted Douglas's "one man, one vote" formulation as the constitutional standard. The Chief Justice dismissed all formulas that attempted to weight certain factors:

> To the extent that a citizen's right to vote is debased, he is that much less a citizen. The weight of a citizen's vote cannot be made to depend on where he lives. . . . A citizen, a qualified voter, is no more nor no less so because he lives in the city or on the farm. This is the clear and strong command of our Constitution's Equal Protection Clause.[95]

In the Colorado case, the state contended that a majority of its voters, by a 2-1 margin, had voluntarily diluted their voting power to protect the rural minority. Warren rejected the argument out of hand; the Court dealt here not with the rights of minorities but with the rights of individuals. "It is a precept of American law," he declared, "that certain rights exist which a citizen cannot trade, barter, or even give away." An individual's constitutional rights could not be infringed because a majority of the people voted to do so.[96]

With Frankfurter now gone from the bench, only Justice Harlan remained to object to the apportionment decisions.[97] The majority opinion, he charged, rested on bad history and bad law, and ignored the special qualities of a pluralist federal system. Harlan would have allowed apportionment formulas to take into account such factors as history, economics, geography, urban-rural balance, theories of bicameralism, and majoritarian preferences of particular schemes. To this the Chief Justice responded that "neither history alone, nor economics or other sorts of group interests are permissible factors in attempting to justify disparities. . . . Citizens, not history or economic interests, cast votes. People, not land or trees or pastures vote."[98]

At Justice Douglas's urging, the Court handed down its decisions in the six cases at the end of the Term in June rather than holding them up until the fall, so that reapportionment could take place before the November elections. This time the Court did not repeat the mistake it had made in *Brown II;* there was no talk of "all deliberate speed" or any other phrase that might be countenanced as inviting delay. The Court clearly indicated that it expected rapid compliance and urged that unless the district courts, which would have primary responsibility for evaluating new plans, found some compelling reason to the contrary, they should allow no more state elections to be held under invalidated plans.

Despite the uproar from rural-dominated legislatures and their allies in Congress that greeted these decisions,[99] the opposition soon faded as new legislatures, elected under court-ordered plans, took control of the state houses. Moreover, influential citizen groups such as the League of Women Voters endorsed *Reynolds* and the one-person, one-vote concept, and conducted educational campaigns to explain the rulings. And, of course, once implemented, reapportionment faced little opposition as formerly dominant minorities could no longer block the majority will. No state, once reapportioned, sought to revive the old system.

Although the one-person, one-vote rule provided a clear and judicially manageable standard, some questions did remain, such as the level of exactitude as well as the reach of the decision. In *Swann* v. *Adams* (1967),[100] the Court invalidated a Florida plan that had only minor aberrations from the formula. Justice White agreed that the Constitution did not require absolute precision, but in this case the statute had failed to provide adequate justification for certain important deviations. As with all equal protection cases, the Court would employ a strict standard of scrutiny, so that states would have to show a compelling reason for any significant deviation. The following year, the Court brought city and county governments under the one-person, one-vote rule;[101] remaining questions, and there were many, would be decided by the Burger Court.

CONCLUSIONS

The apportionment cases seemed a fitting climax to the Warren Court's so-called equal protection revolution. What had been the "last resort of constitutional arguments" had become, in a little over a dozen years, a powerful tool to protect the civil rights and liberties of individuals. In some ways the apportionment cases constitute the most "radical" decisions. Unlike the desegregation cases, in which the Court had chipped away at the separate-but-equal doctrine for many years, apportionment had been a stranger in the courts. Conservatives later seized Justice Frankfurter's argument in *Colgrove* as the proper standard for judicial restraint, yet that argument had never enjoyed support from a majority of his colleagues. Four of the seven justices who heard the case thought it justiciable, but they lacked any idea of how to develop a clear and manageable judicial standard.

By the time the Court agreed on the justiciability of apportionment in *Baker* v. *Carr* in 1962, it had had the experience of the desegregation cases and had learned several valuable lessons. First, the political process cannot always be relied upon to remedy even a clear violation of constitutionally protected rights. Second, if courts intervene to protect such rights, then they must act boldly and set out clear rules. Third, new standards must be implemented without delay. The apportionment decisions showed the wisdom of these lessons; despite some vocal opposition from rural groups who would now lose power, the country quickly accepted the rationale of the decisions and the rightness of the solution.

One could also portray the apportionment decisions as quite conservative. Opponents of judicial activism always justify their call for deference to the legislative will on grounds that elected assemblies represent the will of the people, in whom sovereignty ultimately resides. If one is to take that argument seriously, then it seems absolutely necessary that the legislatures actually and fairly represent the people. If they do not—if a rural minority blocks the will of an urban majority, if older areas have greater voting strength than do newer and more populated districts—then the legislatures do not represent the will of the people. In this sense, the Warren Court fostered greater democracy; it made it possible for the majority to gain control of the political process.

A more complex question involves the nature of federalism and the role of minorities in a pluralist society. The Court, especially in speech and religion cases, has declared that the majority cannot silence a minority. It has also recognized "suspect" classifications, such as race and religion, which trigger strict scrutiny under equal protection analysis. Furthermore, the Constitution, in setting up a federal system, did not establish equality as the criterion. All states, from the largest to the smallest, have two senators, and if one applied the Court's calculus to this system, it would certainly fail under the one-person, one-vote rule. But it is constitutionally mandated, and if the federal system allows such disparities and the use of criteria other than population, then why shouldn't the states also be allowed to set up smaller versions of a federal system, with some counties, no matter how small, assured of the same number of representatives as larger counties in order to protect their rights?

It is a logical argument, but the Court's response is equally logical. The Constitution does not recognize any unit smaller than a state, and from the beginning courts have held that local governments are merely administrative units of the state. Fights for local control of schools, taxes, and other functions clearly show that states are the locus of sovereignty for such matters. One does not find a state constitution that says "We the counties of this state, in order to form a more perfect state . . . " The states and their internal arrangements, therefore, are different from the federal government and its relations with the states.

Finally, should courts be agents of social and political change? Where is the mandate to overturn the majority's desire for segregated schools or legislatures that favor certain areas? Opponents of judicial activism say that courts should not be involved—that social and political change are evolutionary processes that can only be derailed by precipitate action. The answer, Court defenders would say, is in the Constitution. Of what value are guarantees of free speech, due process, or the equal protection of the laws if they can be limited by majority whim? What value is the Constitution itself unless it is obeyed?

The debate, of course, goes on over whether the Court has correctly interpreted the Constitution, but that is a debate which began with the founding of the nation. Perhaps the Court has at times overreached itself and has read more into the Constitution than either its Framers or even current circumstances warranted. Yet it has been the expansion of liberty, not its contraction, that has been the dominant theme in our country's history. Would we really want a Court that took a crabbed and narrow view of our liberties? It is a question that critics of judicial activism often fail to ask.

10

"Not Only Overt Discrimination but also Practices"

The Burger Court and Equal Protection

I n some areas of equal protection analysis, such as racial classification, the Burger Court followed the path laid out by its
predecessor; efforts to segregate on the basis of race, for example, or state
endorsement of discrimination ran into a stone wall of judicial opposition. But
as litigation moved from questions of outright discriminaion to more complex
issues, divisions on the Court became clearer. One could say that here, as in
other issues, the Warren Court had the "easy" cases and left many difficult
questions to be answered later. In non-race-related cases, however, the Burger
Court moved out in completely unanticipated directions and left many people
wondering if perhaps it and not its predecessor had been the most activist bench
in American judicial history.

DESEGREGATION

In the fifteen years following *Brown*, the Warren Court had moved from
the "all deliberate speed" formula of *Brown II*, through the growing impatience
manifested in *Cooper* and *Green*, to proposing specific remedies. The Burger
Court quickly disposed of its first school desegregation case in the fall of 1969.
The Nixon administration, pursuing the so-called southern strategy, had
intervened in a Fifth Circuit case asking Chief Judge John Brown to delay
desegregation orders for thirty Mississippi school districts. On August 18, after
the Justice Department had endorsed this request, a judicial panel granted a
three-month delay. The NAACP immediately appealed to the Supreme
Court, and in *Alexander* v. *Holmes County Board of Education*,[1] the Court summarily reversed the delay and admonished the Fifth Circuit. "The obligation
of every school district," the short per curiam opinion declared, "is to terminate
dual school systems at once."

While technically the *Alexander* decision had been handed down by the Burger Court, in fact the bench that Term hardly differed from the last years of the Warren era; the only change had been in the center chair. Moreover, the case involved straightforward segregation by race, and as such, it still represented the type of discrimination that the Court had tackled in the 1950s and 1960s—a governmental agency intentionally discriminated against someone for no other reason than race, an "overt, garden-variety discrimination," as one scholar called it.[2] While such cases would occasionally surface, the Court's agenda on racial matters changed significantly in the 1970s. Where the Warren Court had dealt with overt de jure segregation (segregation mandated by law), the Burger Court grappled with three far more complex themes: (1) the desegregation of urban school districts, both North and South, where segregation resulted from longstanding residential patterns rather than from law; (2) discriminatory effects in nonschool areas in the absence of a specific purpose to discriminate; and (3) affirmative action, the effort to remedy the effects of past discrimination through current preferential plans.

In the new Chief Justice's second term, the Court handed down its last unanimous school desegregation decision, *Swann* v. *Charlotte-Mecklenburg Board of Education* (1971).[3] Earlier cases had primarily involved rural school districts, where even though blacks and whites lived in close proximity, they went to different schools. In such instances, the remedy had been simple: all students living in one part of the district went to the same school. But in cities with segregated residential patterns, if children went to the school nearest their home, they would be going to an all-white or all-black school. School boards argued that such segregation did not result from state law and therefore should not be subject to forced desegregation. Their arguments, however, ignored the fact that these residential patterns had developed through decades of Jim Crow and that often school boards had gerrymandered districts to make sure that they remained racially segregated. As Justice Powell noted in a later opinion:

> [T]he familiar root cause of segregated schools in *all* the biracial metropolitan areas of our country is essentially the same: one of segregated residential and migratory patterns, the impact of which on the racial composition of the schools was often perpetuated and rarely ameliorated by action of public school authorities.[4]

Speaking for the Court, Chief Justice Burger charged that the current segregation had resulted from past misconduct and therefore had to be remedied. He affirmed the lower court's order that the school board redraw attendance zones and bus students in order to achieve a racial composition at each school approximating the racial mix of the entire district. In a companion case, the Court voided a state antibusing statute that barred school assignments on the basis of race. Although nominally a "colorblind law," in fact it had operated to prevent integration.[5]

The *Swann* case marked a significant departure for the Court aside from the fact that it had begun dealing with the problems of urban segregation. The majority of the Warren Court opinions had been aimed at *desegregating* schools by the stratagem of voiding those statutes which required or preserved racial separation. The underlying philosophy had been that if barriers to integrated schools could be removed, then within a short time the schools would be integrated. The *Swann* court recognized that simply removing old barriers would not be enough, because in addition to the actual laws, a variety of customs and extralegal sanctions still operated to keep blacks and whites separated. In the 1970s, therefore, the Burger Court moved from simply striking down segregation statutes and requiring *integration* plans. In doing so it did not reverse the Warren Court legacy but moved beyond it, taking positive steps to achieve what the earlier Court thought would happen once the overt barriers had been removed.

The remedy which the Court proposed—busing—had been invoked by the Warren Court in one of its last decisions, and it would be the most controversial aspect of school desegregation decisions in the 1970s.[6] Busing as a remedy affected northern as well as southern schools, urban as well as rural, and it led to violence in school districts across the country. White opposition to busing led Congress in 1972 to enact a moratorium on court orders designed to achieve "a balance among students with respect to race, sex, religion, or socioeconomic status" through busing.[7] But in *Drummond* v. *Acree* (1972),[8] Justice Powell, acting as circuit justice, declined to stay a busing decree he characterized as designed to end segregation rather than to achieve a racial balance. He dismissed the 1972 law as inapplicable and said if Congress really wanted to end busing, "it could have used clear and explicit language appropriate to that result."[9]

Congress, under prodding from President Nixon, then enacted in the 1974 Educational Amendments a "priority of remedies" that federal courts and agencies could use to end segregation, and it barred the "transportation of any student to a school other than the school closest or next closest to his place of residence." The law also included a provision that Congress had no intention to diminish federal court authority to enforce the Fifth and Fourteenth Amendments, which in essence meant that the antibusing clause did not apply if the courts believed it a necessary remedy.[10] Later on in the 1970s, Congress barred the use of federal funds to force *desegregated* school districts to bus students, which still left busing available as an antisegregation remedy.[11] Efforts to specifically bar courts from ordering busing except in narrowly defined circumstances came up several times in the early 1980s but failed to gain passage in both houses of Congress.

In light of congressional failure to act, several states took measures designed to curb involuntary busing. In 1982 the Court handed down two decisions on the same day dealing with such state laws. In Washington a state initiative passed following a court-ordered desegregation plan in Seattle would have barred school boards from requiring students to attend any school except the one nearest or next nearest to their homes. Justice Blackmun wrote for the 5-4 majority in invalidating the initiative, holding that the majority could not use the machinery of government to block minorities seeking equal rights, especially when the resulting laws relied heavily on racial classification. The initiative, he declared, had reallocated governmental power in a manner that disadvantaged racial minorities.[12]

Justice Powell, in a strong dissent joined by Burger, Rehnquist, and O'Connor, objected to the Court's "unprecedented intrusion into the structure of a state government." There was no record of de jure segregation and therefore no constitutional obligation to adopt busing as a remedy; given these circumstances, Powell believed it perfectly reasonable for a majority of the people to adopt a proposal barring busing. The Washington initiative "simply does not place unique political obstacles in the way of racial minorities."[13]

In the second case, Powell spoke for an 8-1 majority sustaining a California initiative barring state court-ordered busing as a remedy for de facto segregation, a situation in which segregation obviously existed, but did so in the absence of laws directing that result. The state courts had been attacking de facto segregation, and Proposition I limited state court power to the same level that federal courts could exercise under the Fourteenth Amendment. A state, Powell wrote, may always do more than the Equal Protection Clause mandates but is only required to do no less; if the people of California wanted to limit judicial power to the minimum required, they had the right to do so.[14]

The two cases highlighted one of the significant considerations in the Burger Court's equal protection analysis: the difference between de jure and de facto segregation. The Court would not allow any type of discriminatory classification based on race, and if there had been de jure discrimination in the past, the justices permitted lower courts a greater leeway in fashioning an appropriate remedy. But if no evidence existed of legally established segregation, then the Court gave local governmental units greater flexibility as to how or whether they would respond. Problems arose in the early seventies when the Court began hearing cases aimed at segregation in northern school districts, and the unanimity that had marked the Warren era fell apart.

DESEGREGATION IN THE NORTH

In *Keyes* v. *Denver School District No. 1* (1973),[15] the Court heard its first challenge to a segregated northern school system. Justice Brennan began his opinion by emphasizing that the legal difference between de jure and de facto segregation lay in whether there had been an intent to segregate. While no formal laws required segregation in the Denver schools, the school board had used race as a determinant in drawing attendance zones and siting new schools, and that had the same effect and intent as passing a formal law.

Although Brennan nominally adhered to the de jure/de facto standard, in fact he blurred the distinctions between the two. If "intent" now became the chief criterion, a plaintiff could always find some "evidence" purportedly showing a school official acting to foster continued segregation. Justice Powell's concurrence suggested that the distinction be dropped and that the courts adopt a single standard for integration that would apply to both North and South, in both urban and rural school districts. The Court, he argued, should impose a "constitutional obligation . . . [on] school districts throughout our country to operate *integrated school systems.*" This meant, Powell explained:

> A system would be integrated in accord with constitutional standards if the responsible authorities had taken appropriate steps to (i) integrate faculties and administration; (ii) scrupulously assure equality of facilities, instruction, and curriculum opportunities throughout the district; (iii) utilize their authority to draw attendance zones to promote integration; and (iv) locate new schools, close old ones, and determine the size and grade categories with this same objective in mind.[16]

The following year the Court addressed a most difficult issue: whether the remedy for segregation, even de jure segregation, could cut across jurisdictional lines. The first case of this type to reach the high court involved Richmond, Virginia, where many whites had moved to the surrounding, predominantly white counties, leaving the inner-city school population overwhelmingly black. District Judge Robert R. Merhige ordered the merger of the Richmond city school system with those of neighboring Henrico and Chesterfield counties, which were and still are primarily bedroom suburbs for the city.[17] The Court of Appeals for the Fourth Circuit reversed, holding that the historic district lines between city and county had not been drawn to confine blacks to the city, nor had there been any evidence of conspiracy to maintain segregated schools.[18] When the case reached the Supreme Court, Justice Powell recused himself, presumably because of his earlier connection with the Richmond schools. The remaining justices split 4-4, leaving intact the circuit decision.[19]

Similar situations existed in other areas with predominantly black inner cities and white suburbs. Whether or not de jure segregation had existed, the fact remained that integration could not be achieved with an overwhelmingly black school population. Even if the suburbs had been historically white, the city constituted their reason for being. The city provided the jobs and the services that fueled the entire metropolitan economy. Moreover, the phenomenon known as "white flight," triggered by desegregation and busing orders, had sent tens of thousands of white families and their school-age children out of the cities, effectively resegregating the city systems.[20] All of these considerations, civil rights advocates argued, required the suburbs to share their burden in remedying the problems of inner-city school segregation.

Detroit had a situation similar to that of Richmond, with white suburbs surrounding a black urban core. District Judge Stephen J. Roth had determined that Detroit's schools had been unconstitutionally segregated and that desegregation of the city's 64 percent black schools would send whites fleeing to the suburbs. To prevent resegregation, he ordered the fifty-three surrounding school systems unified with that of Detroit. Justice Powell did not recuse on this case, and by a 5-4 vote in *Milliken* v. *Bradley* (1974),[21] the Court held that federal judges could not order multidistrict remedies without proof that the district lines had originally been drawn in a discriminatory manner. The "scope of the remedy," wrote the Chief Justice, "is determined by the nature and extent of the constitutional violation." The Constitution spoke only to purposeful discrimination, and the Equal Protection Clause could not be invoked to ameliorate problems not caused by state action.

For some people, *Milliken* represented "the sad but inevitable culmination of a national antiblack strategy."[22] The case marked the first time since *Brown* that blacks had lost a school case, and Justice Marshall lamented that "after twenty years of small, often difficult steps toward that great end [of equal justice under law], the Court today takes a great step backwards."[23] But for others, the decision came as a relief, "an act of absolution. Segregated Detroit [s]chools were not the suburb's creation and thus not their burden."[24]

To look on *Milliken* in strictly racial terms, however, would ignore considerations important to the majority, especially Powell and the Chief Justice. "No single tradition," Burger noted, "is more deeply rooted than local control over the operation of the schools; local autonomy has long been thought essential both to the maintenance of community concern and support for public schools and to the quality of the educational process."[25] The Court would not countenance legally sanctioned discrimination, but in combating de facto segregation, it would also look at other values involved.

The Court next dealt with northern urban-school integration in two 1979 Ohio cases, in which the majority extended the logic of *Keyes*.[26] Although neither the Columbus nor Dayton school systems had been segregated by law, the majority sustained the lower court's findings that parts of each system had been deliberately segregated at the time of *Brown;* as a result, the school boards had a constitutional obligation to desegregate.[27] In both cases, Justice White's majority opinion relied heavily on lower-court findings that there had been an intent to preserve racial separation. By placing the burden of proof on the school boards to show that continuing discriminatory patterns had not resulted from official policy, the Court in effect applied the same standards to northern schools as had been applied to southern systems.

In a strong dissent, Justice Rehnquist, joined by Justice Powell, claimed that the Court, while claiming to rely on *Keyes*, had actually ignored the earlier decision, and it swept away the distinction between de facto and de jure segregation. The courts could not just ignore history; judges had to realize that some segregation resulted not from state action or evil intent but rather from other nonmalignant, perhaps even accidental causes. The Constitution neither required nor authorized courts to interfere in such situations.[28]

While lip service had been paid to the de jure/de facto distinction in all of these cases, one wonders if, in the eyes of the Burger majority, it had become a distinction without a difference, a semantic device usefully manipulated to achieve desired results. The legal basis for segregation had been struck down years earlier, and by this time lower courts had voided practically all laws promoting racial classification. But if, for whatever reason, residential patterns had developed along segregated lines, then local schools would also be segregated. If school boards had utilized those lines in drawing school zones, did this constitute evidence of "intent" to foster segregation or intent to preserve neighborhood schools? The majority in the Ohio cases hardly bothered analyzing this question but merely deferred to the lower-court findings that there had been intent. It would have been more logically consistent and doctrinally honest had they adopted Justice Powell's suggestion in *Keyes* that courts stop worrying about the cause of segregation and establish constitutional standards that would apply to all schools.[29]

The justices also would have faced the key issue squarely, or at least what the Warren Court had defined in *Brown* as the key issue—the impact of segregated schools, whatever the cause of that segregation, on minority schoolchildren through the badge of separation and diminished educational opportunity. Does the stigma hurt less if the schools are de facto rather than de jure segregated? Can there be a legitimate constitutional banning of all forms of segregation, whatever the cause, without extending the reach of the state into all private activities? Should the goal be only the ending of purposeful segregation, or should it be the achievement of a true integration? Perhaps these "policy" decisions are beyond the proper bounds of judicial consideration, yet it is hard to talk about the meaning of equal protection, whether legally or otherwise, and ignore these questions.[30]

DISCRIMINATORY INTENT AND IMPACT

One might have expected that by the 1970s, even a "conservative" Court would strike down any facially discriminatory laws which deprived persons of basic rights, such as voting, simply on the basis of race. What is surprising is that the Burger Court went beyond this level and struck down practices which, even if not adopted for discriminatory *intent*, had a disproportionate *impact* on minority groups. The Court held that while the Constitution prohibits intentional discrimination, civil rights statutes went further, barring discriminatory effect as well. As could be expected, the initial unanimity of the Court on this issue dissolved as the cases grew more complex.

At least as early as 1886, in *Yick Wo* v. *Hopkins*,[31] the Court had held that a discriminatory application of an otherwise neutral law violated the Equal Protection Clause of the Constitution. In that case, discrimination had been inferred from the data. A San Francisco ordinance required permits to operate laundries in wooden buildings, a seemingly sensible precaution against fires and a legitimate exercise of the police power. The Board of Supervisors, however, had granted permits to all but one of the non-Chinese applicants, and not a one to the approximately 200 Chinese applicants.

Finding discriminatory impact differs, however, from inferring discriminatory intent. In *Palmer* v. *Thompson* (1971),[32] a 5-4 Court speaking through Justice Black found that Jackson, Mississippi, had not acted unconstitutionally in closing public swimming pools after a court had ordered the city to desegregate the pools. Black ruled that the city had no "affirmative" duty to operate the pools, and he rejected the argument that the closing had been unconstitutional because it had been "motivated by a desire to avoid integration." Black seemed to say that despite some earlier cases in which intent had been taken into account, the Court could not really determine motive; only actions having a clearly discriminatory impact could trigger a constitutional remedy. Here both whites and blacks had been denied use of the pool, so there had been no disproportionate impact.

Justice White insisted in dissent, however, that the closings had not treated blacks and whites equally. "The fact is that closing the pools is an expression of official policy that Negroes are unfit to associate with whites." He denied that courts could not determine motivation; in fact, courts constantly made such judgments.[33]

The Court found clear evidence of discriminatory impact that same Term in *Griggs* v. *Duke Power Company*,[34] a case growing out of Title VII, the employment discrimination section of the 1964 Civil Rights Act. The Chief Justice spoke for a unanimous bench in interpreting the statute as prohibiting employers from imposing general intelligence tests or requiring a high school diploma, where such tests had no relevance to job requirements and effectively disadvantaged black applicants. The law, he explained, "proscribes not only overt discrimination but also practices that are fair in form, but discriminatory in operation."[35]

The Court could not have asked for a better test case of Title VII. The only blacks in the plant had been classified as "laborers," the lowest grade possible, and had wanted to move up one grade to "coal handlers" but had been blocked by the lack of high school diplomas. The company admitted that it had not even considered the relationship of a high school diploma and the intelligence test to the job requirements. Moreover, while Burger disavowed any reliance on "intent" as opposed to "practice," the company did in fact have a history of intentional discrimination.

Although the Court's unanimity evaporated in subsequent cases, the basic principle of *Griggs* remained intact, not only in the courts but also in regulations concerning federal hiring and funding. *Griggs* validated statutory authority to attack facially neutral practices that had discriminatory impact; the Court, however, refused to expand the impact test to the constitutional level, and it made the distinction clear in another employment test case.

In *Washington* v. *Davis* (1976),[36] black applicants challenged a verbal ability test which, they claimed, kept them off the District of Columbia police force. Because Title VII did not apply to the government, the black litigants asked the Court to make the impact criterion constitutional rather than just statutory. Justice White, speaking for a 7-2 majority,[37] refused to read *Griggs* as constitutional, that is, as a guarantee under the Fifth or Fourteenth Amendments. Title VII applied specifically to employment, whereas the expansive language of the Equal Protection Clause could apply to any regulation or situation that disproportionately affected minorities.[38] Moreover, unlike *Griggs* where the high school diploma requirement bore no relevance to the job, verbal skills for police officers met the Title VII standard.

Between the two cases one can pick out a strand that ran fairly consistently through the Burger years. If the plaintiffs could make out a case for intentional discrimination, then such action violated the constitutional promise of equal protection. If they could not show intent, but could demonstrate a disproportionate impact of certain requirements on minorities, then they had a remedy under Title VII. Both cases reaffirmed the nation's commitment to merit and the idea that people ought to be able to compete for jobs on the basis of their ability. *Griggs* said the test had to be fair and relevant to the jobs and could not be a screen for discrimination; *Davis* upheld the validity of tests that were in fact relevant. In such cases, the fact that a greater proportion of blacks than whites failed would not invalidate the tests.[39]

This difference in criteria between constitutional and statutory interpretation also showed up in cases involving voting rights. In 1965 Congress had passed the Voting Rights Act, based on its power under Section 2 of the Fifteenth Amendment, and the Court had read that grant quite broadly in *South Carolina* v. *Katzenbach*.[40] Then in 1970, Congress had extended the Act's provisions, strengthened certain parts, and suspended the use of literacy tests on a nationwide basis. The first test of this act came before the Court that same year, in *Oregon* v. *Mitchell*,[41] taken on original jurisdiction to consolidate several challenges to the law. Although the Court split on several issues, all nine members agreed that Congress had the power under Section 2 to suspend the literacy tests; even Justice Harlan, who took the most restrictive view of congressional power under the Civil War Amendments, agreed that the literacy provision fell within the remedial authority of Congress.

The Voting Rights Act and its subsequent amendments not only protected the individual's right to vote but also prohibited practices that would dilute group voting strength. While voting is an individual right, historically minorities have tended to vote in blocs, and practices that would dilute bloc voting would undermine the individual's right. For example, assume a city had a 40 percent black population, but it drew voting districts in such a manner that no single district had a black majority. As a result, individual black voters would never be able to coalesce in support of a black candidate because they would never have a majority. By thwarting bloc voting, the individual vote would also be devalued. The Voting Rights Act therefore prohibited practices that had the "effect" of "denying or abridging the right to vote on account of race or color."

The language of the statute did not talk about "intent" but about "effect," and the Court upheld the provision in *City of Rome* v. *United States* (1980).[42] Speaking for a 6-3 majority, Justice Marshall endorsed the attorney general's refusal to allow the Georgia city to annex outlying predominantly white areas and change the method by which it elected the city commission, because these changes would effectively dilute the voting strength of Rome's black population. His opinion also reaffirmed Congress's extensive powers under the Fifteenth Amendment to remedy voting rights violations.

That same day, however, in *City of Mobile* v. *Bolden*,[43] a narrow majority of the Court upheld at-large election procedures even though they diluted black voting power. Blacks made up 35 percent of the Alabama city, but no black had ever been elected to the city commission and, under at-large elections, would not likely be in the near future. The difference between the Georgia and Alabama cases is that the former arose under the Voting Rights Act of 1965, which simply called for proof of impact. The latter had been instituted under the Fourteenth and Fifteenth Amendments, and the Court held that in the absence of proof of intent, no constitutional right had been violated.[44]

The Burger Court's record in this area may have disappointed some civil rights groups, who wanted the Court to strike down any form of discrimination, whether de jure or de facto, and this far the Court would not go. The Court made it clear that it would not tolerate any form of de jure discrimination, and it gave Congress an extraordinarily broad reach of power under the Civil War Amendments to protect voting rights for both individuals and groups. Moreover, it also read Title VII extensively, and whether one wishes to read this as judicial deference to the legislature or commitment to equal rights, the result is the same. But not all discrimination is subject to legislative or constitutional remedy, nor is all "disproportionate impact" necessarily the result of discrimination. One might disagree with some of its distinctions, but in this area as in others, the Court under Warren Burger continued and expanded on the precedents set out under Earl Warren.

THE THORNY ISSUE OF AFFIRMATIVE ACTION

It has been remarked at several points in this book that many of the "bold" decisions of the Warren Court were, in fact, the easy cases and that the Burger Court had to deal with much thornier issues. We can look back now and see that it had always been a violation of equal protection to segregate schools and other public facilities by race; on reading *Brown* we are struck by the obviousness of its conclusion. Similarly, we can look at the early stages of the civil rights movements and wonder why anyone ever questioned the rightness of demands for equal treatment without regard to skin color.

In the 1970s, civil rights advocates, while still fighting overt discrimination, began to look at ways by which blacks could truly become equal members of society. The strategy they chose—affirmative action—became one of the most divisive issues in our society. The reasoning behind affirmative action is simple, perhaps even simplistic. Because society discriminated against blacks in so many ways for 300 years, it is unrealistic to assume that mere removal of the old fetters made blacks suddenly equal and able to avail themselves of all opportunities. Rather, the analogy is of a runner kept in prison, without adequate food or exercise, and then expected to compete in the race. Just as no one would consider that a fair race, the argument went, then how could blacks, having been held down for so long, be expected to compete against whites on an equitable basis? Something had to be done to compensate for prior discrimination, so that in the future blacks could take full advantage of equal opportunities.

The answer would be programs granting some preference to blacks to help them overcome the effects of prior discrimination. Colleges would establish different admissions criteria for minority groups; employers would make special efforts to recruit minority members and even hold a certain percentage of jobs aside for them. The most significant affirmative action step came in Executive Order 11246, promulgated by Lyndon Johnson and then greatly strengthened by Richard Nixon, which required federal contractors to take affirmative steps to hire more women and minorities, or they would run the risk of being barred from future government work.

On the surface, affirmative action sounded like a great idea, but in fact it forced society to make some very difficult choices. In the analogy of the runner, one could either postpone the race until the runner regained strength or handicap the other runners to compensate for the weakened condition of the one runner. Jobs, however, differed from races: If you gave preferential treatment to one group, you penalized another. If giving a job to a black man or woman that might have gone to a white person helped the black overcome a heritage of persecution, who paid for it? The white person denied a job may never have discriminated against blacks; his or her ancestors may not even have come to this country until after the end of slavery. One can talk about the collective guilt of white society, or the general disadvantaging of blacks, but in the end individuals paid the price. What some people called affirmative action, others called reverse discrimination.[45] If a white male had been denied a job or a place in a college class or a government contract because it had been reserved for a possibly less-qualified minority member, had not he been deprived of the equal protection of the law? The Civil Rights Act of 1964, in several provisions, barred discrimination against *persons*, that is, individuals, because of race, color, or national origin.

The issue first came before the Court in 1974, and the Court ducked. Marco DeFunis had been accepted by several law schools, but he wanted to live and practice in Seattle, and the University of Washington Law School had twice turned him down. The school had a separate admissions process for blacks, Hispanics, Indians, and Filipinos, and DeFunis learned that of the thirty-seven minority candidates accepted for fall 1971, thirty-six had combined test and grade scores below his. Believing federal courts too sympathetic to minorities, DeFunis sued in state court on claims of racial bias; he won, and the trial court ordered him admitted to the law school. The Washington Supreme Court reversed, upholding the university's affirmative action plan, and then the United States Supreme Court granted certiorari. In the meantime, DeFunis had been attending law school and, thanks to a stay of judgment issued by Justice Douglas, had been registered for his last term by the time the high court heard the case.

Because DeFunis would graduate regardless of the outcome, five members of the Court declared the question moot and thus evaded the substantive issues surrounding affirmative action.[46] Four justices dissented, arguing that the constitutionality of special admissions programs ought to be resolved. "The constitutional issues which are avoided today," declared Justice Brennan, "concern vast numbers of people, organizations and colleges and universities. . . . Few constitutional questions in recent history have stirred as much debate, and they will not disappear."[47]

Brennan of course was right; the issue would not go away, and at best, it gave the political branches a little more time to get their constitutional houses in order. Even as the Court evaded the issue in *DeFunis*, another white male, upset at his rejection from the medical school at the University of California at Davis, began a similar lawsuit.[48]

Davis, a relatively new school, took in 100 students in its medical school each year. It reserved sixteen slots under a special admissions program for minority students, mainly blacks, Hispanics, and Asian-Americans. Allan Bakke, a Vietnam veteran and now an aerospace engineer, wanted to be a doctor and had taken all of the necessary pre-med courses at night. In 1973, at the age of thirty-three, he unsuccessfully applied to a dozen medical schools, including Davis, which turned him down twice. Bakke then learned about the special admissions program and that most of those admitted in the sixteen slots had poorer records and backgrounds compared to his.

Bakke sued in state court, claiming the racial preference shown to minorities under the special admissions program violated his rights as guaranteed under federal and state law. The trial court ruled against the university but denied Bakke the relief he sought, admission to the medical school, because he had failed to prove that the special program had been the direct cause of his rejection. On appeal to the California Supreme Court, normally considered one of the most liberal in the nation, Bakke won, and the court ordered his admission.[49] The university appealed to the Supreme Court, which granted certiorari on February 22, 1977, and stayed Bakke's admission pending review of the case.

This time the Court could not duck, although the decision it handed down settled practically nothing.[50] The Court's opinion came from Justice Powell and did not have the full support of any other member of the Court. Powell flatly rejected the use of quotas and noted that the Court had upheld racial quotas in only a few instances where they supplied a discrete remedy to specified prior discrimination, as determined by an appropriate judicial, legislative, or executive authority. At Davis there had been no record of prior discrimination, and it exceeded the medical faculty's competence or authority to establish a remedial program. But the faculty was within its competence as an educational body in seeking to diversify the student body along as many lines as possible—including racial ones. To use race flexibly, within the context of a comprehensive admissions policy with an educational rather than a societal goal, would be permissible. Therefore, the Davis plan failed, and Powell ordered Bakke admitted to the medical school; but Davis, and other colleges and universities, would be able to take race into account in admissions policies.

Four members of the Court—the Chief Justice, Stevens, Rehnquist, and Stewart—took a strict statutory approach, holding that the Davis program violated Title VI of the 1964 Civil Rights Act, which prohibited discrimination against any *person*—i.e., an individual—because of race, color, or national origin in any institution or program receiving federal assistance. They supported Powell's conclusion that Bakke should be admitted, but they refused to go along with his view that race could be a factor in admissions. Four other justices—Brennan, White, Marshall, and Blackmun—agreed that race could be a factor in admissions and did not believe that the Davis program violated either Title VI or the Fourteenth Amendment; they dissented from ordering Bakke's admission.

Some commentators, such as columnist Anthony Lewis, praised Powell for striking an astute political compromise.[51] One might well call it a transitional decision, one that satisfied neither side but at the same time did not alienate them either. Clearly no majority existed on the Court on all the issues, and while a 5-4 decision is as binding as a 9-0 vote, the Court has long realized that on major issues unanimity carries greater legal as well as moral weight. The "somewhat fuzzy" nature of *Bakke*, declared Paul Freund, "leaves room for development, and on the whole that's a good thing."[52]

Others were far less charitable. Professor Paul Brest condemned Powell's rationale as "nonsense" and claimed that the Court, "whose only justification for meddling in the affairs of other institutions is that its judgments are grounded in principle rather than political expediency," should have forthrightly confronted the central issue—does the Constitution permit the penalization of current members of the majority in order to benefit current members of the minority as recompense for injustices suffered in the past?[53]

Bakke bought time, but it also raised questions that at some point the Court would have to answer. If one could take race into account, how much of a consideration could it be? Might it not, in fact, be the major determinant, even if masked by other factors? How does one determine when race has ceased to be but one consideration among others, and a quota has emerged? What criteria should lower courts use in trying to evaluate the dozens of suits that now flooded in testing both public and private affirmative action plans?

One should always remember that despite its responsibility as the chief interpreter of the Constitution and the court of last resort, the Supreme Court is also a common law court. It must constantly hear new issues—and new variations of old questions—and weighing precedent, law, custom, morality, and common sense, it must fashion an appropriate answer. It does this incrementally, building one step at a time, avoiding a broad doctrinal determination until all of the building blocks are in place. In *Bakke* the Court did decide that race could be a factor in fashioning affirmative action programs; that to remedy past discrimination, providing some preference to minority groups did not per se violate the Fourteenth Amendment or the Civil Rights Act; and that out-and-out quotas, except to remedy specific past de jure segregation, would not be permitted. The Court would now fill in that outline piece by piece.

The first part of that answer came a year later in *United Steelworkers* v. *Weber*.[54] Justice Brennan spoke for a 5-2 majority in sustaining a voluntary program adopted by an agreement between the Kaiser Aluminum & Chemical Company and the United Steelworkers Union. The company had a 98 percent white work force, and the plan created an in-plant craft training program; one-half of all the places in the program would be reserved for minority members until the percentage of black workers in the plant approximated their percentage in the local labor pool. The program turned down Brian Weber's application in favor of a black with less seniority, and he sued under Title VII of the Civil Rights Act. Sections 703(a) and (d) specifically forbade employment discrimination because of race, and 703(j) announced that the act did not require any employer "to grant preferential treatment . . . because of race."

Justice Brennan held the only question to be one of narrow statutory construction, "whether Title VII *forbids* private employers and unions from voluntarily agreeing upon bona fide affirmative action plans that accord racial preferences." The drafters of the act, he noted, had been concerned with the unemployment of blacks, a problem the Kaiser–Steelworkers plan specifically attempted to remedy. Section 703(j) did not forbid preferential treatment but only informed employers that the law did not require it.

While the decision gave a green light to voluntary private plans, it did so cautiously. Justice Brennan carefully explained that the plan did not violate the interests of white employees, it did not require that white workers be fired to make room for blacks, it did not put any barrier in the path of whites seeking advancement, it kept one-half of the spaces in the program for whites; and the program would end when the plant's racial balance reached a specified level. Because the Kaiser plan had been voluntarily adopted by a private employer, Weber could not argue a constitutional deprivation of equal protection, and Brennan's statutory interpretation, while objected to by Burger and Rehnquist, did not appear to most commentators to violate the spirit of the law.

A valid constitutional challenge arose the following year in *Fullilove* v. *Klutznik*.[55] In the Public Works Employment Act of 1977, Congress enacted a "minority business enterprise" (MBE) provision, in which 10 percent of federal funds granted for local public works projects had to be subcontracted to purchase goods or supplies from minority-owned and -controlled businesses. Although six of the nine justices voted to sustain the MBE provision, the Chief Justice's opinion failed to secure a majority. He reviewed the legislative history of the act and concluded that Congress had ample reason to determine that past discrimination had precluded effective minority business participation.

But did the means chosen, the use of racial and ethnic criteria, violate equal protection? While normally Congress must act in a "colorblind" manner, here it had adopted the program to remedy prior discrimination. If courts, with their limited remedial powers, could order quota plans, then Congress, which had far broader remedial powers under the Fourteenth Amendment, could certainly do so.

Only Justices White and Powell joined the Chief's opinion, and Powell wrote separately chiding Burger for failing to articulate the specific standards by which he had measured the MBE provision, and which lower courts could use in evaluating other affirmative action plans. Justices Marshall, Brennan, and Blackmun supported the result but relied entirely on their statutory analysis in *Bakke*. Justice Rehnquist, joined by Stewart, dissented because the MBE program established a specific quota, while Justice Stevens, in his dissent, claimed that Congress had hardly paid attention to the MBE provision in its debates and that, before the Court showed deference to congressional judgment, he wanted some evidence that the legislators had actually considered some of the thorny issues involved.[56]

Beginning in the early 1980s, conservatives within the Reagan administration began a concerted assault on affirmative action, which they condemned as reverse discrimination. Edwin Meese, first as White House counsel and then as attorney general, lobbied unsuccessfully to get President Reagan to revise the old Johnson Executive Order and do away with affirmative action requirements. The man in the Justice Department nominally responsible for civil rights, William Bradford Reynolds, openly opposed affirmative action and tried to pressure states and localities, many of whom had entered into consent agreements after losing a discrimination suit, to renege on those plans. In 1981 Reagan named Sandra Day O'Connor to the Court, and conservatives hoped she would provide a majority to strike down affirmative action. In case after case, Solicitor General Rex Lee entered an amicus brief opposing preferential treatment based on race or gender.

In 1984 the Court for the first time struck down an affirmative action plan in which it had to balance the interests of the minority, not against some vague majority interest but rather against a particular and countervailing interest. In the early 1970s, Memphis adopted a seniority system for all municipal employees. Later in the decade, the city entered a consent decree to increase black employment, although without admitting past purposeful discrimination. In 1981 a budget shortfall forced significant reductions in the city work force, and department heads began to lay off employees on the basis of "last hired, first fired," as required by the seniority system. Although the plan had not been adopted with any intent to discriminate, it disproportionately affected black workers, many of whom had only recently been hired under the consent decree; as the "last hired" they were the "first fired."

Black workers sued, and a lower court ordered the city to stop using the seniority system layoff plan, because it had a racially discriminatory impact of the type banned under Title VII. In a 6-3 decision, the Supreme Court reversed.[57] Justice White held that Title VII prevented a lower federal court from altering a consent decree to disadvantage nonminority workers with protected rights. Title VII, White explained, "protects bona fide seniority systems, and it is inappropriate to deny an innocent employee the benefits of his seniority in order to provide a remedy." Unless proof could be offered that the seniority system had been adopted specifically with an intent to discriminate, it could not be so casually ignored.

In Warren Burger's last Term the Court handed down three more affirmative action decisions and granted certiorari in two cases for argument during the first Term of the Rehnquist Court. If conservatives or liberals had hoped for a clear sign of which way the Court would go, they were sorely disappointed.

In *Wygant* v. *Jackson Board of Education*,[58] the Jackson, Michigan, school board and the local teachers union had reached an agreement that if layoffs became necessary, seniority would determine the order of dismissal except that at no time would a greater percentage of minority teachers be laid off than the percentage then working in the school system. The district had a history of racial discrimination in its hiring policies, and only recently had any significant number of black teachers joined the staff. The school board, with the agreement of the union, wanted to protect the minority teachers from a disproportionate impact under a "last hired, first fired" plan. As a result, the school board laid off some white teachers with greater seniority than the black teachers it retained, and the white teachers sued under the Equal Protection Clause. The Court, by a 5-4 vote, threw out the plan. Justice Powell's opinion found no compelling governmental interest to warrant the racial classifications. The plan also failed in that it had not been narrowly tailored to meet the specific problem, and it placed too great a burden on innocent whites.

Heartened by the decision, the Justice Department stepped up its efforts to have some fifty-one cities and states dismantle their affirmative action plans, while Meese, now attorney general, renewed his call on President Reagan to get rid of the twenty-year-old Executive Order requiring federal contractors to pursue numerical goals in hiring minorities and women. Whatever joy Meese and Reynolds felt was short-lived; on the last day of the Term, the Court handed two decisions upholding affirmative action.

In *Local 93, International Association of Firefighters* v. *City of Cleveland,*[59] the Court by a 6-3 vote upheld a consent decree that included a race-based promotion plan for black and Hispanic firefighters that was not restricted to the actual victims of past discrimination. The Justice Department and the overwhelmingly white union had argued that Section 706(g) of the 1964 Civil Rights Act prohibited consent decrees that included relief for people who had not been the direct victims of discrimination. Justice Brennan disagreed and held that if both parties agreed to the plan because there had been past discrimination, Section 706(g) did not forbid it.

In the second case, *Local 28, Sheet Metal Workers International Association* v. *EEOC,*[60] the Court, again through Justice Brennan, upheld the power of a lower court, faced with a clear record of past discrimination, to fashion an affirmative action plan that included specific hiring goals, even if these worked to the disadvantage of some majority members. Although only three others signed on to Brennan's plurality opinion, six members of the Court, including Justice White in dissent, agreed with Brennan's contention that Section 706(g) had not been intended to tie the hands of courts in fashioning appropriate remedies, and they did not limit the remedies to just identifiable victims of past practices.[61]

The Burger Court's refusal to invalidate affirmative action finally put an end to the efforts of Meese and Reynolds to reverse twenty years of preferential hiring programs. But the majority's avoidance of a total endorsement of affirmative action irked liberals as well and led to denunciations such as this:

> With the exception of Justices Marshall and Brennan, and sometimes Blackmun, the justices do not seem to appreciate the historic injury done

to nonwhites and to women in American society, or the persistence of institutional and structural racism. Little weight is accorded the vital interest a supposedly modern, democratic, pluralistic state has in doing simple justice for its racial minorities. Too much weight is given to the putative interests of so-called innocent parties. Although it is proper for the Court to show concern for all affected parties, it is difficult to see how even the most ordinary and inoffensive white workers, who often got their jobs as a result of biased job markets, are entirely innocent; although they are not directly responsible for the favoritism built into the system, they directly benefit from it.[62]

Not everyone sees the situation so simplistically. One need not agree with the Rehnquist/Burger view that only the specific victims of past discrimination are entitled to race-conscious remedies, but neither is it so clear that people like Wendy Wygant carry more than a minimal share of guilt for racism in American society. The Burger Court's vacillations on the subject disappointed those who wanted a clear answer one way or the other, yet the Court accurately reflected the confusion in American society over the merits and limits of affirmative action. In the simple cases, where one can readily identify the victim and the perpetrator, there is no issue over the legitimacy of race- or gender-conscious remedies. But in many cases the situation is not clear, and courts and the American people have to deal with questions of competing rights and of who will pay for society's efforts to compensate for past injustices. Had the Court been as reactionary as its critics claimed, affirmative action would never have survived *Bakke*.

SETTING LIMITS ON EQUAL PROTECTION ANALYSIS

The Warren Court had intimated in some of its later cases that equal protection analysis might be extended by recognizing new groups, such as the poor, as "suspect categories." Although the Burger Court had several opportunities to embrace this suggestion, it declined to do so.

In 1973 the Court decided *San Antonio Independent School District* v. *Rodriguez*.[63] Parents of Mexican-American school children in a poor Texas area had attacked the state's system of financing public education through local property taxes. Wealthy districts could afford to spend more on their schools than could those with a restricted tax base, and the litigants claimed this inequity violated equal protection. The district court accepted the argument and, applying the strict scrutiny standard for equal protection analysis, ruled poverty a suspect classification and education a fundamental right. Finding no compelling state interest to justify the resulting inequity, the three-judge panel held the entire finance system unconstitutional.[64]

In earlier cases where the Supreme Court had ruled that poor people could not be deprived of certain rights, the rights had been the focus of concern. Although Justice Douglas in the Virginia poll-tax case had declared that "lines drawn on the basis of wealth or poverty, like those of race, are traditionally disfavored,"[65] in fact there had been no such tradition. The Court's analysis had always focused on the nature of the right; once it had determined that a fundamental right existed, then the fact that a person had no money could not lead to the denial of that right. If the right to appeal depended upon having a lawyer or a copy of the transcript, and one had no money to pay for them, then one had been denied a basic right. That conclusion, however, depended on the importance of the right, not the status of the person.

The Court followed this line of reasoning in *Rodriguez*. Justice Powell, speaking for a 5-4 majority, held that poverty did not constitute a suspect classification, nor did education, important as it might be in contemporary society, qualify as a fundamental right protected under the Constitution.[66] Justice Marshall entered an impassioned dissent against what he termed the Court's "rigidified approach to equal protection analysis," and he labeled the majority decision as a retreat from the Court's earlier stance on civil rights.[67] Other commentators also picked up this line of attack and charged Justice Powell and the majority with being insensitive to civil rights, to the needs of the poor, and to the real meaning of equal protection.[68]

A closer look at this criticism reveals that the majority had not been charged with overturning a long established doctrine but instead with failing to inflate poverty to a suspect classification and to raise education to a constitutionally protected right. Critics also attacked the Court for pursuing middle-class values while ignoring the needs of the poor, who had few resources to affect legislative decision making.[69] Other considerations existed, however, and in fact the Burger Court was not insensitive to the needs of the poor.[70]

But, far more than their predecessors, the Burger majority recognized limits on judicial policy making within the confines of the federal system. One important constraint involved the limited resources that the judicial system could put into enforcing its orders. The judiciary has the power of neither purse nor sword, and its effort to remedy wrongs requires a significant investment in monitoring the situation. In two of the great Warren Court decisions—school desegregation and reapportionment—the Supreme Court not only enunciated a clear constitutional standard to guide the lower courts, but then the lower courts heard countless cases in which it applied and enforced the higher court's decisions.

In *Rodriguez*, had the Court chosen to name poverty a suspect classification, how would it have enforced that decision? The particular case involved disparate school districts around San Antonio. The problems of trying to equalize financing across an entire state might well have been considered beyond the ability or resources of the courts. Moreover, if education had been recognized as a fundamental right, then the enjoyment of that right should be the same everywhere, and that would have required action across state lines, in an effort to equalize the differences between rich and poor states.[71] Aside from this issue being an administrative nightmare, one can question if it is an appropriate issue for judicial determination or if variations in educational quality are part of the costs of a diverse federalism.

The Court also refused to extend suspect classification status to disabled and retarded persons, even while it expanded the definition of minimum care and training they could demand from the state.[72] It came as something of a surprise, then, when the Court ordered Texas to admit the children of illegal aliens into its public schools. Justice Brennan, speaking for a 5-4 majority in *Plyler* v. *Doe* (1982),[73] held that depriving these children of an education violated the Equal Protection Clause, which talks about *persons* and not *citizens*. Brennan could legitimately apply a strict scrutiny analysis, because alienage had long been considered a suspect classification. He also implied that education should be considered a fundamental right, an assertion that left Justice Powell uncomfortable. Powell concurred in the result, but not in the reasoning. The five separate opinions filed in the case left many questions open regarding the constitutional status—if any—of equal access to public education. But a majority of the Court clearly opposed creating new suspect categories.

GENDER DISCRIMINATION

In one area, at least, the Burger Court proved far more activist than had its predecessor—too activist, in fact, for many conservatives. The Warren Court, for all its expansive rulings on equal protection, had ignored complaints against discrimination on the basis of sex. Through the Nineteenth Amendment, women had achieved the right to vote and nothing more; evidently, *persons* mentioned in the Fourteenth Amendment were only male persons. As late as 1961, a unanimous Warren Court upheld a Florida statute excusing women from jury duty because the state could rationally find that it should spare women from this obligation in light of their place at "the center of home and family life."[74]

The Burger Court, on the other hand—with a majority supposedly appointed because of their devotion to judicial restraint and strict construction—attacked gender discrimination in a manner similar to its predecessor's assault on racial bias. While the Court did not always measure up to the demands of more militant feminists, the decisions it handed down on equal protection and reproductive choice completely transformed the legal landscape for women.

Down to 1971, courts used a two-tier model to evaluate equal protection claims. If the Court considered the rights involved as fundamental, or the legislation affected suspect classifications, then the courts applied strict scrutiny. To survive this rigorous review, the legislature had to have a compelling interest, the classification had to be necessary and relevant to accomplishing the objective, and the means had to be narrowly tailored to the goal. In all other equal protection cases, the legislation merely had to have a rational relationship to a permissible goal. Thus, in the Florida grand jury case, women were not a suspect group nor did the Court view a fully gender-representative grand jury as a fundamental right; therefore, excusing women from grand jury service rationally served the state's permissible goal of fostering a wholesome family life.[75]

The change began in 1971, when the new Chief Justice spoke for a unanimous Court in *Reed* v. *Reed*,[76] invalidating an Idaho law giving men preference over similarly situated women as administrators of decedents' estates. The Court refused to make gender a suspect classification, and on the surface seemed to be applying the lower-level rationality standard. Yet for the first time, the Court had struck down a gender classification law under the Equal Protection Clause, and the decision made headlines around the country.

Mr. Dooley commented many years ago that the "Court follows the election returns," meaning that the justices are not totally oblivious nor immune to major social, political, and economic changes in our society. *Brown* may have struck the South as radical, but looking back one can see it as part of the broad attack on racial discrimination that emerged from the war against Hitler. The justices deciding the *Reed* case could hardly avoid news about the women's movement, either in their morning papers or evening telecasts. Moreover, Congress in 1963 had passed the Equal Pay Act, mandating equal pay for equal work, and the following year in Title VII of the Civil Rights Act had prohibited employment discrimination on the basis of race, religion, national origins, or sex.[77] Within a few months, Congress would pass the Equal Rights Amendment and send it on to the states for ratification.

The next great leap forward came in 1973 with the landmark case of *Frontiero* v. *Richardson*,[78] in which an 8-1 Court held married women in the armed forces entitled to the same fringe benefits as married men. Under the existing law, men automatically received a housing allowance and health benefits for their civilian wives; women, on the other hand, could not secure these benefits unless they could prove they contributed three-fourths of the family's support (all of their own and one-half of their husband's). The Court did not invalidate the legislation, but in effect cured it of sex bias; it extended to women members of the armed services the same benefits, under the same conditions, as men received.

Although Justice Brennan received seven supporting votes for the result, he failed to get a majority to support his elaborately reasoned argument that women should be considered a suspect classification in equal protection cases. (Only Justices Douglas, White, and Marshall agreed.) The reason may be that although in theory the other justices were moving toward a position of equality before the law, they still believed that in some instances women should be treated differently (not worse, just differently) because, in fact, women *were* different from men.[79]

This ambivalence showed up in several cases decided at this time when men challenged laws favoring women. In *Stanley* v. *Illinois* (1972),[80] the Court used a due process argument to overturn a state regulation that denied an unwed father, who had lived with and supported his children, their custody after the death of their mother. If the state wished to deny a man custody, it would have followed the same procedure as it used with a woman: a hearing to determine parental fitness. But in other child-custody cases it heard in the 1970s, the Court split, sometimes upholding a state regulation favoring women over men and sometimes not.[81]

The Court also upheld some regulations favoring women if it considered the discrimination benign. In *Kahn* v. *Shevin* (1974),[82] for example, it sustained a Florida real-property tax exemption, first enacted in 1885, that provided an annual savings of fifteen dollars for widows, the blind, and the totally disabled, against an equal protection challenge by a widower who wanted the same exemption. Six members of the Court ruled the exemption fair, because it took into account the fact that women normally suffered more economically from the death of a spouse than did men. This benign provision, as the Court noted, helped some women and hurt none.[83]

The following year the Court faced the difficult problem of naval regulations that held male officers to a strict "up or out" system, by which the officer would have to leave the service if twice passed over for promotion, whereas female officers had thirteen years to achieve promotion before mandatory discharge. The navy's argument, which won over a bare majority of the Court in *Schlesinger* v. *Ballard* (1975),[84] rested on the fact that many of the differentials then existing favored men over women and provided them opportunities for training and experience denied to women (such as serving as naval fighter pilots). These other differentials also made it easier to evaluate men in a shorter time. The longer period allowed, for both the navy and for the women, a fairer chance to evaluate a group that had more restricted opportunities. (Interestingly, neither party in this suit, between a male officer denied promotion and the secretary of defense, challenged the existing discriminatory practices that made the longer period necessary.)

If feminists thought the Court about to revert to a pre-*Reed* attitude of condoning sex-based differentiation, a series of decisions showed the Court determinedly moving ahead. In *Taylor* v. *Louisiana* (1975), it struck down a jury-selection scheme exempting women practically identical to the Florida plan upheld in 1961.[85] Two months later, a unanimous Court invalidated the first of several sex-based discriminations in the Social Security program. In *Weinberger* v. *Weisenfeld*,[86] a young widower whose wage-earning wife had died in bearing their son, sued for the same child-care benefits that a woman would have received if her wage-earning husband had died. As in *Frontiero*, the Court did not invalidate the defective legislation but instead directed that henceforth benefits should go equally to men and women similarly situated. Finally that year, the Court struck down a Utah statute that required a parent to support a son until age twenty-one, but a daughter only until eighteen.[87]

All of these cases, even those which supported certain benign classifications, indicate a Court undergoing some consciousness-raising and moving away from traditional cultural stereotypes about men as breadwinners and women as homemakers. In his *Frontiero* opinion, Justice Brennan clearly recognized the heavy price women had paid for such typecasting:

> Our Nation has a long and unfortunate history of sex discrimination. Traditionally, such discrimination was rationalized by an attitude of "romantic paternalism" which, in practical effect, put women, not on a pedestal, but in a cage. As a result of notions such as these, our statute books gradually became laden with gross, stereotyped distinctions between the sexes. . . . It is true, of course, that the position of women in America has improved markedly in recent decades. Nevertheless, it can hardly be doubted that, in part because of the high visibility of the sex characteristic, women still face pervasive, although at times more subtle, discrimination in our educational institutions, in the job market and, perhaps most conspicuously, in the political arena.[88]

Even while the Court had been moving in this direction, it had been searching for some jurisprudential standard to apply to gender cases that would prevent discrimination based solely on a person's sex, yet allow those cases in which a legitimate distinction could be made, but which did qualify as a compelling governmental interest under the strict scrutiny test. (Even benign classification, such as the Florida tax exemption to widows, would fail strict scrutiny.) The majority finally seemed to have found an acceptable middle ground, what some have called "intermediate" or "heightened" scrutiny.

In *Craig* v. *Boren* (1976), the Court struck down an Oklahoma law that allowed girls to purchase 3.2 beer at eighteen but required boys to be twenty-one.[89] Justice Brennan set out the new standard as follows: "To withstand constitutional challenge, previous cases establish that classification by gender must serve important governmental objectives and must be substantially related to achievement of those objectives."[90] Gender did not become a fully suspect classification; the governmental objective must be *important* rather than *compelling;* and the classification must be *substantially related* rather than *necessary* to the goal. Under strict scrutiny, very few sex-based differentials could withstand judicial review; intermediate or heightened scrutiny would allow the courts some flexibility in evaluating particular programs.

A 5-4 Court applied this standard later in the Term in *Califano* v. *Goldfarb* (1977),[91] a fact situation reminiscent of *Frontiero*, except in this case it involved the Social Security system and carried a far higher price tag. Under existing regulations, a widow automatically qualified for survivors' benefits, whereas a widower had to show that his wife had supplied three-fourths of the couple's support. The four members in dissent found nothing wrong with this arrangement, which they characterized as accurately reflecting the station in life of most women, "benignly" favorable to women, and administratively convenient. The majority, however, as Justice Stevens pointed out, saw the arrangement as "merely the accidental by-product of [Congress'] traditional way of thinking about females."[92]

By this time the basic outline of the Burger Court's stance on gender classification had crystallized. In general, the Court would apply a heightened level of scrutiny to any sex-defined program or law, and if it merely perpetuated traditional stereotypes about women and their roles in society, the law would fail an equal protection analysis. However, if a legitimate reason existed for sex-based differentials, such as a conscious effort to overcome past or present discrimination, and if the program had been tailored to fit that objective, it could pass judicial muster.

Thus in *Califano* v. *Webster*,[93] decided a few weeks after *Goldfarb*, the five-man majority upheld a Social Security classification in existence from 1956 to 1972 utilizing a more favorable rate of calculation for retired female than for male workers. Unlike *Goldfarb*, however, here the legislative history clearly indicated that Congress had tried to respond to the fact that women had faced greater discrimination in securing work and had often worked for lower wages than would have been paid to men for doing the same type of work. The congressional scheme thus qualified as "substantially related" to an "important" governmental objective.

In two 1979 decisions, *Orr* v. *Orr*[94] and *Califano* v. *Westcott*,[95] the Burger majority continued the trend, striking down laws that relied solely on traditional stereotypes. In *Orr*, a 6-3 majority invalidated Alabama laws that authorized state courts to impose alimony obligations on husbands but not on wives. In the other case, the Aid to Families with Dependent Children program allowed benefits to families where the father had lost his job, but not where the mother had become unemployed. The Court found this requirement unconstitutionally discriminatory. The following year, by an 8-1 vote, the Court struck down a state survivors' benefit program that discriminated between men and women.[96]

Gender differences existed, however, and the Court grappled with them as best it could. It tried to end the penalization of women for being pregnant, by ruling that public-school teachers in Cleveland could not be arbitrarily dismissed or placed on involuntary leave if pregnant.[97] The following year the majority held that pregnant women able and willing to work could not be denied unemployment compensation if employers refused to hire them because of their condition.[98] In late 1977, in *Nashville Gas Company* v. *Satty*,[99] the Court interpreted Title VII of the 1964 Civil Rights Act to invalidate employers' practices of stripping seniority rights from women who became pregnant. But if a woman should not be punished for pregnancy, she need not be rewarded either. In *Geduldig* v. *Aiello* (1974),[100] the Court ruled that state disability-income plans could exclude pregnancy without violating equal protection, whereas in *General Electric Co.* v. *Gilbert* (1976), it held that a similar omission from private disability plans did not violate Title VII.[101]

In an important series of cases, the Burger Court also disallowed differentials in retirement benefits paid to men and women. Pension plans argued that actuarial tables proved that women on the whole lived longer than men and therefore would draw greater benefits following retirement. To equalize payouts, the companies either had charged women higher preretirement premiums or had paid lower retirement benefits. In *Los Angeles Department of Water and Power* v. *Manhart* (1978),[102] Justice Stevens conceded that women as a group lived longer, but the generalization described a group—and individuals did not necessarily follow the group characteristic. Some women lived longer than the male average, and some died at an earlier age, but women were entitled to their full rights and to protection under Title VII as *individuals*. Applying this same reasoning five years later, the Court struck down a state plan that required equal contributions from men and women but paid out lower pensions to women.[103]

The Court disappointed many feminists, however, following the reinstitution of the military draft in 1980, in which Congress had explicitly and deliberately limited registration to males. The Court heard the expected equal rights challenge in *Rostker* v. *Goldberg*[104] the following year, and by a 6-3 vote rejected the claim. Justice Rehnquist agreed that military considerations alone may not negate constitutional guarantees, but the legislative judgment in this area carried great weight to which the Court deferred. Rehnquist did apply the heightened scrutiny test, however, indicating that he too had finally accepted it as the norm in sex-classification cases. Neither side had questioned the army's decision not to send women into combat; therefore, Congress had an *important* goal of providing enough men for combat troops, and asking men to register for the draft appeared *substantially related* to that objective.

The triumph of heightened scrutiny came in a case that satisfied few people. In *Mississippi University for Women* v. *Hogan* (1982),[105] a slim majority of the Court, speaking through Justice O'Connor, ruled that a state nursing school's refusal to admit qualified males violated the Equal Protection Clause. MUW had been a women's college since its founding in 1884; its nursing school admitted only women but did allow men to audit some courses. Joe Hogan wanted to train as a nurse, but he did not want to travel to other schools in the state that accepted men; he wanted to go to MUW, in his hometown, and he sued, claiming that his exclusion on the basis of sex violated his rights. The district court dismissed the suit, but the Fifth Circuit reversed, holding that any gender discrimination required heightened scrutiny. By this standard, MUW had failed to show a substantial relationship to an important goal; if its ostensible objective had been to provide students with the option of single-sex education, it could not limit this option to women.[106]

Justice O'Connor, joined by Brennan, White, Marshall, and Stevens, agreed. Because women had historically dominated nursing, no case existed for remediation; in fact, the state policy served "to perpetuate the stereotyped view of nursing as an exclusively women's job."[107] O'Connor rejected the state's argument that Title IX of the 1972 Education Amendments exempted historically single-sex schools from the ban on gender discrimination. Even if Congress had intended this, it did not have the power. Section 5 of the Fourteenth Amendment gave only Congress power to enforce the guarantees; "neither Congress nor a State can validate a law that denies the rights guaranteed by the Fourteenth Amendment."[108]

Of the three dissenting opinions, Burger and Blackmun limited their barbs to specific points, but Justice Powell, joined by Rehnquist, entered a powerfully reasoned dissent that shredded O'Connor's arguments. Powell covered not only law but also history and current comments on the value of single-sex schools as an educational option. Ironically, about this time many feminists began reexamining the benefits of single-sex education, and Powell caught their sentiment perfectly in his plea for diversity in education, a diversity that allowed women the choice of going to school with other women.[109]

CONCLUSIONS

Whatever the logical flaws in the *Hogan* case, it marked the complete acceptance by the Court of the heightened scrutiny standard for gender discrimination. If some advocates of women's rights thought that the Burger Court should have gone further, the fact remains that if we compare its decisions with the base it inherited from its predecessors, those rulings laid the foundation for a jurisprudence that looks at gender classification with a skeptical eye and questions whether laws have a legitimate purpose or are merely furthering outmoded stereotypes and prejudice.

Even though the Court did not elevate gender to a suspect category, decisions regarding women took on many of the aspects of the racial classification cases. Out-and-out discrimination affronted the Court no matter who the victim. The Court also recognized that some forms of invidious discrimination cannot be reached by either the Equal Protection Clause or civil rights legislation, and for all its boldness in some areas, the Burger Court remained fairly sensitive to the limits of judicial power. Perhaps some of the confusion that marked decisions on race and gender, as well as poverty, did no more than reflect the confusion of society over these issues as well.

11

"If the Right of Privacy Means Anything . . . "

Personal Autonomy and Due Process

Whatever its accomplishments or failures in other areas, the Burger Court may be remembered primarily for its decisions regarding abortion. It is ironic that the Court which Richard Nixon had promised would show restraint and deference to the political branches handed down the most activist, policy-making decision since the New Deal crisis of the 1930s. In constitutionalizing a woman's right to decide whether or not to terminate a pregnancy, the Court gave feminists one of their greatest victories of the decade and touched off the most emotional and divisive debate on constitutional doctrine since the *Dred Scott* case. The controversy over the moral "rightness" or "wrongness" of abortion is not the concern of this book. What we need to examine is how *Roe* v. *Wade* and its progeny shed light on the Burger Court and its relation to its predecessor. The Warren Court had set out a skeletal doctrinal framework that their successors later fleshed out.

THE "OLD" DUE PROCESS AND THE "NEW"

In the latter part of the nineteenth century, a handful of jurists and legal theorists created the doctrine of substantive due process to identify and protect basic rights, mostly relating to property, against regulation by the state. Men like Justice Stephen Field and Michigan Judge Thomas M. Cooley developed the intellectual and legal arguments to constitutionalize property rights under the Fourteenth Amendment's Due Process Clause.[1]

The phrase "due process" derived from the older notion of a "law of the land," which referred to general legal rules and customs accepted as the normative base of the legal system. From the beginning, due process has meant a bundle of rights, some of which are spelled out in constitutions, statutes, and regulations, and some of which are of common law derivation; some of these rights are substantive, core rights; others are procedural in nature. For example, the right to a trial by jury is a substantive right; how the jurors are chosen, how evidence may be presented, and how the trial should be conducted to ensure fairness are procedural rights. Procedural due process, it has been said, regulates the courts; substantive due process regulates the legislature.

By the turn of the century, conservatives had persuaded the courts that the Fourteenth Amendment's Due Process Clause included substantive rights protecting property from arbitrary regulation by the state.[2] They then used this notion, and the companion idea of freedom of contract, as bulwarks against legislative attempts to regulate property in almost any manner. Courts struck down wage and hour statutes, rate regulations on railroads, employer liability and workers' compensation schemes during the progressive era, and then they attempted to thwart Franklin Roosevelt's New Deal measures to ameliorate the Depression, all of which led to the court-packing plan and the constitutional crisis of 1937.

These excesses of judicial activism had given substantive due process a bad name both among the public and in jurisprudential circles. The idea of substantive due process rights, by itself not necessarily a wrong or foolish notion, came to be associated in the popular mind almost entirely with reactionary judges trying to thwart the will of the people. Even though Justice Brandeis had earlier suggested that the concept could be used to protect individual rights as well as property interests,[3] both liberal activists such as Black and Douglas and conservatives like Frankfurter shied away from any mention of substantive due process.

In 1942, five years after the court-packing crisis, the Court heard a challenge to an Oklahoma statute that provided for the compulsory sterilization of "habitual criminals" but imposed a lesser penalty for an embezzler than for a chicken thief. Only fifteen years earlier the Court had sustained a Virginia sterilization law, and in his opinion, Justice Holmes had derided the equal protection claim as "the usual last resort of constitutional arguments."[4] Thus Justice Douglas, who had been assigned the opinion, found himself precluded from using two constitutional rationales that would have made good sense in this case. So he invented "fundamental rights" analysis, in which certain rights—in this case, procreation—would trigger strict judicial scrutiny if adversely affected by the state. Douglas tied it loosely to the Equal Protection Clause although it really had a greater doctrinal similarity to substantive due process.[5]

Over the next twenty years, the Equal Protection Clause underwent a rebirth, especially in the Warren Court's treatment of racial discrimination, but due process analysis[6] still remained tainted by the earlier excesses of conservative judges. In 1963 the Court sounded what many people interpreted as the death knell of substantive due process. Justice Black spoke for the Court in upholding a Kansas statute prohibiting anyone from engaging in the business of "debt adjusting" except as an incident to "the lawful practice of law." The justices had no interest in the wisdom of the statute, deferring to the legislature in a way that would have even made Felix Frankfurter happy. Black emphasized that the Court had abandoned "the use of the 'vague contours' of the Due Process Clause to nullify laws which a majority of the Court believe to be economically unwise." Although the case involved simple economic regulation, Black gave no hint that due process analysis would be any more likely to come up if it had involved individual rights.[7] So when the Court moved to strike down a Connecticut statute prohibiting the distribution of birth control information or devices to married couples, it again found its hands tied. Although equal protection now enjoyed judicial approbation, the facts of the case did not lend themselves to that analysis; due process seemed a more likely candidate, but the Court had only two years earlier interred that notion. As Justice Douglas explained in the majority opinion:

> We are met with a wide range of questions that implicate the Due Process Clause of the Fourteenth Amendment. Overtones of some arguments suggest that *Lochner* v. *New York* should be our guide. But we decline that invitation. . . . We do not sit as a super-legislature to determine the wisdom, need, and propriety of laws that touch economic problems, business affairs or social conditions.[8]

Douglas then went on to adumbrate his highly controversial "penumbral" analysis of specific rights to show that "emanations" from the First, Third, Fourth, Fifth, and Ninth Amendments "create zones of privacy" and that privacy for married persons is surely a fundamental right.

In his concurring opinion, Justice Harlan (who unlike Douglas had not been personally affected by the Court crisis of the 1930s) had no problem at all in identifying the issue as a due process question. "In my view," he declared, "the proper constitutional inquiry in this case is whether the Connecticut statute infringes the Due Process Clause of the 14th Amendment because the enactment violates basic values 'implicit in the concept of ordered liberty.' . . . I believe that it does."[9]

Eventually the Court came around and openly acknowledged that *Griswold* v. *Connecticut* had been decided on a due process basis; even Justice Stewart, who dissented in the case, later noted that "*Griswold* stands as one in a long line of . . . cases decided under the doctrine of substantive due process, and I now accept it as such."[10] The decision thus opened the door to the Court to identify as fundamental certain individual liberties and then to expand them, much as earlier courts had used due process to expand property rights.

In fact, the analytical differences between the "old" due process, which elevated property rights, and the "new" due process, which protects individual rights, are not that different. Both derive from natural law jurisprudence, which holds that certain rights exist whether or not specifically identified in statute or constitution. Two millennia ago Aristotle declared that "if the written law tells against our case, clearly we must appeal to the universal law, and insist on its greater equity and justice."[11]

The danger—or opportunity—of natural law jurisprudence is that judges can declare new rights as the times change, finding that the people are entitled to some "fundamental right," although it may not be mentioned or even hinted at in the first eight amendments. Justice Black believed in the full range of rights listed in the Bill of Rights and read them as expansively as anyone, but his experience with the old due process led him to oppose reading any new rights into the Constitution through a natural law analysis. In his dissent in *Griswold*, Black charged that if due process formulas based on "natural justice" prevailed, then judges would "determine what is or is not constitutional on the basis of their own appraisal of what laws are unwise or unnecessary." He then went on to point out that judges elevating individual rights they found appealing affronted the Constitution as much as fostering property rights.[12]

Black's warnings fell on deaf ears in an era when the Warren Court consciously expanded the reach of the Bill of Rights and a younger generation of Americans demanded a broader definition of liberty. Moreover, many people could not believe that the Constitution did not protect marital privacy. The image of the state intruding into the bedroom affronted conservatives as well as liberals. Justice Goldberg's suggestion that the Court locate this right in the Ninth Amendment received only limited support. The provisions of that Amendment had been so rarely used, and information on what the Framers had intended so scarce, that no one really knew what it meant.[13] In the end, however, to find a right to privacy in the Ninth Amendment amounted to little more than natural law jurisprudence; due process, at least, had the benefit of decades of analytical treatment and commentary on which the justices could draw.

FROM *GRISWOLD* TO *ROE*

For all of Justice Douglas's free-wheeling declaration of privacy as a fundamental liberty,[14] he never defined exactly what he, or the Court, meant by privacy, and although he referred several times to marital privacy, the opinion never made clear whether the privacy interest applied only to married couples. Depending on how one interpreted the ruling, it could mean no more than the specific holding: that the state could not tell a married couple whether they could learn about or use birth control. Or it could be the first step on the road to creating a far broader right of individual autonomy in which state interference would be prohibited.

The *Griswold* decision came in 1965, and in its remaining terms, the Warren Court never developed the ideas of privacy[15] or personal autonomy. In

1972 the Burger Court dealt with the issue for the first time and, in *Eisenstadt* v. *Baird*,[16] significantly expanded the earlier ruling. In *Griswold* the Court had dealt with the use of contraceptives by married persons; *Eisenstadt* overturned a conviction for the distribution of contraceptives, and the defendant had given the contraceptive foam to an unmarried person. Although Justice Brennan tried to write a narrow opinion and avoid a fundamental rights analysis, his comments definitely set the Court on the road to the far broader autonomy holdings of the abortion cases:

> It is true that in *Griswold* the right of privacy in question inhered in the marital relationship. Yet the marital couple is not an independent entity with a mind and heart of its own, but an association of two individuals each with a separate intellectual and emotional makeup. If the right of privacy means anything, it is the right of the *individual*, married or single, to be free from unwarranted governmental intrusion into matters so fundamentally affecting a person as the decision whether to bear or beget a child.[17]

Richard Posner, now a Court of Appeals judge, described this opinion as "a pure essay in substantive due process,"[18] and there is no doubt that it marked a significant step on the road to an open adoption by the Court of due process analysis. The last line in the section quoted also set the stage for the most controversial decision of the Burger Court, *Roe* v. *Wade*.[19]

Put most simply, the decision invalidated laws that made it a crime to procure an abortion except under very limited circumstances. The lead case tested the Texas statute, which allowed an abortion only when it had been medically determined as necessary to save the life of the mother. A companion case[20] challenged the "modern" Georgia law, enacted in 1968, that followed the American Law Institute's Model Penal Code and allowed abortions when, "based upon the best clinical judgment," continued pregnancy would endanger the life or seriously injure the health of a pregnant woman, or if the fetus would be born with serious defects, or if the pregnancy had resulted from rape. In addition, the statute spelled out certain requirements regarding residency, medical judgments, and where the procedure could be performed. About a dozen other states had laws similar to that of Georgia. By a vote of 7-2, the Court struck down both laws.

Justice Blackmun began with a lengthy review of the history of abortion and then conceded that, although the Constitution "does not explicitly mention any right of privacy," the Court had determined that a right "of personal privacy, or a guarantee of certain areas or zones of privacy, does exist under the Constitution." That right of privacy, he declared in *Roe*,

> whether it be founded in the 14th Amendment's concept of personal liberty and restrictions upon state action, as we feel it is, or, as the District Court

determined, in the [Ninth Amendment], is broad enough to encompass a woman's decision whether or not to terminate her pregnancy.[21]

Blackmun went on to deny that the right was absolute and held that the state had important interests that increased as the pregnancy progressed. As a result, the Court ruled that during the first trimester of pregnancy, a woman enjoyed an absolute right to decide upon an abortion. In the middle trimester, she still had this right, but the state could prescribe conditions under which abortions could be performed to meet its obligations to protect the health and safety of its citizens. In the last trimester, the state's interest in the potential life of the fetus outweighed the liberty interest of the woman, and the state could proscribe abortions.[22]

Blackmun's opinion, as well as the brief concurring opinions of Justices Douglas and Stewart, all based the decision on a constitutionally protected right to privacy, although Blackmun acknowledged that one could not find such a right explicitly mentioned in that document. Stewart, who had dissented in *Griswold*, now said, in essence, privacy is one of those fundamental liberties protected by the Due Process Clause, and rather than beat around the bush, let's call it for what it is.[23] Douglas's concurrence in effect responded to Stewart, and more than three decades after the court crisis, Douglas still shied away from relying on due process. In a footnote Douglas declared:

> My Brother Stewart says that our decision in Griswold reintroduced substantive due process that had been rejected in Ferguson v. Skrupa. [Decisions such as Griswold, Pierce, and Meyer], with all due respect, have nothing to do with substantive due process. One may think they are not peripheral rights to other rights that are expressed in the Bill of Rights. But that is not enough to bring into play the protection of substantive due process.[24]

The public and scholarly community reacted vociferously to the decision, and the tumult has not died down over seventeen years later. People on both sides could not believe what had happened. The pro-abortion groups had not dared dream that they would win so much at one time; as one of the women involved in the case put it, "It scaled the whole mountain. We expected to get there, but not on the first trip." John Cardinal Krol accused the Court of opening the doors to "the greatest slaughter of innocent life in the history of mankind."[25] The intensity of the debate between "pro-choice" and "pro-life" advocates has remained at fever pitch, at times escalating into direct confrontation and violence.

The academic debate, if carried on more decorously, has nonetheless been one of the most intense in recent years. On the public side, one has merely to decide if one favors or opposes abortion to determine whether one agrees with or condemns *Roe*. The debate in the scholarly community has been over the wisdom and integrity of the decision; one can personally approve of a woman's choice to have an abortion and still condemn *Roe* as bad jurisprudence.

A number of charges have been raised against the decision. First, the Court reached out and took the issue too soon. A number of states either had revised their abortion statutes or were in the process of doing so. Because the courts had never before held that women had a right to abortions, it would have been better if the political process had been allowed to play itself out further before the courts intervened.

Much more serious is the charge that the judicial activism of *Roe* is no more acceptable than that of *Lochner*, and once again it evokes the specter of judges using the substantive due process rationale to erect their own prejudices into law. The most compelling statement of this charge came from the pen of John Hart Ely, who saw *Roe* as possibly even less defensible and more dangerous than *Lochner*, because it "sets itself a question the Constitution has not made the Court's business." The criticism by Ely carried a great deal of weight, not only because of his reputation within the scholarly community but also because he favored a woman's right to choose. "Were I a legislator," he wrote, "I would vote for a statute very much like the one the Court ended up drafting."[26] That, of course, went right to the heart of the issue—the extent of judicial policy-making power.

The decision has had its defenders as well. Professor Lawrence Tribe of Harvard Law School first suggested that the Court had not chosen so much between abortion and pregnancy but between the individual and the state deciding on whether the pregnancy should continue. Some types of choices, he argued, "ought to be remanded, on principle, to private decision-makers unchecked by substantive governmental controls."[27] Tribe, however, later had trouble with this rationale and then suggested that in times of moral flux, courts ought to reach out and make such bold decisions to help a moral consensus develop.[28] He failed to convince many people that judges had any greater wisdom than legislators or other folk to make such choices.

Much of the debate centered on whether one favored the use of due process analysis or not and whether the Court had, to use Herbert Wechsler's phrase, employed "neutral principles" to reach its conclusion. But at least one supporter of *Roe* urged his colleagues to expand their vision from a preoccupation with technique and process to what the results meant. In the 1950s and 1960s the Court had recognized and furthered the revolution in civil rights. Now, claimed Kenneth Karst, *Roe, Griswold,* and the gender-discrimination cases "present various faces of a single issue: the roles women are to play in our society. This is a *constitutional* issue, perhaps the most important of the 1970s." Karst found it inconceivable that the *Roe* majority could have been indifferent to the question of women's role.[29]

Whatever their views on the jurisprudential "rightness" or "wrongness" of the case, most commentators do agree that it revived substantive due process analysis, with an emphasis on individual liberty interests rather than on property rights, and that it consolidated the status of privacy as a constitution-ally protected right. There are many other aspects of the decision that have aroused interest and ire, ranging from Justice Blackmun's medical analysis of pregnancy to the sources of judicial morality and the appropriateness of judicial review; it has been, and continues to be, one of the most written about opinions in judicial history. My desire is not to enter the debate but instead to point out that one aspect all the commentators agree upon is that the Burger Court, the vehicle which Richard Nixon had hoped would reverse the runaway activism of the Warren era, itself became with this line of decisions one of the most activist courts in our history.

ABORTION AFTER *ROE*

Unlike the equal protection cases that attacked racial discrimination, the abortion decision had little in the way of either specific precedent or doctrine. The Court had no fall-back position to retreat to in the face of the criticism it had aroused. As a result, both opponents and proponents of abortion seized upon the inevitable adjustments in subsequent cases to declare either a contin-ued victory for women's autonomy or an imminent reversal of *Roe*.

After several unsuccessful efforts to amend the Constitution, opponents of abortion mounted a legislative attack to cut off public funding for abortions, impose procedural stumbling blocks to those seeking abortion, or create a constitutional right to personhood in the unborn. As these issues came to the high court, the original 7 majority faded away, and by the end of the Burger years several decisions on abortion commanded involved 5-4 votes.

In the first major post-*Roe* cases,[30] a 6-3 Court invalidated state laws barring a woman from securing an abortion in the first trimester without spousal consent or, if she were an unmarried minor, without parental consent. As Justice Blackmun explained, the state could not delegate to the husband or parents power that it lacked itself.

The question of parental authority has been one of the more perplexing issues involved in the controversy. Ideally, parents ought to know if their minor children are pregnant and contemplating abortion, so they can be available for advice, help, and comfort. Unfortunately, in many situations of teenage pregnancy, difficulties between parent and child and even fear of the parents have been contributing factors to the girl's problems.

In the *Bellotti* case, Justice Blackmun acknowledged that in the case of a minor, some restrictions might be permissible if they did not "unduly burden" the young woman's rights. Antiabortion forces in Massachusetts tried again, but three years later, this time by an 8-1 vote, the Court voided a state law requiring unmarried minors to obtain the consent of both parents; if they refused, a state judge could authorize the abortion if he or she believed good cause had been shown. Justice Powell set out guidelines that states would have to follow: Minors would have to have alternative procedures; if a young woman feared her parents or did not want to inform them of the pregnancy, she had to be allowed to go directly to an appropriate state authority; if the young woman demonstrated her maturity and showed that she was well informed about the nature of the choices available to her, the state authority had to grant her the permission she sought. While the state could intervene in those instances of demonstrable immaturity or incapacity, the presumption remained on the side of the woman.[31] In 1981 the Court narrowly approved by a 5-4 vote a requirement that physicians "notify if possible" the parent or guardian of a minor seeking an abortion if the minor lived at home, was economically dependent, or otherwise not legally emancipated.[32]

In its last Term the Burger Court struck down a highly restrictive Pennsylvania law whose provisions on informed consent, public disclosure of information, and regulation of medical care, according to Justice Blackmun, only disguised the state's obvious policy of discouraging abortions.[33] The 5-4 vote led opponents of abortion to claim that the Court had finally begun its retreat from *Roe* and that only a few new appointments would secure victory. A closer examination of the vote, however, showed that seven members of the Court still stood by *Roe*, although they differed over where to draw the line between the woman's right to an abortion and the state's legitimate interest in medical supervision and protection of the fetus in the last three months.

The only major defeat for pro-choice advocates came in two cases involving public funding of abortion or, to be more precise, legislative decisions not to pay for abortions with public monies. Women's groups argued that while *Roe* had ended the danger of back alley abortions, poor women still could not afford either the doctors' fees or medical insurance. To exercise their right to choose, the government ought to allow public funds to cover elective abortions; after all, government supported a number of programs to help pregnant woman receive decent medical and prenatal care.

The Court, however, held that previous decisions had only prohibited the state from interfering with a woman's choice; they had not required the state to actively assist women to exercise that right. In *Maher* v. *Roe* (1977),[34] a 6-3 majority sustained a Connecticut law that excluded nontherapeutic and medically unnecessary abortions from a Medicaid program. Three years later, a 5-4 Court upheld the Hyde Amendment, which severely restricted federal payment even for medically necessary abortions. As Justice Stewart explained, "[A]lthough government may not place obstacles in the path of a woman's exercise of her freedom of choice, it need not remove those not of its own creation. Indigency falls in the latter category."[35]

The most interesting abortion decision came in 1983, when the Court considered a variety of restrictive local regulations. The six-man majority applied a strict scrutiny test and voided all of the challenged rules. Justice Powell noted that there had been a continual demand that the Court had erred in interpreting the Constitution and that it ought to abandon *Roe*. He responded that "the doctrine of *stare decisis,* while perhaps never entirely persuasive, is a doctrine that demands respect in a society governed by a rule of law. We respect it today, and reaffirm *Roe* v. *Wade.*"[36]

The three dissenters—Justices White, Rehnquist, and O'Connor—did not call for repeal of *Roe* but instead urged a lower level of scrutiny and greater deference to the legislature and its proposed regulations. Justice O'Connor, in her first major statement on abortion, provided an incisive critique into the weaknesses of the earlier decision. Sound constitutional theory as well as adjudication on the basis of neutral principles could not support an analytical framework that varied according to the stages of pregnancy, especially because medical and technological advances had already made many of the earlier assumptions about pregnancy and fetal viability obsolete. Rather than try to adjust judicial holdings to each change, O'Connor suggested that in place of the trimester scheme and strict scrutiny analysis, the Court adopt a simpler standard: An abortion regulation should not be considered unconstitutional "unless it unduly burdens the right to seek an abortion."[37] O'Connor went on to argue that the state had an interest in the fetus not only as it neared birth but throughout the pregnancy as well; potential life is no less potential in the first weeks of pregnancy than in the last. She urged the Court to reexamine where it wished to draw the line between a woman's right to an abortion on the one hand, and the state's interest on the other, and indicated that she would be willing to move that line to show greater deference to the legislative will.

With the addition of two more conservative justices to the Rehnquist Court, O'Connor's analysis will no doubt receive a renewed and more sympathetic hearing. Opponents of abortion, however, emphasized her call for greater deference to the state, on the assumption that they could lobby for highly restrictive regulations. They failed to note that her opinion, while highly critical of the reasoning in *Roe,* still accepted its conclusion that, as part of personal autonomy, a woman has a right to terminate a pregnancy through abortion. While O'Connor would shift the balance more in favor of state interest, she drew the line at any regulation that proved "unduly burdensome." What this standard means is unclear, but it would seem to indicate that the state could not foreclose all opportunities for those women seeking to exercise their right of choice.

FAMILY RIGHTS AND DUE PROCESS

Once the Burger Court had openly adopted a substantive due process analysis, various groups sought to identify what they considered liberty interests that would now enjoy constitutional protection. With few exceptions, however, the justices did not want to let that genie out of the bottle, and those exceptions came almost entirely in areas where the majority could rely on traditional values, such as in family relations.

Prior to 1970, few cases involving what we would term family law came to the high court. Governance of familial relations, such as marriage, divorce, adoption, child custody, alimony, and the like, had all been considered matters of state law, with no connection to any constitutional rights. The *Griswold* opinion, which extended constitutional protection over marital privacy, led to a number of cases in which litigants tried to establish liberty interests protected by the Due Process Clause. The Burger Court established no clear record in this area, primarily because the justices remained badly divided over a number of issues, including the question of whether they should even be hearing family law cases. While we cannot go into a full-scale exploration of the Court's opinions in this field, once again we find the Burger Court played an activist rather than a restrained role.[38]

In 1977 the Court overturned an East Cleveland zoning ordinance that limited occupancy of a house to members of a single "family," which the regulation defined narrowly. The city council had responded to complaints about large numbers of people, often college students, sharing a house and disturbing otherwise quiet neighborhoods. Normally this would have been considered a simple economic regulation judged on a low-level rational basis test;[39] in fact, it probably would not have even made it to the Court except for the fact situation. Mrs. Moore had been convicted of sharing her home with two of her grandsons, who were first cousins, a relationship not considered close enough to meet the local ordinance's definition of family. The city attorney took a rigid position and argued that if there existed any constitutional right to live together as a family, it extended only to the immediate, nuclear family. By a 5-4 vote, the Court sustained Mrs. Moore and found extended family relationships a fundamental value protected by the Due Process Clause.[40] As such, courts had to look at any laws that affected family ties with the stricter scrutiny demanded when liberty interests were involved. Justice Powell responded directly to the dissents of Justices White and Stewart, who could not accept the due process analysis. "Substantive due process has at times been a treacherous field for this Court," Powell conceded:

> There *are* risks when the judicial branch gives enhanced protection to certain substantive liberties without the guidance of the more specific provisions of the Bill of Rights. As the history of the Lochner era demonstrates, there is reason for concern lest the only limits to such judicial intervention become the predilections of those who happen at the time to be Members of this Court. That history counsels caution and restraint. But it does not counsel abandonment. . . . Appropriate limits on substantive due process come not from drawing arbitrary lines but rather from "careful respect for the teachings of history [and] solid recognition of the basic values that underlie our society." Our decisions establish that the Constitution protects the sanctity of the family. . . .[41]

The majority also relied on tradition in *Zablocki* v. *Redhail* (1978),[42] in which it invalidated a Wisconsin statute that prohibited any divorced person who currently had custody of a minor child or paid child support under a court order from remarrying without the court's permission. The state wanted to make sure that people would be able to meet their current financial obligations before taking on new ones, but the majority ruled that the law violated the Equal Protection Clause. But Justice Marshall's opinion also described the right to marry "as of fundamental importance" and therefore a liberty interest that could not be regulated without strict judicial scrutiny.

A third case, in which the Court did not recognize a liberty interest, nonetheless illustrates the pattern of the Court's thinking. In *Parham* v. *J. R.* (1979),[43] the Court balanced "individual, family and social interests" to conclude that minors did not have a right to a formal adversary hearing when parents sought to commit them to state mental institutions. Chief Justice Burger rejected the fear of parental abuse in the absence of a hearing and stressed that children's rights had always been circumscribed and subject to parental control. The minority opinion of Justice Brennan, joined by Marshall and Stevens, did not dispute the holding that a preadmission hearing was not required but believed there ought to be at least one postadmission hearing to protect the child's liberty interest in not being involuntarily incarcerated.[44]

The underlying thread of the family law cases is that the Burger Court constantly turned to history and tradition—to an idealized view of family relations and obligations—to identify new rights protected by due process. In many ways it is the story of *Griswold:* People assumed that somewhere in the Constitution there ought to be protection for marital privacy. Similarly, there ought to be protection of extended families, of a right to marry, and of parental rights to determine what is best for their children. "Recourse to traditional values," noted one article, "enables the Court to afford protection to rights Americans traditionally have assumed to be part of our nation's scheme of liberty."[45] The danger, of course, is that there are differing values in the American past, and which ones are chosen to be enshrined as fundamental depends very much on the judges' own predilections. Although nonconformity has at times been exalted as an American value, the Burger majority proved very unsympathetic to claims that the Constitution protected variant life styles just as it protected variant speech.

ABERRANT LIFE STYLES

While the Court proved very responsive to the efforts of blacks and women to overcome prejudice, it showed no sympathy to another group seeking equal treatment, namely, homosexuals. In 1976, without oral argument or even an explanation of its decision, it summarily affirmed a lower-court decision upholding Virginia's sodomy law against a challenge by male homosexuals.[46] Justices Brennan, Marshall, and Stevens dissented from the summary disposition and believed the Court should have heard arguments. The three picked up a fourth vote, most likely Justice Blackmun, and heard the issue again in the last term of the Burger era and came within a vote of overturning the Georgia sodomy law.

The logic of *Griswold, Stanley,* and *Eisenstadt* seemed to argue that the state had no business intruding into the bedroom, whether it be occupied by a married couple, an unmarried couple, or a homosexual couple, as long as consenting adults acted of their own free will. In fact, no state seriously enforced its sodomy laws against those who acted discretely and in the privacy of their homes. But in August 1982, a police officer with a valid warrant entered the home of Michael Hardwick to arrest him for having failed to appear in court on a drinking in public charge. One of Hardwick's housemates opened the door and indicated that Hardwick was in his bedroom. On entering the bedroom, the officer immediately arrested Hardwick and a male companion for violating the Georgia sodomy statute. The prosecutor, who had been trying to repair city relations with the gay community, decided to drop the charge, but Hardwick insisted on carrying a test case to the courts.

At the oral argument, the state's deputy attorney general conceded that it would probably be unconstitutional to prosecute a married couple for engaging in sodomy, but he urged the Court to sustain the law lest it open a Pandora's box of attacks on other laws upholding social values. Georgia stood for "a decent and moral society" and adhered "to a centuries-old tradition and the conventional morality of its people." Professor Lawrence Tribe of Harvard asked the Court to strike down the law, not as a sign of approval of homosexual activities but because within their homes people should enjoy the utmost privacy, even if it involved deviant behavior.[47]

The Court, by a narrow 5-4 majority, refused to extend the right of privacy. Justice White phrased the question in such a way that the Court could not have decided otherwise: "The issue presented is whether the Federal Constitution confers a fundamental right upon homosexuals to engage in sodomy." Relying upon tradition, history, and current morality, the majority found that it did not.[48] In fact, if one follows White's reasoning, it may have flown in the face of the privacy logic, but it made sense in terms of the Burger majority's due process analysis.

One could argue that the Framers of the Due Process Clause valued privacy, family support, marriage, and procreation, and would have recognized them as fundamental liberties in a free society; they would not have viewed homosexuality or sodomy in a similar light. If one relied on history and tradition, as Justices Harlan and Powell had urged, then White had reached the correct conclusion. He, and the Court, had refused to create a new right; they had refused to make policy; they had adhered to the traditional social and moral beliefs of the country.

The Court followed a similar reasoning in denying certiorari in a case where two librarians had been fired for living together, while one had still been married to another. The library board had taken the action on the grounds that it did not wish to appear to condone adultery.[49] It also rejected a personal autonomy claim in sustaining a local regulation on the length and style of policemen's hair. Justice Rehnquist's opinion refused to consider whether the average citizen had a liberty interest in how he or she wore their hair, but policemen had to conform to departmental regulations.[50]

THE RIGHT TO A HEARING

One final area in which the Burger Court took significant steps to expand due process rights involved the relations between citizens and their governments. In our time, the state and federal governments touch the lives of all of us, but some more than others. People who depend upon government agencies and programs for food, shelter, and medical care can face terrible problems if that support should suddenly and arbitrarily be cut off. Similarly, many people work for governmental agencies; can they be arbitrarily dismissed for reasons other than poor job performance? Beginning in the early 1970s, advocacy groups for the poor began litigating against arbitrary action and claimed a due process right to a hearing before termination of benefits or employment.

While a hearing is procedural, the underlying issue is substantive—what liberty or property rights do people have in these programs? Does an employee of a state agency have any greater property right in his or her job than does an employee of a private corporation? Starting with the "old" due process cases and extending well into the "new," the Court has always taken an expansive view of the liberty, whether it be the old rights of property or the new rights of personal autonomy. As Boston University Law School Professor Henry Monaghan has pointed out, the phrase "life, liberty and property" has been interpreted in the Due Process Clauses as "a unitary concept embracing all interests valued by sensible men."[51] At the same time, the Court has recognized that in the interest of social order and harmony, liberty interests may at times be infringed upon by the state. The analytical issue then becomes what level of justification must the state show to warrant that infringement. Following the court crisis of the 1930s, the justices adopted a minimal, rational basis standard for the old type of property and a higher level of scrutiny for acknowledged rights, such as free speech.

The expansion of state and federal benefit and entitlement programs led Charles Reich to talk about a "new property" in an often cited 1964 article[52] and in his best-selling book, *The Greening of America* (1970). Reich argued that government had become a major source of wealth through benefits, contracts, franchises, licenses, and employment, which if retracted would be the same as depriving people of property. As a result, just as the government could not take away a person's traditional type of property without due process, so it could not take away this new form of property. And, just as the old due process had invested substantive rights in the old property, so the owners of the new property had similar protected liberties.

The Burger Court followed a somewhat erratic line in delineating these new rights, and in some ways it has been a line of retreat. The first decision came down in 1970 and seemed to indicate the Court's willingness to grapple with the problem. State law had provided that the commissioner of social services could, upon his or her own authority, terminate welfare benefits if the recipient had violated the conditions of the benefit. Justice Brennan, speaking for the majority, ruled that welfare benefits could not be cut off without an evidentiary hearing to determine if in fact there had been a violation. This satisfied the procedural aspect of due process, but Brennan then went on to note that welfare assistance "is not a mere charity, but a means to 'promote the general Welfare, and secure the Blessings of Liberty to ourselves and our Posterity.' " Termination of benefits without a hearing could deprive eligible recipients of the very means of their subsistence—the liberty interest of due process. Not only fairness, therefore, but a substantive property interest required a hearing.[53]

The following year the Court extended this reasoning when Justice Brennan again spoke for the majority in holding that a state could not arbitrarily revoke a driver's license following an accident. The driver had an entitlement to the license and, because he or she might depend upon being able to drive in order to earn a living, had a property interest in that license as well. "In such cases," Brennan concluded, "licenses are not to be taken away without that procedural due process required by the 14th Amendment."[54]

Perhaps aware that this line of reasoning could lead to implications far broader than any of the protections erected under the old due process, the Burger Court began its retreat from this broad view of entitlement rights. In 1972 the Court heard the case of a nontenured faculty member at the University of Wisconsin-Oshkosh who, following an initial one-year appointment, had been told he would not be rehired but had not been given any explanation. The university rules provided that in such situations "no reason for nonretention need be given." Roth claimed that he had been fired because of critical statements he had made about the university administration, and therefore his right to free speech had been violated, and his property interest in his job had been taken away without due process.

Justice Stewart, speaking for a 5-3 Court, acknowledged that the Court had always taken a very broad view of liberty, but not an infinite one. While a tenured faculty member had a property interest in his or her employment, and welfare recipients had a legitimate entitlement to their benefits, mere employment by itself did not constitute a vested property interest. The terms of Roth's employment had been spelled out at the beginning and included the option of nonrenewal at the university's discretion. Roth had accepted employment on those terms and could not claim any more. The university did not, therefore, owe him a hearing.[55]

Subsequent cases, according to Henry Monaghan, seemed to abandon the unitary approach to "life, liberty and property" that had marked earlier decisions and to substitute an analysis that distinguished "liberty" and "property" in a more restricted manner. In *Arnett* v. *Kennedy* (1974), Justice Rehnquist ruled that federal law could circumscribe property interests in employment by spelling out grounds for dismissal that would not require a hearing. If the employee could accept the property interest inherent in the job (the expectation of continued employment), he or she also had to accept the limitations that came with it; they must "take the bitter with the sweet."[56]

Only two other members of the Court—Burger and Stewart—joined Rehnquist's opinion, although a majority concurred in the specific result. However, two years later, in a 5-4 decision, the Court seemed to at least implicitly endorse the Rehnquist view that the government did not have to provide a hearing if it spelled out the conditions ahead of time. In *Bishop* v. *Wood*, the city manager of Marion, North Carolina, discharged a policeman following a poor evaluation by his superior, but without an evidentiary hearing. The policeman, who had worked for the city for several years, claimed that he had a property interest in his continued employment, that the charges of poor performance were false and damaged his reputation, and that due process requirements had not been met. Justice Stevens dismissed the case, and his concluding statement seemed to indicate a major withdrawal by the Court from judicial oversight of governmental employment:

> The federal court is not the appropriate forum in which to review the multitude of personnel decisions that are made daily by public agencies. We must accept the harsh fact that numerous individual mistakes are inevitable in the day-to-day administration of our affairs. The Constitution cannot feasibly be construed to require federal judicial review for every such error. In the absence of any claim that the public employer was motivated by a desire to curtail or to penalize the exercise of an employee's constitutionally protected rights, we must presume that official action was regular and, if erroneous, can best be corrected in other ways. The Due Process Clause is not a guarantee against incorrect or ill-advised personnel decisions.[57]

The decision seemed to signal a return to an older distinction between a right (which cannot be abridged) and a privilege (which exists at the sufferance of the grantor). Almost a century ago Oliver Wendell Holmes, then a state judge, summed it up this way: "The petitioner may have a constitutional right to talk politics, but he has no constitutional right to be a policeman . . . [and] takes the employment on the terms which are offered him."[58] The Burger Court in its latter years seemed to go back and forth between the view that a privilege could be circumscribed if the limitations had been set out aforehand, and that of acknowledging liberty interests that could not be curtailed, but it never developed a consistent rationale that would explain why it decided certain cases in a particular way.[59] The wavering line led John Hart Ely to comment:

> It turns out, you see, that whether it's a property interest is a function of whether you're entitled to it, which means the Court has to decide whether you're entitled to it before it can decide whether you get a hearing on the question whether you're entitled to it.[60]

Justice Powell had tried to avoid this conundrum in a 1976 opinion in which he had suggested a balancing approach taking into account the private interest that would be affected by the public action (whether in terms of entitlements or employment), the risk of erroneous deprivation of that interest through the procedures used, and the effect on the government's interest of imposing a higher level of procedural review.[61] Although the Court invoked this balancing test in some subsequent cases, one often wound up sharing Ely's bemusement at the very subjective, and very circular, judgments made.[62]

CONCLUSION: THE CONTINUITY OF CHANGE

Throughout this study we have seen how both the Warren and the Burger Courts more often than not built and expanded upon precedents handed down to them. Throughout the period, from 1953 to 1986, one would have to characterize the Supreme Court, regardless of its membership, as activist. If the Warren Court initiated a due process revolution in criminal procedure, the Burger majority started an equally revolutionary change in due process in the meaning of personal liberty and autonomy. If there were times when the Burger Court seemed to be hedging in some of the expansive statements made in earlier decisions, the process had actually begun toward the end of Earl Warren's tenure.

That major constitutional changes took place in both Courts is undeniable, but in looking over the decisions of thirty years in the area of individual liberties, one is struck far more by continuity than by change; in fact, one might even talk about the "continuity of change." For all the recent talk about justices sticking to original intent, the fact remains that as the final arbiter of the

Constitution, the Supreme Court is continually faced with having to reconcile the meaning of words written one or two centuries ago with the realities of the latter twentieth century. What did the Framers know, for example, about wiretaps or helicopters or drug testing? They set out certain broad statements about important liberties and left it to subsequent generations to interpret the meaning.

The justices of the Supreme Court have done so ever since, and if they have not always "got it right," their record in protecting individual rights and liberties under the Constitution is on the whole admirable. Whatever one may believe about particular decisions, whatever criticism one can make about erratic doctrinal wanderings, whatever one may believe that the Court went too far in some opinions—the overall view is that the Court has stood for a constant expansion of the meaning of liberty for the past half-century. Even conservative members of the Court would not deny this; their concern has been whether the Court is the proper agency to undertake the task and whether it has sufficiently acknowledged and deferred to the constitutional authority of the other branches of government. That debate will go on so long as we are a nation of laws, not men, and so long as the Supreme Court remains the final interpreter of our Constitution and the laws made pursuant to it.

Notes

Preface

1. Quoted in Alexander Bickel, "Applied Politics and the Science of Law: Writings of the Harvard Period," in Wallace Mendelson, ed., *Felix Frankfurter: A Tribute* (New York: Reynal, 1964), 197.
2. *Texas v. Johnson*, 109 S. Ct. 2533 (1989).
3. The Court's attack on the New Deal certainly played an indirect role in the 1936 election, but Franklin Roosevelt very carefully avoided mention of the Court in his campaign.

Chapter 1
"God Save This Honorable Court"
Continuity and Change on the Supreme Court

1. Oral arguments before the Court are open to the public and are often reported in the press; the decisions of the Court are public documents. The justices, however, have been very reticent about how they work, and the conference, at which they discuss and vote on cases, is closed—not even law clerks or secretaries may enter. The lack of knowledge about the Court, as well as the reverential attitude many people have about it, accounts for some of the notoriety accompanying publication of Bob Woodward and Scott Armstrong, *The Brethren: Inside the Supreme Court* (New York: Simon & Schuster, 1979), a relatively accurate journalistic account of the inner workings of the Court during Warren Burger's first seven terms. Since then there have been many more books on the Court, including one by the current Chief Justice, William H. Rehnquist, *The Supreme Court: How It Was, How It Is* (New York: Morrow, 1987). The best analysis of the Court's operations is David M. O'Brien, *Storm Center: The Supreme Court in American Politics* (New York: Norton, 1986). O'Brien had the inestimable advantage of observing the Court from the inside for a year as a judicial fellow.
2. Federalist No. 78. Edward M. Earle, ed., *The Federalist* (New York: Modern Library, n.d.), 504.
3. Vincent Blasi, ed., *The Burger Court: The Counter-Revolution That Wasn't* (New Haven, Conn.: Yale University Press, 1983).
4. Interview with Mark Tushnet, Georgetown University Law Center, 16 June 1988.
5. Earl Warren, *The Memoirs of Earl Warren* (Garden City, N.Y.: Doubleday, 1977), 260–61. For Warren's life in general, see also G. Edward White, *Earl Warren: A Public Life* (New York: Oxford University Press, 1982), and Bernard Schwartz, *Super Chief: Earl Warren and His Supreme Court* (New York: New York University Press, 1983).

6. Quoted in Richard Kluger, *Simple Justice: The History of Brown v. Board of Education and Black America's Struggle for Equality* (New York: Knopf, 1976), 659.

7. White, *Warren*, 155.

8. For biographical information, see, among others, Gerald T. Dunne, *Hugo Black and the Judicial Revolution* (New York: Simon & Schuster, 1977), and James J. Magee, *Mr. Justice Black: An Absolutist on the Court* (Charlottesville: University Press of Virginia, 1980).

9. Quoted in Alpheus T. Mason, *Harlan Fiske Stone: Pillar of the Law* (New York: Viking, 1956), 469.

10. Frankfurter to Brandeis, 28 May 1938, Felix Frankfurter Papers, Library of Congress, Washington, D.C.

11. *Griswold* v. *Connecticut*, 381 U.S. 479, 507 (1965), Black, J., dissenting.

12. William O. Douglas, *Go East, Young Man* (New York: Random House, 1974), 451.

13. *Id.* at 21. There is no good biography of Reed; probably the best sketch is that of C. Herman Pritchett, "Stanley Reed,"in Leon Friedman and Fred L. Israel, eds., *The Justices of the United States Supreme Court* (New York: Chelsea House, 1969–84), 3:2373. F. William O'Brien, *Justice Reed and the First Amendment: The Religion Clauses* (Washington, D.C.: Georgetown University Press, 1958), is sympathetic toward Reed's accommodationist stance.

14. There is a fair amount of literature about Frankfurter's career on the Court, but one should first see Michael E. Parrish's exemplary study of the pre-Court years, *Felix Frankfurter and His Times: The Reform Years* (New York: Free Press, 1982). Then see Clyde Jacobs, *Justice Frankfurter and Civil Liberties* (Berkeley: University of California Press, 1961); H. N. Hirsch, *The Enigma of Felix Frankfurter* (New York: Basic Books, 1981); and the brilliant introductory essay in Joseph Lash and Jonathan Lash, eds., *From the Diaries of Felix Frankfurter* (New York: Norton, 1975).

15. See Melvin I. Urofsky, "Conflict Among the Brethren: Felix Frankfurter, William O. Douglas, and the Clash of Personalities and Philosophies on the United States Supreme Court,"1988 *Duke Law Journal* 71, 76–81.

16. Frankfurter once stopped Stanley Reed in the hall to inform him that Reed's "error" had resulted from a misreading of a statute. He told Reed that at Harvard he had taught students that in order to construe a statute correctly, they should read it not once but thrice, and he now thought it would be a good idea if Reed did the same. Sidney Fine, *Frank Murphy: The Washington Years* (Ann Arbor: University of Michigan Press, 1984), 159.

17. White, *Warren*, ch. 7.

18. This relationship is explored in James F. Simon, *The Antagonists: Hugo Black, Felix Frankfurter and Civil Liberties in Modern America* (New York: Simon & Schuster, 1989).

19. Douglas wrote several volumes of an autobiography, including one entitled *The Court Years* (New York: Random House, 1980), but it is extremely unreliable and sheds little light on either Douglas or the Court. See the fine biography by James F. Simon, *Independent Journey* (New York: Harper & Row, 1980); see also Melvin I. Urofsky and Philip E. Urofsky, eds., *The Douglas Letters* (Washington, D.C.: Adler & Adler, 1987).

20. Michael Parrish, *Securities Regulation and the New Deal* (New Haven: Yale University Press, 1970), ch. 7.

21. See, for example, *Sunshine Anthracite Coal Co.* v. *Adkins*, 310 U.S. 381 (1941), or *Murdock* v. *Pennsylvania*, 319 U.S. 105 (1943).

22. An extensive critique of Douglas's alleged failings as a judge is put forth in G. Edward White, "The Anti-Judge: William O. Douglas and the Ambiguities of Individuality," 74 *Virginia Law Review* 17 (1988).

23. *Skinner* v. *Oklahoma*, 316 U.S. 535 (1942).

24. *Griswold* v. *Connecticut,* 381 U.S. 479 (1965); see relevant discussion, pp. 252–54.
25. Bernard Schwartz writes that "as a stylist and phrase-maker, Jackson can only be compared with Holmes." *Super Chief,* 36.
26. *Brown* v. *Allen,* 344 U.S. 443, 540 (1953), Jackson, J., concurring.
27. Paul A. Freund, *On Law and Justice* (Cambridge, Mass.: Harvard University Press, 1968), 181–82.
28. Dennis Hutchinson, "Feud over Faith: Justices Jackson and Black," paper delivered at Organization of American Historians, 26 March 1988, Reno, Nevada.
29. *West Virginia State Board of Education* v. *Barnette,* 319 U.S. 624 (1943).
30. There is no good biography of Jackson. Eugene Gerhart, *America's Advocate: Robert H. Jackson* (New York: Bobbs-Merrill, 1957), is admiring, uncritical, and has little on his Court work. Jackson did leave an oral history memoir, large blocks of which are quoted in Philip B. Kurland's sketch in Friedman and Israel, *Justices,* 4:2543. Good analyses of his Court career are in Charles Fairman, "Mr. Justice Jackson: 1892–1954," 55 *Columbia Law Review* 445 (1955), and Paul A. Freund, "Individual and Commonwealth in the Thought of Mr. Justice Jackson," 8 *Stanford Law Review* 9 (1955).
31. Douglas, *Court Years,* 248.
32. Mary F. Berry, *Stability, Security, and Continuity: Mr. Justice Burton and Decision-Making in the Supreme Court, 1945–1958* (Westport, Conn.: Greenwood, 1978), vii. See also David N. Atkinson, "Justice Harold H. Burton and the Work of the Supreme Court," 27 *Cleveland State Law Review* 69 (1978).
33. Kluger, *Simple Justice,* 252.
34. *Shelley* v. *Kraemer,* 334 U.S. 1 (1948).
35. Merle Miller, *Plain Speaking* (New York: Berkley, 1974), 225–26.
36. Fred Rodell, *Nine Men: A Political History of the Supreme Court* (New York: Random House, 1955), 312.
37. Schwartz, *Super Chief,* 58.
38. See relevant discussion, pp. 153–54.
39. Douglas, *Court Years,* 247.
40. Schwartz, *Super Chief,* 59.
41. See the sympathetic sketch by a former law clerk, Henry L. Wallace, "Mr. Justice Minton—Hoosier Justice on the Supreme Court," 34 *Indiana Law Journal* 145 (1959).
42. Urofsky and Urofsky, *Douglas Letters,* 125.
43. 163 U.S. 537 (1896); see relevant discussion, p. 197.
44. Norman Dorsen, "The Second Mr. Justice Harlan: A Constitutional Conservative," 44 *NYU Law Review* 249, 250 (1969).
45. Schwartz, *Super Chief,* 176. For an appreciative assessment of Harlan, see J. Harvie Wilkinson III, "Justice John M. Harlan and the Values of Federalism," 57 *Virginia Law Review* 1185 (1971).
46. Telephone interview with William Cohen (Douglas's law clerk, October 1956 Term), 25 July 1988.
47. Douglas to Fred Rodell, 2 March 1957, Fred Rodell Papers, Haverford College Library, Haverford, Pennsylvania.
48. There is no biography of Brennan, but there are scores of law review articles dealing with his opinions and philosophy. Particularly worthwhile reading are the pieces in the symposium on Brennan in 15 *Harvard Civil Rights–Civil Liberties Law Review* 279 (1980) and the appreciative evaluation by Paul Freund, 86 *Yale Law Journal* 1015 (1977).
49. Schwartz, *Super Chief,* 205–206; White, *Warren,* 185–86.
50. A good example is the 6-3 majority he put together in *Johnson* v. *Transportation Agency, Santa Clara County,* 107 S.Ct. 1442 (1987), a case many observers believed would go in the other direction.

51. In the last eight years of the Warren Court, Brennan dissented from the majority on the average less than six times a term; Warren dissented on the average in thirteen cases. In the first eight terms of the Burger Court, Brennan dissented 60 times a year, and in the 1972 Term he voted against the majority 122 times.

52. William J. Brennan, "The Bill of Rights and the States," 36 *NYU Law Review* 761 (1961). See also Mary C. Porter, "State Supreme Courts and the Legacy of the Warren Court . . . ," 8 *Publius* 55 (1978), and A. E. Dick Howard, "The Renaissance of State Constitutional Law," 63 *Institute of Government Newsletter* 1 (1986).

53. See Brennan's views on the death penalty, discussed on pp. 190–92; and his piece in the symposium, "Construing the Constitution," 19 *University of California at Davis Law Review* 2 (1985). For biographical and evaluative information, see the sketches in Friedman and Israel, *Justices*, by Stephen J. Friedman at 4:2849, and by Nathan Lewin at 5:239; some of his more important early speeches and opinions have been collected in Stephen J. Friedman, ed., *An Affair with Freedom* (New York: Atheneum, 1967).

54. For details, see White, *Warren*, ch. 7.

55. Schwartz, *Super Chief*, 216.

56. *Frank* v. *Maryland*, 359 U.S. 360, 374 (1959), Whittaker, J., concurring; interview with Charles Miller (law clerk to Justice Douglas, October 1958 Term), 2 March 1989.

57. See the story of how Whittaker, unable to write the Court's opinion in *Meyers* v. *United States*, 364 U.S. 410 (1960), gladly accepted Douglas's offer to send over a draft. Douglas had already written the dissent and so wrote both the majority and minority opinions in that case. Douglas, *Court Years*, 173–74. Although Douglas derived some malicious pleasure from recalling this episode, he and his wife went out of their way to help Whittaker when the strain began to take its toll. They convinced him to seek medical help and provided some badly needed emotional support when he resigned from the Court in 1962. Interview with Mercedes Eichholz (formerly Mercedes Douglas), 22 August 1988.

58. Leon Friedman, "Charles Whittaker," in Friedman and Israel, *Justices*, 4:2893, 2904. There is little material other than this piece on Whittaker's short tenure on the Court.

59. Woodward and Armstrong, *The Brethren*, 10.

60. Schwartz, *Super Chief*, 320.

61. Interview with Ellen Borgersen (law clerk to Justice Stewart, October 1977 Term), 30 August 1988; see also her article "On the Power of Balance: A Remembrance of Justice Potter Stewart," 13 *Hastings Constitutional Law Quarterly* 173 (1986).

62. Oliver Wendell Holmes, Jr., *The Common Law* (Boston: Little, Brown, 1881), 5.

63. *Jacobellis* v. *Ohio*, 378 U.S. 184, 197 (1964); see relevant discussion, pp. 82–83.

64. Leon Friedman, "Byron R. White," in Friedman and Israel, *Justices*, 5:345, 346.

65. Schwartz, *Super Chief*, 448. For an analysis of Goldberg's brief tenure on the Court, see Donald Roper, "The Jurisprudence of Arthur Goldberg: A Commentary," 8 *Harvard Civil Rights–Civil Liberties Law Review* 543 (1973).

66. Less than a year after taking his seat, Goldberg agreed to Kennedy's request that he help arbitrate a pending railroad strike. Interestingly, although the railroads were willing to take Goldberg as an arbitrator, the unions rejected the former AFL-CIO counsel.

67. See relevant discussion, pp. 155–56.

68. See Robert Shogan, *A Question of Judgment: The Fortas Case and the Struggle for the Supreme Court* (New York: Bobbs-Merrill, 1972), and Bruce A. Murphy, *Fortas: The Rise and Ruin of a Supreme Court Justice* (New York: Morrow, 1988).

69. Douglas, *Court Years*, 251. When Johnson asked Marshall to resign from the Circuit Court of Appeals and become his solicitor general, his clinching argument was "I want

folks to walk down the hall at the Justice Department and look in the door and see a nigger sitting there." Woodward and Armstrong, *The Brethren*, 50.

70. See Mark Tushnet, *The NAACP's Legal Strategy Against Segregated Education, 1925–1950* (Chapel Hill: University of North Carolina Press, 1987); see also Kluger, *Simple Justice*, and Loren Miller, *The Petitioners* (New York: Pantheon, 1966).

71. Ramsey Clark takes a far more positive view and believes Marshall has carved out a position of sorts in criminal procedure cases. See his sketch of Marshall in Friedman and Israel, *Justices*, 5:385. Marshall has also, of course, been a consistent advocate of civil rights and, along with Brennan, a foe of the death penalty.

72. White, *Warren*, 307.

73. James F. Simon, *In His Own Image: The Supreme Court in Richard Nixon's America* (New York: McKay, 1973), 8.

74. The comments were originally delivered as a speech at Ripon College in Wisconsin and are reprinted as "What to Do About Crime in the U.S.," *U.S. News & World Report*, 7 August 1967, p. 70.

75. Woodward and Armstrong, *The Brethren*, 5–9.

76. See, for example, the articles in Blasi, *The Burger Court*, and Herman Schwartz, ed., *The Burger Court: Rights and Wrongs in the Supreme Court, 1969–1986* (New York: Penguin Books, 1987).

77. Brennan interview in *New York Times Magazine* (5 Oct. 1986); Douglas pulled his punches, but see letters to Burger in Urofsky and Urofsky, *Douglas Letters*, 138–43.

78. Schwartz, *Super Chief*, vii.

79. O'Brien, *Storm Center*, 144–46; Edward A. Tamm and Paul C. Reardon, "Warren E. Burger and the Administration of Justice," 1981 *Brigham Young Law Review* 447 (1981).

80. Marian Faux, *Roe v. Wade* (New York: Macmillan, 1988), 167.

81. Woodward and Armstrong, *The Brethren*, 19.

82. Jon R. Waltz, "The Burger/Blackmun Court," *New York Times Magazine*, 6 December 1970, p. 61.

83. As with many sitting justices, there are no biographies available, but several law review articles do shed light on Blackmun's changing jurisprudence. See, for example, the symposium in 8 *Hamline Law Review* 1 (1985) and Steven R. Schlesinger and Janet Nesse, "Justice Harry Blackmun and Empirical Jurisprudence," 29 *American University Law Review* 405 (1980).

84. Quoted in Michael Pollet, "Harry A. Blackmun," in Friedman and Israel, *Justices*, 5:3, 5.

85. See A. E. Dick Howard, "Mr. Justice Powell and the Emerging Nixon Majority," 70 *Michigan Law Review* 445 (1972), for an evaluation of Powell's career before going on to the Court.

86. *Time*, 1 November 1971, p. 18.

87. Russell W. Galloway, Jr., "The First Decade of the Burger Court: Conservative Dominance (1969–1979)," 21 *Santa Clara Law Review* 891, 930–31 (1981).

88. Christina B. Whitman, "Individual and Community: An Appreciation of Mr. Justice Powell," 68 *Virginia Law Review* 303 (1982).

89. See Paul A. Freund, "Justice Powell—The Meaning of Moderation," 68 *Virginia Law Review* 169 (1982); and Melvin I. Urofsky, "Mr. Justice Powell and Education: The Balance of Competing Values," 13 *Journal of Law & Education* 581 (1984).

90. See relevant discussion, pp. 234–36.

91. *Keyes v. Denver School District No. 1*, 413 U.S. 189, 238, 242 (1973), Powell, J., concurring in part and dissenting in part.

92. David L. Shapiro, "Mr. Justice Rehnquist: A Preliminary View," 90 *Harvard Law Review* 293 (1976), found Rehnquist's early opinions ideologically strong but extremely inflexible; Herman Schwartz, *Packing the Courts: The Conservative Campaign to Rewrite the Constitution* (New York: Scribner's, 1988), 109–17, provides a liberal critique of Rehnquist's career; Donald E. Boles, *Mr. Justice Rehnquist, Judicial Activist: The Early Years* (Ames: Iowa State University Press, 1987), is the first of several projected volumes and tries to take Rehnquist at his word regarding his views.

93. See relevant discussion, p. 259.

94. The general story of the Court-packing plan and the conditions that evoked it can be found in many places; see Paul L. Murphy, *The Constitution in Crisis Times, 1918–1969* (New York: Harper & Row, 1972), ch. 5.

95. Kermit L. Hall, *The Magic Mirror: Law in American History* (New York: Oxford University Press, 1989), 284.

96. Jethro K. Lieberman, *The Litigious Society* (New York: Basic Books, 1981).

97. Phillips Bradley, ed., *Democracy in America* (New York: Knopf, 1960), 1:280.

98. To take just one example, see the opinion written by Chief Justice Rehnquist for a unanimous Court in *Hustler Magazine and Larry C. Flynt* v. *Falwell*, 108 S.Ct. 876 (1988), which rested almost entirely on doctrine developed within the past twenty-five years.

99. See, for example, Louis D. Brandeis's famous call for courts to recognize the facts of modern industrial life, "The Living Law," 10 *Illinois Law Review* 461 (1916).

100. Quoted in Hall, *Magic Mirror*, 311.

Chapter 2
"No Part of the Business of Government"
The Warren Court and the Religion Clauses

1. Part of the discomfort resulted from the shock that issues such as prayer and Bible reading were even open to discussion; many people just assumed the "rightness" of these activities. One reason that these cases came before the Court at this time was that the homogeneity which had marked American society began to disintegrate. While the United States was never a "Christian" nation as some fundamentalist groups have claimed, there was a generalized attitude toward religion that began to fragment in the twentieth century. By midcentury, religious fractionalism had reached a point which, according to some commentators, forced the Court to hear the religion cases.

2. The problem of original intent became more acute during the Burger years; see Chapter 3, pp. 46–49.

3. Radio address of 24 August 1985, 1985 *Public Papers of the Presidents of the United States: Ronald Reagan* 1008 (Washington, D.C.: Government Printing Office, 1988).

4. Congress passed very few laws in the nineteenth century that had any religious impact, and the only one to trigger a major court challenge prohibited bigamy in the western territories. The Mormons, who at the time practiced polygamy, challenged the law as an abridgment of their free exercise of religion, but Chief Justice Morrison Waite rejected their claim. *Reynolds* v. *United States*, 98 U.S. 145 (1879). The Court also upheld, in *Bradfield* v. *Roberts*, 175 U.S. 291 (1899), federal grants to hospitals that provided public wards and ruled that such a grant to a hospital run by a Catholic nursing order did not violate the Establishment Clause.

5. 330 U.S. 1, 15–16 (1947). In this case the Court also incorporated the First Amendment Religion Clauses and held that under the Due Process Clause of

the Fourteenth Amendment, they applied to the states as well as to the federal government.

6. *Id.* at 18.
7. *Id.* at 19.
8. *Id.* at 44–45.
9. 333 U.S. 203 (1948).
10. Stephen L. Wasby, *The Impact of the United States Supreme Court: Some Perspectives* (Chicago: Dorsey, 1970), 127.
11. *Zorach* v. *Clauson*, 343 U.S. 306, 313 (1952).
12. *Id.* at 318.
13. Some people have suggested that Douglas was still interested in running for president at this time and that his opinion reflected political rather than jurisprudential considerations. Whatever its motivation, its hedging nature is uncharacteristic of him.
14. 370 U.S. 421 (1962).
15. Justice Frankfurter was ill and would soon retire, to be replaced by Arthur Goldberg; Justice White had only recently been appointed to take Whittaker's place and did not participate in the decision.
16. 370 U.S. at 430–31.
17. John D. Weaver, *Warren: The Man, The Court, The Era* (Boston: Little, Brown, 1967), 261. See also Bernard Schwartz, *Super Chief: Earl Warren and His Supreme Court* (New York: New York University Press, 1983), 441.
18. Paul L. Murphy, *The Constitution in Crisis Times, 1918–1969* (New York: Harper & Row, 1972), 392.
19. Leo Pfeffer, *Church, State, and Freedom* (Boston: Beacon Press, 1967 rev. ed.), 469. Interestingly enough, two decades later Ervin vigorously opposed school prayers and defended the Court from charges that it was antireligious. Pfeffer, *Religion, State, and the Burger Court* (Buffalo, N.Y.: Prometheus Books, 1984), 83.
20. 108 *Cong. Rec.* 11675 (87th Cong., 2d Sess., 1962).
21. William M. Beaney and Edward N. Beiser, "Prayer and Politics: The Impact of *Engel* and *Schempp* on the Political Process," 13 *Journal of Public Law* 475, 478 (1964). See also Clifford M. Lytle, *The Warren Court and Its Critics* (Tucson: University of Arizona Press, 1968), 47–48.
22. The identification of groups approving and condemning the Court's religion decisions is explored in Francis J. Sorauf, *The Wall of Separation: The Constitutional Politics of Church and State* (Princeton, N.J.: Princeton University Press, 1976).
23. *New York Times*, 28 June 1962, p. 12.
24. 374 U.S. 203 (1963). In a companion case, *Murray* v. *Curlett*, the noted atheist Madelaine Murray and her son challenged a local Baltimore school rule that each school day begin with the "reading, without comment, of a chapter in the Holy Bible and/or use of the Lord's Prayer." The schools did permit children to be excused at the request of parents.
25. *Id.* at 222.
26. 374 U.S. at 291, quoting Frankfurter in *McCollum* v. *Board of Education*, 333 U.S. 203, 227 (1948).
27. *Id.* at 225–26.
28. There were, however, three concurrences. Justice Douglas believed the practice unconstitutional not only because of the state-conducted religious exercises but also because public funds were used to support religious activities. Justice Goldberg, joined by Harlan, spoke of the "unavoidable accommodations" necessary to achieve religious liberty, but the practices required by the state did not permit for meaningful accommodation. The most extensive concurrence came from Justice Brennan, who tried to

distinguish between the myriad but innocuous forms of government involvement with religion and those that violated constitutional standards. Brennan also believed that the majority opinion did not go far enough in developing the historical justification for interpreting the First Amendment to mean strict separation.

29. However, a number of constitutional amendments were introduced in Congress, none of which ever progressed very far down the legislative path. In some areas, especially in the Deep South and the Bible belt, school districts ignored the ruling and got away with it; in such homogeneous communities, most of them small, no one would risk social ostracism to "attack the Bible."

30. A few days after the decision came down, Justice Byron White took part in a swearing-in ceremony at the Justice Department and joked that "I had to borrow this Bible. The only one left in the Supreme Court was Potter Stewart's." Weaver, *Warren*, 263.

31. Even today one hears people who should know better, such as Ronald Reagan, say that the Court outlawed prayer and Bible reading in the schools. The Court has prohibited the state from *imposing required* prayer or Bible reading. Any student who wishes to pray by himself or herself may do so any time they wish; I often see students move their lips in silent prayer or cross themselves as they prepare to take an exam. A student may also read the Bible and may study the Bible as literature or even in a comparative religion class. But students may not be required to read or listen to Bible readings that are designed for moralizing or proselytizing purposes.

32. *Wallace* v. *Jaffree*, 105 S.Ct. 2479, 2497 (1985).

33. According to one scholar: "The Jewish community welcomed [*Schempp*], Protestant leaders were divided but the overwhelming majority of the national leaders approved the decision, and the Catholic Church was firmly opposed to the decision." Ellis Katz, "Patterns of Compliance with the Schempp Decision," 14 *Journal of Public Law* 396, 398 (1965).

34. Justice Rutledge appended a copy to his dissent in *Everson* v. *Board of Education*, 330 U.S. 1, 63–72 (1947). The Remonstrance led directly to the Virginia Statute for Religious Freedom (1786), which is the lineal forebear of the Religion Clauses in the First Amendment.

35. Leonard W. Levy, *The Establishment Clause: Religion and the First Amendment* (New York: Macmillan, 1986), 150; see also Matthew 6:5–6.

36. See Ray Ginger, *Six Days or Forever?* (Boston: Beacon Press, 1958).

37. See her account of the case in Peter Irons, *The Courage of Their Convictions* (New York: Free Press, 1988), ch. 9.

38. *Arkansas* v. *Epperson*, 242 Ark. 922 (1967).

39. *Epperson* v. *Arkansas*, 393 U.S. 97 (1968).

40. Given the centrality of the evolutionary theory to modern biological science, the Court's attribution of religious motivation to the Arkansas legislature was quite supportable. John Hart Ely, *Democracy and Distrust: A Theory of Judicial Review* (Cambridge, Mass.: Harvard University Press, 1980), 141.

41. See relevant discussion, p. 39.

42. *McLean* v. *Arkansas Board of Education*, 529 F.Supp. 1255 (E.D. Ark. 1982).

43. *Edwards* v. *Aguillard*, 107 S.Ct. 2573 (1987).

44. See, for example, *Lovell* v. *Griffin*, 303 U.S. 444 (1938); *Martin* v. *Struthers*, 319 U.S. 141 (1943); and *Kunz* v. *New York*, 340 U.S. 290 (1951). See also the discussion in ch. 3 of Richard E. Morgan, *The Supreme Court and Religion* (New York: Free Press, 1972).

45. *Reynolds* v. *United States*, 98 U.S. 145 (1879).

46. The "truth" of that belief is not a matter of judicial concern. In *United States* v. *Ballard*, 322 U.S. 78 (1944), the defendants had been indicted for mail fraud in soliciting funds

for the "I Am" movement. Among other claims. they represented themselves as "divine messengers" of St. Germain, who had, "by reason of supernatural attainments, the power to heal persons of ailments and diseases." The prosecutor had submitted these claims to the jury as part of his evidence regarding the alleged fraud, but Justice Douglas, speaking for the majority, ruled that the truth or falsity of the beliefs could not be used against the defendants. "Men may believe what they cannot prove. They may not be put to the proof of their religious doctrines or beliefs."

47. *Cantwell* v. *Connecticut,* 310 U.S. 296 (1940).

48. 310 U.S. 586 (1940).

49. 319 U.S. 624 (1943). In an earlier Witness case, *Jones* v. *Opelika,* 316 U.S. 584 (1942), three members of the majority in *Gobitis*—Black, Douglas, and Murphy—joined Stone in dissent and announced that they believed their votes in the flag salute case had been wrong. See David Manwaring, *Render Unto Caesar: The Flag Salute Controversy* (Chicago: University of Chicago Press, 1962).

50. 366 U.S. 420 (1961).

51. In *Two Guys from Harrison-Allentown, Inc.* v. *McGinley,* 366 U.S. 582 (1961), one of the companion cases, the Court ruled that establishment was the only religion claim the appellants could raise and then ruled against that claim.

52. 366 U.S. 599 (1961).

53. There was a fair amount of dissatisfaction within the Court with Warren's opinion. He had to redraft the opinion several times to secure Black's support, while Frankfurter issued a lengthy concurrence, joined by Harlan. Justices Stewart, Douglas, and Brennan dissented.

54. Douglas dissented in all four cases, and in another Sunday closing case a year later, wrote: "By what authority can government compel one person not to work on Sunday because the majority of the populace deem Sunday to be a holy day? . . . Moslems may some day control a state legislature. Could they make criminal the opening of a shop on Friday? Would not we Christians fervently believe, if that came to pass, that government had no authority to make us bow to the scruples of the Moslem majority?" *Arlen's Department Store* v. *Kentucky,* 371 U.S. 218, 219 (1962).

55. *Sherbert* v. *Verner,* 374 U.S. 398 (1963).

56. See the discussion on strict scrutiny at p. 243.

57. Stewart's opinion made a number of other trenchant observations, including his attack on previous religion rulings as "not only insensitive, but positively wooden." He also pointed out that Brennan's efforts to distinguish this case from *Braunfeld* did not work; if South Carolina's rule violated the free exercise of Seventh-Day Adventists, then the Pennsylvania statute similarly affected Jews. That, of course, is exactly what Brennan said in his dissent in the earlier case. Why the Court did not overrule *Braunfeld* is not clear. Certainly the Court tries to avoid overruling cases whenever possible, especially one decided only two terms earlier. It is also likely that Brennan could not have gotten his majority unless he took the approach he did.

58. See relevant discussion, pp. 63–64.

59. Philip B. Kurland, "Of Church and State and the Supreme Court," 29 *University of Chicago Law Review* 1 (1961).

60. Dissenting in *Plessy* v. *Ferguson,* 163 U.S. 537, 552, at 559 (1896).

61. See William M. Wiecek, *The Sources of Antislavery Constitutionalism in America, 1760–1848* (Ithaca, N.Y.: Cornell University Press, 1977).

62. *Selective Draft Law Cases,* 245 U.S. 366 (1918). The Court's deference to the legislature in this area continued when it later upheld a requirement that all male students in land grant colleges take military science courses, over the protests of conscientious objectors. *Hamilton* v. *Regents,* 293 U.S. 243 (1934).

63. 380 U.S. 163 (1965).

Chapter 3
"As Winding as the Famous Serpentine Wall"
The Burger Court and the Religion Clauses

1. The religion issue was not as strong in the early 1970s, when Nixon made his appointments to the Court. At that time, the major criticism dealt with the Court's alleged leniency regarding criminals (see Chapter 7) and its decisions on desegregation (see Chapter 9). The rise of the fundamentalist right occurred in the later seventies and definitely affected Ronald Reagan's appointments to the federal courts. See Herman Schwartz, *Packing the Courts* (New York: Scribner's, 1988), especially Chapter 2.
2. 330 U.S. 1, 16 (1947).
3. An excellent discussion is found in John Hart Ely, *Democracy and Distrust: A Theory of Judicial Review* (Cambridge, Mass.: Harvard University Press, 1980); see also Erwin Chemerinsky, *Interpreting the Constitution* (New York: Praeger, 1987).
4. Edwin L. Meese, Jr., "Construing the Constitution," 19 *University of California at Davis Law Review* 22, 23, 26 (1985).
5. This view is generally supported in Leonard W. Levy, *The Establishment Clause: Religion and the First Amendment* (New York: Macmillan, 1986).
6. This is the view of Gerard V. Bradley, *Church-State Relationships in America* (Westport, Conn.: Greenwood, 1987), and Michael J. Malbin, *Religion and Politics: The Intentions of the Authors of the First Amendment* (Washington, D.C.: American Enterprise Institute, 1978); see, however, Douglas Laycock, " 'Nonpreferential' Aid to Religion: A False Claim about Original Intent," 27 *William & Mary Law Review* 875 (1986).
7. The complexity of early views on religion and the state are well developed in Thomas J. Curry, *The First Freedoms: Church and State in America to the Passage of the First Amendment* (New York: Oxford University Press, 1986), and William Lee Miller, *The First Liberty: Religion and the American Republic* (New York: Knopf, 1986).
8. Leonard W. Levy, *Original Intent and the Framers' Constitution* (New York: Macmillan, 1988).
9. The "Pacificus" essays can be found in Harold Syrett et al., eds., 15 *Papers of Alexander Hamilton* 33 et seq. (New York: Columbia University Press, 1969); the "Helvidius" papers are in T. A. Mason et al., eds., 15 *Papers of James Madison* 66 et seq. (Chicago: University of Chicago Press, 1962).
10. Advocates of original intent find such instances not only embarrassing, but also difficult to explain. To the historian, on the other hand, it makes perfectly good sense, because he or she would take into account the political developments of the intervening years and the emergence of political parties that differed, among other things, on whether one should interpret the Constitution broadly or narrowly.
11. Levy, *Establishment Clause*, ch. 4.
12. Under the doctrine of *Frothingham* v. *Mellon*, 262 U.S. 447 (1923), taxpayers lacked standing to challenge the government's disposition of its tax revenues.
13. 392 U.S. 83 (1968). See the discussion of the case in Richard E. Morgan, *The Supreme Court and Religion* (New York: Free Press, 1972), 96–100.
14. 392 U.S. 236 (1968).
15. For an analysis of the various opinions, see Paul Freund, "Aid to Parochial Schools," 82 *Harvard Law Review* 1687 (1969).
16. *Abington School District* v. *Schempp*, 374 U.S. 203 (1963).
17. 397 U.S. 664 (1970). For a discussion of religious tax exemption, see Dean M. Kelley, "The Supreme Court Redefines Tax Exemption," in Thomas Robbins and Roland

Robertson, eds., *Church-State Relations: Tensions and Transitions* (New York: Transaction Books, 1987), ch. 9.

18.   403 U.S. 602 (1971).

19.   403 U.S. 672 (1971).

20.   Dissenting in *Committee for Public Education and Religious Liberty* v. *Regan*, 444 U.S. 646, 671 (1980). In the first few years, Douglas (whom Stevens replaced) and Black also stood for strict separation of church and state.

21.   In a separate opinion accompanying *Lemon* and *Tilton*, White wrote: "Where a state program seeks to ensure the proper education of its young, in private as well as public schools, free exercise considerations at least counsel against refusing support for students attending parochial schools simply because in that setting they are also being instructed in the tenets of the faith they are constitutionally free to practice." 403 U.S. 661 at 665.

22.   Justice O'Connor replaced Stewart in 1981; while at first she seemed inclined to join the White–Rehnquist group, she later took a more centrist position.

23.   Perhaps the most striking example of this split came in *Meek* v. *Pittenger*, 421 U.S. 349 (1975), when the Court split 3-3-3 in invalidating most parts of a Pennsylvania aid program. Brennan, Marshall, and Douglas voted to void all of the parts; White, Burger, and Rehnquist voted to sustain all parts; Stewart, Blackmun, and Powell voted to sustain some parts and strike the rest.

24.   413 U.S. 472 (1972).

25.   For an analysis of Powell's part in the Burger Court's education decisions, including the Establishment Clause cases, see Melvin I. Urofsky, "Mr. Justice Powell and Education: The Balance of Competing Values," 13 *Journal of Law & Education* 581 (1984).

26.   413 U.S. 734 (1972).

27.   For the three dissenters—Brennan, Douglas, and Marshall—the fact that money had been lent to the Baptist College of Charleston constituted sufficient evidence of entanglement.

28.   413 U.S. 756 (1973)

29.   In the fourth case that day, *Sloan* v. *Lemon* (*Lemon II*), 413 U.S. 825 (1973), the Court struck down a Pennsylvania program of tuition grants. The state had redesigned the law that *Lemon I* had invalidated, but Powell found no significant differences between it and the New York scheme.

30.   413 U.S. at 761.

31.   421 U.S. 349 (1975).

32.   The following year, in a case involving aid to higher education, the Court continued the distinction it had drawn between elementary and secondary schools and colleges. In *Roemer* v. *Maryland Public Works Board*, 426 U.S. 736 (1976), the majority approved annual noncategorical grants to private colleges, including church-related schools; the only restriction was that the monies could not be used for "sectarian purposes." Justice Blackmun's plurality opinion admitted that the statute raised possible entanglement problems, because the state would have to confirm that the funds had been spent for secular purposes. Blackmun's opinion was joined only by Burger and Powell; White, joined by Rehnquist, concurred in the judgment but dismissed the entanglement criterion as "superfluous." Justice Brennan, joined by Marshall, and Justice Stevens entered dissents.

33.   433 U.S. 229 (1977).

34.   Schwartz, *Packing the Courts*, 24.

35.   Despite the failure of the White House to push these issues, Senator Jesse Helms once again introduced a school prayer amendment as well as legislation to strip the courts

36. Wilbur Edel, *Defenders of the Faith: Religion and Politics from the Pilgrim Fathers to Ronald Reagan* (New York: Praeger, 1987), 152–53.
37. 449 U.S. 39 (1980). In addition to the text itself, each school was to post a plaque explaining that the display was a secular application of the Ten Commandments "in its adoption as the fundamental legal code of Western Civilization and the Common Law of the United States."
38. 444 U.S. 646 (1980).
39. Justices Brennan and Marshall joined in Blackmun's opinion. Justice Stevens dissented separately and attacked what he called the majority's ad hoc approach that failed to establish consistent norms.
40. 454 U.S. 263 (1981). Only Justice White dissented.
41. See, for example, *Nartowicz* v. *Clayton County School District*, 736 F.2d 646 (11th Cir. 1984), or *Bell* v. *Little Axe School District*, 766 F.2d 1391 (10th Cir. 1985).
42. Deductible expenses included tuition to attend school outside the student's home district, tuition for summer school and for physically handicapped children, and the costs of transportation and textbooks.
43. 463 U.S. 388 (1983).
44. Justice Marshall, joined by Stevens, Brennan, and Blackmun, wrote a strong dissent charging that the majority had refused to look past the language of the statute at the real facts involved. That the tuition exemption was available to all parents mattered very little, because fewer than 100 of the 90,000 students in Minnesota public schools paid a general tuition. Moreover, of the students in private schools, 96 percent attended a religious school. The practical result of the law, as Marshall noted, was to benefit parents of religious-school students. Justice Rehnquist dismissed Marshall's objection this way: "We would be loath to adopt a rule grounding the constitutionality of a facially neutral law on annual reports reciting the extent to which various classes of private citizens claimed benefits under the law." Compare this dismissal of the effects of the law on the Court's reliance on effect as opposed to facial neutrality in its cases involving racial discrimination, discussed in Chapter 10.
45. 463 U.S. 783 (1983).
46. Norman Redlich, "The Separation of Church and State: The Burger Court's Tortuous Journey," 60 *Notre Dame Law Review* 1094, 1122–26 (1985).
47. 465 U.S. 668 (1984).
48. Burger's manipulation of the *Lemon* test highlighted what had been a problem for both the Court and legal commentators for several years: the lack of precision over exactly what the various components of the test meant. Justice O'Connor, although concurring in the result, wrote a thoughtful opinion suggesting that a clarification of the criteria associated with the Establishment Clause was long overdue. Her suggestion, however, that the Court look primarily at the effects of particular programs did not provide any clearer test than did the one already in effect, although it might have led to the approval of some plans that the Court had struck down.
49. *Id.* at 711–12.
50. See Norman Redlich, "Nativity Ruling Insults Jews," *New York Times*, 26 March 1984, p. A19.
51. Levy, *Establishment Clause*, 157.
52. William Van Alstyne, "Trends in the Supreme Court: Mr. Jefferson's Crumbling Wall—A Commentary on *Lynch* v. *Donnelly*," 1984 *Duke Law Journal* 301 (1984).
53. 459 U.S. 115 (1982).

54. Edel, *Defenders of the Faith*, 126–30.
55. The full prayer read: "Almighty God, You alone are our God. We acknowledge you as the Creator and Supreme judge of the world. May Your justice, Your truth, and Your peace abound this day in the hearts of our countrymen, in the counsels of our government, in the sanctity of our homes and in the classrooms of our schools in the name of our Lord. Amen."
56. *Wallace v. Jaffree* 472 U.S. 38, 57 n.43 (1985). Emphasis added by Justice Stevens.
57. An interesting story, however, is attached to the court challenge to the 1982 amendment with its prescribed prayer. The local federal district judge, W. Brevard Hand, found that, in fact, the statute had been enacted "to encourage a religious activity." Nonetheless, he upheld the law because the Supreme Court had erroneously interpreted the Establishment Clause in its prior rulings! The Fourteenth Amendment, he claimed, never incorporated the First Amendment and Alabama was free to establish a state religion if it so desired. The Eleventh Circuit reversed this decision on the basis of *Engel* v. *Vitale* (1962), and when the state appealed, the Supreme Court summarily and *unanimously* affirmed the Circuit. *Wallace* v. *Jaffree*, 465 U.S. 920 (1984). For an enthusiastic encomium to Hand, however, see James McClellan, "Hand's Writing on the Wall of Separation . . . ," in Robert A. Goldwin and Art Kaufman, eds., *How Does the Constitution Protect Religious Freedom?* (Washington, D.C.: American Enterprise Institute, 1987), 43–68.
58. Justice O'Connor joined in the opinion but also entered a concurrence elaborating on the relation between the Establishment and Free Exercise Clauses. Accommodationists like Burger had used the latter to justify permitting practices that separationists claimed violated the former. She suggested that if the government "lifts a government-imposed burden on the free exercise of religion . . . then the standard Establishment Clause test should be modified accordingly. It is disingenuous to look for a purely secular purpose when the manifest objective of a statute is to facilitate the free exercise of religion by lifting a government-imposed burden." This modification, however, would not save the Alabama law, O'Connor noted, because the state had never imposed any burden on a child's right to pray silently in school. The burden that had been lifted was not one imposed by the state but by the Constitution as interpreted in *Engel* and *Schempp*, and the state had no power to remove burdens imposed by the Constitution. 472 U.S. at 67.
59. Rehnquist relied heavily on Robert L. Cord, *Separation of Church and State: Historical Fact and Current Fiction* (New York: Lambeth Press, 1982), a work dismissed by Leonard Levy as "mostly historical fiction masquerading as scholarship." Although Levy has argued brilliantly that the Framers of the First Amendment did in fact intend to erect a wall of separation, there have been some legitimate works arguing for a nonpreferential view; see, for example, Bradley, *Church-State Relationships*. The use of history in the debate is discussed in David A. Richards, "Interpretation and Historiography," 58 *Southern California Law Review* 489 (1985).
60. 473 U.S. 373 (1985).
61. 473 U.S. 402 (1985).
62. Professor A. E. Dick Howard of the University of Virginia argued the case against the city in *Grand Rapids*, and his strategy assumed that there would be four votes to sustain the program—Burger, White, Rehnquist, and O'Connor—and four to strike it down—Brennan, Marshall, Blackmun, and Stevens. As in so many of these cases, Justice Powell would cast the deciding vote. Howard thus directed his entire oral argument to those issues that he knew concerned Powell, including references to the ideas of Madison and Jefferson. Professor Howard explained this strategy in a talk to my faculty seminar on the Bill of Rights, 24 October 1986.

63. 406 U.S. 205 (1972).
64. Justices Powell and Rehnquist did not participate in this decision. The only dissent came from Justice Douglas, who noted that the subjects of concern—the children—had no voice in this case. The suit had been brought by the parents to satisfy their religious views, but the price of not having sufficient education would be carried by the children, who might not fully share those religious views.
65. Jesse H. Choper, "The Free Exercise Clause: A Structural Overview and an Appraisal of Recent Developments," 27 *William & Mary Law Review* 943, 947–48 (1986). Choper is currently dean of Boalt Hall School of Law at the University of California, Berkeley.
66. The court also suggested that the petitioner's views were more a matter of "personal philosophical choice" than of religious belief.
67. *Thomas* v. *Review Board, Indiana Employment Security Division*, 450 U.S. 707 (1981).
68. See relevant discussion, pp. 41–42.
69. Dean Choper believes that Rehnquist came close to articulating a standard that might have served the Court to adjudicate both Religion Clauses. Choper suggested the following test: Government action violates the Establishment Clause if its purpose is to aid religion and if it significantly endangers religious liberty by coercing, compromising, or influencing religious beliefs. The second prong by itself could be used to evaluate free exercise claims and would not create any tension with the criteria for establishment cases. "The Free Exercise Clause," 948.
70. *Welsh* v. *United States*, 398 U.S. 333 (1970).
71. 401 U.S. 437 (1971). Only Justice Douglas dissented, and his opinion spoke of an "implied First Amendment right . . . of conscience." Moreover, he condemned the law as a species of "invidious discrimination in favor of religious persons and against others with like scruples." See Kent Greenawalt, "All or Nothing at All: The Defeat of Selective Conscientious Objection," 1971 *Supreme Court Review* 31 (1972).
72. 415 U.S. 361 (1974); again, Douglas was the sole dissenter.
73. 455 U.S. 252 (1982).
74. Justice Stevens concurred in the result but disagreed with the reasoning. He did not believe that a strict scrutiny standard, with its burden upon the government to prove it had a compelling state interest, should apply in free exercise cases. "In my opinion," he wrote, "it is the objector who must shoulder the burden of demonstrating that there is a unique reason for allowing him a special exemption from a valid law of general applicability."
75. 461 U.S. 574 (1983).
76. Justice Powell's concurrence and Justice Rehnquist's dissent focused on questions of statutory authority, which in fact comprised the bulk of the Court's opinion. Both, however, explicitly agreed with the majority in rejecting any free exercise claims.
77. *TWA* v. *Hardison*, 432 U.S. 63 (1977). A later Title VII case involved a public employer, a school system in which an employee had sought paid leave to observe holy days unique to his sect; the school board had countered with an offer of unpaid leave. Although the Court remanded the case to a lower court for further factual findings, it held that unpaid leave to observe certain holy days was not a reasonable accommodation when paid leave was provided for all purposes except religious ones. *Ansonia Board of Education* v. *Philbrook*, 107 S.Ct. 367 (1986).
78. 472 U.S. 703, 708–709 (1985).
79. Levy, *Establishment Clause*, 162–63.

Chapter 4
"The Central Meaning of the First Amendment"
The Warren Court and Free Speech

1. *Palko* v. *Connecticut*, 302 U.S. 319, 327 (1937).
2. For earlier developments, see David M. Rabban, "The First Amendment: The Forgotten Years," 90 *Yale Law Journal* 514 (1981); Paul L. Murphy, *World War I and the Origin of Civil Liberties in the United States* (New York: Norton, 1979); and the classic Zechariah Chafee, Jr., *Free Speech in the United States* (Cambridge, Mass.: Harvard University Press, 1941 rev. ed.).
3. E. E. Dennis, D. M. Gillmor, and D. L. Grey, eds., *Justice Hugo Black and the First Amendment* (Ames: Iowa State University Press, 1978).
4. Sir William Blackstone, 4 *Commentaries of the Laws of England* 151 (1783 ed.).
5. Common law developed four such libels: seditious libel (the criticism of government and public officials), private libel (the defamation of private citizens), blasphemous libel (the utterance of heretical, immoral, or antireligious sentiment), and obscene libel (the publication of "lewd" or sexually stimulating materials).
6. For the English experience in general, see Fredrick S. Siebert, *Freedom of Speech in England: 1476–1776* (Urbana: University of Illinois Press, 1952).
7. Leonard Levy depicted a restrictive society in *Freedom of Speech and Press in Early American History: Legacy of Suppression* (New York: Harper & Row, 1963), in which he relied on the statutes as a guide to the level of free speech in the colonies. Subsequent studies indicated, however, that in practice the colonists enjoyed a wide latitude for free expression; see, for example, Lawrence Leder, *Liberty and Authority: Early American Political Ideology, 1689–1763* (Chicago: Quadrangle Books, 1968). Recently Levy revised his earlier opinion, and he now believes that despite the existence of formal restraints on speech, the colonists enjoyed true freedom. *Emergence of a Free Press* (New York: Oxford University Press, 1985).
8. James Alexander, *A Brief Narrative of the Case and Trial of John Peter Zenger (1736)*, Stanley N. Katz, ed. (Cambridge, Mass.: Harvard University Press, 1972).
9. James Morton Smith, *Freedom's Fetters: The Alien and Sedition Laws and American Civil Liberties* (Ithaca, N.Y.: Cornell University Press, 1956), 421–22.
10. Over a century later, Justice Oliver Wendell Holmes, Jr., embraced the Blackstonian view that free speech meant no more than lack of prior restraint. *Patterson* v. *Colorado*, 205 U.S. 454 (1907). A dozen years later, however, Holmes grudgingly acknowledged that it "may well be that the prohibition of laws abridging the freedom of speech is not confined to previous restraints, although to prevent them may have been the main purpose." *Schenck* v. *United States*, 249 U.S. 47, 51–52 (1919).
11. Chafee, *Free Speech in the United States*, 21.
12. *Id.* at 35. Chafee's influence on Holmes, which led to his eloquent defense of free speech in the *Abrams* case, is explored in Fred D. Ragan, "Justice Oliver Wendell Holmes, Jr., Zechariah Chafee, Jr., and the Clear and Present Danger Test for Free Speech: The First Year, 1919," 58 *Journal of American History* 24 (1971). See also the analysis of Holmes and Chafee in Harry Kalven, Jr., *A Worthy Tradition: Freedom of Speech in America* (New York: Harper & Row, 1988), 130–38. Perhaps the one single Court opinion that sums up the Chafee view on the value of political speech is Justice Brandeis's concurrence (in fact a dissent) in *Whitney* v. *California*, 274 U.S. 357, 372 (1927).
13. Chafee, *Free Speech in the United States*, 150; *Chaplinsky* v. *New Hampshire*, 315 U.S. 568 (1942). Justice Murphy, one of the most liberal members of the wartime Court, wrote

the opinion, in which both Justices Black and Douglas joined. Later on the two men took a far more expansive view of protected speech.

14. Alexander Meiklejohn, *Political Freedom: The Constitutional Powers of the People* (New York: Oxford University Press, 1960), 28. The notion of political speech as having the highest value is elaborated upon in Lillian BeVier, "The First Amendment and Political Speech: An Inquiry into the Substance and Limits of Principle," 30 *Stanford Law Review* 299 (1978); a narrower view of what constitutes protected political speech is Robert Bork, "Neutral Principles and Some First Amendment Problems," 47 *Indiana Law Journal* 1 (1971). Meiklejohn's influence within the Court is acknowledged in William Brennan, "The Supreme Court and the Meiklejohn Interpretation of the First Amendment," 79 *Harvard Law Review* 1 (1965).

15. *Political Freedom*, 37.

16. Chafee, Review of Meiklejohn, *Free Speech and Its Relation to Self-Government* (New York: Harper's, 1949), in 62 *Harvard Law Review* 891 (1949).

17. See relevant discussion, pp. 76–77.

18. Emerson's ideas are laid out most fully in *Toward a General Theory of the First Amendment* (New York: Random House, 1966) and *The System of Freedom of Expression* (New York: Vintage, 1970).

19. Hugo L. Black, *A Constitutional Faith* (New York: Knopf, 1968), 45.

20. *Brandenburg* v. *Ohio*, 395 U.S. 444, 454 (1969); see also Douglas to Alden Whitman, 24 January 1972, in Urofsky and Urofsky, *Douglas Letters*, 202–203.

21. 54 Stat. 670 (1940).

22. See Michael Belknap, *Cold War Political Justice: The Smith Act, the Communist Party, and American Civil Liberties* (Westport, Conn.: Greenwood Press, 1977).

23. 341 U.S. 494 (1951). Former Attorney General Tom Clark, who had recently been appointed to the Court, did not participate in the decision.

24. Vinson actually spoke for only himself and three other justices. Frankfurter concurred in the result, but not in Vinson's reasoning. He believed that the balancing of values must accompany the weighing of immediate danger. Justice Jackson also concurred, and he focused his attention on whether Congress had a right to punish conspiracy, which he believed it did.

25. The case evoked extensive commentary in the legal press. See, among others, Wallace Mendelson, "Clear and Present Danger—From Schenck to Dennis," 52 *Columbia Law Review* 313 (1952), and John A. Gorfinkel and Julian W. Mack II, "Dennis v. United States and the Clear and Present Danger Rule," 39 *California Law Review* 475 (1951).

26. John P. Frank, *Marble Palace: The Supreme Court in American Life* (Westport, Conn.: Greenwood Press, 1961), 252; Paul L. Murphy, *The Constitution in Crisis Times, 1918–1969* (New York: Harper & Row, 1972), 301.

27. *Id.* at 320.

28. *Quinn* v. *United States*, 349 U.S. 155, 161 (1955); the other two cases were *Emspak* v. *United States*, 349 U.S. 190 (1955), and *Bart* v. *United States*, 349 U.S. 219 (1955). That same Term, in *Peters* v. *Hobby*, 349 U.S. 331 (1955), the Court carefully skirted the First Amendment attack against the government's security program by ruling that the Loyalty Board lacked jurisdiction in the matter.

29. *Pennsylvania* v. *Nelson*, 350 U.S. 497 (1956); see Roger C. Cramton, "The Supreme Court and State Power to Deal with Subversion and Loyalty," 43 *Minnesota Law Review* 1025 (1959).

30. *Slochower* v. *SACB*, 350 U.S. 513 (1956); *Communist Party* v. *SACB*, 351 U.S. 115 (1956).

31. *Yates* v. *United States*, 354 U.S. 298 (1957). Justices Brennan and Whittaker did not participate in the decision; Justice Black concurred in part and dissented in part, and only Justice Clark fully dissented.

32. Kalven, *A Worthy Tradition*, 211.

33. The Communists had been organized in the United States as early as 1919, but in 1945 the old apparatus was disbanded and reconstituted as the Communist Party of the United States. All of the defendants had been members since before 1945, but the government used the reorganization date of 1945 as the baseline and thus could indict people who had been involved in the movement for many years before that. But a three-year statute of limitations existed on conspiracy, and the indictments had not been brought until 1951, six years after the baseline date. The government could not have it both ways; if it wanted to use 1945 as the date to catch older members, it could not bring it forward to evade the statute of limitations.

34. 354 U.S. 178 (1957).

35. 354 U.S. 234 (1957).

36. 354 U.S. 363 (1957).

37. 367 U.S. 203 (1961).

38. *Noto* v. *United States*, 367 U.S. 290 (1961).

39. *Communist Party* v. *SACB*, 367 U.S. 1 (1961).

40. *Albertson* v. *SACB*, 382 U.S. 70 (1965).

41. *Aptheker* v. *Secretary of State*, 378 U.S. 500 (1964); *United States* v. *Robel*, 389 U.S. 258 (1967).

42. 395 U.S. 444 (1969).

43. 249 U.S. 47 (1919).

44. 250 U.S. 616 (1919).

45. The major cases on this trail would include *Abrams* v. *United States*, 250 U.S. 616 (1919) (Holmes and Brandeis dissenting); *Gitlow* v. *New York*, 268 U.S. 652 (1925) (applying the First Amendment to the states through the Fourteenth Amendment); *Whitney* v. *California*, 274 U.S. 357 (1927) (Brandeis and Holmes concurring); *DeJonge* v. *Oregon*, 299 U.S. 353 (1937) (overturning conviction for state criminal syndicalism law); and *Herndon* v. *Lowry*, 301 U.S. 242 (1937) (overturning insurrection charge against Negro who advocated racial equality).

46. *Whitney* v. *California*, 274 U.S. 357 (1927). Ten years later the Court reversed a conviction under a similar Oregon statute on First Amendment grounds but did not reach the issue of whether the statute itself was constitutional. *DeJonge* v. *Oregon*, 299 U.S. 353 (1937).

47. Justices Black and Douglas entered concurring opinions objecting to *any* form of clear and present danger test, believing that there could be no constitutional distinction between advocacy of abstract ideas and advocacy of political action. Their objections arose from the Court's reference to *Dennis*, but in fact the actual words "clear and present danger" do not even appear in the decision. The strategy of the Court to in fact overturn *Dennis* without saying so is explored in Kalven, *A Worthy Tradition*, 231–34.

48. In Gerald Gunther's opinion, the decision combines the most useful aspects of Learned Hand's incitement test in the 1917 *Masses* case as well as the protection of the clear and present danger doctrine as expounded by Holmes and Brandeis. Gunther, "Learned Hand and the Origins of Modern First Amendment Doctrine: Some Fragments of History," 27 *Stanford Law Review* 719, 722 (1975). The case is *Masses Publishing Co.* v. *Patten*, 244 Fed. 535 (S.D.N.Y. 1917).

49. *Queen* v. *Read*, 88 Eng. Rep. 935 (1708), cited in Frederick F. Schauer, *The Law of Obscenity* (Washington, D.C.: Bureau of National Affairs, 1976), 5.

50. *Rex* v. *Curll*, 93 Eng. Rep. 849 (1727), *id.* 5–6.

51. *Regina* v. *Hicklin*, L.R. 3 Q.B. 360, 371 (1868). For a brief overview of obscenity laws in Great Britain and the United States in the nineteenth century, see Felice Flanery Lewis, *Literature, Obscenity and Law* (Carbondale: Southern Illinois University Press, 1976), 7–12.

52. *United States* v. *One Book Called "Ulysses,"* 5 F.Supp. 182 (1933).

53. The Court, after three separate hearings, did strike down a New York law that prohibited publication of material devoted primarily to "criminal news, police reports, or accounts of criminal deeds" on overbreadth grounds; that is, the state had spread its net too widely and in doing so restricted dissemination of legitimate news. But Justice Reed emphasized that the decision did not prevent the state, using a properly drawn statute, from regulating "objectionable" material, such as pornography. *Winter* v. *New York*, 333 U.S. 507 (1948).

54. 335 U.S. 848 (1948). Justice Frankfurter, a personal friend of Wilson's, recused himself, thus creating the tie vote.

55. 352 U.S. 380, 383–84 (1957).

56. 354 U.S. 476 (1957). The Court heard *Roth*, which involved a federal obscenity statute, along with *Alberts* v. *California*, which derived from conviction under a similar state law.

57. *United States* v. *Roth*, 237 F.2d 796, 806 (2d Cir. 1956).

58. *A Worthy Tradition*, 33–34.

59. Richard Y. Funston, *Constitutional Counterrevolution?* (New York: Schenkman, 1977), 263.

60. The problems that the novel had with the censor are recounted in Charles Rembar, *The End of Obscenity* (New York: Random House, 1968), 59–160.

61. *Kingsley International Pictures Corp.* v. *Regents*, 175 N.Y.S.2d 39 (Ct.App. 1958). Judge Conway's opinion is carefully analyzed in Harry M. Clor, *Obscenity and Public Morality* (Chicago: University of Chicago Press, 1969), 44–51. It should be noted that the Supreme Court had ruled as early as 1915 that states could license films. Justice Joseph McKenna described motion pictures as a "business, pure and simple," and like a circus, "not to be regarded . . . as part of the press of the country." *Mutual Film Corporation* v. *Industrial Commission of Ohio*, 236 U.S. 230 (1915). Not until 1952 did the Court reject the commercial speech rationale of film licensing and admit that expression of ideas in motion pictures enjoyed First Amendment protection. *Burstyn* v. *Wilson*, 343 U.S. 495 (1952). The Court, however, still placed obscenity outside constitutional protection and therefore continued to permit state boards to censor films by withholding exhibition licenses. In 1965 the Court imposed strict procedural standards on film review boards in *Freedman* v. *Maryland*, 380 U.S. 51 (1965), which excluded the idiosyncratic standards of individual censors. In the wake of the ruling, most state film boards simply collapsed; in 1981 the last such board, that of Maryland, went out of existence.

62. 360 U.S. 684 (1959).

63. Some useful survey articles are C. Peter Magrath, "The Obscenity Cases: Grapes of Roth," 1966 *Supreme Court Review* 7 (1967), and Note, "Obscenity in the Supreme Court: Nine Years of Confusion," 19 *Stanford Law Review* 167 (1966).

64. 370 U.S. 478 (1962).

65. 378 U.S. 184 (1964).

66. *Id.* at 197.

67. 383 U.S. 413 (1966).

68. For the story of the trial, and *Fanny Hill*'s tribulations elsewhere, see Rembar, *The End of Obscenity*, 222 et seq.

69. 383 U.S. at 418.
70. 383 U.S. 502 (1966).
71. 383 U.S. 463 (1966).
72. Kalven, *A Worthy Tradition*, 43. Ginzburg himself may have affronted the Court by his reference to their decisions in his advertisements. The Court cited one such ad which claimed that *Eros* "is the result of recent court decisions that have realistically interpreted America's obscenity laws and that have given to this country a new breadth of freedom of expression. . . . *Eros* takes full advantage of this new freedom. It is *the* magazine of sexual candor."
73. 383 U.S. at 480–81.
74. *Redrup* v. *New York*, 386 U.S. 767, 771 (1967). Following this decision, the Court began a six-year policy of issuing summary reversals without opinion when at least five justices, each applying his own standard, believed that First Amendment protection existed.
75. *Ginsberg* v. *New York*, 390 U.S. 629 (1968). A number of commentators who argued against censorship as a per se violation of the First Amendment had nonetheless accepted protection of children as constitutionally permissible. See, for example, J. Rex Dibble, "Obscenity: A State Quarantine to Protect Children," 39 *Southern California Law Review* 345 (1966).
76. *Stanley* v. *Georgia*, 394 U.S. 557 (1969).
77. See *United States* v. *Reidel*, discussed at pp. 97–98.
78. Under common law, spoken defamation, or slander, was not actionable as criminal libel. In a number of modern statutes, however, spoken defamation may be prosecuted in the same manner as libel.
79. In general, see Norman L. Rosenberg, *Protecting the Best Men: An Interpretive History of the Law of Libel* (Chapel Hill: University of North Carolina Press, 1986), which, as its title implies, argues that defamation laws were designed for the protection of the upper classes and used almost entirely by them.
80. *Shelley* v. *Kraemer*, 334 U.S. 1 (1948).
81. *Beauharnais* v. *Illinois*, 343 U.S. 250 (1952).
82. *Id.* at 267, 269, 274.
83. *Id.* at 284, 286. Illinois, it should be noted, later repealed this statute, but some other states still have group libel laws on their books. The Court has never dealt with group libel since this case, and while subsequent decisions have significantly altered the law of libel in general, *Beauharnais* has never been overruled. Although there have been some expressions in the lower courts that it no longer governs, in one of the cases growing out of the Nazi effort to march in Skokie, Justice Blackmun, joined by Justice Rehnquist, noted that "*Beauharnais* has never been overruled or formally limited in any way." *Smith* v. *Collins*, 436 U.S. 953 (1978). For group libel, see Emerson, *System of Freedom of Expression*, ch. 10.
84. Kalven, *A Worthy Tradition*, 62.
85. 376 U.S. 254 (1964).
86. See Harry Kalven, Jr., "The New York Times Case: A Note on 'The Central Meaning of the First Amendment,' " 1964 *Supreme Court Review* 191 (1965).
87. For example, the advertisement stated that Dr. King had been jailed seven times; in fact, he had been arrested four times.
88. Joseph J. Hemmer, Jr., *The Supreme Court and the First Amendment* (New York: Praeger, 1986), 164.
89. 376 U.S. at 276.
90. *Barr* v. *Matteo*, 360 U.S. 564 (1959).
91. *Gertz* v. *Robert Welch, Inc.*, 418 U.S. 323, 343 (1974).

92. For a defense of this so-called definitional balancing, see Melville B. Nimmer, "The Right to Speak from Times to Time," 56 *California Law Review* 935 (1968).
93. *Rosenblatt* v. *Baer*, 383 U.S. 75, 95 (1966), Justice Black (joined by Justice Douglas) concurring.
94. Despite a general belief—or wish—by the press that the case had abolished all liability, the majority never said this either explicitly or implicitly. Much of the criticism of the Burger Court's press decisions arose from the misinterpretation of *New York Times*. See Chapter 6.
95. 379 U.S. 64 (1964).
96. *Id.* at 75.
97. The Court expanded upon the actual malice standard and the burden of proof that the plaintiff had to carry the following year in *Beckley Newspapers Corporation* v. *Hanks*, 389 U.S. 31 (1967).
98. 388 U.S. 130 (1967).
99. Harry Kalven, Jr., "The Reasonable Man and the First Amendment: Hill, Butts and Walker," 1967 *Supreme Court Review* 267 (1968).

Chapter 5
"Free Speech Is Powerful Medicine"
The Burger Court and Free Speech

1. Emerson, *System of Freedom of Expression*, 15–16.
2. See pp. 50–51. Former Chief Justice Burger says that the Court never viewed the *Lemon* criteria as a "test" but that law teachers so named it and then complained when the Court did not use it as they thought it should be used. Interview with Warren Burger, 4 October 1988.
3. *NAACP* v. *Alabama*, 377 U.S. 288, 307 (1964).
4. 389 U.S. 258, 268 (1967). *Robel* dealt with that provision of the Communist Control Act which made it a crime for any member of the Communist Party to work in a defense facility.
5. *United States* v. *Butler*, 297 U.S. 1 (1936).
6. Gerald Gunther, "Reflections on Robel: It's Not What the Court Did But the Way That It Did It," 20 *Stanford Law Review* 1140, 1147 (1968); see also Ely, *Democracy and Distrust*, 106, that while evaluation may be taking place "at the margin" in this case, "it remains evaluation nonetheless."
7. *Aptheker* v. *Secretary of State*, 378 U.S. 500, 505 (1964).
8. *Keyishian* v. *Board of Regents*, 385 U.S. 589 (1967).
9. For an extended critique of the strengths and weaknesses of the overbreadth doctrine, see Martin H. Redish, *Freedom of Expression: A Critical Analysis* (Charlottesville, Va.: Michie, 1984), ch. 5.
10. See *Coates* v. *Cincinnati*, 402 U.S. 611 (1971), and *Gooding* v. *Wilson*, 405 U.S. 518 (1972).
11. *Younger* v. *Harris*, 401 U.S. 37, 52 (1971).
12. When a majority reversed, on overbreadth grounds, a conviction for using the word "mother-fucker" at a school board meeting with women and children in the audience, the Chief Justice complained that "when we undermine the general belief that the law will give protection against fighting words and profane and abusive language . . . we take steps to return to the law of the jungle." *Rosenfeld* v. *New Jersey*, 408 U.S. 901, 902 (1972).

13.   413 U.S. 601 (1973); Burger's suggestion had come in his dissent in the *Gooding* case, in which a 4-3 Court had invalidated a state conviction for use of "opprobrious and abusive language," that phrase being termed too vague and overbroad.
14.   413 U.S. at 615.
15.   *Id.* at 621.
16.   See *Lovell* v. *Griffin*, 303 U.S. 444 (1938); *Buckley* v. *Valeo*, 424 U.S. 1 (1976); and *Village of Schaumburg* v. *Citizens for a Better Environment*, 444 U.S. 620 (1980).
17.   Redish, *Freedom of Expression*, 247.
18.   *New York* v. *Ferber*, 458 U.S. 747, 780–81 (1982).
19.   *City Council of Los Angeles* v. *Taxpayers for Vincent*, 466 U.S. 789, 800 (1984).
20.   416 U.S. 134 (1974).
21.   *Lewis* v. *City of New Orleans*, 415 U.S. 130 (1974).
22.   *Village of Schaumburg* v. *Citizens for a Better Environment*, 444 U.S. 620 (1980).
23.   394 U.S. 557 (1969); see pp. 85–86.
24.   A list of articles that espoused this view is cited in Frederick F. Schauer, *The Law of Obscenity* (Washington, D.C.: BNA, 1976), 64 n.33.
25.   402 U.S. at 355.
26.   402 U.S. 351 (1971). The case was decided after Warren Burger had taken the center chair, and Harry Blackmun had replaced Abe Fortas, but before Lewis Powell and William Rehnquist joined the Court.
27.   *Id.* at 356. The Court emphasized the limits of the *Stanley* principle in several other cases around this time, including *United States* v. *Thirty-seven Photographs*, 402 U.S. 363 (1971) (no right to bring obscene photographs through customs, even for one's own viewing), and *United States* v. *Orito*, 413 U.S. 139 (1973) (no right to transport privately owned "lewd, lascivious and filthy materials" on airlines, in this case eighty-three reels of pornographic film).
28.   Harry Kalven, Jr., *A Worthy Tradition: Freedom of Speech in America* (New York: Harper & Row, 1988), 47–48.
29.   *Miller* v. *California*, 413 U.S. 15, 73 (1973), Justice Brennan dissenting.
30.   The report came under immediate criticism from conservative groups for its conclusions, and a number of scholars questioned the scope and quality of the empirical studies that the Commission had used.
31.   In fact, the Court handed down eight obscenity decisions that day, each dealing with a different substantive or procedural aspect of regulation. The two most important, which are discussed here, involved the rationale for state regulation and a new definition of obscenity.
32.   413 U.S. 49 (1973). The case involved a Georgia civil proceeding to stop the showing of allegedly obscene films at so-called adult theaters. The evidence at the trial consisted primarily of the films and photographs of the theater entrance. The former depicted simulations of various sexual practices, while the latter showed a rather nondescript building with a sign reading "Atlanta's Finest Mature Feature Films." On the door a notice had been posted that one had to be twenty-one and able to prove it in order to enter the theater and that if one found viewing the nude body offensive, one should not enter.
33.   *Id.* at 61.
34.   413 U.S. 15 (1973).
35.   *Id.* at 24.
36.   *Id.* at 46.
37.   413 U.S. 15, 49, 73–74.
38.   418 U.S. 153 (1974).
39.   *Id.* at 161.

40. An anonymous author, in satirizing the Obscenity and Pornography Commission report, put his or her finger on one of the major problems with juries applying community standards:

> The genius of the local jury is that it does not apply the local community standard as reflected in the actual behavior of the people. Rather, the local jury applies the *expected or anticipated moral standard.* This anticipated moral standard is what each member of the jury thinks other members of the jury expect him to possess. Thus, when a prosecutor presents a piece of smut to the jury . . . it is simply unlikely that any man or woman in the jury room would be brazen enough to suggest that his moral standards are so lax that he would permit himself or his children to read or look at smut, the actual facts notwithstanding. [Quoted in David S. Bogen, *Bulwark of Liberty: The Court and the First Amendment* (Port Washington, N.Y.: Associated Faculty Press, 1984), 72.]

41. 418 U.S. 87 (1974).
42. In *Smith* v. *United States*, 431 U.S. 291 (1977), the majority held that the determination of local community standards in federal prosecutions remained the prerogative of the jury, even in a case where the defendant had mailed the allegedly obscene material solely intrastate in a state that had no laws prohibiting sales to adults. State law, Justice Blackmun declared, "is not conclusive as to the issue of contemporary community standards for appeal to the prurient interest and patent offensiveness."
43. 458 U.S. 747 (1982).
44. Justice Brennan, joined by Marshall, concurred in most of the opinion, but noted that there was a possibility of scientific films depicting children engaged in sexual conduct that would be protected by the *Miller* test but would run afoul of this law. Justice Stevens concurred only in the judgment, while Justice O'Connor also submitted a separate concurrence.
45. Eric L. Dauber, "Child Pornography: A New Exception to the First Amendment," 10 *Florida State University Law Review* 684 (1983).
46. Stephen L. Wasby, *Continuity and Change: From the Warren Court to the Burger Court* (Pacific Palisades, Calif.: Goodyear, 1976), 154.
47. Richard Funston notes that the difficulties experienced by the Court

> have been the result of an inadequacy in our classical free speech theory. Neither Mill nor Meiklejohn provide much assistance in discovering why artistic expression should be protected by the First Amendment. Similarly, the famous First Amendment opinions of Hand, Holmes, and Brandeis have emphasized the interrelationship of freedom of communication and the democratic process. But it makes little sense to consider artistic expression in this framework. [Funston, *Constitutional Counterrevolution?* (New York: Schenkman, 1977), 283.]

48. *New York Times*, 25 October 1970, p. 1.
49. The state law prohibited "maliciously and willfully disturb[ing] the peace or quiet of any neighborhood or person [by] offensive conduct."
50. *Cohen* v. *California*, 403 U.S. 15 (1971).
51. *Id.* at 20.
52. Justice Blackmun, joined by the Chief Justice and Justice Black, entered a short dissent that labeled Cohen's "absurd and immature antic" as conduct rather than speech, and therefore unprotected, and he decried the "Court's agonizing over First Amendment values" as "misplaced and unnecessary" in this case. *Id.* at 27.
53. *Rosenfeld* v. *New Jersey*, 408 U.S. 901; *Lewis* v. *City of New Orleans*, 408 U.S. 913; and *Brown* v. *Oklahoma*, 408 U.S. 914—all 1972.

54.   *Id.* Two years later the Lewis case came before the Court again, 415 U.S. 130 (1974), and Justice Powell then joined the majority to reverse the conviction on overbreadth grounds, because the wording of the statute "confers on police a virtually unrestrained power."

55.   422 U.S. 205 (1975).

56.   *Id.* at 209.

57.   427 U.S. 50 (1976).

58.   Justice Stevens spoke for four members of the Court—himself, the Chief Justice, and Justices Rehnquist and White. Justice Powell concurred in the result, but not the reasoning, to make the majority.

59.   438 U.S. 726 (1978).

60.   Lucas A. Powe, Jr., *American Broadcasting and the First Amendment* (Berkeley: University of California Press, 1987), 185–88.

61.   438 U.S. at 763–64.

62.   403 U.S. at 25–26.

63.   447 U.S. 530 (1980).

64.   *Id.* at 538.

65.   Justice Stevens concurred in the judgment, agreeing that in this case the speech which the government had attempted to regulate consisted of just the type protected by the Constitution. But he objected to the majority reasoning that did not allow for differentiation in order to establish appropriate levels of protection.

66.   *Bolger* v. *Young's Drug Products Corp.*, 463 U.S. 60, 73 (1983).

67.   *Schad* v. *Mount Ephraim*, 452 U.S. 61 (1981). Once again Justice Stevens concurred only in the result, and believed that the majority had misused and thus trivialized the First Amendment by applying it to this type of expression.

68.   *Cohen* v. *California*, 403 U.S. at 27.

69.   See the crititical treatment of this issue in Powe, *American Broadcasting*.

70.   Norman Dorsen and Joel Gora, "The Burger Court and the Freedom of Speech," in Vincent Blasi, ed., *The Burger Court: The Counter-Revolution That Wasn't* (New Haven, Conn.: Yale University Press, 1983), 30–31.

71.   The judgment depends on one's views. For example, in 1977 a unanimous Court struck down a local ordinance banning "For Sale" and "Sold" signs on residential property. The municipality had enacted the regulation in an effort to prevent "block-busting" and white flight when black families bought into previously all-white neighborhoods. The NAACP Legal Defense Fund supported the ordinance; the American Civil Liberties Union did not. *Linmark Association* v. *Willingboro*, 431 U.S. 85 (1977).

72.   *Marsh* v. *Alabama*, 326 U.S. 501 (1946).

73.   391 U.S. 308 (1968).

74.   407 U.S. 551 (1972).

75.   *Id.* at 569.

76.   424 U.S. 507 (1976).

77.   *Id.* at 521.

78.   334 U.S. 1 (1948).

79.   The public function analysis provided an alternative ground in Justice Douglas's majority opinion in *Evans* v. *Newton*, 382 U.S. 296 (1966), involving a segregated park established by a private trust.

80.   *Jackson* v. *Metropolitan Edison Co.*, 419 U.S. 345 (1974), involved a federal due process claim against a privately owned and state-licensed and regulated utility. Her service had been cut off for nonpayment, and she claimed that because the utility was state-licensed, its actions were the state's actions and she was entitled to a hearing. In *Flagg Bros., Inc.* v. *Brooks*, 436 U.S. 149 (1978), the owner of seized goods under a

warehouseman's lien claimed that because the sale took place under conditions of the Uniform Commercial Code, it constituted state action. The Court rejected both claims.

81. In 1951 Justice Douglas dissented, however, from a ruling upholding a local ordinance regulating door-to-door solicitation for magazine subscriptions. He argued that such subscriptions were a form of expression entitled to First Amendment protection. *Breard* v. *Alexandria*, 341 U.S. 622, 649 (1951), Justice Douglas dissenting. Douglas's comment came in *Cammarano* v. *United States*, 358 U.S. 498, 514 (1959), and he concluded that the original ruling "has not survived reflection."

82. 316 U.S. 552 (1942). The decision did not come from a constitutional blank slate; for the background and precedents of *Valentine*, see Edwin P. Rome and William H. Roberts, *Corporate and Commercial Free Speech* (Westport, Conn.: Quorum Books, 1985), 11–20.

83. 413 U.S. 376 (1973).

84. 421 U.S. 376 (1975).

85. In 1977 the Court followed a similar rationale in *Carey* v. *Population Services International*, 431 U.S. 678 (1977), striking down a ban against advertising mail-order sale of contraceptives. The Court rejected New York's argument that the ads were offensive or embarrassing to many people and said that the fact that protected speech, dealing with "the free flow of commercial information" which reflected "substantial individual and societal interests," could not be suppressed because it offended some people.

86. 425 U.S. 748 (1976).

87. Justice Stewart concurred, noting that he did not believe the opinion precluded regulations against deceptive advertising. The Chief Justice also concurred, emphasizing a footnote in the majority opinion reserving the question of whether different professions might be subject to differing regulations. Justice Stevens, who had recently taken his seat on the bench, did not participate. Only Justice Rehnquist dissented.

88. 425 U.S. at 762.

89. The Court did, in fact, follow through on this caveat. In *Ohralik* v. *Ohio State Bar Association*, 436 U.S. 447 (1978), the Court sustained a suspension from law practice for soliciting contingent fees in "a classic example of ambulance chasing." And in *Friedman* v. *Rogers*, 440 U.S. 1 (1979), a 7-2 Court sustained a Texas statute prohibiting the practice of optometry under a trade name. Justice Powell declared that the state had a "substantial and well-demonstrated" interest in protecting the public "from the deceptive and misleading use of optometrical trade names."

90. *Bates* v. *State Bar of Arizona*, 433 U.S. 350 (1977). Although Justice Powell dissented in this case, he wrote the majority opinion in two other cases supporting lawyer advertising. In 1982 he spoke for a unanimous Court in striking down a wide range of restrictions Missouri had placed on language that could be used in informing the public of legal services; the state had even restricted the audience to which the traditional cards announcing the opening of law offices or addition of partners could be mailed. *In re R.M.J.*, 455 U.S. 191 (1982). In 1978 the Court set aside disciplinary action against an attorney who did volunteer work for the ACLU and who had written a letter to a woman who had been involuntarily sterilized asking whether she wished to bring suit. A state may not punish a lawyer who is "seeking to further political and ideological goals" and discloses "that free legal service is available from a nonprofit organization." *In re Primus*, 436 U.S. 412 (1978).

91. *Central Hudson Gas Co.* v. *Public Service Commission*, 447 U.S. 557, 567 (1980).

92. 425 U.S. at 782.

93. Thomas H. Jackson and John Calvin Jeffries, Jr., "Commercial Speech: Economic Due Process and the First Amendment," 65 *Virginia Law Review* 1 (1979).

94. In *Metromedia, Inc.* v. *San Diego*, 453 U.S. 490 (1981), the Court struck down a billboard ordinance for excessively restricting noncommercial speech. The plurality opinion by Justice White made it clear that restricting commercial billboards would be permissible.
95. 435 U.S. 765 (1978).
96. 424 U.S. 1 (1976). The Court issued a per curiam opinion in which only Justices Stewart, Brennan, and Powell joined fully. The Chief Justice and Justices White, Marshall, Blackmun, and Rehnquist joined in certain parts and dissented in others, though not together. Justice Stevens did not participate. The assemblage of plaintiffs was among the most diverse in any case ever heard by the Court, which identified them as "a candidate for the Presidency of the United States [Eugene McCarthy], a United States Senator who is a candidate for reelection [Buckley], a potential contributor, the Committee for a Constitutional Presidency—McCarthy '76, the Conservative Party of the State of New York, the Mississippi Republican Party, the Libertarian Party, the New York Civil Liberties Union, Inc., the American Conservative Union, the Conservative Victory Fund, and Human Events, Inc." The Socialist Labor Party was among the many groups filing amici curiae briefs.
97. The case elicited widespread comment in the law reviews. See, among others, Daniel D. Polsby, "Buckley v. Valeo: The Special Nature of Political Speech," 1976 *Supreme Court Review* 1 (1977); J. Skelley Wright, "Politics and the Constitution: Is Money Speech?" 85 *Yale Law Journal* 1001 (1976); and Note, "Buckley v. Valeo: The Supreme Court and Federal Campaign Reform," 76 *Columbia Law Review* 852 (1976).
98. *Citizens Against Rent Control* v. *City of Berkeley*, 454 U.S. 290 (1981).

Chapter 6
"A Press That Is Alert, Aware, and Free"
The Press Clause in the Court

1. Quoted in Thomas I. Emerson, "Freedom of the Press Under the Burger Court," in Vincent Blasi, ed., *The Burger Court: The Counter-Revolution That Wasn't* (New Haven, Conn.: Yale University Press, 1983), 2.
2. Sidney Zion, "Freedom of the Press: A Tale of Two Libel Theories," in Herman Schwartz, ed., *The Burger Years: Rights and Wrongs in the Supreme Court, 1969–1986* (New York: Penguin, 1987), 45. See also works such as John Hohenberg, *A Crisis for the American Press* (New York: Columbia University Press, 1978).
3. *Bose Corp.* v. *Consumers Union*, 466 U.S 485 (1984), in which the Court ruled against the manufacturer of audio speakers and in favor of the magazine.
4. A noted First Amendment attorney, Floyd Abrams, believes the press has overreacted to the obvious inconsistency in Burger Court decisions, and he notes such other friends of the press and of the First Amendment as Marc Franklin, Anthony Lewis, and William J. Brennan as concurring in this view. Abrams, "The Burger Court and the First Amendment . . . An Analysis," in Bill F. Chamberlin and Charlene J. Brown, *The First Amendment Reconsidered: New Perspectives on the Meaning of Freedom of Speech and Press* (New York: Longmans, 1982), 138–39.
5. The debate over the meaning of the Press Clause has been vigorous, but inconclusive. As David Lange concluded: "The Framers have left us language in the first amendment which justifies the present debate—language which, under almost any view one takes, is less than clear." Lange, "The Speech and Press Clauses," 23 *UCLA Law Review* 77,

88 (1975). See also the discussion in William W. Van Alstyne, *Interpretations of the First Amendment* (Durham, N.C.: Duke University Press, 1984), 50–53.

6. 435 U.S. 765, 795 (1978). The Chief Justice noted that the press issue was not central to the case but commented on it nonetheless.

7. *Id.* at 802.

8. Potter Stewart, "Or of the Press," 26 *Hastings Law Journal* 631, 633 (1975).

9. 408 U.S. 665, at 721 (1972).

10. 283 U.S. 697 (1931).

11. For the background of the case, see Fred W. Friendly, *Minnesota Rag* (New York: Random House, 1981).

12. 283 U.S. at 713, 716.

13. *Times Film Corp.* v. *Chicago,* 365 U.S. 43, 49 (1961).

14. *Freedman* v. *Maryland,* 380 U.S. 51 (1965).

15. In *Kingsley Books, Inc.* v. *Brown,* 354 U.S. 436 (1957), the Court sustained a New York statute that allowed an injunctive procedure against the distribution and sale of allegedly obscene books. But the law also required that a trial to determine the obscenity take place within one day after the injunction and that a determination be made within two days after the end of the trial.

16. Frederick Schauer, *Free Speech: A Philosophical Enquiry* (New York: Cambridge University Press, 1982), 152.

17. Martin H. Redish, *Freedom of Expression: A Critical Analysis* (Charlottesville, Va.: Michie Co., 1984), 127–72. For other voices in the debate, see John C. Jeffries, "Rethinking Prior Restraint," 92 *Yale Law Journal* 409 (1983); Vincent Blasi, "Toward a Theory of Prior Restraint: The Central Linkage," 66 *Minnesota Law Review* 11 (1981); and Justice Frankfurter's discussion of the relative value of prior restraint against the fear of subsequent criminal punishment in *Kingsley Books,* 354 U.S. at 441.

18. *Bantam Books, Inc.* v. *Sullivan,* 372 U.S. 58 (1963).

19. An excellent chronology, including summaries of the contents of the initial articles and the Nixon administration responses, is Chapter 1 of Martin Shapiro, ed., *The Pentagon Papers and the Courts: A Study in Foreign Policy-Making and Freedom of the Press* (San Francisco: Chandler, 1972).

20. Normally, cases in the circuit courts are heard by three-judge panels. In cases where major issues are involved or the three judges are closely divided and believe a larger court should hear the case, all the members of the circuit will hear the case en banc.

21. The only comparable case that comes to mind is *Ex parte Quirin,* 317 U.S. 1 (1942), decided in the midst of World War II. Eight Nazi saboteurs put ashore on Long Island and Florida had been caught and tried before a military tribunal, which sentenced six of them to death. They appealed for habeas corpus, and the Supreme Court agreed to convene a special summer session to hear the arguments. After the hearing, the Court verbally announced its decision, which upheld the use of a military proceeding; only after the Court reconvened in the fall did Chief Justice Stone hand down the elaborate written decision. See Cyrus Bernstein, "The Nazi Saboteur Trial: A Case History," 11 *George Washington Law Review* 131 (1943).

22. *New York Times Co.* v. *United States,* 403 U.S. 713 (1971).

23. *Id.* at 731.

24. *Id.* at 728.

25. *Id.* at 753, 748, 751. For details about the maneuverings in the Court, see Bob Woodward and Scott Armstrong, *The Brethren* (New York: Simon & Schuster, 1979), 161–74.

26. See statement of Daniel Ellsberg, in Shapiro, ed., *Pentagon Papers,* 87–88.

27. *Id.* at 5. The arrogance of Taylor's comment betrayed the reflected the view of those who managed the war in Vietnam, a belief that they knew what was best for the nation. See David Halberstam, *The Best and the Brightest* (New York: Random House, 1972).
28. 403 U.S. at 751.
29. Woodward and Armstrong, *The Brethren*, 174.
30. Justice Harlan, although writing in dissent in the Pentagon papers, pointed the way in his historical review of executive authority in foreign affairs. When that authority came into conflict with some constitutional provision, the judiciary could not blindly uphold the president's claim to sole responsibility. The judiciary must first

    [satisfy] itself that the subject matter of the dispute does lie within the proper compass of the President's foreign relations power. . . . Moreover, the judiciary may properly insist that the determination that disclosure of the subject matter would irreparably impair the national security be made by the head of the Executive Department concerned—here the Secretary of State or the Secretary of Defense—after actual personal consideration by that officer. . . .

    But in my judgment the judiciary may not properly go beyond these two inquiries and redetermine for itself the probable impact of disclosure on the national security. [403 U.S. at 747.]

    For a clear exposition of the problems involved in creating an appropriate review mechanism, see Archibald Cox, *The Court and the Constitution* (Boston: Houghton Mifflin, 1987), ch. 12.
31. *Snepp* v. *United States*, 444 U.S. 507 (1980). In an earlier case, *United States* v. *Marchetti*, 466 F.2d 1309 (4th Cir. 1972), cert. denied, 409 U.S. 1063 (1972), the Court had refused to review a case involving the CIA's demands that changes be made in a book co-authored by a former employee. The lower court initially granted an injunction to stop publication in 1972, and three years later it upheld the agency's demands that some 168 deletions be made in order to protect national security interests.
32. 444 U.S. at 509 n.3.
33. See, for example, Morton H. Halperin, "The National Security State: Never Question the President," in Schwartz, ed., *Burger Years*, 50–55.
34. The most criticized case of this time was decided not in the Supreme Court but in the Western District of Wisconsin. In *United States* v. *Progressive, Inc.*, 467 F.Supp. 990 (W.D. Wis. 1979), the government sought an injunction against publication of an article that it claimed would make it easier for small nations and terrorist groups to make thermonuclear bombs. While most of the information in the article was in the public domain, as the government conceded, the synthesis of that material provided new information that constituted a threat to national security. The district judge granted a preliminary injunction, distinguishing the facts from those in the Pentagon papers case. The case never reached the high court because the government soon after abandoned the proceedings before a hearing for a permanent injunction could be had, apparently because other magazines had published similar materials while the case had been under way.
35. 427 U.S. 539 (1976).
36. *Id.* at 559.
37. *Id.* at 572. See Woodward and Armstrong, *The Brethren*, 500–503.
38. 427 U.S. at 617.
39. See the discussion of this case in Stephen R. Barnett, "The Puzzle of Prior Restraint," 29 *Stanford Law Review* 539 (1977)
40. 427 U.S. at 571.

41. *Seattle Times Co.* v. *Rhinehart,* 467 U.S. 20 (1984).
42. Justice Brennan's concurrence, joined by Justice Marshall, noted that Powell had in fact used traditional First Amendment scrutiny in his reference to the substantial state interest and the least restrictive alternative. *Id.* at 37.
43. Lyle Denniston, "The Burger Court and the Press," in Schwartz, ed., *Burger Years,* 34.
44. For background and claims regarding the journalists' privilege, see Donald M. Gillmor and Jerome A. Barron, *Mass Communication Law,* 4th ed. (St. Paul, Minn.: West, 1984), 377–432. See also the discussion in AEI Round Table, *Freedom of the Press* (Washington, D.C.: American Enterprise Institute, 1975).
45. The Court joined two other cases involving reporters' claims. Paul Pappas, a Massachusetts television reporter, was allowed to stay in Black Panther headquarters on condition that he disclose nothing he witnessed. He kept his word, broadcasting no report and refusing to tell a grand jury what he had seen. Earl Caldwell had written several articles for the *New York Times* on the Black Panthers after interviewing their leaders. He refused to appear before a federal grand jury investigating possible violation of criminal statutes by the Panthers. The trial court issued a protective order that allowed Caldwell to withhold confidential information unless the government could show "a compelling national interest" in his testimony that could not be served "by any alternative means." Caldwell labeled the order inadequate, refused to appear, and was sentenced for contempt. An appeals court set aside Caldwell's conviction; those of Branzburg and Pappas had been affirmed by Kentucky and Massachusetts courts.
46. See Richard O. Lempert and Stephen A. Saltzburg, *A Modern Approach to Evidence,* 2nd ed. (St. Paul, Minn.: West, 1982), 652–731.
47. 408 U.S. 665 (1972).
48. *Id.* at 697.
49. *Id.* at 726 n.2.
50. See the discussion by Benno C. Schmidt, Jr., "Journalists' Privilege: One Year After Branzburg," in Earl Warren Symposium, *The First Amendment and the News Media: Final Report* (Cambridge, Mass.: American Trial Lawyers Foundation, 1973), 41–53.
51. *Zurcher* v. *Stanford Daily,* 436 U.S. 547, 565 (1978).
52. *Id.* at 570. In response to lobbying efforts begun in response to this decision, Congress passed the Privacy Protection Act of 1980, which requires federal and state officials to use subpoena procedures rather than search warrants to secure documents from persons in the communications industry. Search warrants are allowed only when there is a reasonable fear that materials would be destroyed rather than handed over in response to a subpoena. The law has not been tested, but there is a question whether Congress can pass legislation regulating state police procedures when no constitutional right is affected.
53. 417 U.S. 817 (1974).
54. 417 U.S. 843 (1974).
55. 417 U.S. at 834, 835.
56. *Id.* at 835 (emphasis added).
57. 417 U.S. at 863.
58. 438 U.S. 1 (1978). KQED, a San Francisco television station, sought access to the Alameda County jail to investigate charges of deplorable conditions in one part of the facility. After the suit had been filed, Sheriff Houchins modified his no-access rule, which applied to both the press and the public, and launched monthly tours limited to twenty-five persons. People on the tour could not take photographs nor interview inmates. A lower court granted KQED and other news media access to the prison "at

reasonable times and hours" and authorized the use of photographic and sound equipment, as well as inmate interviews.

59.   443 U.S. 368 (1979).
60.   Gillmor and Barron, *Mass Communication Law,* 512.
61.   448 U.S. 555 (1980). Justices White and Stevens joined the Chief Justice's opinion, and also entered separate concurrences, as did Justices Brennan (joined by Marshall), Blackmun, and Stewart. Only Justice Rehnquist dissented. Justice Powell did not participate in this case, but several of the opinions cited his earlier concurrences and noted that his ideas had now been adopted by the Court.
62.   *Id.* at 576–77.
63.   For speculation about the implications of *Richmond Newspapers,* see Archibald Cox, "Freedom of Expression in the Burger Court," 94 *Harvard Law Review* 1 (1980).
64.   457 U.S. 596 (1982).
65.   464 U.S. 501 (1984).
66.   One might note, however, the Court's invalidation of a Minnesota use tax on ink and paper which, because of a $100,000 exemption, applied to only 14 of the 388 newspapers in the state. Although exemptions are normal in most taxation schemes, Justice O'Connor's opinion for a 7-2 Court found the tax discriminated against newspapers and therefore violated the First Amendment. *Minneapolis Star* v. *Minnesota Commissioner of Revenue,* 460 U.S. 575 (1983).
67.   *FCC* v. *Pacifica Foundation,* 438 U.S. 726 (1978); see relevant discussion, pp. 106–107.
68.   The history of control of the broadcast media, and the related First Amendment problems, are discussed in Lucas A. Powe, Jr., *American Broadcasting and the First Amendment* (Berkeley: University of California Press, 1987).
69.   319 U.S. 192 (1943).
70.   395 U.S. 367 (1969).
71.   Gerald J. Baldesty and Roger A. Simpson, "The Deceptive 'Right to Know': How Pessimism Rewrote the First Amendment," 56 *Washington Law Review* 365 (1981).
72.   418 U.S. 241 (1974).
73.   See the discussion of this case and the concept of right-to-know in Benno C. Schmidt, Jr., *Freedom of the Press vs. Public Access* (New York: Praeger, 1976).
74.   412 U.S. 94 (1973).
75.   *Id.* at 148. At one time Douglas had embraced the scarcity doctrine and the necessity for public "ownership" of the airwaves. William O. Douglas, *The Right of the People* (Garden City, N.Y.: Doubleday, 1958), 76–77.
76.   47 U.S.C. § 312(a)(7).
77.   *CBS, Inc.* v. *FCC,* 453 U.S. 367, 396 (1981). Justice White, joined by Justices Rehnquist and Stevens, strongly dissented.
78.   The Court has confronted the specter of cable in several cases. In the lead case, *United States* v. *Southwestern Cable Co.,* 392 U.S. 157 (1968), the Warren Court, through Justice Harlan, ruled that the FCC had authority, under the 1934 Communications Act, to regulate cable television systems. For a critique of the FCC's efforts to regulate cable, and judicial response, see Powe, *American Broadcasting,* ch. 12.
79.   468 U.S. 364 (1984).
80.   *Id.* at 380.
81.   William J. Brennan, Jr., "The Supreme Court and the Meiklejohn Interpretation of the First Amendment," 79 *Harvard Law Review* 1 (1965).
82.   Denniston, in Schwartz, ed., *Burger Years,* 25–26.
83.   *Id.* at 27. Denniston's analysis is far more sophisticated than appears here and deserves far more time and elaboration to do it full justice.

84. The Court upheld a libelous statement about a candidate's personal life, because some people might consider it relevant in considering his fitness for public office; *Monitor Patriot Co.* v. *Roy*, 401 U.S. 265 (1971). A radio station called a subsequently exonerated magazine distributor a "smut peddler," and the Court overturned a libel conviction because the news story had involved a matter of public interest; *Rosenbloom* v. *Metromedia*, 403 U.S. 29 (1971). It held that federal law, which favored "uninhibited, robust and wide-open debate in labor disputes," superceded state libel law and reversed a judgment against a union for accurately listing a person as a scab; *Old Dominion Branch, Letter Carriers* v. *Austin*, 418 U.S. 264 (1974).
85. 418 U.S. 323 (1974).
86. For divorce, see *Time* v. *Firestone*, 424 U.S. 448 (1976); for public funds, *Hutchinson* v. *Proxmire*, 443 U.S. 111 (1979); and for crime, *Wolston* v. *Reader's Digest*, 443 U.S. 157 (1979).
87. 441 U.S. 153 (1979). The decision opened up several more years of discovery in the libel suit, which was ultimately dismissed without resolution nearly twelve years after it had begun.
88. This term refers to a ruling by the trial court relating to the fact-gathering process that precedes the trial and which concerned one of the issues in the suit, but which did not settle the merits of that issue. See the discussion of this issue in Abrams, "Analysis," in Chamberlin and Brown, *First Amendment Reconsidered*, 139–40.
89. 465 U.S. 770 (1984).
90. *Dun & Bradstreet* v. *Greenmoss Builders*, 472 U.S. 749, 760 (1985), citing *Harley-Davidson* v. *Markley*, 279 Ore. 361, 366 (1977).
91. *Philadelphia Newspapers* v. *Hepps*, 106 S.Ct. 1558 (1986).
92. Denniston, "The Burger Court and the Press," in Schwartz, ed., *Burger Years*, 25.
93. Without denying the importance of freedom of the press, one might note the conclusion of a recent study of press adherence to constitutional guarantees when its own interests were not at stake:

    One clear impression emerges from this survey of more than 175 years of press reaction to various freedom of expression issues in the United States. It is that, except when their own freedom was discernibly at stake, established general circulation newspapers have tended to go along with efforts to suppress deviations from the prevailing political and social orthodoxies of their time and place rather than to support the right to dissent. [John Lofton, *The Press as Guardian of the First Amendment* (Columbia: University of South Carolina Press, 1980), 279.]

94. Emerson, "Freedom of the Press," in Blasi, ed., *Burger Court*, 2–3. Emerson, however, does believe that the Court's refusal to expand *Sullivan* has had a detrimental effect on freedom of the press.
95. *Hustler Magazine and Larry C. Flynt* v. *Jerry Falwell*, 108 S.Ct. 876 (1988). Many of the First Amendment issues raised in the case, as well as the implications of *New York Times* v. *Sullivan*, are discussed with great clarity in Rodney A. Smolla, *Jerry Falwell v. Larry Flynt: The First Amendment on Trial* (New York: St. Martin's, 1988). Considering the great emphasis Chief Justice Rehnquist gave to *Sullivan*, one might note the pessimistic tone of Lyle Denniston a little over a year earlier, when he characterized Rehnquist as "a determined foe even of the *Sullivan* principles." In Schwartz, ed., *Burger Years*, 43.
96. Abrams, "An Analysis," in Chamberlin and Brown, *First Amendment Reconsidered*, 143.

Chapter 7
" . . . *In No Way Creates a Constitutional Straightjacket"*
The Warren Court and Criminal Procedure

1. Quoted in Archibald Cox, *The Warren Court: Constitutional Decision as an Instrument of Reform* (Cambridge, Mass.: Harvard University Press, 1968), 88.
2. For the general historical background of these rights, see Robert Rutland, *The Birth of the Bill of Rights* (Boston: Northeastern University Press, 1983 rev. ed.).
3. *Barron* v. *Baltimore*, 7 Pet. 243 (1833).
4. 16 Wall. 36 (1873).
5. *Hurtado* v. *California*, 110 U.S. 516 (1884).
6. *Twining* v. *New Jersey*, 211 U.S. 78 (1908).
7. *Powell* v. *Alabama*, 287 U.S. 45 (1932).
8. See relevant discussion, Part II.
9. 302 U.S. 319, 325 (1937).
10. 332 U.S. 46 (1947).
11. Neither Cardozo nor Frankfurter suggested that the Court could add rights through the Fourteenth Amendment. Justices Murphy and Rutledge, however, believed that the Due Process Clause of the Fourteenth Amendment meant the Bill of Rights plus more recently recognized liberties and that both state and federal governments would be bound by these standards. A good example of this "Bill of Rights *plus*" is the "proof beyond a reasonable doubt" standard for guilt, a criterion not to be found in the first eight amendments.
12. These exceptions include a search incident to an arrest, the arrest of a person apprehended during commission of a crime, searches of automobiles, and so on, and by themselves form an interesting chapter in Fourth Amendment law. Because this book is not primarily a study of criminal procedure, the interested reader is referred to Stephen A. Saltzburg, *American Criminal Procedure* (St. Paul, Minn.: West, 1980), ch. 2.
13. Anthony Amsterdam, "Perspectives on the Fourth Amendment," 58 *Minnesota Law Review* 335 (1974).
14. The Fourth Amendment was not, however, a major source of cases for two reasons. First, the Federal Bureau of Investigation had adopted fairly stringent standards that easily met strict constitutional requirements. Second, prior to its incorporation, the Fourth Amendment did not apply to the states, so there were practically no appeals of state cases.
15. *Nathanson* v. *United States*, 190 U.S. 41 (1933).
16. 331 U.S. 145 (1947).
17. *Johnson* v. *United States*, 333 U.S. 10 (1948).
18. *Giordenello* v. *United States*, 357 U.S. 480 (1958).
19. 367 U.S. 643 (1961).
20. 378 U.S. 108 (1964).
21. *Spinelli* v. *United States*, 393 U.S. 410 (1969).
22. Charles Moylan, Jr., "Hearsay and Probable Cause: An *Aguilar* and *Spinelli* Primer," 25 *Mercer Law Review* 741 (1974). Moylan was then an associate judge of the Maryland Court of Special Appeals and, according to Stephen Saltzburg, "has explained as well as anyone what the case means. It is unfortunate that the Supreme Court was not as clear." Saltzburg, *American Criminal Procedure*, 69.
23. 395 U.S. 752 (1969).

24. Two prior decisions of the Vinson Court, which seemed to give police wider scope in these searches, were overruled: *Harris* v. *United States*, 331 U.S. 145 (1947), and *United States* v. *Rabinowitz*, 339 U.S. 56 (1950).
25. Fred P. Graham, *The Self-Inflicted Wound* (New York: Macmillan, 1970), 208.
26. 386 U.S. 300 (1967).
27. 387 U.S. 294 (1967).
28. *Terry* v. *Ohio*, 392 U.S. 1 (1968).
29. *Olmstead* v. *United States*, 277 U.S. 438, 468 (1928).
30. *Nardone* v. *United States*, 302 U.S. 379 (1937); *Schwartz* v. *Texas*, 344 U.S. 199 (1952).
31. *Goldman* v. *United States*, 316 U.S. 129 (1942); *On Lee* v. *United States*, 343 U.S. 747 (1952).
32. *Benanti* v. *United States*, 355 U.S. 96 (1957).
33. 365 U.S. 505, 512 (1961). Three years later a per curiam opinion applied *Silverman* to an electronic eavesdropping device stuck in an adjoining wall by a thumbtack. *Clinton* v. *Virginia*, 377 U.S. 158 (1964).
34. See *Lopez* v. *United States*, 373 U.S. 427 (1963); *Lewis* v. *United States*, 385 U.S. 206 (1966); *Hoffa* v. *United States*, 385 U.S. 293 (1966); and *Osborn* v. *United States*, 385 U.S. 323 (1966).
35. Alan Westin, "Science, Privacy and Freedom," 66 *Columbia Law Review* 1003, 1017 (1966).
36. *Berger* v. *New York*, 388 U.S. 41 (1967).
37. *Katz* v. *United States*, 389 U.S. 347 (1967). The privacy decision is *Griswold* v. *Connecticut*, discussed at pp. 252–54.
38. 18 U.S.C. §§ 2510–2520. The evolution of the law, and the specific cases it attacks, are discussed in Adam C. Breckenridge, *Congress Against the Court* (Lincoln: University of Nebraska Press, 1970). For a critical view of the statute, see Herman Schwartz, "The Legitimation of Electronic Eavesdropping: The Politics of 'Law and Order,' " 67 *Michigan Law Review* 455 (1969).
39. 232 U.S. 383, 393–94 (1914).
40. *Silverthorne Lumber Co.* v. *United States*, 251 U.S. 385, 392 (1919).
41. 338 U.S. 25 (1949).
42. *Id.* at 44. The Court split 6-3 in this case, but all the justices agreed that illegal searches violated the Fourteenth Amendment. The three dissenters objected to the lack of a remedy.
43. *Mapp* v. *Ohio*, 367 U.S. 643, 645 (1961).
44. There are, however, some exceptions to the exclusionary rule. The doctrines of "independent source" and "inevitable discovery" may permit the utilization of evidence otherwise illegally seized. See relevant discussion, p. 179–84.
45. For a vigorous defense of the rule, see Yale Kamisar, "The Exclusionary Rule in Historical Perspective: The Struggle to Make the Fourth Amendment More than 'An Empty Blessing,' " 62 *Judicature* 337 (1979).
46. *People* v. *Defore*, 242 N.Y. 13, 21 (1926).
47. *Bivens* v. *Six Unknown Named Federal Agents*, 403 U.S. 388, 414 (1971), Chief Justice Burger dissenting.
48. *Olmstead* v. *United States*, 277 U.S. 438, 485 (1928).
49. See the discussion and the sources cited in Jesse H. Choper, *Judicial Review and the National Political Process* (Chicago: University of Chicago Press, 1980), 95–96.
50. 367 U.S. at 659. One should also see the lucid explanation of why the rule is necessary by one of the nation's outstanding state judges, Roger Traynor of California. Traynor had originally opposed the exclusionary rule but changed his mind in 1955. He

explains his change of heart, as well as why he thinks *Mapp* is correct, in "Mapp v. Ohio at Large in the 50 States," 1962 *Duke Law Journal* 319.

51.   William H. Beany, *The Right to Counsel in American Courts* (Ann Arbor: University of Michigan Press, 1955), 8–15.

52.   *Johnson* v. *Zerbst*, 304 U.S. 458 (1938).

53.   *Powell* v. *Alabama*, 287 U.S. 45 (1932). For details of the egregious conduct of the trial by local officials and lawyers, see Dan T. Carter, *Scottsboro: A Tragedy of the American South* (Baton Rouge: Louisiana State University Press, 1969).

54.   316 U.S. 455, 472 (1942).

55.   Jerold Israel, "Gideon v. Wainwright: The 'Art' of Overruling," 1963 *Supreme Court Review* 211, 260.

56.   The story of this case is rivetingly told in Anthony Lewis, *Gideon's Trumpet* (New York: Random House, 1964).

57.   Choper, *Judicial Review*, 97.

58.   *Gideon* v. *Wainwright*, 372 U.S. 335 (1963). Justices Douglas, Clark, and Harlan wrote separate concurring opinions.

59.   Note, "The Right to Counsel: The Impact of Gideon v. Wainwright in the Fifty States," 3 *Creighton Law Review* 103 (1970).

60.   *Argersinger* v. *Hamlin*, 407 U.S. 25 (1972).

61.   *United States* v. *Wade*, 388 U.S. 218 (1967). That same day, the Court applied this rule to the states in *Gilbert* v. *California*, 388 U.S. 263.

62.   388 U.S. at 224.

63.   389 U.S. 128 (1967).

64.   *Douglas* v. *California*, 372 U.S. 353 (1963).

65.   351 U.S. 12 (1956).

66.   Leonard Levy, *The Origins of the Fifth Amendment* (New York: Oxford University Press, 1968), 330.

67.   Levy, *id.*, ch. 12, argues for a broad coverage; Lewis Mayers, *Shall We Amend the Fifth Amendment* (New York: Harper's, 1959), 178–96, maintains that the early history supports only a limited coverage.

68.   Henry J. Friendly, "The Fifth Amendment Tomorrow: The Case for Constitutional Change," 37 *University of Cincinnati Law Review* 679, 680 (1968).

69.   116 U.S. 616 (1886).

70.   *Counselman* v. *Hitchcock*, 142 U.S. 547 (1892).

71.   Both the Warren and the Burger Courts have ruled on questions of when is a proceeding criminal; what type of evidence may be required and what is protected; to whom the privilege applies; the production of records; and other technical matters.

72.   *Brown* v. *Mississippi*, 297 U.S. 278 (1936).

73.   *Fikes* v. *Alabama*, 352 U.S. 191 (1957).

74.   *Payne* v. *Arkansas*, 356 U.S. 560 (1958).

75.   *Culombe* v. *Connecticut*, 367 U.S. 568 (1961).

76.   *Blackburn* v. *Alabama*, 361 U.S. 199 (1960).

77.   *Mallory* v. *United States*, 354 U.S. 449 (1957). This case involved a specific Federal Rule of Criminal Procedure, 5(a), which required prompt arraignment. Federal agents had kept Mallory overnight in order to question him and induce a confession before taking him to the magistrate.

78.   Otis H. Stephens, Jr., *The Supreme Court and Confessions of Guilt* (Knoxville: University of Tennessee Press, 1973), chs. 4, 5.

79.   *Spano* v. *New York*, 360 U.S. 315 (1959).

80.   *Crooker* v. *California*, 357 U.S. 433, 444–45 (1958).

81.   377 U.S. 201 (1964).

82. For comment on the case, see David Robinson, Jr., "Massiah, Escobedo and Rationales for the Exclusion of Confessions" 56 *Journal of Criminal Law* 412 (1965), and Arnold N. Enker and Sheldon H. Elsen, "Counsel for the Suspect: Massiah v. United States," 49 *Minnesota Law Review* 47 (1964).

83. 378 U.S 478 (1964).

84. *Id.* at 485, 488.

85. For discussions of the case, see Yale Kamisar, "Equal Justice in the Gatehouses and Mansions of American Criminal Procedure," in A. E. Dick Howard, ed., *Criminal Justice in Our Time* (Charlottesville: University Press of Virginia, 1965), 1, and Donald C. Dowling, "Escobedo and Beyond: The Need for a Fourteenth Amendment Code of Criminal Procedure," 56 *Journal of Criminal Law, Criminology, and Police Science* 143 (1965).

86. Stephens, *Supreme Court and Confessions*, 122–28. For a discussion of *Escobedo's* historical roots, see "Comment," 73 *Yale Law Journal* 1000 (1964).

87. All quotes can be found at 384 U.S. at 440 n.3.

88. *Malloy* v. *Hogan*, 378 U.S. 1 (1964).

89. 384 U.S. 436 (1966).

90. *Id.* at 517.

91. *Id.* at 467. The Chief Justice also cited a number of police manuals suggesting different forms of psychological coercion to get suspects to confess.

92. For a defense of the majority approach, see Yale Kamisar, "A Dissent from the Miranda Dissents: Some Comments on the 'New' Fifth Amendment and the Old 'Voluntariness' Test," 65 *Michigan Law Review* 59 (1966).

93. Many of the more progressive police departments in the country, as well as the Federal Bureau of Investigation, had been adhering to such practices for years and promptly announced that informing suspects of their rights did not hamper effective police work. See the symposium on "The Supreme Court and the Police: 1966," in 57 *Journal of Criminal Law, Criminology, and Police Science* 238 (1966).

94. Although in some places the number of confessions declined immediately after *Miranda*, police conviction rates did not suffer once they adopted the warnings as part of their routine. Richard H. Seeburger and R. Stanton Wettick, "Miranda in Pittsburgh—A Statistical Study," 29 *University of Pittsburgh Law Review* 1 (1967); Note, "Interrogations in New Haven: The Impact of Miranda," 76 *Yale Law Journal* 1519 (1967); and Stephens, *Supreme Court and Confessions*, ch. 7.

95. 384 U.S. at 467.

96. *Id.* at 542.

97. Stephens, *Supreme Court and Confessions*, 139–42. For more on the storm of criticism against *Miranda*, see Paul L. Murphy, *The Constitution in Crisis Times, 1919–1969* (New York: Harper & Row, 1972), 427–32, and Clifford M. Lytle, *The Warren Court and Its Critics* (Tucson: University of Arizona Press, 1968), 82–93.

98. *Mapp* v. *Ohio*, 367 U.S. 643 (1961).

99. *Benton* v. *Maryland*, 395 U.S. 784 (1969).

100. *Malloy* v. *Hogan*, 378 U.S. 1 (1964).

101. *Klopfer* v. *North Carolina*, 386 U.S. 213 (1967).

102. *Duncan* v. *Louisiana*, 391 U.S. 145 (1968).

103. *Pointer* v. *Texas*, 380 U.S. 400 (1965).

104. *Washington* v. *Texas*, 388 U.S. 14 (1967).

105. *Gideon* v. *Wainwright*, 372 U.S. 335 (1963).

106. *Robinson* v. *California*, 370 U.S. 660 (1962).

107. Cox, *Warren Court*, 74.

108. See the interview of Warren by Anthony Lewis, originally published in *The New York Times Magazine*, 19 October 1969, and reprinted in Leonard W. Levy, ed., *The Supreme Court under Earl Warren* (New York: Quadrangle, 1972), 165–70.
109. See sources cited in notes 93 and 94.
110. *Warden* v. *Hayden*, 387 U.S. 294 (1967).
111. 392 U.S. at 13.
112. Yale Kamisar, "The Warren Court (Was It Really So Defense-Minded?), the Burger Court (Is It Really So Prosecution-Oriented?), and Police Investigatory Practices," in Vincent Blasi, ed., *The Burger Court: The Counter-Revolution That Wasn't* (New Haven, Conn.: Yale University Press, 1983), 64–65.
113. *McCray* v. *Illinois*, 386 U.S. 300 (1967).

Chapter 8
"The Time Has Come to Modify the . . . Rule"
The Burger Court and Criminal Procedure

1. A Harris poll in November 1966 showed 54 percent of the public rating the Court negatively, and 65 percent opposing *Miranda*. See discussion of public opinion in Stephen L. Wasby, *The Impact of the United States Supreme Court: Some Perspectives* (Chicago: Dorsey, 1970), 233–42. The congressional reaction is traced in Adam C. Breckenridge, *Congress Against the Court* (Lincoln: University of Nebraska Press, 1970).
2. James F. Simon, *In His Own Image: The Supreme Court in Richard Nixon's America* (New York: McKay, 1973), 8.
3. The Burger speech at Ripon College was reprinted as "What to Do About Crime in U.S.," 63 *U.S. News & World Report* 70 (7 August 1967).
4. Yale Kamisar, "The Warren Court (Was It Really So Defense-Minded?), the Burger Court (Is It Really So Prosecution-Oriented?), and Police Investigatory Practices," in Vincent Blasi, ed., *The Burger Court: The Counter-Revolution That Wasn't* (New Haven, Conn.: Yale University Press, 1983), 68. A similar view is expressed by Jerold Israel, "Criminal Procedure, the Burger Court, and the Legacy of the Warren Court," 75 *Michigan Law Review* 1319 (1977). There are, however, some dissenting views; see, for example, Leonard Levy, *Against the Law: The Nixon Court and Criminal Justice* (New York: Harper & Row, 1974), 421–41. Levy wrote, it should be noted, in what Kamisar calls the "first" Burger Court period, before the Court shifted back toward the center.
5. Quoted in Yale Kamisar, "The 'Police Practices' Phases of the Criminal Process and the Three Phases of the Burger Court," in Herman Schwartz, ed., *The Burger Years: Rights and Wrongs in the Supreme Court, 1969–1986* (New York: Penguin, 1987), 145.
6. Wasby, *Impact of the Supreme Court*, 149–54.
7. 388 U.S. 218 (1967).
8. 388 U.S. 263 (1967).
9. 388 U.S. at 228.
10. Felix Frankfurter, *The Case for Sacco and Vanzetti* (Boston: Little, Brown, 1927), 30. For a full discussion of the problems inherent in witness identification, and a sampling of the large body of scholarly literature attacking its reliability, see Stephen A. Saltzburg, *American Criminal Procedure* (St. Paul, Minn.: West, 1980), 487–99.
11. Fred Graham, *The Self-Inflicted Wound* (New York: Macmillan, 1970), 224.
12. Wasby, *Impact of the Supreme Court*, 206.
13. 406 U.S. 682 (1972).

14. Saltzburg, *Criminal Procedure*, 521.
15. Joseph D. Grano, "*Kirby, Biggers,* and *Ash:* Do Any Constitutional Safeguards Remain Against the Danger of Convicting the Innocent?" 72 *Michigan Law Review* 717, 730 (1974).
16. *United States* v. *Marion*, 404 U.S. 307 (1971). Some post-*Kirby* decisions reaffirm the idea that an arrest is the initial stage of a criminal prosecution. See *United States* v. *Robinson*, 414 U.S. 218, 228 (1973).
17. 388 U.S. 293 (1967). The decision, written by Justice Brennan, is also known for its refusal to apply the *Wade–Gilbert* rule retroactively.
18. 409 U.S. 188 (1972).
19. *Id.* at 198, 199, quoting *Simmons* v. *United States*, 390 U.S. 377, 384 (1968).
20. 413 U.S. 300 (1973).
21. 432 U.S. 98 (1977).
22. 432 U.S. at 114.
23. The Burger Court reaffirmed this in *Moore* v. *Illinois*, 434 U.S. 220 (1977).
24. In Schwartz, ed., *Burger Years*, 147.
25. In *Douglas* v. *California*, 372 U.S. 353 (1963), the Warren Court had extended the right to counsel to include first appeals as of right, that is, those appeals from certain convictions guaranteed by state statute or constitution. In *Ross* v. *Moffitt*, 417 U.S. 600 (1974), a 6-3 majority, speaking through Justice Rehnquist, refused to extend this right to discretionary appeals, that is, those undertaken at the initiative of the defendant on any number of real or imagined legal grounds.
26. *Coleman* v. *Alabama*, 399 U.S. 1 (1970).
27. *Argersinger* v. *Hamlin*, 407 U.S. 25, 37 (1972). Justice Brennan wrote a concurring opinion, in which Douglas and Stewart joined; Justice Powell entered a concurrence, joined by Rehnquist, while Chief Justice Burger filed a separate concurrence.
28. 440 U.S. 367 (1979).
29. 422 U.S. 806 (1975).
30. 435 U.S. 475 (1978).
31. 466 U.S. 648 (1984).
32. *Cronic* v. *United States*, 675 F.2d 1126, 1128 (10th C.C.A. 1982).
33. 287 U.S. 45 (1932).
34. 466 U.S. at 654–55. Specific citations omitted.
35. Justice O'Connor dealt with this issue at length in *Strickland* v. *Washington*, 466 U.S. 668 (1984), and in essence concluded that trial and appellate judges could recognize ineffective counsel when they saw it. She also made it clear that guilty verdicts or severe punishment by themselves did not constitute legitimate evidence of ineffectiveness.
36. Herbert Packer, *The Limits of the Criminal Sanction* (Stanford, Calif.: Stanford University Press, 1968), 163.
37. Potter Stewart, "The Road to Mapp v. Ohio and Beyond: The Origins, Development and Future of the Exclusionary Rule in Search-and-Seizure Cases," 83 *Columbia Law Review* 1365, 1397 (1983).
38. See relevant discussion, pp. 146–48.
39. 403 U.S. 573 (1971).
40. *Id.* at 584; see also the discussion of the exclusionary rule on pp. 152–55.
41. Saltzburg, *American Criminal Procedure*, 84.
42. In Blasi, ed., *Burger Court*, 74.
43. 399 U.S. 30 (1970).
44. 267 U.S. 132 (1925).
45. 399 U.S. 42 (1970).

46. 403 U.S. 443 (1971).
47. 407 U.S. 297 (1972).
48. 412 U.S. 218 (1973).
49. 414 U.S. 218 (1973).
50. 415 U.S. 800 (1974).
51. 415 U.S. 164 (1974).
52. 427 U.S. 463 (1976).
53. 428 U.S. 364 (1976).
54. 425 U.S. 438 (1976).
55. 433 U.S. 1 (1977).
56. 442 U.S. 735 (1979).
57. 445 U.S. 573 (1980).
58. 453 U.S. 454 (1981).
59. 462 U.S. 213, 238 (1983).
60. 462 U.S. 640 (1983).
61. 460 U.S. 276 (1983).
62. 466 U.S. 170 (1984).
63. 468 U.S. 517 (1984).
64. 468 U.S. 705 (1984).
65. 469 U.S. 325 (1985).
66. 106 S.Ct. 1809 (1986).
67. 367 U.S. 643, 655 (1961).
68. Wasby, *Impact of the Supreme Court*, 163–68.
69. Police, however, do not always search a house to secure evidence or seize a person in order to charge him or her with a crime. In some instances they act in order to develop leads or, to put it bluntly, harass certain individuals into being more cooperative. Some studies indicate that when police are serious about gathering evidence or making an arrest, they have no trouble abiding by the warrant requirements or remembering to read suspects their *Miranda* rights.
70. 367 U.S. at 653.
71. Dallin H. Oaks, "Studying the Exclusionary Rule in Search and Seizure," 37 *University of Chicago Law Review* 754 (1970), argued that the rule has no deterrent impact at all and should be replaced by a civil action tort remedy. Anthony Amsterdam, "The Supreme Court and the Rights of Suspects in Criminal Cases," 45 *NYU Law Review* 785 (1970), responded that such a remedy would be totally ineffective for the class of people affected by police misbehavior, "marginal types who are quite happy, once out of police clutches, to let well enough alone." Moreover, "juries are not sympathetic to suits against the police."
72. *Bivens* v. *Six Unknown Named Federal Agents*, 403 U.S. 388, 416 (1971), Burger dissenting.
73. Burger relied on studies such as Oaks, cited in note 71; see, however, Bradley C. Canon, "Is the Exclusionary Rule in Failing Health? Some New Data and a Plea Against a Precipitous Conclusion," 62 *Kentucky Law Journal* 681 (1974).
74. 414 U.S. 338 (1974). The balancing test had previously been suggested by Chief Justice Burger in his dissent in *Bivens* v. *Six Unknown Named Federal Agents*, 403 U.S. 388, 411 (1971).
75. 414 U.S. at 348, 354. For an extensive critique of this case, see Thomas S. Schrock and Robert C. Welsh, "Up from Calandra: The Exclusionary Rule As a Constitutional Requirement," 659 *Minnesota Law Review* 251 (1974). Justice Brennan, in a dissent joined by Justices Douglas and Marshall, played down the deterrent effect of the

exclusionary rule and emphasized instead the need for the police and the courts to avoid unconstitutional practices.

76.   428 U.S. 465, 486 (1976). For a contrary view on the "original intent" of the rule, see Yale Kamisar, "Does (Did) (Should) the Exclusionary Rule Rest on a 'Principled Basis' Rather than an 'Empirical Proposition'?" 16 *Creighton Law Review* 565 (1983).

77.   428 U.S. at 496.

78.   *United States* v. *Janis*, 428 U.S. 433 (1976).

79.   *United States* v. *Havens*, 446 U.S. 620 (1980), that evidence inadmissible in the case-in-chief could be used to impeach defendant's credibility in cross-examination; *United States* v. *Payner*, 447 U.S. 727 (1980), an unbending application of the rule unacceptably impedes the truth-finding functions of judge and jury; and *Illinois* v. *Gates*, 462 U.S. 213 (1983), affirming a totality-of-the-circumstances test instead of strict adherence to technical warrant requirements.

80.   *United States* v. *Leon*, 468 U.S. 897 (1984).

81.   *Id.* at 905.

82.   *Id.* at 926.

83.   468 U.S. 981 (1984).

84.   In 1982 the Court had asked counsel in *Illinois* v. *Gates* to reargue the case, with attention to the question of whether the exclusionary rule should be modified to allow a good faith exception. Evidently a majority of the Court could not agree at the time on how such an exception could be defined, and when the decision came down Justice Rehnquist said, "with apologies to all," that the Court was not yet ready to answer the question.

85.   Justices Brennan and Marshall dissented in both cases; Justice Stevens dissented in *Leon* but concurred in *Sheppard*.

86.   For comment, most of it critical, see Wayne LaFave, "The Seductive Call of Expediency: U.S. v. Leon, Its Rationale and Ramifications," 1984 *University of Illinois Law Review* 895 (1984); Donald A. Dripps, "Living with Leon," 95 *Yale Law Journal* 906 (1986); and Craig M. Bradley, "The 'Good Faith Exception' Cases: Reasonable Exercises in Futility," 60 *Indiana Law Journal* 287 (1985).

87.   468 U.S. 1032 (1984).

88.   384 U.S. 436 (1966); see relevant discussion, pp. 162–64.

89.   See, for example, Kamisar, "Police Practices," in Schwartz, ed., *Burger Years*, 148–49.

90.   Paul L. Murphy, *The Constitution in Crisis Times, 1919–1969* (New York: Harper & Row, 1972), 479 n.49.

91.   Quoted in Wasby, *Impact of the Supreme Court*, 155.

92.   See the results of several studies reported in *id.* 156–62, and citations on 277, notes 21–36.

93.   401 U.S. 222 (1971).

94.   See John Hart Ely and Alan Dershowitz, "Harris v. New York: Some Anxious Observations on the Candor and Logic of the Emerging Nixon Majority," 80 *Yale Law Journal* 1198 (1971), for a devastating attack on Burger's opinion. It showed "a total absence of analysis and provides no support for its results."

95.   420 U.S. 714 (1975).

96.   417 U.S. 433 (1974). The police questioning had occurred before *Miranda* had been decided, but the trial took place afterward. Tucker's own statements had been excluded, but incriminating evidence came from a witness identified through the questioning. The Court held that the witness' testimony could be admitted—a narrow holding on narrow grounds. Justices Stewart, Brennan, Marshall, and White concurred with the holding but not with Rehnquist's exposition; only Justice Douglas dissented.

97. 426 U.S. 610 (1976).
98. Prior to this case the Court had imposed limits on the use of silence for impeachment, but as an evidentiary rather than as a constitutional rule.
99. 430 U.S. 387 (1977).
100. Justices Marshall, Powell, and Stevens entered concurring opinions; the Chief Justice dissented, as did Justice White, with whom Blackmun and Rehnquist joined, and Blackmun, with whom White and Rehnquist joined. For a thorough analysis of this case, see Yale Kamisar, "Brewer v. Williams, Massiah and Miranda: What Is 'Interrogation'? When Does It Matter?" 67 *Georgetown Law Journal* 1 (1978).
101. *Nix* v. *Williams*, 467 U.S. 431 (1984). Williams claimed that he had had no part in the murder, but had agreed to dispose of the body because the actual murderer threatened to turn in Williams, who had escaped from a mental institution, and he feared being returned to the hospital.
102. 446 U.S. 291 (1980).
103. *Id.* at 300–301.
104. *Id.* at 304.
105. 451 U.S. 477 (1981).
106. In an earlier case, *Michigan* v. *Mosely*, 423 U.S. 96 (1975), the Court had found no *Miranda* violation if police renewed interrogation of a suspect after he had chosen to remain silent, provided they read him his rights each time they resumed questioning.
107. 467 U.S. 649 (1984).
108. *Id.* at 656.
109. *Oregon* v. *Elstad*, 105 S.Ct. 1285, 1296 (1985).
110. 106 S.Ct. 1135 (1986).
111. *Id.* at 1148, n.4.
112. In Schwartz, ed., *Burger Years*, 150.
113. See, for example, *Jackson* v. *United States*, 390 U.S. 570 (1968), which struck down a provision of the Lindberg Act allowing a jury but not a judge to impose a death sentence, and *Witherspoon* v. *Illinois*, 391 U.S. 510 (1968), in which the Court voided the systematic exclusion in capital cases of those opposed to the death penalty.
114. Graham, *Self-Inflicted Wound*, 113. By 1968 about 500 inmates sat on death rows across the country, nearly all of them having filed one or more petitions for habeas corpus.
115. *Rudolph* v. *Alabama*, 375 U.S. 889 (1963); see also a memorandum by William O. Douglas, dated 17 October 1963, in Melvin I. Urofsky and Philip E. Urofsky, eds., *The Douglas Letters* (Bethesda, Md.: Adler & Adler, 1987), 189. Douglas did not at the time believe the death sentence unconstitutional, but activist that he was, stood willing to hear anything that raised a constitutional issue. In 1971, even after he voted to strike down the Arkansas capital punishment law, he noted that "I don't see how anyone would entertain the thought that as a matter of constitutional law the death penalty was prohibited in a straight, clear-cut first degree murder case." Memorandum to the Conference, 3 June 1971, *id.* at 192.
116. 398 U.S. 262 (1970); see also Bob Woodward and Scott Armstrong, *The Brethren* (New York: Simon & Schuster, 1979), 242–43.
117. 402 U.S. 183 (1971).
118. *Crampton* v. *Ohio*, decided with *McGautha* at *id.*
119. *Furman* v. *Georgia*, 408 U.S. 238 (1972).
120. 428 U.S. 153 (1976).
121. *Profitt* v. *Florida*, 428 U.S. 242 (1976), and *Jurek* v. *Texas*, 428 U.S. 262 (1976), decided the same day as *Gregg*, upheld the Florida and Texas statutes. In *Woodson* v. *North Carolina*, 428 U.S. 280 (1976), and *Roberts* v. *Louisiana*, 428 U.S. 325 (1976), the Court struck down mandatory death sentence statutes. The following year, in *Coker* v.

Georgia, 433 U.S. 584 (1977), the majority held the death sentence too severe for rape. In *Lockett* v. *Ohio*, 438 U.S. 586 (1978), the Court struck down the Ohio law as too restrictive on the defendant's ability to introduce mitigating evidence at the penalty stage. The Court found in *Godfrey* v. *Georgia*, 446 U.S. 420 (1980), that a jury had wrongly applied statutory criteria in sentencing a man to death for shooting his mother-in-law. Questions of racial bias in sentencing and the imposition of the death penalty on minors were not taken up until after Burger's retirement.

122. David Rudovsky, "Criminal Justice: The Accused," in Norman Dorsen, ed., *Our Endangered Rights* (New York: Pantheon, 1984), 205.
123. Kamisar, "Police Practices," in Schwartz, ed., *Burger Years*, 145.
124. Schwartz, "The Burger Court and the Prisoner," in *ibid.*, 177.

Chapter 9
"People, Not Land or Trees or Pastures Vote"
The Warren Court and Equal Protection

1.   16 Wall. 36, 81 (1873).
2.   *Buck* v. *Bell*, 274 U.S. 200, 208 (1927). The Court did on occasion utilize equal protection arguments, but in economic rather than civil rights cases. In *Gulf, C. & S. F. Ry.* v. *Ellis*, 165 U.S. 150 (1897), the Court struck down on equal protection grounds a state statute requiring railroads, but not other defendants, to pay attorneys' fees to successful plaintiffs in certain cases. See also Justice Jackson's concurrence in *Railway Express Agency* v. *New York*, 336 U.S. 106, 111 (1949).
3.   109 U.S. 3 (1883).
4.   163 U.S. 537, 544 (1896).
5.   For the development of racial segregation following Reconstruction, see C. Vann Woodward, *The Strange Career of Jim Crow*, 3rd ed. (New York: Oxford University Press, 1974).
6.   245 U.S. 600 (1917). The Court had reaffirmed *Plessy* a few years earlier but said that railroads wishing to offer luxury cars for white passengers had to offer them for blacks as well, regardless of the demand for those services. *McCabe* v. *Atchison, Topeka & Santa Fe Ry.*, 235 U.S. 151 (1914).
7.   The Court did, of course, hear cases in other areas in which race played an important role; see, for example, *Powell* v. *Alabama*, 287 U.S. 45 (1932), in which black youths accused of rape had been railroaded through trial without effective assistance of counsel.
8.   *Missouri ex rel. Gaines* v. *Canada*, 305 U.S. 339 (1938).
9.   *United States* v. *Carolene Products Co.*, 304 U.S. 144, 152 (1938).
10. Approval of the forced evacuation of Japanese-Americans from the West Coast and their resettlement in concentration camps did not survive the wartime hysteria, and the Court's validation of the program ran into immediate censure. The relocation cases are analyzed and attacked in Eugene V. Rostow, "The Japanese-American Cases—a Disaster," 54 *Yale Law Journal* (1945), and in Peter Irons, *Justice at War* (New York: Oxford University Press, 1983).
11. *Sipuel* v. *Board of Regents of the University of Oklahoma*, 332 U.S. 631 (1948).
12. *McLaurin* v. *Oklahoma State Regents*, 339 U.S. 637 (1950).
13. *Shelley* v. *Kraemer*, 334 U.S. 1 (1948). In a companion case, the Court struck down restrictive covenants in the District of Columbia in *Hurd* v. *Hodge*, 334 U.S. 24 (1948). Although the Fourteenth Amendment does not apply to the federal government, Chief

Justice Vinson found that such actions violated the 1866 Civil Rights Act and that it went against public policy to allow a federal court to enforce an agreement that was unenforceable in state courts. See Clement E. Vose, *Caucasians Only: The Supreme Court, the NAACP, and the Restrictive Covenant Cases* (Los Angeles: University of California Press, 1959), which examines the cases culminating in *Shelley*.

14. For an extremely lucid and illuminating discussion of the Legal Defense Fund and its work, see Mark V. Tushnet, *The NAACP's Legal Strategy against Segregated Education, 1925–1950* (Chapel Hill: University of North Carolina Press, 1987).
15. 339 U.S. 626 (1950).
16. Tushnet, *NAACP's Strategy*, 135.
17. It is told exceedingly well in Richard Kluger's magisterial *Simple Justice* (New York: Random House, 1975).
18. *Id.* at 671.
19. See, for example, Alfred H. Kelley, "The Fourteenth Amendment Reconsidered: The Segregation Question," 54 *Michigan Law Review* 1049 (1955), and Alexander Bickel, "The Original Understanding and the Desegregation Decision," 69 *Harvard Law Review* 1 (1955); the latter was originally prepared as a research memorandum for Justice Frankfurter the year that Bickel served as his law clerk.
20. *Brown* v. *Board of Education*, 347 U.S. 483, 492 (1954).
21. *Id.* at 493, 494.
22. President Roosevelt had, during the war, issued an executive order directing that Negroes be accepted into job-training programs in defense plants, and he had set up a Fair Employment Practices Commission to investigate charges of racial discrimination. Congress killed the agency immediately after the war and refused President Truman's request that it establish a permanent FEPC. Truman later appointed a presidential commission on civil rights, which made broad-ranging proposals that he recommended to Congress in February 1948. Under threat of a filibuster by southern lawmakers, Congress again refused to act, and later that year, under his authority as commander-in-chief, Truman ordered the desegregation of the armed forces. See Donald R. McCoy and Richard T. Ruetten, *Quest and Response: Minority Rights in the Truman Administration* (Lawrence: University of Kansas Press, 1973).
23. Kenneth B. Clark, Effect of Prejudice and Discrimination on Personality Development (Midcentury White House Conference on Children and Youth, 1950). See Clark's defense of the use of this evidence in "The Desegregation Cases: Criticism of the Social Scientist's Role," 5 *Villanova Law Review* 224 (1959), as well as a response by Ernest Van den Haag, "Social Science Testimony in the Desegregation Cases," 6 *Id.* 69 (1960).
24. The various uses as well as some misuses of social sciences in various legal areas are explored in John Monahan and Laurens Walker, *Social Science in Law: Cases and Materials* (Mineola, N.Y.: Foundation Press, 1985).
25. Edmund Cahn, "Jurisprudence," 30 *NYU Law Review* 150, 157 (1955).
26. C. K. Brown, "White South Is a Minority Group: Supreme Court Cannot Bestow White Man's Inheritance on Another Race," 17 *Alabama Lawyer* 438, 441 (1956).
27. J. Harvie Wilkinson III, *From Brown to Bakke: The Supreme Court and School Integration, 1954–1978* (New York: Oxford University Press, 1979), 33.
28. *Id.*, 33–34. For a discussion of scientific racism and desegregation, see Idus A. Newby, *Challenge to the Court: Social Scientists and the Defense of Segregation, 1954–1966* (Baton Rouge: Louisiana State University Press, 1967).
29. The article by Wechsler, "Toward Neutral Principles of Constitutional Law," 73 *Harvard Law Review* 1 (1959), generated an immediate controversy over its view toward *Brown*; see, for example, Louis H. Pollak, "Racial Discrimination and Judicial Integ-

rity: A Reply to Professor Wechsler," 108 *University of Pennsylvania Law Review* 1 (1959), and Charles L. Black, Jr., "The Lawfulness of the Segregation Decisions," 69 *Yale Law Journal* 421 (1960). Although the ideal of "neutral principles" enjoyed much esteem in the 1960s, it later came under attack for its supposed impracticability. See John Hart Ely, *Democracy and Distrust: A Theory of Judicial Review* (Cambridge, Mass.: Harvard University Press, 1980), 54–55; Robert Bork, "Neutral Principles and Some First Amendment Problems," 47 *Indiana Law Journal* 1 (1971); and Jan G. Deutsch, "Neutrality, Legitimacy, and the Supreme Court: Some Intersections between Law and Political Science," 20 *Stanford Law Review* 169 (1968).

30. Both quoted in Wilkinson, *Brown to Bakke*, 35.
31. See especially the uproar over the abortion decisions, pp. 253–57.
32. Wilkinson, *Brown to Bakke*, 39.
33. *Brown* v. *Board of Education*, 349 U.S. 294 (1955), referred to hereafter as *Brown II*.
34. Kluger, *Simple Justice*, 711.
35. From the start, the NAACP saw the issue not just in terms of *desegregating* schools, which meant the end of legal separation, but of *integrating* them as well, that is, of taking positive steps to ensure that schools were comprised of both black and white children. The Court's decisions, especially in the 1950s and 1960s, focused only on abolishing legal segregation.
36. Woodward, *Strange Career of Jim Crow*, 153.
37. See Jack W. Peltason, *Fifty-Eight Lonely Men: Southern Federal Judges and School Desegregation* (New York: Harcourt, Brace & World, 1961), a sympathetic examination of federal judges in the South.
38. By 1964 a scant 2.3 percent of southern blacks were enrolled in desegregated schools. The often-tragic story of desegregation and southern resistance is told in a number of sources. See Robert C. Smith, *They Closed Their Schools: Prince Edward County, Virginia* (Chapel Hill: University of North Carolina Press, 1965), and Nunan V. Bartley, *The Rise of Massive Resistance: Race and Politics in the South during the 1950s* (Baton Rouge: Louisiana State University Press, 1969).
39. Woodward, *Strange Career of Jim Crow*, 159.
40. John D. Weaver, *Warren: The Man, the Court, the Era* (Boston: Little, Brown, 1967), 18.
41. The story is well told in Tony A. Freyer, *The Little Rock Crisis: A Constitutional Interpretation* (Westport, Conn.: Greenwood Press, 1984).
42. 358 U.S. 1 (1958).
43. 1 Cr. 137 (1803).
44. 358 U.S. at 18.
45. See, for example, Gerald Gunther, "The Subtle Vices of the 'Passive Virtues'—A Comment on Principles and Expediency in Judicial Review," 64 *Columbia Law Review* 1 (1964), and Daniel A. Farber, "The Supreme Court and the Rule of Law: Cooper v. Aaron Revisited," 1983 *University of Illinois Law Review* 387.
46. *Griffin* v. *County School Board*, 377 U.S. 218, 229 (1964). See also Justice Goldberg's comment in *Watson* v. *City of Memphis*, 373 U.S. 526, 530 (1963).
47. 373 U.S. 683 (1963).
48. 377 U.S. 218 (1964).
49. 391 U.S. 431 (1968).
50. *Mayor of Baltimore* v. *Dawson*, 350 U.S. 877 (1955).
51. *Gayle* v. *Browder*, 352 U.S. 903 (1956).
52. *Holmes* v. *Atlanta*, 350 U.S. 879 (1955).
53. *New Orleans City Improvement Assn.* v. *Detiege*, 358 U.S. 54 (1958).
54. 373 U.S. 61 (1963).

55. *Muir* v. *Louisiana Park Theatrical Assn.*, 347 U.S. 971 (1955).
56. *Derrington* v. *Plummer*, 353 U.S. 924 (1957).
57. *Burton* v. *Wilmington Parking Authority*, 356 U.S. 17 (1961).
58. See, for example, *Gilmore* v. *Montgomery*, 417 U.S. 556 (1974), upholding a lower-court injunction barring a city from permitting private segregated schools as well as racially discriminatory nonschool groups to use municipal recreational facilities. In *Moose Lodge No. 107* v. *Irvis*, 407 U.S. 163 (1972), however, the Court held that a state liquor license did not provide the necessary state action nexus to a racially discriminatory private club.
59. *Pace* v. *Alabama*, 106 U.S. 583 (1883).
60. *McLaughlin* v. *Florida*, 379 U.S. 184, 198 (1964).
61. *Naim* v. *Naim*, 350 U.S. 891 (1955), dismissed per curiam for lack of a sufficient record; brought back and dismissed the following year, 350 U.S. 985 (1956), for want of a federal question. See a defense of the Naim decisions in Alexander M. Bickel, *The Least Dangerous Branch: The Supreme Court at the Bar of Politics* (New Haven, Conn.: Yale University Press, 1962), 71, and criticism in Gunther, "Subtle Vices," 11–12.
62. 388 U.S. 1, 12 (1967).
63. 379 U.S. 19 (1964).
64. 390 U.S. 333 (1968).
65. See, however, *New York State Club Association* v. *City of New York*, 108 S.Ct. 2225 (1988).
66. In *Garner* v. *Louisiana*, 368 U.S. 157 (1961), the majority dismissed convictions for lack of "evidentiary support." In *Taylor* v. *Louisiana*, 370 U.S. 154 (1962), the protesters had been arrested in a bus terminal, and the Court noted that segregation in interstate transportation facilities violated federal law. The Court relied on the First Amendment in *Edwards* v. *South Carolina*, 372 U.S. 229 (1963), with Justice Stewart noting that when a hostile crowd gathered in response to a peaceful protest in front of the state capitol, police had the obligation to protect the protesters' freedom of speech—not to arrest them.
67. *Bell* v. *Maryland*, 378 U.S. 226 (1964).
68. 379 U.S. 241 (1964).
69. 379 U.S. 294 (1964).
70. 383 U.S. 301 (1966).
71. Some question existed as to whether South Carolina had proper standing to sue. Ever since *Massachusetts* v. *Mellon*, 262 U.S. 447 (1923), the Court had held that a state could not bring suit to shield its citizens against the operation of a federal statute. The Court, however, had often ignored this issue when it considered state interests sufficiently affected.
72. The Fifteenth Amendment read in full:

    Sec. 1. The right of citizens of the United States to vote shall not be denied or abridged by the United States or by any State on account of race, color, or previous condition of servitude.

    Sec. 2. Congress shall have power to enforce this article by appropriate legislation.

73. "Brief of Plaintiff . . . ," in Philip Kurland and Gerhard Casper, eds., 62 *Landmark Briefs* . . . 119 (1975).
74. Black concurred with all of the major points but believed that one section of the law was unconstitutional—that section prohibiting a state from changing its electoral procedures without the attorney general's permission.
75. 383 U.S. at 355. The argument that all states had to be treated equally received short shrift from the Court; all it meant was that they had to be admitted to the Union on

an equal footing, after which nothing precluded Congress from treating local evils with discrete remedies. The Court also dismissed the separation of powers claim, because congressional findings supported the belief that case-by-case adjudication would only delay the remedy.

76. 383 U.S. 663 (1966).
77. *Id.* at 668.
78. *Id.* at 669.
79. 351 U.S. 12 (1956).
80. *Douglas* v. *California,* 372 U.S. 353 (1963).
81. *Shapiro* v. *Thompson,* 394 U.S. 618 (1969).
82. See relevant discussion, p. 240–42.
83. The academic comments on this problem have been quite extensive. See, among others, Gerald Gunther, "Foreword: In Search of Evolving Doctrine on a Changing Court: A Model for a Newer Equal Protection," 86 *Harvard Law Review* 1 (1972); Frank I. Michelman, "Welfare Rights in a Constitutional Democracy," 1979 *Washington University Law Quarterly* 659; Kenneth L. Karst, "Justice Douglas and the Return of the 'Natural-Law-Due-Process Formula,' " 16 *UCLA Law Review* 716 (1969); Ralph K. Winter, Jr., "Poverty, Economic Equality, and the Equal Protection Clause," 1972 *Supreme Court Review* 51; and Note, "Developments," 82 *Harvard Law Review* 1065 (1969).
84. 7 How. 1 (1849); see also *Pacific States Telephone & Telegraph Co.* v. *Oregon,* 223 U.S. 118 (1912).
85. See Marvin E. Gettleman, *The Dorr Rebellion* (New York: Random House, 1973), and George M. Dennison, *The Dorr War* (Lexington: University of Kentucky Press, 1976). The constitutional issues are explored in William M. Wiecek, *The Guarantee Clause of the U.S. Constitution* (Ithaca, N.Y.: Cornell University Press, 1972).
86. 328 U.S. 549, 552, 553–54 (1946).
87. *South* v. *Peters,* 339 U.S. 276 (1950).
88. *Gomillion* v. *Lightfoot,* 364 U.S. 339 (1960).
89. 369 U.S. 186 (1962).
90. In *Powell* v. *McCormack,* 395 U.S. 486 (1969), however, the Court accepted and decided a case that many commentators thought a perfect example of a political question, the power of a house of Congress to determine the credentials of its own members. Following that decision, handed down in the last weeks of Warren's tenure, one could well believe that the political question boundary, already narrowed in *Carr,* had vanished; a political question was, and is, whatever the justices say is a political question. See Kent M. Weeks, *Adam Clayton Powell and the Supreme Court* (New York: Dunellen, 1971).
91. 369 U.S. at 266, 270.
92. *Id.* at 330, 334.
93. *Gray* v. *Sanders,* 372 U.S. 368 (1963). The county unit system, which applied to statewide primaries, assigned each county a number of units, only some of which depended on population; rural counties had more units than did heavily populated urban areas.
94. *Wesberry* v. *Sanders,* 376 U.S. 1 (1964).
95. 377 U.S. 533, 567, 568 (1964).
96. *Lucas* v. *Forty-Fourth General Assembly of Colorado,* 377 U.S. 713, 736–37 (1964).
97. Harlan entered a dissent covering all six cases; Justices Stewart and Clark dissented only in the Colorado and New York cases.
98. *Reynolds* v. *Sims,* 377 U.S. at 579–80.

99. After a proposed constitutional amendment to override the decisions faltered in Congress, conservative groups mounted a drive to call a constitutional convention by petition of the states. By mid-1967, thirty-two states had approved the call, two shy of the necessary number.
100. 385 U.S. 440 (1967).
101. *Avery* v. *Midland County*, 390 U.S. 474 (1968).

Chapter 10
"Not Only Overt Discrimination but also Practices"
The Burger Court and Equal Protection

1. 396 U.S. 19 (1969).
2. Paul Brest, "Race Discrimination," in Vincent Blasi, ed., *The Burger Court: The Counter-Revolution That Wasn't* (New Haven, Conn.: Yale University Press, 1983), 113.
3. 402 U.S. 1 (1971). For a detailed account of the case's origin and resolution, see Bernard Schwartz, *Swann's Way* (New York: Oxford University Press, 1986).
4. *Keyes* v. *Denver School District No. 1*, 413 U.S. 189, 258 (1973), dissenting opinion.
5. *North Carolina State Board of Education* v. *Swann*, 402 U.S. 43 (1971).
6. See Gary Orfield, *Must We Bus? Segregated Schools and National Policy* (Washington, D.C.: Brookings Institution, 1978).
7. Higher Education Act of 1972, 86 Stat. 372.
8. 409 U.S. 1228 (1972).
9. *Id.* at 1229.
10. 88 Stat. 484 (1974).
11. 90 Stat. 1434 (1976).
12. *Washington* v. *Seattle School District No. 1*, 458 U.S. 457 (1982). Blackmun relied heavily on *Hunter* v. *Erickson*, 393 U.S. 385 (1969), in which the Court had struck down an amendment to the Akron, Ohio, city charter as placing impediments in the way of fair housing legislation.
13. 458 U.S. at 488, 489, 497.
14. *Crawford* v. *Los Angeles Board of Education*, 438 U.S. 527 (1982).
15. 413 U.S. 189 (1973). Brennan spoke for himself, Warren Court holdovers Douglas, Stewart, and Marshall, and one Nixon appointee, Blackmun. Chief Justice Burger concurred in the result; Powell concurred in part and dissented in part; and Rehnquist dissented. White took no part in the decision.
16. *Id.* at 235, 236.
17. *Bradley* v. *Richmond School Board*, 338 F.Supp. 67 (E.D. Va. 1972).
18. *Bradley* v. *Richmond School Board*, 462 F.2d. 1058 (4th Cir. 1972).
19. *Richmond School Board* v. *Virginia Board of Education*, 412 U.S. 92 (1973).
20. The Court could not, of course, prevent people from leaving the cities or enrolling their children in white schools, but it did act if the state appeared to be encouraging this trend. The Court limited state aid to racially restrictive private schools, forbidding textbook loans in *Norwood* v. *Harrison*, 413 U.S. 455 (1973), and exclusive temporary use of public facilities, in *Gilmore* v. *Montgomery*, 417 U.S. 556 (1974). Further, by a 7-2 vote the Court sustained a § 1983 suit against a segregated private school in *Runyon* v. *McCrary*, 427 U.S. 160 (1976). While parents had a First Amendment association right to send their children to schools promoting the idea of racial segregation, Justice Stewart wrote, this did not protect the *practice* of excluding minorities from such schools.

21. 418 U.S. 717 (1974).
22. Nathaniel R. Jones, "An Anti-Black Strategy and the Supreme Court," 4 *Journal of Law & Education* 203 (1975).
23. 418 U.S. at 782.
24. J. Harvie Wilkinson III, *From Brown to Bakke: The Supreme Court and School Integration, 1954–1978* (New York: Oxford University Press, 1970), 224.
25. 418 U.S. at 741–42.
26. *Columbus Board of Education* v. *Penick*, 443 U.S. 449 (1979), and *Dayton Board of Education* v. *Brinkman*, 443 U.S. 526 (1979).
27. Note, "Columbus Board of Education v. Penick: Regarding the Concept of State Sanctioned Segregation," 32 *Baylor Law Review* 153, 161 (1980).
28. The Rehnquist dissents are at 447 U.S. 489 and 542. Justice Stewart, joined by the Chief Justice, concurred in the results in the *Columbus* case, where the District Court had found for the plaintiff, but dissented in *Dayton*. He believed that appellate courts should defer to the findings of fact in the court of first hearing.
29. Powell's suggestion might be seen in another light, the response of a man with years of schoolboard experience seeking a clear standard for school officials to follow. See Melvin I. Urofsky, "Mr. Justice Powell and Education: The Balancing of Competing Values," 13 *Journal of Law & Education* 581 (1984).
30. Kenneth L. Karst, "Not One Law at Rome and Another at Athens: The Fourteenth Amendment in Nationwide Application," 1972 *Washington University Law Quarterly* 383.
31. 118 U.S. 356 (1886).
32. 403 U.S. 217 (1971). For more on this case, see Paul Brest, "Palmer v. Thompson: An Approach to the Problem of Unconstitutional Legislative Motive," 1971 *Supreme Court Review* 95.
33. 403 U.S. at 240–41.
34. 401 U.S. 424 (1971).
35. *Id.* at 431.
36. 426 U.S. 229 (1976).
37. Justice Stewart joined the constitutional part of the opinion, while Justice Stevens concurred on narrow grounds. Justices Brennan and Marshall dissented on the statutory claim and did not reach the constitutional argument.
38. In his opinion, Justice White made it a point that racially disproportionate impact by itself did not violate the Constitution or civil rights statutes. The impact had to be in areas such as voting or employment specifically covered by the law. The following year, in *Arlington Heights* v. *Metropolitan Housing Corporation*, 429 U.S. 252 (1977), the Court upheld a Chicago suburb's single-family zoning requirement that, in effect, kept black families out. Without evidence of discriminatory intent, which would have triggered the Equal Protection Clause, the fact that the zoning ordinance worked more against blacks than whites did not violate any statute.
39. For a discussion of other ramifications to the two cases, see Brest, "Race Discrimination," 120–24.
40. See relevant discussion pp. 213–14.
41. 400 U.S. 112 (1970).
42. 446 U.S. 156 (1980).
43. 446 U.S. 55 (1980).
44. The Court did find proof of discriminatory intent in *Rogers* v. *Lodge*, 458 U.S. 613 (1982), in which it upheld a district court finding that an at-large system in Burke County, Georgia, while "racially neutral when adopted, is being *maintained* for invidious purposes" in violation of Fourteenth and Fifteenth Amendment rights.

45.   The literature on this subject is immense and growing. See Robert K. Fullinwider, *The Reverse Discrimination Controversy: A Moral and Legal Analysis* (Savage, Md.: Rowman & Littlefield, 1980), and W. E. Bloch and M. A. Walker, eds., *Discrimination, Affirmative Action, and Equal Opportunity: An Economic and Social Perspective* (Vancouver, British Columbia, Can.: Fraser, 1982).

46.   *DeFunis* v. *Odegaard*, 416 U.S. 312 (1974).

47.   *Id.* at 350. Only Justice Douglas reached the merits and declared that even benign racial classifications violated the Constitution. The entire opinion, as Harvie Wilkinson described it, "was a celebration of individualism, a Thoreauvian remonstrance against the powerful homogenizing forces of American life." *Brown to Bakke*, 258.

48.   The literature on the *Bakke* case is quite extensive, indeed overwhelming. See, among others, Alan P. Sindler, *Bakke, DeFunis and Minority Admissions: The Quest for Equal Opportunity* (New York: Longman, 1978); Joel Dreyfuss and Charles Lawrence III, *The Bakke Case: The Politics of Inequality* (New York: Harcourt Brace Jovanovich, 1979); and especially Wilkinson, *Brown to Bakke*, ch. 10.

49.   *Bakke* v. *University of California*, 553 P.2d 1152 (1976).

50.   *Regents of the University of California* v. *Bakke*, 438 U.S. 265 (1978).

51.   *New York Times*, 2 July 1978, p. IV-1.

52.   *Time*, 10 July 1978, p. 9.

53.   In Blasi, ed., *Burger Court*, 128.

54.   443 U.S. 193 (1979).

55.   448 U.S. 448 (1980).

56.   In *Richmond* v. *J. A. Croson Company*, 109 S.Ct. 706 (1989), the Court by a 6-3 vote struck down a city set-aside program that required 30 percent of city contracts to be subcontracted to minority firms. The majority opinion by Justice O'Connor distinguished between the power of a city and that of the federal government to adopt preferential programs, but although some commentators jumped to the conclusion that this marked a major turnaround by the Court, a closer reading justifies some caution. The city had evidently set 30 percent as an arbitrary number, without any justification on the basis of past discrimination, available minority contractors, or other data. The city used a fixed quota, which the Court had repeatedly disallowed except as a specific remedy for de jure segregation. The construction industry had invested heavily in this case, and within the next few years there will be further cases testing particular set-aside programs. Among those there will undoubtedly be one that is carefully tailored to the situation and that was adopted after examining sufficient evidence of prior discrimination. That case, when it gets to the high court, will provide a far better clue to the future of affirmative action.

57.   *Firefighters* v. *Stotts*, 467 U.S. 561 (1984). Justice Blackmun, joined by Brennan and Marshall, dissented. Justice O'Connor filed a separate opinion concurring with the majority, while Justice Stevens joined only in the result.

58.   106 S.Ct. 1842 (1986).

59.   106 S.Ct. 3063 (1986).

60.   106 S.Ct. 3019 (1986).

61.   Supporters of affirmative action cheered the following year when the Rehnquist Court handed down a major decision supporting a gender-based voluntary affirmative action plan, *Johnson* v. *Transportation Agency, Santa Clara County*, 107 S.Ct. 1442 (1987). The Court also upheld a quota program to add blacks to the Alabama Department of Public Safety in light of a clear record of four decades of systematic racial exclusion. *United States* v. *Paradise*, 107 S.Ct. 1053 (1987).

62.   Haywood Burns, "The Activism Is Not Affirmative," in Herman Schwartz, ed., *The Burger Years: Rights and Wrongs in the Supreme Court, 1969–1986* (New York: Penguin,

1988), 104. Burns is president of the National Lawyers Guild and chair emeritus of the National Conference of Black Lawyers.

63. 411 U.S. 1 (1973).
64. *Rodriguez* v. *San Antonio Independent School District*, 337 F.Supp. 280 (W.D. Texas 1971).
65. *Harper* v. *Virginia Board of Elections*, 383 U.S. 663, 668 (1966).
66. For an elaboration of Powell's opinion, see Urofsky, "Justice Powell and Education," 596–600.
67. 411 U.S. at 70, 98.
68. See, for example, John E. Coon, "Introduction: 'Fiscal Neutrality' after *Rodriguez*," 38 *Law & Contemporary Problems* 299, 301 (1974), and Comment, "*San Antonio Independent School District* v. *Rodriguez*: Chaotic, Unjust—and Constitutional," 2 *Journal of Law & Education* 461–62 (1973).
69. See, for example, Mark Tushnet, " ' . . . And Only Wealth Will Buy You Justice'— Some Notes on the Supreme Court 1972 Term," 1974 *Wisconsin Law Review* 177.
70. See Robert W. Bennett, "The Burger Court and the Poor," in Blasi, ed., *The Burger Court*, 46–61.
71. Moreover, as Justice Powell noted in his opinion, monetary resources are but one factor in determining the quality of education. If the Court had required equal financing, would it then have had to order an economic desegregation, so that the socioeconomic mix of students would be approximately the same in every school? And, carrying this argument to an extreme, would it then have sought some homogenization of neighborhoods, so that the children's out-of-school environments would have been more nearly equal?
72. *Youngburg* v. *Romeo*, 457 U.S. 307 (1982).
73. 457 U.S. 202 (1982).
74. *Hoyt* v. *Florida*, 368 U.S. 57, 62 (1961).
75. In *Goesaert* v. *Cleary*, 335 U.S. 464 (1948), Justice Frankfurter spoke for a 6-3 Court in upholding a Michigan law denying women bartender's licenses unless "the wife or daughter of the male owner." The state could, he declared, "beyond question, forbid all women from working behind a bar. This is so despite the vast changes in the social and legal position of women. . . . The Constitution does not require legislatures to reflect sociological insight, or shifting social standards, any more than it requires them to keep abreast of the latest scientific standards."
76. 404 U.S. 71 (1971).
77. The Court had, in fact, already heard its first sex-discrimination case under Title VII, *Phillips* v. *Martin-Marietta Corporation*, 400 U.S. 542 (1971). In a per curiam decision a few months earlier, the Court had held that firms willing to hire fathers, but not mothers, with preschool children were guilty of sex discrimination within the meaning of Title VII. The Court indicated that the employer might prevail if it could show proof that "conflicting family obligations [are] demonstrably more relevant to job performance for a woman than for a man." This would allow the employer to come up with a so-called bona fide occupational qualification. Six years later the Court flatly repudiated this view. There has, however, been one case in which the Court has found gender a bona fide qualification. In *Dothard* v. *Rawlinson*, 433 U.S. 321 (1977), it upheld a men-only rule for contract guards in the violent, overcrowded male maximum-security sections of Alabama's prisons.
78. 411 U.S. 677 (1973).
79. In some instances, the justices' recognition of these differences smacked a great deal of the paternalism they claimed to be abandoning. In *Michael M.* v. *Superior Court*, 450 U.S. 464 (1981), the Court upheld a California statutory rape law that punished the

male participant in intercourse when the female was under eighteen years old, but did not operate reciprocally. The plurality admitted difficulty in fitting the decision into normal gender-discrimination analysis, but it believed that the legislature had acted rationally, because girls, and not boys, got pregnant.

80. 405 U.S. 645 (1972).
81. In *Quilloin* v. *Walcott*, 434 U.S. 246 (1978), a unanimous Court held that an unwed father who had never had custody or provided support could not block an adoption approved by the mother. In *Caban* v. *Mohammed*, 441 U.S. 380 (1979), a 5-4 Court held that a state violated equal protection by permitting adoption of an illegitimate child solely on the mother's consent, although the father had demonstrated a significant parental relationship. That same day, however, in *Parham* v. *Hughes*, 441 U.S. 347 (1979), also by a 5-4 vote, the Court permitted a state to condition an unwed father's parental rights on legitimation of the child by court order. The common theme in all of the parental rights cases is simple common sense. Men and women are not similarly situated, and therefore entitled to equal treatment, because maternity is rarely in doubt, whereas proof of paternity may be difficult to produce. All of these cases were decided before the introduction of genetic identification, which would have settled the issue of paternity, but it would not have addressed the larger social policy issue of the rights of wed versus unwed parents to determine their children's futures.
82. 416 U.S. 351 (1974).
83. To feminists, however, even benign classification is unacceptably discriminatory. Wendy W. Williams wrote:

> All widows, rich or poor . . . were presumed destitute after the death of their spouse. The Court preserved a negligible economic benefit that failed to address the underlying causes of women's persistently inferior economic status. . . . When the Court defines affirmative action in the sloppy way it did in *Kahn*, it does women no favor. ["Sex Discrimination: Closing the Law's Gender Gap," in Schwartz, ed., *Burger Years*, 123.]

Ms. Williams teaches law at Georgetown University, and has practiced with Equal Rights Advocates, a public-interest firm specializing in sex-discrimination issues. It is not at all clear that the Court even considered this an affirmative action case; *Bakke* was still a few years down the road.

84. 419 U.S. 498 (1975).
85. 419 U.S. 522 (1975). When Missouri, which included women in the jury pool but then allowed them to opt out, misinterpreted the decision, the Court reaffirmed its earlier ruling that the state's exemption of "any woman" from jury service violated equal protection. *Duren* v. *Missouri*, 439 U.S. 357 (1979).
86. 420 U.S. 636 (1975). The case marked one of the rare appearances of Justice Rehnquist in opposition to gender discrimination. However, four years later, in *Califano* v. *Boles*, 443 U.S. 282 (1979), he recanted and declared that his vote in *Weisenfeld* had been a big mistake, based on an erroneous reading of the legislative history.
87. *Stanton* v. *Stanton*, 421 U.S. 7 (1975).
88. 411 U.S. at 684–86.
89. 429 U.S. 190 (1976). It is interesting that the Court used a law protective of males to establish the new criteria, but as Judge Ruth Bader Ginsburg pointed out, "One senses the justices' evolving appreciation that discrimination by gender cuts with two edges and is seldom, if ever, a pure favor to women." Ginsburg, "The Burger Court's Grapplings with Sex Discrimination," in Blasi, ed., *Burger Court*, 140.
90. 429 U.S. at 197.
91. 430 U.S. 199 (1977).

92. 430 U.S. at 217, 222, Justice Stevens concurring.
93. 430 U.S. 313 (1977).
94. 440 U.S. 268 (1979).
95. 443 U.S. 76 (1979). The Court divided 5-4 on the appropriate remedy; the majority extended the benefits to families of unemployed mothers, whereas the dissenters would have invalidated the entire program and left new policy to Congress. However, all nine members of the Court agreed on the constitutional issue and the equal protection analysis.
96. *Wengler* v. *Druggists Mutual Insurance Company*, 446 U.S. 142 (1980).
97. *Cleveland Board of Education* v. *LaFleur*, 414 U.S. 632 (1974).
98. *Turner* v. *Department of Employment Security*, 423 U.S. 44 (1975).
99. 434 U.S. 136 (1977).
100. 417 U.S. 484 (1974).
101. 429 U.S. 125 (1976). Two years later Congress overruled the Court by amending Title VII to say explicitly that classification on the basis of sex includes classification on the basis of pregnancy. Congress could do this because the Court's decision involved a statutory interpretation of congressional intent, and it is understood that if the Court gets it wrong, then Congress can repass legislation making its intent clearer. Obviously, this power does not exist in cases where the Court relies on constitutional interpretation.
102. 435 U.S. 702 (1978).
103. *Arizona Governing Committee* v. *Norris*, 463 U.S. 1073 (1983).
104. 453 U.S. 57 (1981).
105. 458 U.S. 718 (1982).
106. *Hogan* v. *Mississippi University for Women*, 646 F.2d 1116 (5th Cir. 1981).
107. 458 U.S. at 729.
108. *Id*. at 732–33.
109. 458 U.S. at 735, Justice Powell dissenting.

Chapter 11
"If the Right of Privacy Means Anything . . . "
Personal Autonomy and Due Process

1. See Arnold M. Paul, *Conservative Crisis and the Rule of Law: Attitudes of Bar and Bench, 1887–1895* (Ithaca, N.Y.: Cornell University Press, 1960); Clyde E. Jacobs, *Law Writers and the Courts* (Berkeley: University of California Press, 1954); and the relevant chapters on law in Robert G. McCloskey, *American Conservatism in the Age of Enterprise, 1865–1910* (New York: Harper & Row, 1964).
2. The Supreme Court accepted the notion of a substantive due process in *Allgeyer* v. *Louisiana*, 165 U.S. 578 (1897).
3. *Gilbert* v. *Minnesota*, 254 U.S. 325, 334, 336 (1920), Justice Brandeis dissenting. Justice McReynolds, one of the most conservative members of the Court, employed due process analysis in individual rights cases in *Meyer* v. *Nebraska*, 262 U.S. 290 (1923) and *Pierce* v. *Society of Sisters*, 268 U.S. 510 (1925). In the former case, McReynolds declared that liberty denotes

   not merely freedom from bodily restraint but also the right of the individual to contract, to engage in any of the common occupations of life, to acquire useful knowledge, to marry, to establish a home and bring up children, to worship God according to the dictates of his own conscience, and generally to enjoy those privileges long recognized at common law as essential to the orderly pursuit of happiness by free men. [262 U.S. at 399.]

4. *Buck* v. *Bell*, 274 U.S. 200, 207–208 (1927).

5. *Skinner* v. *Oklahoma*, 316 U.S. 535, 541–42 (1942).

6. We are talking throughout this chapter of *substantive* due process; the Warren Court, of course, initiated what many called a due process revolution in criminal procedure, expanding both procedural and substantive rights in that area. But outside of criminal law, the Warren Court majority tried to avoid anything that sounded like a resurgence of the old analysis.

7. *Ferguson* v. *Skrupa*, 372 U.S. 726, 731 (1963).

8. *Griswold* v. *Connecticut*, 381 U.S. 479, 481–82 (1965). The reference to *Lochner* (198 U.S. 45 [1905]) is to one of the most notorious cases in which judges had used a combination of substantive due process and freedom of contract to strike down a ten-hour workday law for bakery workers.

9. *Id.* at 499, 500. In an earlier challenge to this statute, which the Court had evaded, Harlan had entered a lengthy dissent against the refusal to take the case, and there had developed the due process rationale. *Poe* v. *Ullman*, 367 U.S. 497, 522 (1961).

10. *Roe* v. *Wade*, 410 U.S. 113, 167, 168 (1973), Justice Stewart concurring.

11. Quoted in John Hart Ely, *Democracy and Distrust: A Theory of Judicial Review* (Cambridge, Mass.: Harvard University Press, 1980), 49n.

12. 381 U.S. at 507, 511–12, Justice Black dissenting.

13. *Id.* at 486. For the Ninth Amendment, see Bennett B. Patterson, *The Forgotten Ninth Amendment* (Indianapolis: Bobbs- Merrill, 1955), and Norman Redlich, "Are There Certain Rights Retained by the People?" 37 *NYU Law Review* 787 (1962). Goldberg himself could cite only a handful of older cases, none of them apposite to *Griswold*, in which the Court had even referred to the Ninth Amendment.

14. See the critique in G. Edward White, "The Anti-Judge: William O. Douglas and the Ambiguities of Individuality," 74 *Virginia Law Review* 17, 68–72 (1988).

15. It did rely on a privacy rationale in one case, *Stanley* v. *Georgia*, 394 U.S. 557 (1969); see relevant discussion pp. 85–86.

16. 405 U.S. 438 (1972).

17. *Id.* at 453.

18. Richard Posner, "The Uncertain Protection of Privacy by the Supreme Court," 1979 *Supreme Court Review* 173, 198; for a critique that sees Brennan's *Eisenstadt* reasoning as freewheeling as that of Douglas in *Griswold*, see Harry Wellington, "Common Law Rules and Constitutional Double Standards," 83 *Yale Law Journal* 221 (1973).

19. 410 U.S. 113 (1973). A detailed account of the case is Marian Faux, *Roe* v. *Wade* (New York: Macmillan, 1988); see also the account of the debate within the Court in Bob Woodward and Scott Armstrong, *The Brethren: Inside the Supreme Court* (New York: Simon & Schuster, 1979), 271 et seq.

20. *Doe* v. *Bolton*, 410 U.S. 179 (1973).

21. 410 U.S. at 153.

22. Justice White entered a biting dissent covering both cases; Justice Rehnquist entered two briefer and more dispassionate but still scathing dissents. Both men also took the unusual step of summarizing their dissents from the bench. The Chief Justice had stumbled into the majority because of his ineptitude in trying to control the writing assignment, and his short concurrence tried to put some distance between himself and the majority.

23. Stewart's turnabout confused many people. How could he oppose a right to privacy in 1965, on grounds that it had no constitutional basis, and then support it only a few

years later, because it now did have such a basis? In 1983, after his retirement, Stewart spoke at Columbia University and said that he was a believer in stare decisis and therefore felt bound by *Griswold*. This raised some eyebrows because Stewart, as the good common law judge he was, ignored past precedents when he felt it necessary to do so. A more convincing story, if true, is that Stewart's wife had long been active in Planned Parenthood and had been appalled at his vote in *Griswold*. She had not given him a moment's peace on the subject, and in *Roe* he atoned for his past error. Faux, *Roe v. Wade*, 302.

24. 410 U.S. at 209, 212n.

25. Faux, *Roe v. Wade*, 305.

26. Ely, "The Wages of Crying Wolf: A Comment on Roe v. Wade," 82 *Yale Law Journal* 920, 926 (1973); see also his "Foreword: On Discovering Fundamental Values," 92 *Harvard Law Review* 5 (1978).

27. Tribe, "Foreword: Toward a Model of Roles in the Due Process of Life and Law," 87 *Harvard Law Review* 1, 32 (1973).

28. "Structural Due Process," 10 *Harvard Civil Rights–Civil Liberties Law Review* 269 (1975).

29. Kenneth L. Karst, Book Review, 89 *Harvard Law Review* 1028, 1036 (1976); see also his "Foreword: Equal Citizenship Under the Fourteenth Amendment," 91 *Id*. 1 (1977); Sylvia A. Law, "Rethinking Sex and the Constitution," 132 *University of Pennsylvania Law Review* 955 (1984); and Ruth Bader Ginsburg, "Gender and the Constitution," 44 *University of Cincinnati Law Review* 1 (1975).

30. *Planned Parenthood of Missouri* v. *Danforth*, 428 U.S. 52 (1976), involved spousal consent; *Bellotti* v. *Baird*, 428 U.S. 132 (1976), dealt with parental consent.

31. *Bellotti* v. *Baird* (*Bellotti II*), 443 U.S. 622 (1979).

32. *H. L.* v. *Matheson*, 450 U.S. 398 (1981).

33. *Thornburgh* v. *American College of Obstetricians and Gynecologists*, 106 S.Ct. 2169 (1986).

34. 432 U.S. 464 (1977).

35. *Harris* v. *McRae*, 448 U.S. 297 (1980).

36. *Akron* v. *Akron Center for Reproductive Health*, 462 U.S. 416, 420 (1983).

37. *Id*. at 452, 453, quoting *Bellotti* v. *Baird*, 428 U.S. 132, 147 (1976).

38. Some cases, such as *Loving* v. *Virginia*, 388 U.S. 1 (1967), a late Warren Court decision, were primarily concerned with racial discrimination, but had an important impact on marital law. *Boddie* v. *Connecticut*, 401 U.S. 371 (1971), an equal protection case, voided state regulations that denied access to divorce for those too poor to pay the $60 fee. The birth control and abortion cases obviously affected family law, as did the equal protection cases involving custody of children, such as *Stanley* v. *Illinois*, 405 U.S. 645 (1972), and *Quilloin* v. *Walcott*, 434 U.S. 246 (1978). For a survey of these developments covering most of the Burger years, see Note, "The Constitution and the Family," 93 *Harvard Law Review* 1156 (1980). For a more critical look, see Robert A. Burt, "The Constitution of the Family," 1979 *Supreme Court Review* 329.

39. In fact, Justice Douglas had applied just such a test in *Belle Terre* v. *Boraas*, 416 U.S. 1 (1974), rejecting a privacy claim against a zoning ordinance excluding unrelated groups. The ordinance represented no more than economic and social legislation and therefore deserved the utmost deference from the courts. There have, of course, been a number of decisions that have protected associational rights under the First Amendment, but the Burger Court never extended a fundamental liberty status to general associational preferences.

40. *Moore* v. *East Cleveland*, 431 U.S. 494 (1977). Although a 5-4 vote, Chief Justice Burger dissented not on the due process argument but because he believed Mrs. Moore had failed to exhaust her state remedies, and therefore the case should not have been heard.

41. *Id*. at 502–503; the quote is from Harlan's concurrence in *Griswold*, 381 U.S. at 501.

42.   434 U.S. 374 (1978).

43.   442 U.S. 584 (1979).

44.   The Court did establish that institutionally confined mentally ill and mentally retarded persons had a liberty interest in a safe environment, no undue physical restraint, and minimally adequate and reasonable training, although it balanced this right against "relevant state interests." *Youngburg* v. *Romeo,* 457 U.S. 307 (1982). In previous cases dealing with this issue, the Court had avoided ruling on whether such a liberty interest existed; its extent is still unclear. See Note, "The Right to Treatment Dilemma and the Mentally Retarded," 47 *Albany Law Review* 179 (1982).

45.   "Constitution and the Family" at 1186.

46.   *Doe* v. *Commonwealth's Attorney,* 425 U.S. 901 (1976).

47.   Peter Irons, *The Courage of Their Convictions* (New York: Free Press, 1988), 381, 388.

48.   *Bowers* v. *Hardwick,* 106 S.Ct. 2841, 2843 (1986). It would appear that originally Justice Powell agreed with the view that privacy ought to cover the situation but then changed his mind. Several questions concerning the status and rights of homosexuals are currently working their way through state and federal courts and without the overt sexual issue will certainly challenge the Court in its equal protection analysis.

49.   *Hollenbaugh* v. *Carnegie Free Library,* 439 U.S. 1052 (1978).

50.   *Kelley* v. *Johnson,* 425 U.S. 238 (1976). One might note a letter Justice Douglas wrote in 1965 to a Florida high school student, who had asked whether school regulations on hair length and dress violated his constitutional rights:

> Our Bill of Rights, as you indicate, is designed for the protection of a minority. But it does not cover all of man's idiosyncracies. And you are talking about a field that is beyond the penumbra of any constitutional guarantees. The price that all of us pay for living in a civilized society is a certain degree of regimentation, and the pressures of conformity are always great. The part of wisdom is to find out when to bow and when to rebel. Most people find it better in the long run to make their fights on basic issues. [Melvin I. Urofsky and Philip E. Urofsky, eds., *The Douglas Letters* (Bethesda, Md.: Adler & Adler, 1987), 153.]

51.   Henry Paul Monaghan, "Of 'Liberty' and 'Property,' " 62 *Cornell Law Review* 405, 409 (1977).

52.   "The New Property," 73 *Yale Law Journal* 733 (1964); see also his "Individual Rights and Social Welfare: The Emerging Legal Issues," 74 *Id.* 1245 (1965).

53.   *Goldberg* v. *Kelly,* 397 U.S. 254, 265 (1970).

54.   *Bell* v. *Burson,* 402 U.S. 535, 539 (1971).

55.   *Board of Regents* v. *Roth,* 408 U.S. 564 (1972). In a companion case, *Perry* v. *Sindermann,* 408 U.S. 593 (1972), the Court held that Sindermann was entitled to an evidentiary hearing on his First Amendment claim because he had been employed at the school for several years. While the school had no formal tenure policy, it had a de facto one that gave him a protectable property interest in his job.

56.   416 U.S. 134, 154 (1974).

57.   *Bishop* v. *Wood,* 426 U.S. 341, 349–50 (1976).

58.   *McAuliffe* v. *Mayor of New Bedford,* 29 N.E. 517 (Mass. 1892).

59.   For example, in the highly criticized case of *Paul* v. *Davis,* 424 U.S. 693 (1976), a sharply divided Court supported Justice Rehnquist's assertion that reputation did not constitute part of the liberty covered under due process. However, in *Vitek* v. *Jones,* 445 U.S. 480 (1980), Justice White acknowledge a "stigma" ingredient of liberty, when the state moved a prisoner to a mental hospital without a hearing. In *Goss* v. *Lopez,* 419 U.S. 565 (1975), a majority ruled that high school students threatened with even brief disciplinary suspensions, much less dismissal, were entitled to at least an informal

evidentiary hearing. But in *Ingraham* v. *Wright*, 430 U.S. 651 (1977), the Court ruled that while corporal punishment in schools affects a "protected liberty interest," inflictment of that punishment did not require a prior hearing.

60.   Ely, *Democracy and Distrust*, 19.

61.   *Mathews* v. *Eldridge*, 424 U.S. 319 (1976). For a criticism of this balancing test, see Jerry L. Mashaw, "The Supreme Court's Due Process Calculus . . . Three Factors in Search of a Theory of Value," 44 *University of Chicago Law Review* 28 (1976).

62.   See, for example, *Dixon* v. *Love*, 431 U.S. 105 (1977), involving revocation of a driver's license; *Barry* v. *Barchi*, 443 U.S. 55 (1979), suspension of a horse trainer's license; *Landon* v. *Plasencia*, 459 U.S. 21 (1982), deportation proceedings; and *Santosky* v. *Kramer*, 455 U.S. 745 (1982), proceedings to terminate parental rights.

Index of Cases

General Index